Peter Norton's Assembly Language Book

for the IBM PC

Revised and Expanded

Peter Norton

and

John Socha

Brady
New York

BRADY

Simon & Schuster, Inc.
15 Columbus Circle
New York, NY 10023

DISTRIBUTED BY PRENTICE HALL TRADE

Manufactured in the United States of America

2 3 4 5 6 7 8 9 10

Library of Congress Cataloging-in-Publication Data

Norton, Peter, 1943–
    Peter Norton's assembly language book for the IBM PC.

    1. IBM Personal Computer—Programming.   2. Assembler
language (Computer program language)   I. Socha, John,
1958–   . II. Title.   III. Title: Assembly language
book for the IBM PC.
QA76.8.I2594N66   1989   005.265   89-17439

Contents

Trademarks

IBM, IBM PC, XT, and AT are registered trademarks of International Business Machines Corporation.

COMPAQ is a registered trademark of Compaq Computer Corporation.

MS-DOS and Microsoft are registered trademarks of Microsoft Corporation.

SideKick and SuperKey are trademarks of Borland International.

ProKey is a trademark of Rosesoft.

Lotus and 1-2-3 are trademarks of Lotus Development Corporation.

Intel is a registered trademark of Intel Corporation.

Limits of Liability and Disclaimer of Warranty

The authors and publisher of this book have used their best efforts in preparing this book and the programs contained in it. These efforts include the development, research, and testing of the theories and programs to determine their effectiveness. The authors and publisher make no warranty of any kind, expressed or implied, with regard to these programs or the documentation contained in this book. The authors and publisher shall not be liable in any event for incidental or consequential damages in connection with, or arising out of, the furnishing, performance, or use of these programs.

Introduction

By the time you finish reading this book, you'll know how to write full-scale, assembly language programs: text editors, utilities, and so on. Along the way, you'll learn many techniques that professional programmers use to make their work simpler. These techniques, which include modular design and step-wise refinement, will double or triple your programming speed, as well as help you write more readable and reliable programs.

The technique of step-wise refinement, in particular, takes a lot of the work out of writing complex programs. If you've ever had that sinking, "where-do-I-start feeling," you'll find that step-wise refinement gives you a simple and natural way to write programs. And it's also fun!

This book isn't all theory, though. We'll build a program, too. The program is called Dskpatch (for Disk Patch), and you'll find it useful for several reasons. First of all, you'll see step-wise refinement and modular design at work in a real program, so you'll have an opportunity to see why these techniques are so useful. Also, as you'll see shortly, Dskpatch is, in its own right, a general-purpose, full-screen editor for disk sectors—one that you can continue to use both in whole and in part long after you've finished with this book.

Why Assembly Language?

We'll assume that you've picked up this book because you're interested in learning assembly language. But you may not be exactly certain why you want to learn it.

One reason, perhaps the least obvious, is that assembly language programs are at the heart of any IBM PC (AT, PS/2, or compatible) computer. (IBM PC in this book refers to any of the PC, AT, PS/2, or compatible computers.) In relation to all other programming languages, assembly language is the lowest common denominator. It takes you closer to the machine than higher level languages do, so learning assembly language also means learning to understand the microprocessor inside your computer, which may be an 8088, 80286, or 80386 microprocessor. (8088 in this book refers to the 8088, 80286, and 80386 family of microprocessors.) We'll teach you the instructions of the 8088 microprocessor, as do the authors of other introductory books, but we'll go much farther and also cover *advanced* material that you'll find invaluable when you start to write your own programs.

Once you understand the 8088 microprocessor inside your IBM PC, many elements you'll see in other programs and in high-level languages will have greater meaning for you. For example, you may have noticed that the largest integer you can have in BASIC is 32767. Where did this number come from? It's an odd number for an upper limit. But as you'll see later, the number 32767 is directly related to the way your IBM PC stores numbers.

Then, too, you may be interested in speed or size. As a rule, assembly language programs are much faster than those written in any other languages. Typical assembly language programs are two to three times faster than equivalent C or Pascal programs, and they generally outpace interpreted BASIC programs by 15 times or more. Assembly language programs are also smaller. The Dskpatch program we'll build in this book will be full-grown at about one kilobyte. Compared with programs in general, that's small. A similar program written in C or Pascal would be about ten times that size. For these reasons, among others, the Lotus Development Corporation wrote 1-2-3 entirely in assembly language.

Assembly language programs also provide you with full access to the features in your computer. A number of programs, such as SideKick, ProKey, and SuperKey, stay in memory after you run them. Such programs change the way your machine works, and they use system features available only to assembly language programs. We'll show how to write such programs at the end of this book.

Dskpatch

In our work with assembly language, we'll look directly at disk sectors, displaying characters and numbers stored there by DOS in hexadecimal notation. Dskpatch is a full-screen editor for disks, and it will allow us to change these characters and numbers in a disk sector. Using Dskpatch you could, for example, look at the sector where DOS stores the directory for a disk and you could change file names or other information. Doing so is a good way to learn how DOS stores information on a disk.

You'll get more out of Dskpatch than just one program, though. Dskpatch contains about 50 subroutines. Many of these are general-purpose subroutines you'll find useful when you write your own programs. Thus, not only is this book an introduction to the 8088 and assembly language programming, it's also a source of useful subroutines.

In addition, any full-screen editor needs to use features specific to the IBM PC family of computers. Through the examples in this book, you'll also learn how to write useful programs for IBM PCs, ATs, or compatible computers, such as the Compaq.

Equipment Requirements

What equipment will you need to run the examples in this book? You'll need an IBM PC or compatible with at least 256K of memory and one disk drive. You'll also need version 2.00 or later of PC-DOS (or MS-DOS). And, starting in Part II, you'll need an assembler, which can be the IBM or the Microsoft Macro Assembler version 5.0 or later, the Turbo Assembler from Borland International, or OPTASM from SLR Systems.

Organization of This Book

This book is divided into four parts, each with a different emphasis. Whether you know anything about microprocessors or assembly language you'll find sections of interest.

Part I focuses on the 8088 microprocessor. Here, you'll learn the mysteries of bits, bytes, and machine language. Each of the seven chapters contains a wealth of real examples that use a program called Debug, which comes on your DOS disk. Debug will allow us to look *inside* the famous 8088 microprocessor nestled deep in your IBM PC as it runs DOS. Part I assumes only that you have a rudimentary knowledge of BASIC and know how to work with your computer.

Part II, Chapters 8 through 16, moves on to assembly language and to writing programs in the assembler. The approach is gentle, and rather than cover all the details of the assembler itself, we'll concentrate on a set of assembler commands we need to write useful programs.

We'll use the assembler to rewrite some of the programs from Part I and then move on to begin creating Dskpatch. We'll build this program slowly, so you'll learn how to use step-wise refinement in building large programs. We'll also cover techniques like modular design that help in writing clear programs. As mentioned, these techniques will simplify programming by removing some of the complexities usually associated with writing assembly language programs.

In Part III, which includes Chapters 17 to 28, we'll concentrate on using more advanced features found in IBM PCs. These features include moving the cursor and clearing the screen.

In Part III we'll also discuss techniques for debugging larger assembly language programs. Assembly language programs grow very quickly and can easily be two or more pages long without doing very much (Dskpatch will be longer). Even though we'll use these debugging techniques on programs larger than a few pages, you'll find them useful with small programs, too.

Part IV covers several advanced topics that will be of interest to you when you start to write real programs. The first two chapters cover details about .COM programs, which you'll need to write sometimes, and more on segments. Then there is a chapter on writing directly to screen memory for very fast screen displays. Next, there is a chapter on writing assembly language procedures that you can use in your C programs. And finally, we finish Part IV with a chapter on RAM-resident programs, complete with a program called DISK-LITE that adds a disk light to your screen.

Now, without further ado, let's jump into the 8088 and take a look at the way it stores numbers.

PART I

Machine Language

1

DEBUG AND ARITHMETIC

Before we begin to look at assembly language, a few words are in order about microprocessors. Currently (as of 1989) there are three main microprocessors used in the IBM PC, AT, PS/2, and compatible computers: the 8088, 80286, and 80386 microprocessors. The 8088 microprocessor was first used in the original IBM PC and is the slowest and least powerful microprocessor. Next came the 80286 in the IBM AT, which was about four times faster, and the first computer capable of running IBM's OS/2. Finally we have even faster computers built around the 80386 microprocessor that are even faster and more powerful than 80286 computers.

Both the 80286 and the 80386 are *supersets* of the 8088 microprocessor, which means any programs written for the 8088 microprocessor will run on any of the others. In fact, programs written for MS-DOS (or PC-DOS) computers are almost always written using just 8088 features so they'll run on all MS-DOS computers. We'll cover the 8088 in this book, which means all the programs in this book run on any MS-DOS computer. So whenever you see 8088, we're also referring to the 8088 subset of features in the 80286 and 80386 (and someday the 80486).

Elementary Counting

Let's begin our foray into assembly language by learning how computers count. That may sound simple enough. After all, we count to 11 by starting at one and counting up: 1, 2, 3, 4, 5, 6, 7, 8, 9, 10, 11.

But a computer doesn't count that way. Instead, it counts to five like this: 1, 10, 11, 100, 101. The numbers 10, 11, 100, and so on are binary numbers, based a number system with only two digits, one and zero, instead of the ten associated with our more familiar decimal numbers. Thus, the binary number 10 is equivalent to the decimal number we know as two.

We're interested in binary numbers because they are the form in which numbers are used by the 8088 microprocessor inside your IBM PC. But while computers thrive on binary numbers, those strings of ones and zeros can be long and cumbersome to write out. The solution? Hexadecimal numbers—a far more compact way to write binary numbers. In this chapter, you'll learn both ways to write numbers: hexadecimal and binary. And as you learn how computers count, you'll also learn about how they store numbers—in bits, bytes, and words.

If you already know about binary and hexadecimal numbers, bits, bytes, and words, you can skip to the chapter summary.

Hexadecimal Numbers

Since hexadecimal numbers are easier to handle than binary numbers—at least in terms of length—we'll begin with hexadecimal (hex for short), and use DEBUG.COM, a program you'll find on your PC-DOS supplemental disk. We'll be using Debug here and in later chapters to enter and run machine-language programs one instruction at a time. Like BASIC, Debug provides a nice, interactive environment. But unlike BASIC, it doesn't know decimal numbers. To Debug, the number 10 is a hexadecimal number—not ten. And since Debug speaks only in hexadecimal, you'll need to learn something about hex numbers. But first, let's take a short side trip and find out a little about Debug itself.

Debug

Why does this program carry the name Debug? *Bugs*, in the computer world, are mistakes in a program. A working program has no bugs, while a non-working or "limping" program has at least one bug. By using Debug to run a program one instruction at a time, and watching how the program works, we can find mistakes and correct them. This is known as *debugging*, hence the name Debug.

According to computer folklore, the term debugging stems from the early days of computing—in particular, a day on which the Mark I computer at Harvard failed. After a long search, the technicians found the source of their troubles: a small moth caught between the contacts of a relay. The technicians removed the moth and wrote a note in the log book about "debugging" the Mark I.

Find Debug on your DOS supplemental disk and we'll get started. If you're not using a hard disk, you should also have a work disk handy, and you'll want to copy DEBUG.COM to it. We'll make heavy use of Debug in Part I of this book.

Note: From here on, in interactive sessions like this one, the text you type will be against a gray background to distinguish it from your computer's responses:

```
A>DEBUG
```

Type the gray text, (DEBUG in this example), press the Enter key, and you should see a response similar to the ones we show in these sessions. You won't always see exactly the same responses, because your computer probably has a different amount of memory from the computer on which we wrote this

> book. (We'll begin to encounter such differences in the next chapter.) In addition, note that we use uppercase letters in all examples. This is only to avoid any confusion between the lowercase letter l (el) and the number 1 (one). If you prefer, you can type all examples in lowercase letters.

Now, with those few conventions noted, start Debug by typing its name after the DOS prompt (which is A> in this example):

```
A>DEBUG
-
```

The hyphen you see in response to your command is Debug's prompt symbol, just as A> is a DOS prompt. It means Debug is waiting for a command.

To leave Debug and return to DOS, just type Q (for *Quit*) at the hyphen prompt and press Enter. Try quitting now, if you like, and then return to Debug:

```
-Q
A>DEBUG
-
```

Now we can get down to learning about hex numbers.

Hexarithmetic

We'll use a Debug command called H. H is short for *Hexarithmetic*, and, as its name suggests, it adds and subtracts two hex numbers. Let's see how H works by starting with 2 + 3. We know that 2 + 3 = 5 for decimal numbers. Is this true for hex numbers? Make sure you're still in Debug and, at the hyphen prompt, type the following screened text:

```
-H 3 2
0005    0001
```

Debug prints both the sum (0005) and the difference (0001) of 3 and 2. The Hexarithmetic command always calculates the sum and difference of two numbers, as it did here. And so far, the results are the same for hex and decimal numbers: 5 is the sum of 3 + 2 in decimal, and 1 is the difference (3 − 2). But sometimes, you can encounter a few surprises.

For example, what if we typed *H 2 3*, to add and subtract 2 and 3, instead of 3 and 2? If we try it:

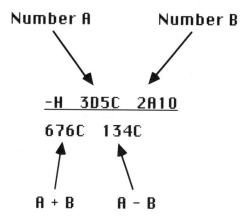

Number A   **Number B**

```
-H  3D5C  2A10
    676C  134C
```

A + B   A - B

Figure 1-1. The Hexarithmetic Command.

```
-H 2 3
0005  FFFF
```

we get FFFF instead of −1, for 2 − 3. Strange as it may look, however, FFFF is a number. In fact, it is hex for −1.

We'll come back to this rather unusual −1 shortly. But first, let's explore the realm of slightly larger numbers to see how an F can appear in a number.

To see what the Hexarithmetic command does with larger numbers, let's try 9 plus 1, which would give us the decimal number 10:

```
-H 9 1
000A 0008
```

How does 9 + 1 = A? A is the hex number for ten. Now, what if we try for an even larger number, such as 15:

```
-H 9 6
000F 0003
```

If you try other numbers between 10 and 15, you'll find 16 digits altogether— 0 through F (0 through 9 and A through F). The name hexadecimal comes from hexa- (6), plus deca- (10) which, when combined, represent 16. The digits 0 through 9 are the same in both hexadecimal and decimal; the hexadecimal digits A through F are equal to the decimals 10 through 15.

Why does Debug speak in hexadecimal? Soon you'll see that we can write 256 different numbers with two hex digits. As you may already suspect, 256 also bears some relationship to the unit known as a byte, and the byte plays a major

Decimal	Hex digit
0	0
1	1
2	2
3	3
4	4
5	5
6	6
7	7
8	8
9	9
10	A
11	B
12	C
13	D
14	E
15	F

Figure 1-2. Hexadecimal Digits.

role in computers and in this book. You'll find out more about bytes near the end of this chapter, but for now we'll continue to concentrate on learning hex, the only number system known to Debug, and hex math.

Converting Hexadecimal to Decimal

So far we've looked at single-digit hex numbers. Now, let's see how to represent larger hex numbers and how to convert these numbers to decimal numbers.

Just as with decimal numbers, we build multiple-digit hex numbers by adding more digits on the left. Suppose, for example, we add the number 1 to the largest single-digit decimal number, 9. The result is a two-digit number, 10 (ten). What happens when we add 1 to the largest single-digit hex number, F? We get 10 again.

But wait, 10 in hex is really 16, not ten. This could become rather confusing. We need some way to tell these two 10s apart, so from now on we'll place the letter h after any hex number. Thus, we'll know that 10h is hexadecimal 16 and 10 is decimal ten.

```
7     -->   7  *   16  =    112
C     --> 12  *    1  =     12
7Ch               =         124


3     -->   3  *  256  =    768
 F    -->  15  *   16  =    240
  9   -->   9  *    1  =      9
3F9h              =        1,017


A       -->  10  *  4,096  =  40,960
 F      -->  15  *    256  =   3,840
  1     -->   1  *     16  =      16
   C    -->  12  *      1  =      12
AF1Ch              =          44,828


3       -->   3  *  65,536  =  196,608
 B      -->  11  *   4,096  =   45,056
  8     -->   8  *     256  =    2,048
   D    -->  13  *      16  =      208
    2   -->   2  *       1  =        2
3B8D2h             =           243,922
```

Figure 1-3. More Hexadecimal to Decimal Conversions.

Now we come to the question of how to convert numbers between hex and decimal. We know that 10h is 16, but how do we convert a larger hex number, such as D3h, to a decimal number without counting up to D3h from 10h? Or, how do we convert the decimal number 173 to hex?

We can't rely on Debug for help, because Debug can't speak in decimal. In Chapter 10, we'll write a program to convert a hex number into decimal notation so that our programs can talk to us in decimal. But right now, we'll have to do these conversions by hand, so let's begin by returning to the familiar world of decimal numbers.

What does the number 276 mean? In grade school, we learned that 276 means we have two hundreds, seven tens, and six ones. Or, more graphically:

```
  2   * 100 =  200
  7   *  10 =   70
  6 *   1 =    6
276          =  276
```

That certainly helps us visualize the meanings of those digits. Can we use the same graphic method with a hex number? Of course.

Consider the number D3h we mentioned earlier. D is the hexadecimal digit 13, and there are 16 hex digits, versus 10 for decimal, so D3h is thirteen six-teens and three ones. Or, presented graphically:

```
D  → 13 * 16 =  208
3  →  3 *  1 =    3
D3h          =  211
```

For the decimal number 276, we multiplied the digits by 100, 10, and 1; for the hex number D3, we multiplied the digits by 16 and 1. If we had four decimal digits we'd multiply by 1000, 100, 10, and 1. Which four numbers would we use with four hex digits?

For decimal, the numbers 1000, 100, 10, and 1 are all powers of 10:

```
10³ = 1000
10² =  100
10¹ =   10
10⁰ =    1
```

We can use exactly the same method for hex digits, but with powers of 16, instead of 10, so our four numbers are:

```
16³ = 4096
16² =  256
16¹ =   16
16⁰ =    1
```

Let's convert 3AC8h to decimal using the four numbers we just calculated:

```
3    →  3 * 4096 = 12288
A    → 10 *  256 =  2560
C    → 12 *   16 =   192
8    →  8 *    1 =     8
3AC8h            = 15048
```

Now let's discover what happens when we add hex numbers that have more than one digit. For this, we'll use Debug and the numbers 3A7h and 1EDh:

```
-H 3A7 1ED
0594  01BA
```

```
        1                  1                   1
       3A7                F451                  C
     + 92A              + CB03                + D
       CD1              1BF54                 19


      1111                    1 1
      BCD8                    BCD8
    + FAE9                  + 0509
     1B7C1                   C1E1
```

Figure 1-4. More Examples of Hexadecimal Addition.

So we see that 3A7h + 1EDh = 594h. You can check the results by converting these numbers to decimal and doing the addition (and subtraction, if you wish) in decimal form; if you're more adventurous, do the calculations directly in hex.

Five-Digit Hex Numbers

So far, hex math is quite straightforward. What happens when we try adding even larger hex numbers? Let's try a five-digit hex number:

```
-H 5C3F0 4BC6
         ^ Error
-
```

That's an unexpected response. Why does Debug say we have an error here? The reason has to do with a unit of storage called the *word*. Debug's Hex-arithmetic command works only with words, and words happen to be long enough to hold four hex digits, no more.

We'll find out more about words in a few pages, but for now, remember that you can work only with four hex digits. Thus, if you try to add two four-digit hex numbers, such as C000h and D000h (which should give you 19000h), you get 9000h, instead:

```
-H C000 D000
9000   F000
-
```

Debug keeps only the four rightmost digits of the answer.

Converting Decimal to Hex

So far we've only looked at the conversion from hex to decimal. Now we'll learn how to convert decimal numbers to hex. As noted earlier, in Chapter 10 we'll create a program to write the 8088's numbers as decimal numbers; in Chapter 23, we'll write another program to read decimal numbers into the 8088. But, as with decimal-to-hex conversions, let's begin by learning how to do the conversions by hand. Again, we'll start by recalling a bit of grade-school math.

When we first learned division, we would divide 9 by 2 to get 4 with a remainder of 1. We'll use the remainder to convert decimal numbers to hex.

Let's see what happens when we repeatedly divide a decimal number, in this case 493, by 10:

```
493 / 10   =   49 remainder 3

 49 / 10   =    4 remainder 9

  4 / 10   =    0 remainder 4
                              4 9 3
```

The digits of 493 appear as the remainder in reverse order—that is, starting with the rightmost digit (3). We saw in the last section that all we needed for our hex-to-decimal conversion was to replace powers of 10 with powers of 16. For our decimal-to-hex conversion, can we divide by 16 instead of 10? Indeed, that's our conversion method.

For example, let's find the hex number for 493. Dividing by 16, as shown here:

```
493 / 16   =   30 remainder 13 (Dh)

 30 / 16   =    1 remainder 14 (Eh)

  1 / 16   =    0 remainder  1 (1h)
493                =                1 E D h
```

We find that 1EDh is the hex equivalent of decimal 493. In other words, keep dividing by 16, and form the final hex number from the remainders. That's all there is to it.

Figure 1-5. More Examples of Hexadecimal Conversions.

Negative Numbers

If you recall, though, we still have an unanswered puzzle in the number FFFFh. We said that FFFFh is actually −1. Yet, if we convert FFFFh to decimal, we get 65535. How can that be? Does it behave as a negative number?

Well, if we add FFFFh (alias −1) to 5, the result should be 4, because 5 − 1 = 4. Is that what happens? Using Debug's H command to add 5 and FFFFh, we find:

```
-H 5 FFFF
0004  0006
-
```

Debug *seems* to treat FFFFh as −1. But FFFFh won't always behave as −1 in programs we'll write. To see why not, let's do this addition by hand.

When we add two decimal numbers, we often find ourselves *carrying* a 1 to the next column, like this:

```
1 1
  9 5
+ 5 8
1 5 3
```

The addition of two hex numbers isn't much different. Adding 3 to F gives us 2, with a carry into the next column:

```
  1
    F
+   3
  1 2 h
```

Now, watch what happens when we add 5 to FFFFh:

```
1 1 1 1
  0 0 0 5 h
+ F F F F h
1 0 0 0 4 h
```

Since Fh + 1h = 10h, the successive carries neatly move a 1 into the far left position. And, if we ignore this 1, we have the correct answer for 5 − 1: namely, 4. Strange as it seems, FFFFh behaves as −1 when we ignore this *overflow*. It's called an overflow because the number is now five digits long, but Debug keeps only the last (rightmost) four digits.

Is this overflow an error, or is the answer correct? Well, yes and yes. We can choose either answer. Don't the answers contradict each other? Not really, because we can view these numbers in either of two ways.

Let's suppose we take FFFFh as equal to 65536. This is a positive number, and it happens to be the largest number we can write with four hex digits. We say that FFFFh is an *unsigned* number. It is unsigned because we've just defined all four digit numbers as positive. Adding 5 to FFFFh gives us 10004h;

no other answer is correct. In the case of unsigned numbers, then, an overflow is an error.

On the other hand, we can also treat FFFFh as a negative number, as Debug did when we used the H command to add FFFFh to 5. FFFFh behaves as −1 as long as we ignore the *overflow*. In fact, the numbers 8000h through FFFFh all behave as negative numbers. For *signed* numbers, as here, the overflow isn't an error.

The 8088 microprocessor can view numbers either as unsigned or signed; the choice is yours. There are slightly different instructions for each, and we'll explore these differences in later chapters as we begin to use numbers on the 8088. Right now, before you can learn to actually write the negative of, say, 3C8h, we need to unmask the bit and see how it fits into the scheme of bytes, words, and hex.

Bits, Bytes, Words, and Binary Notation

It's time for us to dig deeper into the intricacies of your IBM PC—time to learn about the arithmetic of the 8088: binary numbers. The 8088 microprocessor, with all its power, is rather dumb. It knows only the two digits 0 and 1, so any number it uses must be formed from a long string of zeros and ones. This is the *binary* (base 2) number system.

When Debug prints a number in hex, it uses a small program to convert its internal numbers from binary to hexadecimal. In Chapter 5, we'll build such a program to write binary numbers in hex notation, but first we need to learn more about binary numbers themselves.

Let's take the binary number 1011b (the b stands for binary). This number is equal to the decimal 11, or Bh in hex. To see why, multiply the digits of 1011b by the number's base, 2:

Powers of 2:

$$
\begin{aligned}
2^3 &= 8 \\
2^2 &= 4 \\
2^1 &= 2 \\
2^0 &= 1
\end{aligned}
$$

So that:

```
1 * 8  =  8
0 * 4  =  0
1 * 2  =  2
1 * 1  =  1
1011b  =  11    or    Bh
```

Binary	Decimal	Hexadecimal
0000	0	0
0001	1	1
0010	2	2
0011	3	3
0100	4	4
0101	5	5
0110	6	6
0111	7	7
1000	8	8
1001	9	9
1010	10	A
1011	11	B
1100	12	C
1101	13	D
1110	14	E
1111	15	F

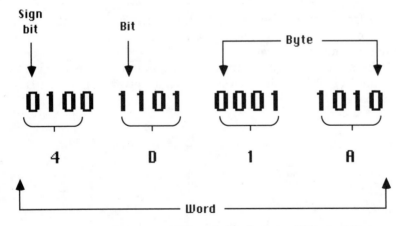

Figure 1-7. A Word is Made Out of Bits and Bytes.

Likewise, 1111b is Fh, or 15. And 1111b is the largest unsigned four-digit binary number we can write, while 0000b is the smallest. Thus, with four binary digits we can write 16 different numbers. There are exactly 16 hex digits, so we can write one hex digit for every four binary digits.

A two-digit hex number, such as 4Ch, can be written as 0100 1100b. It's composed of eight digits, which we separate into groups of four for easy reading. Each one of these binary digits is known as a bit, so a number like 0100 1100b, or 4Ch, is eight bits long.

Very often, we find it convenient to number each of the bits in a long string, with bit 0 farthest to the right. The 1 in 10b then is bit number 1, and the leftmost bit in 1011b is bit number 3. Numbering bits in this way makes it easier for us to talk about any particular one, as we'll want to later on.

A group of eight binary digits is known as a *byte*, while a group of 16 binary digits, or two bytes, is a *word*. We'll use these terms frequently throughout this book, because bits, bytes, and words are all fundamental to the 8088.

We can see now why hexadecimal notation is convenient; two hex digits fit exactly into one byte (four bits per hex digit), and four digits fit exactly into one word. We can't say the same for decimal numbers. If we try to use two decimal digits for one byte, we can't write numbers larger than 99, so we lose the values from 100 to 255—more than half the range of numbers a byte can hold. And if we use three decimal digits, we must ignore more than half the three-digit decimal numbers, because the numbers 256 through 999 can't be contained in one byte.

Two's Complement—An Odd Sort of Negative Number

Now we're ready to learn more about negative numbers. We said before that the numbers 8000h through FFFFh all behave as negative numbers when we ignore the overflow. There is an easy way to spot negative numbers when we write them in binary:

```
Positive numbers:
        0000h            0000 0000 0000 0000b
          .                       .
          .                       .
          .                       .
        7FFFh            0111 1111 1111 1111b

Negative numbers:
        8000h            1000 0000 0000 0000b
          .                       .
          .                       .
          .                       .
        FFFFh            1111 1111 1111 1111b
```

In the binary forms for all the positive numbers, the left most bit (bit 15) is always 0. For all negative numbers, this left most bit is always 1. This difference is, in fact, the way that the 8088 microprocessor knows when a number is negative: It looks at bit 15, the *sign bit*. If we use instructions for unsigned numbers in our programs, the 8088 will ignore the sign bit, and we will be free to use signed numbers at our convenience.

These negative numbers are known as the *two's complement* of positive numbers. Why complement? Because the conversion from a positive number, such as 3C8h, to its two's-complement form is a two-step process, with the first being the conversion of the number to its *complement*.

We won't need to negate numbers often, but we'll do the conversion here just so you can see how the 8088 microprocessor negates numbers. The conversion will seem a bit strange. You won't see why it works, but you will see that it does work.

To find the two's-complement form (negative of) any number, first write the number in binary, ignoring the sign. For example, 4Ch becomes 0000 0000 0100 1100b.

To negate this number, first reverse all the zeros and ones. This process of reversing is called *complementing*, and taking the complement of 4Ch, we find that:

```
          0 0 0 0    0 0 0 0    0 1 0 0    1 1 0 0
becomes:
          1 1 1 1    1 1 1 1    1 0 1 1    0 0 1 1
```

In the second step of the conversion, we add 1:

```
                                       1  1
     1 1 1 1    1 1 1 1    1 0 1 1    0 0 1 1
  +                                          1
     1 1 1 1    1 1 1 1    1 0 1 1    0 1 0 0
                                     -4Ch = FFB4h
```

The answer, FFB4h, is the result we get if we use Debug's H command to subtract 4Ch from 0h.

If you wish, you can add FFB4h to 4Ch by hand, to verify that the answer is 10000h. And from our earlier discussion, you know that you should ignore this leftmost 1 to get 0 (4C + (−4C) = 0) when you do two's-complement addition.

Summary

This chapter has been a fairly steep climb into the world of hexadecimal and binary numbers, and it may have required a fair amount of mental exercise.

Soon, in Chapter 3, we'll slow down to a gentler pace—once you've learned enough to converse with Debug in hex. Now, let's take a breath of fresh air and look back on where we've been and what we've found.

We started out by meeting Debug. In chapters to come, we'll become intimate friends with Debug but, since it doesn't understand our familiar decimal numbers, we've begun the friendship by learning a new numbering system, hexadecimal notation.

In learning about hex numbers, you also learned how to convert decimal numbers to hex, and hex numbers to decimal. We'll write a program to do these translations later, but for now it's been necessary to learn the language itself.

Once we'd covered the basics of hexadecimal notation, we were able to wander off for a look at bits, bytes, words, and binary numbers—important characters you'll encounter frequently as we continue to explore the world of the 8088 and assembly language programming.

Finally, we moved on to learn about negative numbers in hex—the two's-complement numbers. They led us to signed and unsigned numbers, where we also witnessed overflows of two different types: one in which an overflow leaves the correct answer (addition of two signed numbers), and one in which the overflow leads to the wrong answer (addition of two unsigned numbers).

All this learning will pay off in later chapters, because we'll use our knowledge of hex numbers to speak with Debug, and Debug will act as an interpreter between us and the 8088 microprocessor waiting inside your IBM PC.

In the next chapter, we'll use the knowledge we've gained so far to learn about the 8088. We'll rely on Debug again, and use hex numbers, rather than binary, to talk to the 8088. We'll learn about the microprocessor's registers—the places where it stores numbers—and in Chapter 3 we'll be ready to write a real program that will print a character on the screen. We'll also learn more about how the 8088 does its math; by the time we reach Chapter 10, we'll be able to write a program to convert binary numbers to decimal.

2

8088 ARITHMETIC

Knowing something of Debug's hex arithmetic and the 8088's binary arithmetic, we can begin to learn how the 8088 does its math. It uses internal commands called *instructions*.

Registers as Variables

Debug, our guide and interpreter, knows much about the 8088 microprocessor inside the IBM PC. We'll use it to delve into the inner workings of the 8088, and begin by asking Debug to display what it can about small pieces of memory called *registers*, in which we can store numbers. Registers are like variables in BASIC, but they are not exactly the same. Unlike the BASIC language, the 8088 microprocessor contains a fixed number of registers, and these registers are not part of your IBM PC's memory.

We'll ask Debug to display the 8088's registers with the R, for *Register,* command:

```
-R
AX=0000  BX=0000  CX=0000  DX=0000  SP=FFEE  BP=0000  SI=0000  DI=0000
DS=3756  ES=3756  SS=3756  CS=3756  IP=0100   NV UP DI PL NZ NA PO NC
3756:0100 E485            IN      AL,85
-
```

(You'll probably see different numbers in the second and third lines of your display; those numbers reflect the amount of memory in a computer. You'll continue to see such differences, and later we'll learn more about them.)

For now, Debug has certainly given us a lot of information. Let's concentrate on the first four registers—AX, BX, CX, and DX—all of which Debug tells us are equal to 0000, both here and on your display. These registers are the *general-purpose* registers. The other registers, SP, BP, SI, DI, DS, ES, SS, CS, and IP, are special-purpose registers we'll deal with in later chapters.

The four-digit number following each register name is in hex notation. In Chapter 1, we learned that one word is described exactly by four hex digits. Here, you can see that each of the 13 registers in the 8088 is one word, or 16 bits, long. This is why computers based on the 8088 microprocessor are known as 16-bit machines.

We mentioned that the registers are like BASIC variables. That means we should be able to change them, and we can. Debug's R command does more than display registers. Followed by the name of the register, the command tells Debug that we wish to view the register, and then change it. For example, we can change the AX register like this:

```
-R AX
AX 0000
:3A7
-
```

Let's look at the registers again to see if the AX register now contains 3A7h:

```
-R
AX=03A7  BX=0000  CX=0000  DX=0000  SP=FFEE  BP=0000  SI=0000  DI=0000
DS=3757  ES=3756  SS=3756  CS=3756  IP=0100   NV UP DI PL NZ NA PO NC
3756:0100 E485          IN      AL,85
-
```

It does. Furthermore, we can put any hex number into any register with the R command by specifying the register's name and entering the new number after the colon, as we just did. From here on, we'll be using this command whenever we need to place numbers into the 8088's registers.

You may recall seeing the number 3A7h in Chapter 1, where we used Debug's Hexarithmetic command to add 3A7h and 1EDh. Back then, Debug did the work for us. This time, we'll use Debug merely as an interpreter so we can work directly with the 8088. We'll give the 8088 instructions to add numbers from two registers: We'll place a number in the BX register and then instruct the 8088 to add the number in BX to the number in AX and put the answer back into AX. First, we need a number in the BX register. This time, let's add 3A7h and 92Ah. Use the R command to store 92Ah into BX.

Memory and the 8088

The AX and BX registers should, respectively, contain 3A7h and 92Ah, as we can verify with the R command:

```
AX=03A7  BX=092A  CX=0000  DX=0000  SP=FFEE  BP=0000  SI=0000  DI=0000
DS=3756  ES=3756  SS=3756  CS=3756  IP=0100   NV UP DI PL NZ NA PO NC
3756:0100 E485          IN      AL,85
```

Now that we have our two numbers in the AX and BX registers, how do we tell the 8088 to add BX to AX? We put some numbers into the computer's memory.

Your IBM PC probably has at least 128K of memory—far more than we'll need to use here. We'll place two bytes of *machine code* into a corner of this vast amount of memory. In this case, the machine code will be two binary numbers that tell the 8088 to add the BX register to AX. Then, so we can watch what happens, we'll *execute* this instruction with the help of Debug.

Where in memory should we place our two-byte instruction, and how will we tell the 8088 where to find it? As it turns out, the 8088 chops memory into 64K pieces known as *segments*. Most of the time, we'll be looking at memory within one of these segments without really knowing where the segment starts. We can do this because of the way the 8088 labels memory.

All bytes in memory are labeled with numbers, starting with 0h and working up. But remember the four-digit limitation on hex numbers? That means the highest number the 8088 can use is the hex equivalent of 65535, which means the maximum number of labels it can use is 64K. Even so, we know from experience that the 8088 can call on more than 64K of memory. How does it do this? By being a little bit tricky: It uses two numbers, one for each 64K segment, and one for each byte, or *offset*, within the segment. Each segment begins at a multiple of 16 bytes, so by overlapping segments and offsets, the 8088 effectively can label more than 64K of memory. In fact, this is precisely how the 8088 uses up to one million bytes of memory.

All the addresses (labels) we'll be using are offsets from the start of a segment. We'll write addresses as a segment number, followed by the offset within the segment. For example, 3756:0100 will mean we are at an offset of 100h within segment 3756h.

Later, in Chapter 11, we'll learn more about segments and see more about why we have such a high segment number. But for now, we'll simply trust Debug to look after the segments for us so that we can work within one segment without having to pay attention to segment numbers. And for the time being, we'll refer to addresses only by their offsets. Each of these addresses refers to one byte in the segment, and the addresses are sequential, so 101h is the byte following 100h in memory.

Written out, our two-byte instruction to add BX to AX looks like this: ADD AX,BX. We'll place this instruction at locations 100h and 101h, in whatever segment Debug starts to use. In referring to our ADD instruction, we'll say that it's *at* location 100h, since this is the location of the first byte of the instruction.

Debug's command for examining and changing memory is called E, for *Enter*. Use this command to enter the two bytes of the ADD instruction, as follows:

```
-E 100
3756:0100  E4.01
-E 101
3756:0101  85.D8
-
```

The numbers 01h and D8h are the 8088's machine language for our ADD instruction at memory locations 3756:0100 and 3756:0101. The segment number you see will probably be different, but that difference won't affect our program. Likewise, Debug probably displayed a different two-digit number for each of your E commands. These numbers (E4h and 85h in our example) are the old numbers in memory at offset addresses 100h and 101h of the segment Debug chose—that is, the numbers are data from previous programs left in

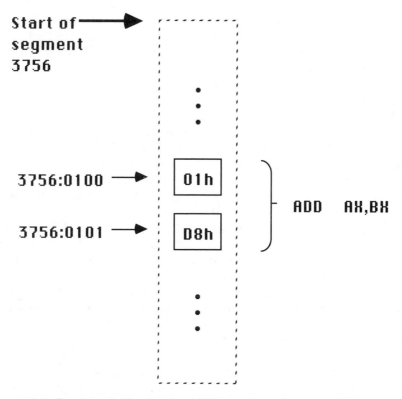

Figure 2-1. Our instruction begins 100 bytes from the start of the segment.

memory when you started Debug. (If you just started your computer, the numbers should be 00.)

Addition, 8088 Style

Now your register display should look something like this:

```
AX=03A7  BX=092A  CX=0000  DX=0000  SP=FFEE  BP=0000  SI=0000  DI=0000
DS=3756  ES=3756  SS=3756  CS=3756  IP=0100   NV UP DI PL NZ NA PO NC
3756:0100 01D8          ADD     AX,BX
```

Our ADD instruction is neatly placed in memory, just where we want it to be. We know this from reading the third line of the display. The first two numbers, 3756:0100, give us the address (100h) for the first number of our ADD instruction. Next to this, we see the two bytes for ADD: 01D8. The byte equal to 01h is at address 100h, while D8h is at 101h. Finally, since we entered our instruction in *machine language*—numbers that have no meaning to us, but that the 8088 will interpret as an add instruction—the message *ADD AX,BX* confirms that we entered the instruction correctly.

Even though we've placed our ADD instruction in memory, we're not quite ready to run it through the 8088 (*execute* it). First, we need to tell the 8088 where to find the instruction.

The 8088 finds segment and offset addresses in two special registers, CS and IP, which you can see listed in the preceding register display. The segment number is stored in the CS, or *Code Segment*, register, which we'll discuss shortly. If you look at the register display, you can see that Debug has already set the CS register for us (CS = 3756, in our example). The full starting address of our instruction, however, is 3756:0100.

The second part of this address (the offset within segment 3756) is stored in the IP (*Instruction Pointer*) register. The 8088 uses the offset in the IP register to actually find our first instruction. We can tell it where to look by setting the IP register to the address of our first instruction—IP = 0100.

But the IP register is already set to 100h. We've been clever: Debug sets IP to 100h whenever you first start it. Knowing this, we've deliberately chosen 100h as the address of our first instruction and have thus eliminated the need to set the IP register in a separate step. It's a good point to keep in mind.

Now, with our instructions in place and the registers set correctly, we'll tell Debug to execute our one instruction. We'll use Debug's T (*Trace*) command, which executes one instruction at a time and then displays the registers. After each trace, the IP should point to the next instruction. In this case, it will point to 102h. We haven't put an instruction at 102h, so in the last line of the register display you see an instruction left from some other program.

Let's ask Debug to trace one instruction with the T command:

```
-T
AX=0CD1  BX=092A  CX=0000  DX=0000  SP=FFEE  BP=0000  SI=0000  DI=0000
DS=3756  ES=3756  SS=3756  CS=3756  IP=0102   NV UP DI PL NZ AC PE NC
3756:0102 AC            LODSB
-
```

That's it. The AX register now contains CD1h, which is the sum of 3A7h and 92Ah. And the IP register points to address 102h, so the last line of the register display shows some instruction at memory location 102h, rather than 100h.

We mentioned earlier that the instruction pointer, together with the CS register, always points to the next instruction for the 8088. If we typed T again, we'd execute the next instruction, but don't do it just yet—your 8088 might head for limbo.

AX: 03A7   BX: 092A

ADD   AX,BX
LODSB

Figure 2-2. Before we execute the ADD instruction.

AX: 0CD1   BX: 092A

ADD   AX,BX
LODSB

Figure 2-3. After we execute the ADD instruction.

Instead, what if we want to execute our ADD instruction again, adding 92Ah to CD1h and storing the new answer in AX? For that we need to tell the 8088 where to find its next instruction, which we want to be our ADD instruction at 0100h. Can we just change the IP register to 0100h? Let's try it. Use the R command to set IP to 100 and look at the register display:

```
AX=0CD1  BX=092A  CX=0000  DX=0000  SP=FFEE  BP=0000  SI=0000  DI=0000
DS=3756  ES=3756  SS=3756  CS=3756  IP=0100   NV UP DI PL NZ AC PE NC
3756:0100              ADD     AX,BX
```

That's done it. Try the T command again and see if the AX register contains 15FBh. It does.

> **Note:** You should always check the IP register and the instruction at the bottom of an R display before using the T command. That way, you'll be sure the 8088 executes the instruction you want it to.

Now, set the IP register to 100h once again, make certain the registers contain AX = 15FB, BX = 092A, and let's try subtraction.

Subtraction, 8088 Style

We're going to write an instruction to subtract BX from AX so that, after two subtractions, we'll have 3A7h in AX: the point from which we started before our two additions. You'll also see how we can save a little effort in entering two bytes into memory.

When we entered the two bytes for our ADD instruction, we typed the E command twice: once with 0100h for the first address, and once with 0101h for the second address. The procedure worked, but as it turns out we can actually enter the second byte without another E command if we separate it from the first byte with a space. When you've finished entering bytes, pressing the Enter key will exit from the Enter command. Try this method for our subtract instruction:

```
-E 100
3756:0100  01.29  D8.D8
```

The register display (remember to reset the IP register to 100h) should now show the instruction *SUB AX,BX*, which subtracts the BX register from the AX register and leaves the result in AX. The order of AX and BX may seem backwards, but the instruction is like the BASIC statement AX = AX − BX except that the 8088, unlike BASIC, always puts the answer into the first variable (register).

Execute this instruction with the T command. AX should contain CD1. Change IP to point back to this instruction, and execute it again (remember to check the instruction at the bottom of the R display first). AX should now be 03A7.

Negative Numbers in the 8088

In the last chapter, we learned how the 8088 uses the two's-complement form for negative numbers. Now, let's work directly with the SUB instruction to calculate negative numbers. Let's put the 8088 to a little test, to see if we get

FFFFh for −1. We'll subtract one from zero and, if we're right, the subtraction should place FFFFh (−1) into AX. Set AX equal to zero and BX to one, then trace through the instruction at address 0100h. Just what we expected: AX = FFFFh.

While you have this subtraction instruction handy, you may wish to try some different numbers to gain a better feel for two's-complement arithmetic. For example, see what result you get for −2.

Bytes in the 8088

All our arithmetic thus far has been performed on words, hence the four hex digits. Does the 8088 microprocessor know how to perform math with bytes? Yes, it does.

Since one word is formed from two bytes, each general-purpose register can be divided into two bytes, known as the *high byte* (the first two hex digits) and the *low byte* (the second two hex digits). Each of these registers can be called by its letter (A through D), followed by X for a word, H for the high byte, or L for the low byte. For example, DL and DH are byte registers, and DX is a word register. (This terminology can become somewhat confusing, however, because words stored in memory have their low byte first and the high byte second.)

Let's test byte-size math with an ADD instruction. Enter the two bytes 00h and C4h, starting at location 0100h. At the bottom of the register display, you'll see the instruction *ADD AH, AL,* which will add the two bytes of the AX register and place the result in the high byte, AH.

Next, load the AX register with 0102h. This places 01h in the AH register and 02h in the AL register. Set the IP register to 100h, execute the T command,

Figure 2-4. **A register (AX) can be split into two byte registers (AH and AL).**

Figure 2-5. Before we execute the MUL instruction.

and you'll find that AX now contains 0302. The result of 01h + 02h is 03h, and that value is in the AH register.

But suppose you hadn't meant to add 01h and 02h. Suppose you really meant to add 01h and 03h. If the AX register already contained 0102, could you use Debug to change the AL register to 03h? No. You would have to change the entire AX register to 0103h. Why? Because Debug allows us to change only *word* registers. There isn't a way to change just the low or high part of a register with Debug. But, as you saw in the last chapter, this isn't a problem. With hex numbers, we can split a word into two bytes by breaking the four-digit hex number in half. Thus, the word 0103h becomes the two bytes 01h and 03h.

To try this ADD instruction, load the AX register with 0103h. Your ADD AH,AL instruction is still at memory location 0100h, so reset the IP register to 100h and, with 01h and 03h now in the AH and AL registers, trace through this instruction. This time, AX contains 0403h: 04h, the sum of 01h + 03h is now in the AH register.

Multiplication and Division, 8088 Style

We've seen the 8088 add and subtract two numbers. Now we'll see that it can also multiply and divide—a clever processor. The multiply instruction is called

Figure 2-6. After we execute the MUL instruction: The result is in the DX:AX pair of registers.

MUL, and the machine code to multiply AX and BX is F7h E3h. We'll enter this into memory, but first a word about the MUL instruction.

Where does the MUL instruction store its answer? In the AX register? Not quite; we have to be careful here. As you'll soon see, multiplying two 16-bit numbers can give a 32-bit answer, so the MUL instruction stores its result in two registers, DX and AX. The higher 16 bits are placed in the DX register; the lower, into AX. We will write this register combination as DX:AX, from time to time.

Let's get back to Debug and the 8088. Enter the multiply instruction, F7h E3h, at location 0100h, just as you did for the addition and subtraction instructions, and set AX = 7C4Bh and BX = 100h. You'll see the instruction in the register display as *MUL BX*, without any reference to the AX register. To multiply words, as here, the 8088 *always* multiplies the register you name in the instruction by the AX register, and stores the answer in the DX:AX pair of registers.

Before we actually execute this MUL instruction, let's do the multiplication by hand. How do we calculate 100h * 7C4Bh? The three digits 100 have the same effect in hex as in decimal, so to multiply by 100h simply add two zeros to the right of a hex number. Thus, 100h * 7C4Bh = 7C4B00h. This result is too long to fit into one word, so we'll split it into the two words 007Ch and 4B00h.

Figure 2-7. Before we execute the DIV instruction. DIV BX calculates DX:AX / BX.

Figure 2-8. After we execute the DIV instruction, the result is in the AX, and the remainder is in the DX register.

Use Debug to trace through the instruction. You'll see that DX contains the word 007Ch, and AX contains the word 4B00h. In other words, the 8088 returned the result of the *word-multiply* instruction in the DX:AX pair of registers. Since multiplying two words together can never be longer than two words but will often be longer than one word (as we just saw), the word-multiply instruction *always* returns the result in the DX:AX pair of registers.

And what about division? When we divide numbers, the 8088 keeps both the result and the remainder of the division. Let's see how the 8088's division works. First, place the instruction F7h F3h at 0100h (and 101h). Like the MUL instruction, DIV uses DX:AX without being told, so all we see is *DIV BX*. Now, load the registers so that DX = 007Ch and AX = 4B12h; BX should still contain 0100h.

Again, we'll first calculate the results by hand: 7C4B12h / 100h = 7C4Bh, with 12h left over. When we execute our division instruction at 0100h, we find that AX = 7C4Bh, the result of our division, and DX = 0012h, which is the remainder. (We'll put this remainder to very good use in Chapter 10, when we write a program to convert decimal numbers to hex by using the remainders, just as we did in Chapter 1.)

Summary

It's almost time for us to write a real program—one to print a character on the screen. We've put in our time learning the basics. Let's take a look at the ground we've covered, and then we'll be all set to push on.

We began this chapter by learning about registers and noticing their similarity to variables in BASIC. Unlike BASIC, however, we saw that the 8088 has a small, fixed number of registers. We concentrated on the four general-purpose registers (AX, BX, CX, and DX), with a quick look at the CS and IP registers, which the 8088 uses to locate segment and offset addresses.

After learning how to change and read registers, we moved on to build some single-instruction programs by entering the machine codes to add, subtract, multiply, and divide two numbers with the AX and BX registers. In future chapters we'll use much of what we learned here, but you won't need to remember the machine codes for each instruction.

We also learned how to tell Debug to execute, or trace through, a single instruction. We'll come to rely heavily on Debug to trace through our programs.

Of course, as our programs grow in size, this tracing will become both more useful and more tedious. Later on we'll build on our experience and learn how to execute more than one instruction with a single Debug command.

Let's turn back to real programs and learn how to make a program that speaks.

3

PRINTING CHARACTERS

Now we know enough to do something solid, so roll up your sleeves and flex your fingers. We're going to begin by instructing DOS to send a character to the screen, then we'll move on to even more interesting work. We'll build a small program with more than one instruction and from there, learn another way to put data into registers—this time, from within a program. Now, let's see if we can get DOS to speak.

INT—The Powerful Interrupt

To our four math instructions, ADD, SUB, MUL, and DIV, we'll add a new instruction called INT (for *Interrupt*). INT is something like BASIC's GOSUB statement. We'll use the INT instruction to ask DOS to print a character, A, on the screen for us.

Before we learn how INT works, let's run through an example. Start Debug and place 200h into AX and 41h into DX. The INT instruction for DOS functions is INT 21h—in machine code, CDh 21h. This is a two-byte instruction like the DIV instruction in the last chapter. Put INT 21h in memory, starting at location 100h, and use the R command to confirm that the instruction reads INT 21 (remember to set IP to 100h if it isn't already there).

Now we're ready to execute this instruction, but we can't use the trace command here as we did in the last chapter. The trace command executes one instruction at a time, but the INT instruction calls upon a large program in DOS to do the actual work, much as BASIC programs can call a subroutine with the GOSUB statement.

We don't want to execute each of the instructions in the entire DOS "subroutine" by tracing through it one instruction at a time. Instead, we want to *run* our one-line program, but stop before executing the instruction at location 102h. We can do this with Debug's G (*Go till*) command, followed by the address at which we want to stop:

```
-G 102
A
AX=0241  BX=0000  CX=0000  DX=0041  SP=FFEE  BP=0000  SI=0000  DI=0000
DS=3970  ES=3970  SS=3970  CS=3970  IP=0102  NV UP DI PL NZ NA PO NC
3970:0102 8BE5           MOV     SP,BP
```

DOS printed the character A and then returned control to our small program. (Remember, the instruction at 102h is just data left behind by another program, so you'll probably see something different.)

Our small program here is, in a sense, two instructions long, the second instruction being whatever is at location 102h. That is, it is something like this:

```
INT     21
MOV     SP,BP          (Or whatever is on your computer)
```

We'll soon replace this random second instruction with one of our own. For now, since it isn't anything we want to execute, we told Debug to run our program, stop execution when it reached this second instruction, and display the registers when it was done.

And how did DOS know to print the A? The 02h in the AH register told DOS to print a character. Another number in AH would tell DOS to execute a different function. (We'll see others later, but if you're curious right now, you can find a list of functions in your DOS Technical Manual. You can also find a list of functions in Appendix E that we use in this book.)

As for the character itself, DOS uses the number in the DL register as the ASCII code for the character to print when we ask it to send a character to the screen. We stored 41h, the ASCII code for an uppercase A.

In Appendix E, you'll find a chart of ASCII character codes for all the characters your IBM PC can display. For your convenience, the numbers are in both decimal and hex notation. But since Debug reads hex only, here is a good chance for you to practice converting decimal numbers to hex. Pick a character from the table and convert it to hex on your own. Then, verify your conversion by typing your hex value into the DL register and running the INT instruction again (remember to reset IP to 100h).

You may have wondered what would have happened if you had tried the trace command on the INT instruction. We'll pretend we had not executed the G 102 command and, instead, trace a short distance through, to see what happens. If you try this yourself, don't go too far: You may find your IBM PC doing something strange. After you've traced through a few steps, exit Debug with the Q command. This will clean up any mess you've left behind.

```
-R
AX=0200  BX=0000  CX=0000  DX=0041  SP=FFEE  BP=0000  SI=0000  DI=0000
DS=3970  ES=3970  SS=3970  CS=3970  IP=0100   NV UP DI PL NZ NA PO NC
3970:0100 CD21           INT     21
-T

AX=0200  BX=0000  CX=0000  DX=0041  SP=FFE8  BP=0000  SI=0000  DI=0000
DS=3970  ES=3970  SS=3970  CS=3372  IP=0180   NV UP DI PL NZ NA PO NC
3372:0180 80FC4B         CMP     AH,4B
-T

AX=0200  BX=0000  CX=0000  DX=0041  SP=FFE8  BP=0000  SI=0000  DI=0000
DS=3970  ES=3970  SS=3970  CS=3372  IP=0183   NV UP DI NG NZ AC PE CY
3372:0183 7405           JZ      018A
-T

AX=0200  BX=0000  CX=0000  DX=0041  SP=FFE8  BP=0000  SI=0000  DI=0000
```

```
DS=3970  ES=3970  SS=3970  CS=3372  IP=0185   NV UP DI NG NZ AC PE CY
3372:0185 2E            CS:
3372:0186 FF2EAB0B      JMP     FAR [0BAB]                CS:0BAB=0BFF
-Q
```

Notice that the first number of the address changed here, from 3970 to 3372. These last three instructions were part of DOS, and the program for DOS is in another segment. In fact, there are many, many more instructions that DOS executes before it prints a single character; even such an apparently simple task is not as easy as it sounds. Now you can see why we used the G command to run our program to location 102h. Otherwise, we'd have seen a torrent of instructions from DOS. (If you're using a different version of DOS than we used, the instructions you see when you try this may be different.)

A Graceful Exit—INT 20h

Remember that our INT instruction was 21h? If we changed the 21h to a 20h, we'd have INT 20h, instead. INT 20h is another interrupt instruction, and it tells DOS we want to exit our program, so DOS can take full control again. In our case, INT 20h will send control back to Debug, since we're executing our programs from Debug, rather than from DOS.

Enter the instruction CDh 20h, starting at location 100h, then try the following (remember to check the INT 20h instruction with the R command):

```
-G 102

Program terminated normally
-R
AX=0000  BX=0000  CX=0000  DX=0000  SP=FFEE  BP=0000  SI=0000  DI=0000
DS=3970  ES=3970  SS=3970  CS=3970  IP=0100   NV UP DI PL NZ NA PO NC
3970:0100 CD20            INT     20
-G

Program terminated normally
-R
AX=0000  BX=0000  CX=0000  DX=0000  SP=FFEE  BP=0000  SI=0000  DI=0000
DS=3970  ES=3970  SS=3970  CS=3970  IP=0100   NV UP DI PL NZ NA PO NC
3970:0100 CD20            INT     20
```

The command G, with no number after it, executes the entire program (which is just one instruction now, because INT 20 is an *exit* instruction), and then returns to the start. IP has been reset to 100h, which is where we started. The registers in this example are 0 only because we started Debug afresh.

We can use this INT 20h instruction at the end of a program to return control gracefully to DOS (or Debug), so let's put this instruction together with INT 21h and build a two-line program.

A Two-Line Program—Putting the Pieces Together

Starting at location 100h, enter the two instructions INT 21h, INT 20h (CDh 21h CDh 20h) one after the other. (From now on, we'll always start programs at location 100h).

When we had only one instruction we could "list" that instruction with the R command, but now we have two instructions. To see them, we have the U (*Unassemble*) command, which acts like BASIC's List command:

```
-U 100
3970:0100 CD21         INT     21
3970:0102 CD20         INT     20
3970:0104 D98D460250B8 ESC     09,[DI+0246][DI+B850]
3970:010A 8D00         LEA     AX,[BX+SI]
3970:010C 50           PUSH    AX
3970:010D E82A23       CALL    243A
3970:0110 8BE5         MOV     SP,BP
3970:0112 83C41A       ADD     SP,+1A
3970:0115 5D           POP     BP
3970:0116 C3           RET
3970:0117 55           PUSH    BP
3970:0118 83EC02       SUB     SP,+02
3970:011B 8BEC         MOV     BP,SP
3970:011D 823E0E0000   CMP     BYTE PTR [000E],00
```

The first two instructions we recognize as the two instructions we just entered. The other instructions are remnants left in memory. As our program grows, we'll fill this display with more of our own code.

Now, fill the AH register with 02h and the DL register with the number for any character (just as you did earlier when you changed the AX and DX registers), then simply type the G command to see your character. For example, if you place 41h into DL, you'll see:

```
-G
A
Program terminated normally
-
```

Try this a few times with other characters in DL before we move on to other ways to set these registers.

Entering Programs

From here on, most of our programs will be more than one instruction long, and to present these programs we'll use an unassemble display. Our last program would thus appear like this:

```
3970:0100 CD21         INT     21
3970:0102 CD20         INT     20
```

So far, we've entered the instructions for our programs directly as numbers, such as CDh, 21h. But that's a lot of work, and, as it turns out, there is a much easier way to enter instructions.

Besides the unassemble command, Debug includes an A (*Assemble*) command, which allows us to enter the mnemonic, or human-readable, instructions directly. So rather than entering those cryptic numbers for our short program, we can use the assemble command to enter the following:

```
-A 100
3970:0100 INT 21
3970:0102 INT 20
3970:0104
-
```

When you've finished assembling instructions, all you have to do is press the Enter key, and the Debug prompt reappears.

Here, the A command told Debug that we wished to enter instructions in mnemonic form, and the 100 in our command told Debug to start entering instructions at location 100h. Since Debug's assemble command makes entering programs much simpler, we'll use it from now on to enter instructions.

MOVing Data into Registers

Although we've relied on Debug quite a bit so far, we won't always run programs with it. Usually, a program would set the AH and DL registers itself before an INT 21h instruction. To do this, we'll learn about another instruction, MOV. Once we know enough about this instruction, we'll be able to take our small program to print a character and make a real program—one that we can execute directly from DOS.

Soon, we'll use the MOV instruction to load numbers into registers AH and DL. But let's start learning about MOV by moving numbers between registers. Place 1234h into AX (12h into the AH register, and 34h in AL) and ABCDh into DX (ABh in DH, and CDh in DL). Now, enter the following instruction with the A command:

```
396F:0100 88D4        MOV     AH,DL
```

This instruction *moves* the number in DL into AH by putting a copy of it into AH; DL is not affected. If you trace through this one line, you'll find that AX = CD34h and DX = ABCDh. Only AH has changed. It now holds a copy of the number in DL.

Like the BASIC statement LET AH = DL, a MOV instruction copies a number from the second register to the first, and for this reason we write AH before DL. Although there are some restrictions, which we'll find out about later, we can use other forms of the MOV instruction to copy numbers between other pairs of registers. For example, reset IP and try this:

```
396F:0100 89C3        MOV     BX,AX
```

You've just moved words, rather than bytes, between registers. The MOV instruction always works between words and words, or bytes and bytes; never between words and bytes. It makes sense, for how would you move a word into a byte?

We originally set out to move a number into the AH and DL registers. Let's do so now with another form of the MOV instruction:

```
396F:0100 B402        MOV     AH,02
```

This instruction moves 02h into the AH register without affecting the AL register. The second byte of the instruction, 02h, is the number we wish to move. Try moving a different number into AH: Change the second byte to another, such as C1h, with the E 101 command.

Now, let's put all the pieces of this chapter together and build a longer program. This one will print an asterisk, *, all by itself, with no need for us to set the registers (AH and DL). The program uses MOV instructions to set the AH and DL registers before the INT 21h call to DOS:

```
396F:0100 B402        MOV     AH,02
396F:0102 B22A        MOV     DL,2A
396F:0104 CD21        INT     21
396F:0106 CD20        INT     20
```

Enter the program and check it with the U command (U 100). Make sure IP points to location 100h, then try the G command to run the entire program. You should see the * character appear on your screen:

```
-G
*
Program terminated normally
-
```

Now that we have a complete, self-contained program, let's write it to disk as a .COM program, so we will be able to execute it directly from DOS. We can run a .COM program from DOS simply by typing its name. Since our program doesn't yet have a name, we need to give it one.

The Debug command N (*Name*) gives a name to a file before we write it to disk. Type:

```
-N WRITESTR.COM
```

to give the name WRITESTR.COM to our program. This command doesn't write our file to the disk, though—it simply names the file.

Next, we must give Debug a byte count, telling it the number of bytes in our program so it will know how much memory we want to write to our file. If you refer to the unassemble listing of our program, you can see that each instruction is two bytes long (this won't always be true). We have four instructions, so our program is 4 * 2 = 8 bytes long. (We could also put Debug's H command to work and use Hexarithmetic to determine the number of bytes in our program. Typing *H 108 100* to subtract the first address after our program, 108, from 100 will produce 8.)

Once we have our byte count, we need somewhere to put it. Debug uses the pair of registers BX:CX for the length of our file, so putting 8h into CX tells Debug that our program is eight bytes long. Finally, since our file is only eight bytes long, we also need to set BX to zero.

Once we've set the name and length of our program, we can then write it to disk with Debug's W (for *Write*) command:

```
-W
Writing 0008 bytes
-
```

We now have a program on our disk called WRITESTR.COM, so let's exit Debug, with a Q, and look for it. Use the DOS Dir command to list the file:

```
A>DIR WRITESTR.COM

 Volume in drive A has no label
 Directory of  A:\

WRITESTR COM        8   6-30-83  10:05a
        1 File(s)      18432 bytes free

A>
```

The directory listing tells us that WRITESTR.COM is on the disk and that it's eight bytes long, just as it should be. To run the program, simply type *Writestr* at the DOS prompt. You'll see a * appear on the display. Nothing to it.

Writing a String of Characters

As a final example for this chapter, we'll use INT 21h, with a different function number in the AH register, to write a whole string of characters. We'll have to store our string of characters in memory and we'll have to tell DOS where to find the string, so in the process, we'll also learn more about addresses and memory.

We've already seen that function number 02h for INT 21H prints one character on the screen. Another function, number 09h, prints an entire string, and stops printing characters when it finds a $ symbol in the string. Let's put a string into memory. We'll start at location 200h, so the string won't become tangled with the code for our program. Enter the following numbers, using the instruction E 200:

```
48        65        6C        6C
6F        2C        20        44
4F        53        20        68
65        72        65        2E
24
```

The last number, 24h, is the ASCII code for a $ sign, and it tells DOS that this is the end of our string of characters. You'll see what this string says in a minute, when you run the program we'll enter now:

```
396F:0100 B409        MOV     AH,09
396F:0102 BA0002      MOV     DX,0200
396F:0105 CD21        INT     21
396F:0107 CD20        INT     20
```

200h is the address of the string we entered, and loading 200h into the DX register tells DOS where to find the string of characters. Check your program with the U command, then run it with a G command:

```
-G
Hello, DOS here.
Program terminated normally
```

Now that we've stored some characters in memory, it's time to meet another Debug command, D (for *Dump*). The dump command dumps memory to the screen somewhat like U lists instructions. Just as when you use the U command, simply place an address after D to tell Debug where to start the dump. For example, type the command D 200 to see a dump of the string you just entered:

```
-D 200
396F:0200  48 65 6C 6C 6F 2C 20 44-4F 53 20 68 65 72 65 2E   Hello, DOS here.
396F:0210  24 5D C3 55 83 EC 30 8B-EC C7 06 10 00 00 00 E8   $]CU.10.1G.....h
    .
    .
    .
```

After each pair of address numbers (such as 396F:0200 in our example), we see 16 hex bytes, followed by the 16 ASCII characters for these bytes. Thus, on the first line you see most of the ASCII codes and characters you typed in. The ending $ sign you typed is the first character on the second line; the remainder of that line is a miscellaneous assortment of characters.

Wherever you see a period (.) in the ASCII window, it represents either a period or a special character, such as the Greek letter pi. Debug's D command displays only 96 of the 256 characters in the IBM PC character set, so a period is used for the remaining 160 characters.

We'll use the D command in the future to check numbers we enter for data, whether those data are characters or ordinary numbers. (For more information, refer to the Debug section in your DOS manual.)

Our string-writing program is complete, so we can write it to the disk. The procedure is the same one we used to write WRITESTR.COM to disk, except this time we have to set our program length to a value long enough to include the string at 200h. Our program begins at line 100h, and we can see from the memory dump just performed that the first character (]) following the $ sign that ends our string is at location 211h. Again, we can use the H command to find the difference between these two numbers. Find 211h − 100h and store this value into the CX register, again setting BX to zero. Use the N command to give the program a name (add the .COM extension to run the program directly from DOS), then use the W command to write the program and data to a disk file.

That's it for writing characters to the screen—aside from one final note: You may have noticed that DOS never sends the $ character. Quite so, because DOS uses the $ sign to mark the end of a string of characters. That means we can't use DOS to print a string with a $ in it, but in a later chapter, we'll see how to print a string with a $ sign or any other special character.

Summary

Our preparations in the first two chapters brought us to the point where we could work on a real program. In this chapter, we used our knowledge of hex numbers, Debug, 8088 instructions, and memory to build short programs to print a character and a string of characters on the screen. In the process we also learned some new things.

First we learned about INT instructions—not in much detail, but enough for us to write two short programs. In later chapters, we'll gain more knowledge about interrupt instructions as we increase our understanding of the 8088 microprocessor tucked under the cover of your IBM PC.

Debug has, once again, been a useful and faithful guide. We've been relying heavily on Debug to display the contents of registers and memory, and in this chapter we used its abilities even more. Debug ran our short programs with the G command.

We also learned about the INT 20 exit instruction, and the MOV instruction for moving numbers into and between registers. The exit instruction (INT 20) allowed us to build a complete program that we could write to the disk and run directly from DOS without the help of Debug. And the MOV instruction gave us the ability to set registers before an INT 21 (print) instruction, so we could write a self-contained program to print one character.

Finally, we rounded out the chapter with the INT 21h function to print an entire string of characters. We'll use all these instructions heavily throughout the rest of this book, but as you saw from using the Debug assemble and unassemble commands, you won't need to remember the machine codes for these instructions.

Now we know enough to move on to printing binary numbers. In the next chapter we'll build a short program to take one byte and print it on the screen as a string of binary digits (zeros and ones).

4

PRINTING BINARY NUMBERS

In this chapter we'll build a program to write binary numbers to the screen as strings of zeros and ones. We have most of the knowledge we need, and our work here will help solidify ideas we've already covered. We'll also add a few instructions to those we know, including another version of ADD and some instructions to help us repeat parts of our program. Let's begin by learning something completely new.

Rotations and the Carry Flag

In Chapter 2, when we first encountered hex arithmetic, we found that adding 1 to FFFFh should give 10000h, but doesn't. Only the four hex digits to the right fit into one word; the 1 doesn't fit. We also found that this 1 is an overflow and that it is not lost. Where does it go? It is put into something called a *flag*—in this case, the *Carry Flag*, or *CF*. Flags contain one-bit numbers, so they can hold either a zero or a one. If we need to carry a one into the fifth hex digit, it goes into the carry flag.

Let's go back to our ADD instruction of Chapter 2 (ADD AX,BX). Put FFFFh into AX and 1 into BX, then trace through the ADD instruction. At the end of the second line of Debug's R display, you'll see eight pairs of letters. The last of these, which can read either NC or CY, is the carry flag. Right now, because your add instruction resulted in an overflow of 1, you'll see that the carry status reads CY (*Carry*). The carry bit is now 1 (or, as we'll say, it's set).

Just to confirm that we've stored a seventeenth bit here (it would be the ninth bit for a byte addition), ADD one to the zero in AX by resetting IP to 100h and tracing through the add instruction again. The carry flag is affected by each ADD instruction, and this time there shouldn't be any overflow, so the carry should be reset. And, indeed, the carry does become zero, as indicated by the NC, which stands for *No Carry*, in the R display.

(We'll learn about the other status flags later, but if you're curious, you can find information about them right now under Debug's R command in your DOS manual.)

Let's review the task of printing a binary number to see how the carry information could be useful. We print only one character at a time, and want to pick off the bits of our number, one by one, from left to right. For example, the first character we would want to print in the number 1000 0000b would be the one. If we could move this entire byte left one place, dropping the one into the carry flag and adding a 0 to the right side, then repeat the process for each succeeding

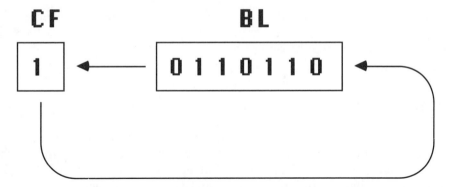

Figure 4-1. The RCL BL,1 instruction moves the bits left one position through the carry flag.

digit, the carry flag would pick off our binary digits. And we can do just this with a new instruction called RCL (*Rotate Carry Left*).

To see how it works, enter the short program:

```
3985:0100 D0D3          RCL     BL,1
```

This instruction *rotates* the byte in BL to the left by one bit (hence the ,1), and it does so through the carry flag. The instruction is called rotate, because RCL moves the leftmost bit into the carry flag, while moving the bit currently in the carry flag into the rightmost bit position (0). In the process, all the other bits are moved, or rotated, to the left. After enough rotations (17 for a word, nine for a byte) the bits are moved back into their original positions, and you get back the original number.

Place B7h in the BX register, then trace through this rotate instruction several times. Converting your results to binary, you'll see the following:

```
Carry           BL register
   0        1 0 1 1   0 1 1 1     B7h      We start here
   1        0 1 1 0   1 1 1 0     6Eh
   0        1 1 0 1   1 1 0 1     DDh
   1        1 0 1 1   1 0 1 0     BAh
                      .
                      .
                      .
   0        1 0 1 1   0 1 1 1     B7h      After 9 rotations
```

In the first rotation, bit 7 of BL moves into the carry flag, the bit in the carry flag moves into bit 0 of BL, and all the other bits move left one position. Succeeding moves continue rotating the bits to the left until, after nine rotations, the original number is back in the BL register.

We're getting closer to building our program to write binary numbers to the screen, but we still need a few other pieces. Let's see how we can convert the bit in the carry flag into the character 0 or 1.

Adding With the Carry Flag

The normal ADD instruction, for example, ADD AX,BX, simply adds two numbers. Another instruction, ADC (*Add with Carry*) adds three numbers: the two, as before, *plus* one bit from the carry flag. If you look in your ASCII table, you'll discover that 30h is the character 0 and 31h is the character 1. So, adding the carry flag to 30h gives the character 0 when the carry is clear, and 1 when the carry is set. Thus, if DL = 0 and the carry flag is set (1), executing:

```
ADC  DL,30
```

adds DL (0) to 30h ('0') and to 1h (the carry) to give 31h ('1'). And, with one instruction we've converted the carry to a character we can print.

At this point, rather than run through an example of ADC, let's wait for our complete program. Once we've built our program, we'll execute its instructions one at a time, in a procedure called *single-stepping*, and through this, we'll see both how the ADC instruction works and how it fits nicely into

Figure 4-2. The LOOP Instruction.

our program. But first we need one more instruction, which we'll use to repeat our RCL, ADC, and INT 21h (print) instructions eight times: once for each bit in a byte.

Looping

As noted, the RCL instruction isn't limited to rotating bytes; it can also rotate entire words. We'll use this ability to demonstrate the *LOOP* instruction. LOOP is something like a FOR-NEXT loop in BASIC, but it's not as general. As with BASIC's FOR-NEXT loop, however, we need to tell LOOP how many times to run through a loop. We do this by placing our repeat count in register CX. Each time through the loop, the 8088 subtracts one from CX, and, when CX becomes zero, LOOP ends the loop.

Why the CX register? The C in CX stands for *Count*. We can use this register as a general-purpose register, but, as you'll see in the next chapter, the CX register is used with other instructions when we wish to repeat operations.

Here's a simple program that rotates the BX register left eight times, moving BL into BH (but not the reverse, since we rotate through the carry flag):

```
396F:0100 BBC5A3     MOV     BX,A3C5
396F:0103 B90800     MOV     CX,0008
396F:0106 D1D3       RCL     BX,1
396F:0108 E2FC       LOOP    0106
396F:010A CD20       INT     20
```

Our loop starts at 106h (RCL BX,1) and ends with the LOOP instruction. The number following LOOP (106h) is the address of the RCL instruction. When we run the program, LOOP subtracts one from CX, then jumps to address 106h if CX is not zero. The instruction RCL BX,1 (Rotate Carry Left, one place) is executed eight times here, because CX is set to eight before the loop.

You may have noted that, unlike the FOR-NEXT loop in BASIC, the LOOP instruction is at the end of our loop (where we'd put the NEXT statement in BASIC). And the start of the loop, the RCL instruction at 106h, has no special instruction like FOR has in BASIC. If you know a language like Pascal, you can see that the LOOP instruction is somewhat akin to the REPEAT-UNTIL pair of instructions, where the REPEAT instruction just labels the start of the block of instructions to loop through.

There are different ways you could execute our small program. If you simply type G, you won't see any change in the register display, because Debug saves all the registers before it starts carrying out a G command. Then, if it encounters an INT 20 instruction (as it will in our program), it restores all the registers. Try G. You'll see that IP has been reset to 100h (where you started), and that the other registers don't look any different, either.

If you have the patience, you can trace through this program, instead. Taking it one step at a time, you can watch the registers change at each step:

```
-R
AX=0000  BX=0000  CX=0000  DX=0000  SP=FFEE  BP=0000  SI=0000  DI=0000
DS=0CDE  ES=0CDE  SS=0CDE  CS=0CDE  IP=0100   NV UP DI PL NZ NA PO NC
0CDE:0100 BBC5A3        MOV     BX,A3C5
-T

AX=0000  BX=A3C5  CX=0000  DX=0000  SP=FFEE  BP=0000  SI=0000  DI=0000
DS=0CDE  ES=0CDE  SS=0CDE  CS=0CDE  IP=0103   NV UP DI PL NZ NA PO NC
0CDE:0103 B90800        MOV     CX,0008
-T

AX=0000  BX=A3C5  CX=0008  DX=0000  SP=FFEE  BP=0000  SI=0000  DI=0000
DS=0CDE  ES=0CDE  SS=0CDE  CS=0CDE  IP=0106   NV UP DI PL NZ NA PO NC
0CDE:0106 D1D3          RCL     BX,1
-T

AX=0000  BX=478A  CX=0008  DX=0000  SP=FFEE  BP=0000  SI=0000  DI=0000
DS=0CDE  ES=0CDE  SS=0CDE  CS=0CDE  IP=0108   OV UP DI PL NZ NA PO CY
0CDE:0108 E2FC          LOOP    0106
-T
AX=0000  BX=478A  CX=0007  DX=0000  SP=FFEE  BP=0000  SI=0000  DI=0000
DS=0CDE  ES=0CDE  SS=0CDE  CS=0CDE  IP=0106   OV UP DI PL NZ NA PO CY
0CDE:0106 D1D3          RCL     BX,1
                               .
                               .
                               .

 -T

AX=0000  BX=C551  CX=0001  DX=0000  SP=FFEE  BP=0000  SI=0000  DI=0000
DS=0CDE  ES=0CDE  SS=0CDE  CS=0CDE  IP=0108   NV UP DI PL NZ NA PO CY
0CDE:0108 E2FC          LOOP    0106
-T

AX=0000  BX=C551  CX=0000  DX=0000  SP=FFEE  BP=0000  SI=0000  DI=0000
DS=0CDE  ES=0CDE  SS=0CDE  CS=0CDE  IP=010A   NV UP DI PL NZ NA PO CY
0CDE:010A CD20          INT     20
```

Or, you can type G 10A to execute the program up to, but not including, the INT 20 instruction at 10Ah; then the registers will show the result of our program.

If you try this, you'll see CX = 0 and either BX = C551 or BX = C5D1, depending on the value of the carry flag before you ran the program. The C5 our program's MOV instruction put into BL at the start is now in the BH register, but BL doesn't contain A3, because we rotated BX *through* the carry. Later, we'll see other ways of rotating without going through the carry. Let's get back to our goal of printing a number in binary notation.

Writing a Binary Number

We've seen how to strip off binary digits one at a time and convert them to ASCII characters. If we add an INT 21h instruction to print our digits, our program will be done. Here's the program; the first instruction sets AH to 02 for the INT 21h function call (recall, 02 tells DOS to print the character in the DL register):

```
3985:0100 B402        MOV     AH,02
3985:0102 B90800      MOV     CX,0008
3985:0105 B200        MOV     DL,00
3985:0107 D0D3        RCL     BL,1
3985:0109 80D230      ADC     DL,30
3985:010C CD21        INT     21
3985:010E E2F5        LOOP    0105
3985:0110 CD20        INT     20
```

We've seen how all the pieces work and will put them together now. We rotate BL (with the instruction RCL BL,1) to pick off the bits of a number, so pick a number you want printed in binary, load it into the BL register, then run this program with a G command. After the INT 20h instruction, the G command restores the registers to the values they had before, so BL still contains the number you see printed in binary.

The ADC DL,30 instruction in our program converts the carry flag to a zero or a one character. The instruction MOV DL,0 sets DL to zero first, then the ADC instruction adds 30h to DL, and then finally adds the carry. Since 30h is the ASCII code for a 0, the result of ADC DL,30 is the code for 0 when the carry is clear (NC) or 1 if the carry is set (CY).

If you want to see what happens when you run this program, trace through it. Keep in mind that you'll need to be a bit careful in single-stepping through it with the T command. It contains an INT 21h instruction and, as you saw when we first encountered INT 21h, DOS does a great deal of work for that one instruction. That's why you can't use T on the INT 21.

You can, however, trace through all the other instructions in this program except the final INT 20, which won't concern you until the very end. During your tracing, each time you loop through and reach the INT 21h instruction, type G 10E. Your G command, followed by an address, will tell Debug to continue running the program, but to stop when IP becomes the address (10E) you entered. That is, Debug will execute the INT 21h instruction without your tracing through it, but stops before executing the LOOP instruction at 10E, so you can return to tracing through the program. (The number you type after G is known as a *breakpoint* in the DOS manual; breakpoints are very useful when you're trying to understand the inner workings of programs.)

Finally, terminate the program when you reach the INT 20h instruction by typing the G command by itself.

The Proceed Command

Whether or not you tried out the instructions to trace through our program, you've seen that an instruction like G 10E allows us to trace *over* an INT instruction that starts at, say, 10Ch. But that means each time we want to trace over an INT instruction, we need to find the address of the instruction immediately following the INT instruction.

As it turns out, there is a Debug command that makes tracing through INT instructions much simpler. The P (*Proceed*) command does all the work for us. To see, trace through the program, but this time, when you reach the INT 21h instruction, type P, rather than G 10E, as described before.

We'll make heavy use of the P command in the rest of this book, because it's a very nice way to trace over commands like INT, which call on large programs, such as the routines inside DOS. Before going on, though, we should mention one thing about the P command—it wasn't documented in the DOS manuals for versions of DOS before 3.00. This lack of documentation may have been an oversight or, more likely, because Microsoft didn't have time to test the P command completely before delivering version 2.00 of DOS. Whatever the reason, if you have a version of DOS before 3.00, you should be aware that the P command *may not* work all the time—although we've never had any problems using it.

That's about all we'll do for printing binary numbers as strings of zeros and ones, but here's a simple exercise for you to practice on: See if you can modify this program to print a *b* at the end of our binary number (**Hint**: The ASCII code for b is 62h).

Summary

In this chapter, we had a chance to catch our breath a bit after our hard work on new concepts in Chapters 1 through 3. So where have we been and what have we seen?

We had our first encounter with flags and had a look at the carry flag, which was of special interest here, because it made our job of printing a binary number quite simple. It did so as soon as we learned about the rotate instruction RCL, which rotates a byte or word to the left, one bit at a time.

Once we learned about the carry flag and rotating bytes and words, we tucked a new version of the ADD instruction, ADC, under our belts and were almost ready to build our program to print a number in binary notation.

This is where the LOOP instruction entered the scene. By loading the CX register with a loop count, we could keep the 8088 executing a loop of instructions a number of times. We set CX to 8, to execute a loop eight times.

That's all we needed to write our program. We'll use these tools again in the following chapters. In the next chapter we'll print a binary number in hexadecimal notation, just as Debug does, so by the time we finish Chapter 5, we'll have a better idea of how Debug translates numbers from binary to hex. Then, we'll move on to the other end of Debug: reading the numbers typed in hex and converting them to the 8088's binary notation.

5

PRINTING IN HEX

Our program in Chapter 4 was fairly straightforward. We were lucky because the carry flag made it easy to print a binary number as a string of 0 and 1 characters. Now we'll move on to printing numbers in hex notation. Here, our work will be a bit less direct, and we'll begin to repeat ourselves in our programs, writing the same sequence of instructions more than once. But that type of repetition won't last forever: In Chapter 7, we'll learn about procedures, or subroutines, that eliminate the need to write more than one copy of a group of instructions. First, let's learn some more useful instructions and see how to print numbers in hex.

Compare and Status Bits

In the last chapter, we learned something about status flags and examined the carry flag, which is represented as either CY or NC in Debug's R display. The other flags, which are equally useful, keep track of the *status* for the last arithmetic operation. There are eight flags altogether, and we'll learn about them as they are needed.

Recall that CY means the carry flag is 1, or set, whereas NC means the carry flag is 0. In all flags 1 means *true* and 0 means *false*. For example, if a SUB instruction results in 0, the flag known as the Zero Flag would be set to 1—true—and you would see it in the R display as ZR (*Zero*). Otherwise, the zero flag would be reset to 0—NZ (*Not Zero*).

Let's look at an example that tests the zero flag. We'll use the SUB instruction to subtract two numbers. If the two numbers are equal, the result will be zero, and the zero flag will appear as ZR on your display. Enter the following subtract instruction:

```
396F:0100 29D8        SUB     AX,BX
```

Now, trace through the instruction with a few different numbers, watching for ZR or NZ to appear in the zero flag. If you place the same number (F5h in the following example) into both the AX and BX registers, you'll see the zero flag set after one subtract instruction, and cleared after another:

```
-R
AX=00F5  BX=00F5  CX=0000  DX=0000  SP=FFEE  BP=0000  SI=0000  DI=0000
DS=0CDE  ES=0CDE  SS=0CDE  CS=0CDE  IP=0100   NV UP DI PL NZ NA PO NC
0CDE:0100 29D8        SUB     AX,BX
-T

AX=0000  BX=00F5  CX=0000  DX=0000  SP=FFEE  BP=0000  SI=0000  DI=0000
```

```
DS=0CDE   ES=0CDE   SS=0CDE   CS=0CDE   IP=0102   NV UP DI PL ZR NA PE NC
0CDE:0102 3F                   AAS
-R IP
IP 0102
:100
-R
AX=0000   BX=00F5   CX=0000   DX=0000   SP=FFEE   BP=0000   SI=0000   DI=0000
DS=0CDE   ES=0CDE   SS=0CDE   CS=0CDE   IP=0100   NV UP DI PL ZR NA PE NC
0CDE:0100 29D8                   SUB     AX,BX
-T

AX=FF0B   BX=00F5   CX=0000   DX=0000   SP=FFEE   BP=0000   SI=0000   DI=0000
DS=0CDE   ES=0CDE   SS=0CDE   CS=0CDE   IP=0102   NV UP DI NG NZ AC PO CY
0CDE:0102 3F                   AAS
```

If we subtract one from zero, the result is FFFFh, which, as we saw in Chapter 1, is -1 in two's-complement form. Can we tell from the R display whether a number is positive or negative? Yes, another flag, called the Sign Flag, changes between NG (*Negative*) and PL (*Plus*), and is set to 1 when a number is a negative two's-complement number.

And another new flag we'll be interested in is the Overflow Flag, which changes between OV (*Overflow*) when the flag is 1 and NV (*No Overflow*) when the flag is 0. The overflow flag is set if the sign bit changes when it shouldn't. For example, if we add two positive numbers, such as 7000h and 6000h, we get a negative number, D000h, or -12288. This is an error because the result overflows the word. The result should be positive, but isn't, so the 8088 sets the overflow flag. (Remember, if we were dealing with unsigned numbers, this wouldn't be an error, in which case we would ignore the overflow flag.)

Try several different numbers to see if you can set and reset each of these flags, trying them out until you're comfortable with them. For the overflow, subtract a large negative number from a large positive number— for example, 7000h $-$ 8000h, since 8000h is a negative number equal to -32768 in two's-complement form.

Now we're ready to look at a set of instructions called the *conditional jump* instructions. They allow us to check status flags more conveniently than we've been able to so far. The instruction JZ (*Jump if Zero*) jumps to a new address if the last arithmetic result was zero. Thus, if we follow a SUB instruction with, say, JZ 15A, a result of zero for the subtraction would cause the 8088 to jump to, and start executing, statements at address 15Ah, rather than at the next instruction.

The JZ instruction tests the zero flag, and, if it's set (ZR), does a jump just like a jump with the BASIC statement IF A = 0 THEN 100. The opposite of JZ is JNZ (*Jump if Not Zero*). Let's look at a simple example that uses JNZ and subtracts one from a number until the result is zero:

```
396F:0100 2C01                   SUB     AL,01
396F:0102 75FC                   JNZ     0100
396F:0104 CD20                   INT     20
```

Put a number like three in AL, so you'll go through the loop a few times, then trace through this program, one instruction at a time, to see how conditional branches work. We put the INT 20h instruction at the end so typing G by accident won't drop off the end of our program: It's a good defensive practice.

You may have noticed that using SUB to compare two numbers, as we just did, has the potentially undesirable side effect of changing the first number. Another instruction, CMP (*Compare*) allows us to do the subtraction without storing the result anywhere and without changing the first number. The result is used only to set the flags, so we can use one of the many conditional jump instructions after a compare. To see what happens, set both AX and BX to the same number, F5h, and trace through this instruction:

```
-A 100
0CDE:0100 CMP AX,BX
0CDE:0102
-T

AX=00F5  BX=00F5  CX=0000  DX=0000  SP=FFEE  BP=0000  SI=0000  DI=0000
DS=0CDE  ES=0CDE  SS=0CDE  CS=0CDE  IP=0102   NV UP DI PL ZR NA PE NC
0CDE:0102 3F            AAS
```

The zero flag is now set (ZR), but F5h remains in both registers.

Let's use CMP to print a single hex digit. We'll create a set of instructions that use flags to alter the flow of our program, as LOOP did in the last chapter, in a manner similar to BASIC's IF-THEN statement. This new set of instructions will use the flags to test for such conditions as less than, greater than, and so on. We won't have to worry about which flags are set when the first number is less than the second; the instructions know which flags to look at.

Printing a Single Hex Digit

Let's start by putting a small number (between 0 and Fh) into the BL register. Since any number between 0 and Fh is equivalent to one hex digit, we can convert our choice to a single ASCII character and then print it. Let's look at the steps we need to take to do the conversion.

The ASCII characters 0 through 9 have the values 30h through 39h; the characters A through F, however, have the values 41h through 46h. Herein lies a problem: These two groups of ASCII characters are separated by seven characters. As a result, the conversion to ASCII will be different for the two groups of numbers (0 through 9 and Ah through Fh), so we must handle each group differently. A BASIC program to do this two-part conversion looks like this:

```
100 IF  BL < &H0A
       THEN BL = BL + &H30
       ELSE BL = BL + &H37
```

Character	ASCII Code (Hex)
/	2F
0	30
1	31
2	32
3	33
4	34
5	35
6	36
7	37
8	38
9	39
:	3A
;	3B
<	3C
=	3D
>	3E
?	3F
@	40
A	41
B	42
C	43
D	44
E	45
F	46
G	47

Figure 5-1. Part of the ASCII table showing the characters used by hex digits.

Our BASIC conversion program is fairly simple. Unfortunately, the 8088's machine language doesn't include an ELSE statement; it's far more primitive than BASIC is, so we'll need to be somewhat clever. Here's another BASIC program, this time one that mimics the method we'll use for our machine-language program:

```
100 BL = BL + &H30
110 IF BL >= &H3A
    THEN BL = BL + &H7
```

You can convince yourself that this program works by trying it with some choice examples. The numbers 0, 9, Ah, and Fh are particularly good because these four numbers cover all the *boundary* conditions—areas where we often run into problems.

Here, 0 and Fh are, respectively, the smallest and largest single-digit hex numbers, so by using 0 and Fh, we check the bottom and top of our range. The numbers 9 and 0Ah, although next to each other, require two different conversion schemes in our program. By using 9 and 0Ah, we confirm that we've chosen the correct place to switch between these two conversion schemes.

(Note that we wrote 0Ah for the number A, rather than AH, so we wouldn't confuse the number Ah with the register AH. So, we'll often place a zero before hex numbers in situations that could be confusing. In fact, since it never hurts to place a zero before a hex number, it's a good idea to place a zero before *all* hex numbers.)

The machine-language version of this program contains a few more steps, but it's essentially the same as the BASIC version. It uses the CMP instruction, as well as a conditional jump instruction called JL (*Jump if Less Than*). Here's the program to take a single-digit hex number in the BL register and print it in hex:

```
3985:0100 B402        MOV     AH,02
3985:0102 88DA        MOV     DL,BL
3985:0104 80C230      ADD     DL,30
3985:0107 80FA3A      CMP     DL,3A
3985:010A 7C03        JL      010F
3985:010C 80C207      ADD     DL,07
3985:010F CD21        INT     21
3985:0111 CD20        INT     20
```

The CMP instruction, as we saw before, subtracts two numbers (DL − 3Ah) to set the flags, but it doesn't change DL. So if DL is less than 3Ah, the JL 10F instruction skips to the INT 21h instruction at 10Fh. Place a single-digit hex number in BL and trace through this example to get a better feeling for CMP and our algorithm to convert hex to ASCII. Remember to use either the G command with a breakpoint or the P command when you run the INT instructions.

Another Rotate Instruction

Our program works for any single-digit hex number, but if we wish to print a two-digit hex number, we need a few more steps. We need to isolate each digit (four bits, which are often called a *nibble*) of this two-digit hex number. In this section, we'll see that we can easily isolate the first, or higher, four bits, and in

Figure 5-2. The JL Instruction.

the next section, we'll encounter a concept known as a *logical operation*, which we'll use to isolate the lower four bits—the second of our two hex digits.

To begin, recall that the RCL instruction rotates a byte or a word to the left, through the carry flag. In the last chapter we used the instruction RCL BL,1, in which the 1 told the 8088 to rotate BL by one bit. We can rotate by more than one bit if we want, but we can't simply write the instruction RCL BL,2. (**Note**: Although RCL BL,2 isn't a legal 8088 instruction, it works just fine with the 80286 and 80386 processors found in IBM ATs and PS/2s. But since there are still many IBM PCs, it's best to write your programs for the lowest common denominator—the older 8088.) For rotations by more than one bit, we must place a rotate count in the CL register.

The CL register is used here in much the same way as the CX register is used by the LOOP instruction to determine the number of times to repeat a loop. The 8088 uses CL for the number of times to rotate a byte or word, rather than the CX register, because it makes no sense to rotate more than 16 times; thus the eight-bit CL register is more than large enough to hold our maximum shift count.

How does all this tie in with printing a two-digit hex number? Our plan now is to rotate the byte in DL four bits to the right. To do so, we'll use a slightly different rotate instruction called SHR (*Shift Right*). Using SHR, we will be able to move the upper four bits of our number to the rightmost nibble (four bits).

We also want the upper four bits of DL set to zero, so that the entire register becomes equal to the nibble we are shifting into the right nibble. If we were to enter SHR DL,1, our instruction would move the byte in DL one bit to the right, and at the *same* time, it would move bit 0 into the carry flag, while *shifting* a zero into bit 7 (the highest, or leftmost, bit in DL). If we do that three more times, we'll have just what we want: The upper four bits will end up shifted right into the lower four bits, while the upper four bits will all have had zeroes

Figure 5-3. The SHR DL,1 instruction moves the bits right one position into the carry flag.

shifted into them. We can do all that shifting in one instruction, using the CL register as the *shift count*. By setting CL to four before the instruction SHR DL,CL, we will ensure that DL becomes equal to the upper hex digit.

Let's see how this works. Place 4 into CL and 5Dh into DL, then enter and trace through the following SHR instruction:

```
3985:0100 D2EA        SHR    DL,CL
```

DL should now be 05h, which is the first digit in the number 5Dh, and we can now print this digit with a program like the one we used earlier. Thus, putting together the pieces we have so far, we can build the following program to take a number in the BL register and print the first hex digit:

```
3985:0100 B402        MOV    AH,02
3985:0102 88DA        MOV    DL,BL
3985:0104 B104        MOV    CL,04
3985:0106 D2EA        SHR    DL,CL
3985:0108 80C230      ADD    DL,30
3985:010B 80FA3A      CMP    DL,3A
3985:010E 7C03        JL     0113
3985:0110 80C207      ADD    DL,07
3985:0113 CD21        INT    21
3985:0115 CD20        INT    20
```

Logic and AND

Now that we can print the first of the two digits in a hex number, let's see how we can isolate and print the second digit. Here, we'll learn how to clear the upper four bits of our original (unshifted) number to zero, leaving DL equal to the lower four bits. It's simple: Set the upper four bits to zero with an instruction called AND. The AND instruction is one of the *logical* instructions—those that have their roots in formal logic. Let's see how AND works.

In formal logic, we can say, "A is true, if B *and* C are both true." But if either B or C is false, then A must also be false. If we take this statement, substitute one for true and zero for false, then look at the various combinations of A, B, and C, we can create what is known as a *truth* table. Here's the truth table for ANDing two bits together:

```
AND │ F   T                  AND │ O   1
────┼──────          =       ────┼──────
 F  │ F   F                   O  │ O   O
 T  │ F   T                   1  │ O   1
```

Down the left and across the top are the values for the two bits. The results for the AND are in the table, so you see that 0 AND 1 gives 0.

The AND instruction works on bytes and words by ANDing together the bits of each byte or word that are in the same position. For example, the statement AND BL,CL successively ANDs bits 0 of BL and CL, bits 1, bits 2, and so on, and places the result in BL. Let's make this clearer with an example in binary:

```
      1 0 1 1   0 1 0 1
AND   0 1 1 1   0 1 1 0
      ───────────────────
      0 0 1 1   0 1 0 0
```

Furthermore, by ANDing 0Fh to any number, we can set the upper four bits to zero:

```
      0 1 1 1   1 0 1 1
AND   0 0 0 0   1 1 1 1
      ───────────────────
      0 0 0 0   1 0 1 1
```

Let's put this logic into a short program that takes the number in BL, isolates the lower hex digit by ANDing 0Fh to the upper four bits, and then prints the result as a character. We saw most of the details of this program when we printed the upper hex digit; the only new detail is the AND instruction.

```
3985:0100 B402        MOV    AH,02
3985:0102 88DA        MOV    DL,BL
3985:0104 80E20F      AND    DL,0F
3985:0107 80C230      ADD    DL,30
3985:010A 80FA3A      CMP    DL,3A
3985:010D 7C03        JL     0112
3985:010F 80C207      ADD    DL,07
3985:0112 CD21        INT    21
3985:0114 CD20        INT    20
```

Try this with some two-digit hex numbers in BL before we move on to put the pieces together to print both digits. You should see the rightmost hex digit of your number in BL on the screen.

Putting It All Together

There really isn't much to change when we put all the pieces together. We need only change the address of the second JL instruction we used to print the second hex digit. Here is the complete program:

```
3985:0100 B402        MOV     AH,02
3985:0102 88DA        MOV     DL,BL
3985:0104 B104        MOV     CL,04
3985:0106 D2EA        SHR     DL,CL
3985:0108 80C230      ADD     DL,30
3985:010B 80FA3A      CMP     DL,3A
3985:010E 7C03        JL      0113
3985:0110 80C207      ADD     DL,07
3985:0113 CD21        INT     21
3985:0115 88DA        MOV     DL,BL
3985:0117 80E20F      AND     DL,0F
3985:011A 80C230      ADD     DL,30
3985:011D 80FA3A      CMP     DL,3A
3985:0120 7C03        JL      0125
3985:0122 80C207      ADD     DL,07
3985:0125 CD21        INT     21
3985:0127 CD20        INT     20
```

Once you've entered this program, you'll have to type *U 100*, followed by *U*, to see the entire unassembled listing. Note that we've repeated one set of five instructions: the instructions at 108h through 113h, and 11Ah through 125h. In Chapter 7 we'll see how to write this sequence of instructions just once by using an instruction similar to BASIC's GOSUB statement.

Summary

In this chapter, we learned more about how Debug translates numbers from the 8088's binary format to a hex format we can read. What did we add to our growing store of knowledge?

First, we learned about some of the two-letter flags we see on the right side of the register (R) display. These status bits give us a great deal of information about our last arithmetic operation. By looking at the zero flag, for example, we could tell whether the result of the last operation was zero. We also found we could compare two numbers with a CMP instruction.

Next, we learned how to print a single-digit hex number. And, armed with this information, we went on to learn about the SHR instruction, which enabled us to move the upper digit of a two-digit hex number into the lower four bits of BL. That done, we could print the digit, just as we've done before.

Finally, we found that the AND instruction allowed us to isolate the lower hex digit from the upper. And, putting all these pieces together, we wrote a program to print a two-digit hex number.

We could have continued on to print a four-digit hex number, but at this point, we'd find ourselves repeating instructions. Before we try to print a four-digit hex number, we'll learn about procedures in Chapter 7. Then, we'll know enough to write a procedure to do the job. By then we'll also be ready to learn about the assembler—a program that will do much of our work for us. But now, let's move on to reading hex numbers.

READING CHARACTERS

$\mathbf{N}$ow that we know how to print a byte in hex notation, we're going to reverse the process by reading two characters—hex digits—from the keyboard and converting them into a single byte.

Reading One Character

The DOS INT 21h function call we've been using has an input function, number 1, that reads a character from the keyboard. When we learned about function calls in Chapter 4, we saw that the function number must be placed in the AH register before an INT 21h call. Let's try function 1 for INT 21h. Enter INT 21h at location 0100h:

```
396F:0100 CD21        INT     21
```

Then, place 01h into AH and type either *G 102* or *P* to run this one instruction. Nothing happens? It doesn't seem to—all you'll see is the blinking cursor. But actually, DOS has paused and is waiting until you press a key (don't do so yet). Once you press a key, DOS will place the ASCII code for that character into the AL register. We'll use this instruction later, to read the characters of a hex number, but right now, let's see what happens when we press a key like the F1 key.

Try pressing the F1 key. DOS will return a 0 in AL, and you'll also see a semi-colon (;) appear just after Debug's hyphen prompt.

This is what happened. F1 is one of a set of special keys with *extended codes*, which DOS treats differently from the keys representing normal ASCII characters. (You'll find a table listing these extended codes in Appendix D, as well as at the end of your BASIC manual.) For each of these special keys, DOS sends *two* characters, one right after the other. The first character returned is always zero, indicating that the next character is the *scan code* for a special key.

To read both characters, we'd need to execute INT 21h twice. But in our example, we read only the first character, the zero, and left the scan code in DOS. When Debug finished with the G 102 (or P) command, it began to read characters, and the first character it read was the scan code left behind from the F1 key: namely, 59, which is the ASCII code for a semicolon.

Later, when we develop our Dskpatch program, we'll begin to use these extended codes to bring the cursor and function keys to life. Until then, we'll just work with the normal ASCII characters.

Reading a Single-Digit Hex Number

Let's reverse the conversion used in Chapter 5, when we transformed a single-digit hex number to the ASCII code for one of the characters in 0 through 9 or A through F. To convert one character, such as C or D, from a hex character to a byte, we must subtract either 30h (for 0 through 9) or 37h (for A through F). Here is a simple program that will read one ASCII character and convert it to a byte:

```
3985:0100 B401      MOV     AH,01
3985:0102 CD21      INT     21
3985:0104 2C30      SUB     AL,30
3985:0106 3C09      CMP     AL,09
3985:0108 7E02      JLE     010C
3985:010A 2C07      SUB     AL,07
3985:010C CD20      INT     20
```

Most of these instructions should be familiar now, but there is one new one, JLE (*Jump if Less than or Equal*). In our program, this instruction jumps if AL is less than or equal to 9h.

To see the conversion from hex character to ASCII, you need to see the AL register just before the INT 20h is executed. Since Debug restores the registers when it executes the INT 20h, you'll need to set a breakpoint, as you did in Chapter 4. Here, type *G 10C*, and you'll see that AL will contain the hex number converted from a character.

Try typing some characters, such as *k* or a lowercase *d*, that are not hex digits, to see what happens. You'll notice that this program works correctly only when the input is one of the digits 0 through 9 or the uppercase letters A through F. We'll correct this minor failing in the next chapter, when we learn about subroutines, or procedures. Until then, we'll be sloppy temporarily and ignore error conditions: We'll have to type correct characters for our program to work properly.

Reading a Two-Digit Hex Number

Reading two hex digits isn't much more complicated than reading one, but it does require many more instructions. We'll begin by reading the first digit, then we'll place its hex value in the DL register and multiply it by 16. To perform this multiplication, we'll shift the DL register left four bits, placing a hex zero (four zero bits) to the right of the digit we just read. The instruction SHL DL,CL, with CL set to four does the trick by inserting zeros at the right. In fact, the SHL (*Shift Left*) instruction is known as an *arithmetic shift*, because it has

Figure 6-1. The SHL DL,1 instruction moves the bits left one position into the carry flag.

the same effect as an arithmetic multiplication by two, four, eight, and so on, depending on the number (such as one, two, or three) in CL.

Finally, with the first digit shifted over, we'll add the second hex digit to the number in DL (the first digit * 16). You can see and work through all these details in this program:

```
3985:0100 B401          MOV     AH,01
3985:0102 CD21          INT     21
3985:0104 88C2          MOV     DL,AL
3985:0106 80EA30        SUB     DL,30
3985:0109 80FA09        CMP     DL,09
3985:010C 7E03          JLE     0111
3985:010E 80EA07        SUB     DL,07
3985:0111 B104          MOV     CL,04
3985:0113 D2E2          SHL     DL,CL
3985:0115 CD21          INT     21
3985:0117 2C30          SUB     AL,30
3985:0119 3C09          CMP     AL,09
3985:011B 7E02          JLE     011F
3985:011D 2C07          SUB     AL,07
3985:011F 00C2          ADD     DL,AL
3985:0121 CD20          INT     20
```

Now that we've got a working program, it's a good idea to check the boundary conditions to confirm that it's working properly. For these boundary conditions, use the numbers 00, 09, 0A, 0F, 90, A0, F0, and some other number, such as 3C. Use a breakpoint to run the program without executing the INT 20h instruction. (Make sure you use uppercase letters for your hex input.)

Summary

We've finally had a chance to practice what we learned in previous chapters without being flooded with new information. Using a new INT 21 function (number 1) to read characters, we developed a program to read a two-digit hex number. Along the way, we emphasized the need to test programs with all the boundary conditions.

Now we're ready to wrap up Part I by learning about procedures in the 8088.

PROCEDURES—COUSINS TO SUBROUTINES

In the next chapter, we'll meet MASM, the macro assembler, and begin to use *assembly* language. But before we leave Debug, we'll look at one last set of examples, and learn about subroutines and a special place to store numbers called the stack.

Procedures

A procedure is a list of instructions that we can execute from many different places in a program, rather than having to repeat the same list of instructions at each place they're needed. In BASIC such lists are called *subroutines*, but we'll call them *procedures* for reasons that will become clear later.

We move to and from procedures just as we do in BASIC. We call a procedure with one instruction, *CALL*, which is just like BASIC's GOSUB. And we return from the procedure with a *RET* instruction, which is just like BASIC's RETURN.

Here's a simple BASIC program we'll soon rewrite in machine language. This program calls a subroutine ten times, each time printing one character, starting with A and ending with J:

```
10 A = &H41               'ASCII for 'A'
20 FOR I = 1 TO 10
30 GOSUB 1000
40 A = A + 1
50 NEXT I
60 END

1000 PRINT CHR$(A);
1200 RETURN
```

The subroutine, following a common practice in BASIC programs, begins at line 1000 to leave room for us to add more instructions to the main program without affecting our subroutine. We'll do the same with our machine-language procedure by putting it at 200h, far away from our main program at 100h. We'll also replace GOSUB 1000 with the instruction CALL 200h, which *calls* the procedure at memory location 200h. The CALL sets IP to 200h, and the 8088 starts executing the instructions at 200h.

The FOR-NEXT loop of the BASIC program, as we saw in Chapter 4, can be written as a LOOP instruction. The other pieces of the main program (except for the INC instruction) should be familiar.

Figure 7-1. The CALL and RET Instructions.

```
3985:0100 B241        MOV     DL,41
3985:0102 B90A00      MOV     CX,000A
3985:0105 E8F800      CALL    0200
3985:0108 FEC2        INC     DL
3985:0108 E2FB        LOOP    0105
3985:010A CD20        INT     20
```

The first instruction places 41h (ASCII for A) into the DL register, because the INT 21h instruction prints the character given by the ASCII code in DL. The INT 21h instruction itself is located some distance away, in the procedure at location 200h. INC DL, the new instruction, *increments* the DL register. That is, it adds one to DL, setting DL to the next character in the alphabet. Here's the procedure you should enter at 200h:

```
3985:0200 B402        MOV     AH,02
3985:0202 CD21        INT     21
3985:0204 C3          RET
```

Recall that the 02h in AH tells DOS to print the character in DL when we execute the INT 21h instruction. RET is a new instruction that *returns* to the first instruction (LOOP) following the CALL in our main program.

Type G to see the output of this program, then single-step through it to see how it works (remember to use either a breakpoint or the P command to run the INT 21 instruction).

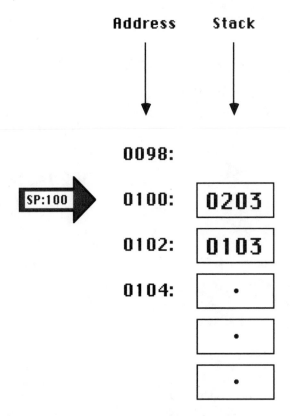

Figure 7-2. The Stack Just Before Executing the CALL 400 Instruction.

The Stack and Return Addresses

The CALL instruction in our program needs to save the *return address* somewhere so the 8088 will know where to resume executing instructions when it sees the RET instruction. For the storage place itself, we have a portion of memory known as the stack. And for tracking what's on the stack, there are two registers that we can see on the R display: the SP (*Stack Pointer*) register, which points to the top of the stack, and the SS (*Stack Segment*), which holds the segment number.

In operation, a stack for the 8088 is just like a stack of trays in a cafeteria, where placing a tray on the top covers the trays underneath. The last tray on the stack is the first to come off, so another name for a stack is LIFO, for *Last In,*

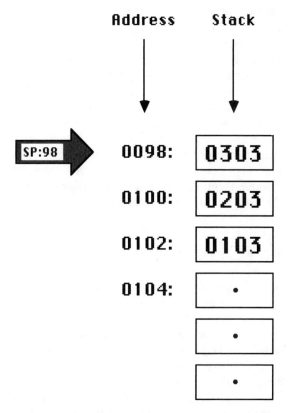

Figure 7-3. The Stack Just After Executing the CALL 400 Instruction.

First Out. This order, LIFO, is precisely what we need for retrieving return addresses after we make *nested* CALLs like this one:

```
396F:0100 E8FD00        CALL    0200
                                  .
                                  .
                                  .
396F:0200 E8FD00        CALL    0300
396F:0203 C3            RET
                                  .
                                  .
                                  .
396F:0300 E8FD00        CALL    0400
396F:0303 C3            RET
                                  .
                                  .
                                  .
396F:0400 C3            RET
```

Here, the instruction at 100h calls one at 200h, which calls one at 300h, which calls one at 400h, where we finally see a return (RET) instruction. This RET returns to the instruction following the *previous* CALL instruction, at 300h, so the 8088 resumes executing instructions at 303h. But there it encounters a RET instruction at 303h, which pulls the next oldest address (203h) off the stack. So the 8088 resumes executing instructions at 203h, and so on. Each RET *pops* the topmost return address off the stack, so each RET follows the same path backward as the CALLs did forward.

Try entering a program like the preceding one. Use multiple calls and trace through the program to see how the calls and returns work. Although the process may not seem very interesting right now, there are other uses for this stack, and a good understanding of how it works will come in handy. (In a later chapter, we'll go looking for the stack in memory.)

PUSHing and POPping

The stack is a useful place to store words of data for a while, provided we're careful to restore the stack before a RET instruction. We've seen that a CALL instruction *pushes* the return address (one word) onto the top of the stack, while a RET instruction *pops* this word off the top of the stack, loads it into the IP register, and exposes the word that was lying underneath it. We can do much the same thing with the instructions PUSH and POP, which allow us to push and pop words. When might we want to do this?

It's often convenient to save the values of registers at the beginning of a procedure and restore them at the end, just before the RET instruction. Then we're free to use these registers in any way we like within the procedure, as long as we restore their values at the end.

Programs are built from many levels of procedures, with each level calling the procedures at the next level down. By saving registers at the beginning of a procedure and restoring them at the end, we remove unwanted interactions between procedures at different levels, and this makes our job of programming much easier. You'll see more about saving and restoring registers in Chapter 13, when we talk about modular design. But right now, here's an example (don't enter it) that saves and restores CX and DX:

```
396F:0200 51        PUSH    CX
396F:0201 52        PUSH    DX
396F:0202 B90800     MOV     CX,0008
396F:0205 E8F800     CALL    0300
396F:0208 FEC2       INC     DL
396F:020A E2F9       LOOP    0205
396F:020C 5A         POP     DX
396F:020D 59         POP     CX
396F:020E C3         RET
```

Notice that the POPs are in reverse order from the PUSHes, because a POP removes the word placed most recently on the stack, and the old value of DX is on top of the old CX.

Saving and restoring CX and DX allows us to change these registers in the procedure that begins at 200h, but without changing the values used by any procedure that calls this one. And once we've saved CX and DX, we can use these registers to hold *local* variables—variables we can use within this procedure without affecting the values used by the calling program.

We'll use such local variables to simplify our programming tasks. As long as we're careful to restore the original values, we won't have to worry about our procedures changing any of the registers used by the calling program. This will become clearer in the next example, which is a procedure to read a hex number. Unlike the program in Chapter 6, our program now will allow only valid characters such as A, but not K.

Reading Hex Numbers with More Class

We want to create a procedure that keeps reading characters until it receives one it can convert to a hex number between 0 and Fh. We don't want to display any invalid characters, so we'll sift our input by using a new INT 21h function, number 8, that reads a character but doesn't pass it on to the screen. That way we can *echo* (display) characters only if they are valid.

Place 8h into the AH register and run through this instruction, typing an A just after you type G 102:

```
3985:0100 CD21        INT     21
```

The ASCII code for A (41h) is now in the AL register, but the A didn't appear on the screen.

Using this function, our program can read characters without echoing them until it reads a valid hex digit (0 through 9 or A through F), which it will then echo. Here is the procedure to do this and to convert the hex character to a hex number:

```
3985:0200 52          PUSH    DX
3985:0201 B408        MOV     AH,08
3985:0203 CD21        INT     21
3985:0205 3C30        CMP     AL,30
3985:0207 72FA        JB      0203
3985:0209 3C46        CMP     AL,46
3985:020B 77F6        JA      0203
3985:020D 3C39        CMP     AL,39
3985:020F 770A        JA      021B
3985:0211 B402        MOV     AH,02
3985:0213 88C2        MOV     DL,AL
3985:0215 CD21        INT     21
```

```
3985:0217 2C30        SUB     AL,30
3985:0219 5A          POP     DX
3985:021A C3          RET
3985:021B 3C41        CMP     AL,41
3985:021D 72E4        JB      0203
3985:021F B402        MOV     AH,02
3985:0221 88C2        MOV     DL,AL
3985:0223 CD21        INT     21
3985:0225 2C37        SUB     AL,37
3985:0227 5A          POP     DX
3985:0228 C3          RET
```

The procedure reads a character in AL (with the INT 21h at 203h) and checks to see if it's valid with the CMPs and conditional jumps. If the character just read is not a valid character, the conditional jump instructions send the 8088 back to location 203, where the INT 21h reads another character. (JA is *Jump if Above*, and JB is *Jump if Below*; both treat the two numbers as unsigned numbers, whereas the JL instruction we used earlier treated both as signed numbers.)

By line 211h, we know that we have a valid digit between 0 and 9, so we subtract the code for the character 0 and return the result in the AL register, remembering to pop the DX register, which we saved at the beginning of the procedure. The process for hex digits A through F is much the same. Note that we have two RET instructions in this procedure; we could have had more, or we could have had just one.

Here is a very simple program to test the procedure:

```
3985:0100 E8FD00        CALL    0200
3985:0103 CD20          INT     20
```

As you've done before, use either the G command, with a breakpoint, or use the P command. You want to execute the CALL 200h instruction without executing the INT 20h instruction, so you can see the registers just before the program terminates and the registers are restored.

You'll see the cursor at the left side of the screen, waiting patiently for a character. Type *k*, which isn't a valid character. Nothing should happen. Now, type any of the uppercase hex characters. You should see the character's hex value in AL and the character itself echoed on the screen. Test this procedure with the boundary conditions: '\' (the character before zero), 0, 9, ':' (the character just after 9), and so on.

Now that we have this procedure, the program to read a two-digit hex number, with error handling, is fairly straightforward:

```
3985:0100 E8FD00        CALL    0200
3985:0103 88C2          MOV     DL,AL
3985:0105 B104          MOV     CL,04
3985:0107 D2E2          SHL     DL,CL
3985:0109 E8F400        CALL    0200
3985:010C 00C2          ADD     DL,AL
3985:010E B402          MOV     AH,02
3985:0110 CD21          INT     21
3985:0112 CD20          INT     20
```

You can run this program from DOS, since it reads in a two-digit hex number and then displays the ASCII character that corresponds to the number you typed in.

Aside from the procedure, our main program is much simpler than the version we wrote in the last chapter, and we haven't duplicated the instructions to read characters. We did add error handling, though, and even if it did complicate our procedure, it also ensures that the program now accepts only valid input.

Here we can also see the reason for saving the DX register in the procedure. The main program stores the hex number in DL, so we don't want our procedure at 200h to change DL. On the other hand, the procedure at 200h must use DL itself to echo characters. So, by using the instruction PUSH DX at the beginning of the procedure, and POP DX at the end, we save ourselves from problems.

From now on, to avoid complicated interactions between procedures, we'll be very strict about saving any registers used by a procedure.

Summary

Our programming is becoming more sophisticated. We've learned about procedures, which allow us to reuse the same set of instructions without rewriting them each time. We've also discovered the stack and seen that a CALL stores a return address on the top of the stack, while a RET instruction returns to the address on the top of the stack.

We saw how to use the stack for more than just saving return addresses. We used the stack to store the values of registers (with a PUSH instruction) so we could use them in a procedure. By restoring the registers (with a POP instruction) at the end of each procedure, we avoided unwanted interactions between procedures. By always saving and restoring registers in procedures that we write, we can CALL other procedures without worrying about which registers are used within the other procedure.

And finally, armed with this knowledge, we moved on to build a better program to read hex numbers—this time, with error checking. The program we built here is similar to one we'll use in later chapters, when we begin to develop the Dskpatch program.

Now we're ready to move on to Part II, where we'll learn how to use the assembler. In the next chapter, we'll see how to use the assembler to convert a program to machine language. We'll also see that there won't be any reason to leave room between procedures, as we did in this chapter, when we put our procedure way up at location 200h.

PART II

Assembly Language

8

WELCOME TO THE ASSEMBLER

At long last we're ready to meet the assembler, a DOS program that will make our programming much simpler. From now on, we'll write mnemonic, human-readable instructions directly, using the assembler to turn our programs into machine code.

Of necessity, this chapter and the next will be somewhat heavy with details on the assembler, but learning these details will be well worth the effort. Once we know how to use the assembler, we'll get back on course in learning how to write assembly language programs. Meanwhile, let's jump right in.

A Program Without Debug

Up to this point, we've just typed *DEBUG*, and then typed in our program instructions. Now we're about to leave Debug behind and to write programs without it, and we'll have to use either an editor or a word processor to create text, or human-readable, files containing our assembly language instructions.

We begin by creating a *source file*—the name for the text version of an assembly language program. We'll create a source file now, for the program we built and named Writestr back in Chapter 3. To refresh your memory, here is our Debug version:

```
396F:0100 B402        MOV   AH,02
396F:0102 B22A        MOV   DL,2A
396F:0104 CD21        INT   21
396F:0106 CD20        INT   20
```

Use your editor to enter the following lines of code into a file named WRITESTR.ASM (the extension .ASM means this is an assembler source file). Here, as with Debug, lowercase works just as well as uppercase, but we'll continue to use uppercase letters to avoid confusion between the number 1 (one) and the lowercase letter l (el):

```
.MODEL  SMALL
.CODE

        MOV   AH,2h
        MOV   DL,2Ah
        INT   21h
        INT   20h

        END
```

This is the same program we created in Chapter 3, but it contains a few necessary changes and additions. Ignoring for now the three new lines in our source file, notice that there is an *h* after each hex number. This *h* tells the assembler that the numbers are in hexadecimal. Unlike Debug, which assumes all numbers are in hexadecimal, the assembler assumes all numbers are decimal. We tell it otherwise by placing an *h* after any hexadecimal number.

> **Note:** Here's a warning before we move on: The assembler can become confused by numbers, such as ACh, that look like a name or an instruction. To avoid this, always type a zero before a hex number that begins with a letter. For example, type 0ACh—*not* ACh.

MOV   DL,ACh

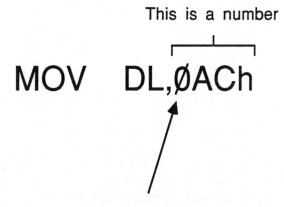

MOV   DL,ØACh

The 0 tells MASM
that this is a number

Figure 8-1. You must put a 0 before hexadecimal numbers that start with a letter, otherwise the assembler will treat the number as a name.

Watch what happens when we assemble a program with ACh, rather than 0ACh. Here's the program:

```
.MODEL   SMALL
.CODE
         MOV    DL,ACh
         INT    20h

         END
```

Here's the output:

```
A>MASM TEST;
Microsoft (R) Macro Assembler   Version 5.10
Copyright (C) Microsoft Corp 1981, 1988.  All rights reserved.

test.ASM(4) : error A2009: Symbol not defined: ACH

  49842 + 224473 Bytes symbol space free

      0 Warning Errors
      1 Severe  Errors

A>
```

Definitely not encouraging. But changing the ACh to 0ACh satisfies the assembler.

Also note the spacing of the commands in our assembler program. We used tabs to align everything neatly and make the source text more readable. Compare the program you entered with this version:

```
.MODEL SMALL
.CODE
MOV AH,2h
MOV DL,2Ah
INT 21h
INT 20h
END
```

A bit of a mess; the assembler doesn't care but we do.

Now let's return to the three new lines in our source file. The three new lines are all *directives* (also sometimes called *pseudo-ops,* or pseudo-operations). They're called directives because, rather than generate instructions, they just supply information and directions to the assembler. The END pseudo-op marks the end of the source file, so the assembler knows it's done when it sees an END. Later on, we'll see that END is useful in other ways, too. But right now, let's put aside any further discussion of it or the other two directives and see how to use the assembler.

Creating Source Files

Even though you've entered the lines of WRITESTR.ASM, there's one more consideration before we move on to actually assemble our program. The assembler can use source files that contain standard ASCII characters only. If you are using a word processor, bear in mind that not all word processors write disk files using only the standard ASCII characters. WordStar is one such culprit; Microsoft Word is another. For both word processors, use the non-document, or unformatted, mode when you save your files.

Before you try assembling WRITESTR.ASM, make sure it's still ASCII. From DOS, type:

```
A>TYPE WRITESTR.ASM
```

You should see the same text you entered. If you see strange characters in your program (many word processors put additional formatting information into the file, which the assembler treats as errors) you may have to use a different editor or word processor to enter programs. You'll also need a blank line after the END statement in your file.

Now, let's begin to assemble Writestr. (If you're using Borland's Turbo Assembler, type TASM whenever you see MASM; if you're using SLR Systems' OPTASM, type OPTASM in place of MASM.) Be sure to type the semicolon:

```
A>MASM WRITESTR;
Microsoft (R) Macro Assembler Version 5.10
Copyright (C) Microsoft Corp 1981, 1988. All rights reserved.

  49822 + 219323 Bytes symbol space free

      0 Warning Errors
      0 Severe  Errors

A>
```

We're not done yet. At this point, the assembler has produced a file called WRITESTR.OBJ, which you'll now find on your disk. This is an intermediate file, called an *object file*. It contains our machine-language program, along with a lot of bookkeeping information used by another DOS program called the *Linker*.

Linking

Right now, we want the linker to take our .OBJ file and create an .EXE version of it. Copy LINK.EXE from your DOS disk to the disk containing your source file and the assembler (or onto your hard disk). Then, link WRITESTR.OBJ by typing:

```
A>LINK WRITESTR;

Microsoft (R) Overlay Linker Version 3.64
Copyright (C) Microsoft Corp 1983-1988. All rights reserved.

LINK: warning L4021: no stack segment

A>
```

Even though the linker warns us that there is no stack segment, we don't need one right now. After we learn how to add more of the trappings, we'll see why we might want a stack segment.

Now we have our .EXE file, but this still isn't the last step. We have one more step—to create a .COM version, which is just what we created with Debug. Again, you'll see later why we need all these steps. For now, let's create a .COM version of Writestr.

For our final step, we need the program EXE2BIN.EXE from the DOS supplemental disk. Exe2bin, as its name implies, converts an .EXE file to a .COM, or binary (bin) file. There's a difference between .EXE and .COM files, but we won't deal with the differences until Chapter 11; for now let's just create the .COM file. Type:

```
A>EXE2BIN WRITESTR WRITESTR.COM

A>
```

The response didn't tell us very much. To see whether Exe2bin worked, let's list all the Writestr files we've created so far:

```
A>DIR WRITESTR.*

 Volume in drive A has no label
 Directory of  A:\

WRITESTR ASM       76   4-27-89   4:49p
WRITESTR OBJ      105   4-27-89   4:52p
WRITESTR EXE      520   4-27-89   4:52p
WRITESTR COM        8   4-27-89   4:52p
        4 File(s)     585728 bytes free

A>
```

This is quite a number of files, including WRITESTR.COM. Type *writestr* to run the .COM version and verify that your program functions properly (recall that it should print an asterisk on your screen). The exact sizes DOS reports for the first three files may vary a bit.

The results may seem a little anticlimactic, since we are seemingly back where we were in Chapter 3, but we aren't: We've gained a great deal. It will all become much clearer when we deal with calls again. Notice that we never once had to worry about where our program was put in memory, as we did about IP in Debug. The addresses were all taken care of for us.

Very soon you'll come to appreciate this feature of the assembler: It will make programming much easier. For example, recall that in the last chapter we wasted space by having our main program at 100h and the procedure we called at 200h. We'll see that using the assembler allows us to place the procedure immediately after the main program without any gap. But first, let's see how our program looks to Debug.

Back in Debug

Let's read our .COM file into Debug and unassemble it to see how Debug reconstructs our program from the machine code of WRITESTR.COM:

```
A>DEBUG WRITESTR.COM
-U
397F:0100 B402          MOV     AH,02
397F:0102 B22A          MOV     DL,2A
397F:0104 CD21          INT     21
397F:0106 CD20          INT     20
                 .
                 .
                 .
```

Exactly what we had in Chapter 3. This is all Debug sees in WRITESTR.COM. The END and the two lines at the start of our source file didn't make it through at all. What happened to them?

These instructions don't appear in the final machine-language version of the program because they are directives, and directives are for bookkeeping only. The assembler takes care of much bookkeeping at the cost of some extra lines. We'll make good use of directives to simplify our job and we'll see how they affect our program when we take a closer look at segments in Chapter 11.

Comments

Since we are no longer operating directly with Debug, we're free to add more to our program that the assembler sees but won't pass on to the 8088. Perhaps the most important such additions we can make are comments, which are invaluable in making a program clear. In assembly language programs, we place comments after a semicolon, which works like a single quotation mark (')

in BASIC. The assembler ignores anything on the line after a semicolon, so we can add anything we want. If we add comments to our brief program:

```
.MODEL  SMALL
.CODE
        MOV     AH,2h           ;Select DOS function 2, character output
        MOV     DL,2Ah          ;Load the ASCII code for '*' to be printed
        INT     21h             ;Print it with INT 21h
        INT     20h             ;And exit to DOS

        END
```

we see quite an improvement—we can understand this program without having to think back and remember what each line means.

Labels

To round off this chapter, let's look at another bookkeeping feature of the assembler that makes programming smoother: labels.

Until now, when we wanted to jump from one part of a program to another with one of the jump commands, we had to know the specific address we were jumping to. In everyday programming, inserting new instructions forces us to change the addresses in jump instructions. The assembler takes care of this problem with *labels*—names we give to the addresses of any instructions or memory locations. A label takes the place of an address. As soon as the assembler sees a label, it replaces the label with the correct address before sending it on to the 8088.

Labels can be up to 31 characters long and can contain letters, numbers, and any of the following symbols: a question mark (?), a period (.), an *at* symbol (@),

Figure 8-2. The assembler substitutes addresses for the labels that we write.

an underline (_), or a dollar sign ($). They can't start with a digit (0 through 9), and a period can be used only as the first character.

As a practical example, let's take a look at our program from Chapter 6 that reads a two-digit hex number. It contains two jumps, JLE 0111 and JLE 011F. Here's the old version:

```
3985:0100 B401        MOV     AH,01
3985:0102 CD21        INT     21
3985:0104 88C2        MOV     DL,AL
3985:0106 80EA30      SUB     DL,30
3985:0109 80FA09      CMP     DL,09
3985:010C 7E03        JLE     0111
3985:010E 80EA07      SUB     DL,07
3985:0111 B104        MOV     CL,04
3985:0113 D2E2        SHL     DL,CL
3985:0115 CD21        INT     21
3985:0117 2C30        SUB     AL,30
3985:0119 3C09        CMP     AL,09
3985:011B 7E02        JLE     011F
3985:011D 2C07        SUB     AL,07
3985:011F 00C2        ADD     DL,AL
3985:0121 CD20        INT     20
```

It's certainly not obvious what this program does, and if it's not fresh in your mind, you may have to work a little to understand the program again. Let's add labels and comments to clarify its function:

```
.MODEL  SMALL
.CODE
        MOV     AH,1h       ;Select DOS function 1, character input
        INT     21h         ;Read a character, and return ASCII code in AL
        MOV     DL,AL       ;Move ASCII code into DL
        SUB     DL,30h      ;Subtract 30h to convert digit to 0 - 9
        CMP     DL,9h       ;Was it a digit between 0 and 9?
        JLE     DIGIT1      ;Yes, we have the first digit (four bits)
        SUB     DL,7h       ;No, subtract 7h to convert letter A - F
DIGIT1:
        MOV     CL,4h       ;Prepare to multiply by 16
        SHL     DL,CL       ;Multiply by shifting, becomes upper four bits
        INT     21h         ;Get next character
        SUB     AL,30h      ;Repeat conversion
        CMP     AL,9h       ;Is it a digit 0 - 9?
        JLE     DIGIT2      ;Yes, so we have the second digit
        SUB     AL,7h       ;No, subtract 7h
DIGIT2:
        ADD     DL,AL       ;ADD second digit
        INT     20h         ;And exit

        END
```

The labels here, DIGIT1 and DIGIT2, are of a type known as *NEAR* labels, because a colon (:) appears after the labels when they're defined. The term *NEAR* has to do with segments, which we'll talk about in Chapter 11, along with the .MODEL, and .CODE directives. Here, if you assembled the preceding program and then unassembled it with Debug, you'd see DIGIT1 replaced by 0111h and DIGIT2 replaced by 011Fh.

Summary

This has been quite a chapter. It's as if we've stepped into a new world, and, in a sense, we have. The assembler's much simpler to work with than Debug was, so we can now begin to write real programs, because the assembler does much of the bookkeeping for us.

What have we learned here? We began by learning how to create a source file and then go through the steps of assembling, linking, and converting it from an .OBJ file to an .EXE, and then a .COM file, using a simple program from Chapter 3. The assembly language program we created contained a few directives, which we've never seen before. But they'll become familiar once we've become more comfortable using the assembler. In fact, we'll place .MODEL, .CODE, and END directives in all our programs from now on, since we need them, even though we won't really see the reason why until Chapter 11.

Next, we learned about comments. You may have wondered how we could survive without comments. We won't from now on. Comments add so much to the readability of programs that we won't skimp on them.

Finally came labels, to make our programs even more readable. We'll use all these ideas and methods throughout the rest of this book. Let's move on to the next chapter and see how the assembler makes procedures easier to use.

9

PROCEDURES AND THE ASSEMBLER

Now that we've met the assembler, let's become a little more comfortable with writing assembly language programs. In this chapter, we'll return to the subject of procedures. You'll see how we can write procedures much more easily with the help of our hard-working assembler. Then, we'll move on to build some useful procedures, which we'll use when we begin to develop our Dskpatch program a few chapters from now.

We'll begin with two procedures to print a byte in hexadecimal. Along the way, we'll meet several directives. But, like .MODEL, .CODE, and END in the last chapter, we'll leave them pretty much undefined until Chapter 11, where we'll learn more about segments.

The Assembler's Procedures

When we first learned about procedures, we left a large gap between the main program and its procedures, so that we'd have room for changes without having to worry about our main program overlapping a procedure. But now we have the assembler, and since it does all the work of assigning addresses to instructions, we no longer need to leave a gap between procedures. With the assembler, each time we make a change, we just assemble the program again.

In Chapter 7, we built a small program with one CALL. The program did nothing more than print the letters A through J, and it looked like this:

```
3985:0100 B241        MOV     DL,41
3985:0102 B90A00       MOV     CX,000A
3985:0105 E8F800       CALL    0200
3985:0108 FEC2         INC     DL
3985:010A E2F9         LOOP    0105
3985:010C CD20         INT     20

3985:0200 B402         MOV     AH,02
3985:0202 CD21         INT     21
3985:0204 C3           RET
```

Let's turn this into a program for the assembler. It will be hard to read without labels and comments, so we'll add those embellishments to make our program far more readable:

Listing 9-1. The Program PRINTAJ.ASM

```
.MODEL     SMALL
.CODE

PRINT_A_J PROC
        MOV   DL,'A'            ;Start with the character A
        MOV   CX,10             ;Print 10 characters, starting with A
```

```
PRINT_LOOP:
    CALL WRITE_CHAR          ;Print character
    INC  DL                  ;Move to the next char in the alphabet
    LOOP PRINT_LOOP          ;Continue for 10 characters
    INT  20h                 ;Return to DOS
PRINT_A_J ENDP

WRITE_CHAR      PROC
    MOV  AH,2                ;Set function code for character output
    INT  21h                 ;Print the character already in DL
    RET                      ;Return from this procedure
WRITE_CHAR      ENDP

    END  PRINT_A_J
```

There are two new directives here: PROC, and ENDP. PROC and ENDP are directives for defining procedures. As you can see, both the main program and the procedure at 200h are surrounded by matching pairs of the directives PROC and ENDP.

PROC defines the beginning of a procedure; ENDP defines the end. The label in front of each is the name we give to the procedure they define. Thus, in the main procedure, PRINT_A_J, we can replace our CALL 200 instruction with the more readable CALL WRITE_CHAR. Just insert the name of the procedure and the assembler assigns the addresses.

Since we have two procedures, we need to tell the assembler which to use as the main procedure—where the 8088 should start executing our program. The END directive takes care of this detail. By writing END PRINT_A_J, we've told the assembler that PRINT_A_J is the main procedure. Later in our work, we'll see that the main procedure can be anywhere. Right now, however, we are dealing with .COM files, and we'll need to place the main procedure first in our source file.

You're ready to go, so if you haven't done so yet, enter the program into a file called PRINTAJ.ASM and generate the .COM version, using the same steps you did in the last chapter (remember to substitute TASM or OPTASM for MASM if you're using either the Turbo Assembler or OPTASM):

```
MASM PRINTAJ;
LINK PRINTAJ;
EXE2BIN PRINTAJ PRINTAJ.COM
```

Then give Printaj a try. (Make sure you've run Exe2bin *before* you run Printaj. Otherwise, you'll end up running the .EXE version of Printaj, which will crash when it encounters the INT 20h instruction, for reasons we'll see in Chapter 11.)

> **Note:** If you encounter any error messages that you don't recognize, check that you've typed in the program correctly. If that fails, you might want to check Appendix C, which lists some common errors.

When you're satisfied, use Debug to unassemble the program and see how the assembler fits the two procedures together. Recall that we can read a particular file into Debug by typing its name as part of the command line. For example, we can type *DEBUG PRINTAJ.COM*, and when we do, we see:

```
-U
3985:0100 B241       MOV      DL,41
3985:0102 B90A00     MOV      CX,000A
3985:0105 E80600     CALL     010E
3985:0108 FEC2       INC      DL
3985:010A E2F9       LOOP     0105
3985:010C CD20       INT      20
3985:010E B402       MOV      AH,02
3985:0110 CD21       INT      21
3985:0112 C3         RET
```

Our program is nice and snug, with no gap between the two procedures.

The Hex-Output Procedures

We've seen hex-output procedures twice before: once in Chapter 5, where we learned how to print a number in hex, and again in Chapter 7, where we saw how to simplify the program, using a procedure to print one hex digit. Now we're going to add yet another procedure to print one character. Why? Well, let's just call it foresight.

By using a central procedure to write a character to the screen, we can change the way this procedure writes characters without affecting the rest of the program. We will change it several times.

Enter the following program into the file VIDEO_IO.ASM:

Listing 9-2. The New File VIDEO_IO.ASM

```
.MODEL     SMALL
.CODE

TEST_WRITE_HEX PROC
           MOV      DL,3Fh              ;Test with 3Fh
           CALL     WRITE_HEX
           INT      20h                 ;Return to DOS
TEST_WRITE_HEX ENDP

           PUBLIC   WRITE_HEX
;---------------------------------------------------------------------;
; This procedure converts the byte in the DL register to hex and writes ;
; the two hex digits at the current cursor position.                  ;
;                                                                     ;
; On Entry:   DL   Byte to be converted to hex.                       ;
;                                                                     ;
; Uses:         WRITE_HEX_DIGIT                                        ;
;---------------------------------------------------------------------;
WRITE_HEX     PROC                ;Entry point
           PUSH     CX                  ;Save registers used in this procedure
           PUSH     DX
```

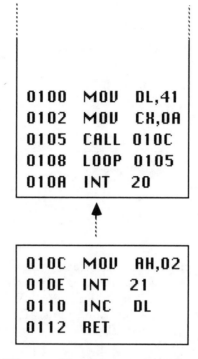

Figure 9-1. MASM assembles separate procedures without a gap.

```
        MOV     DH,DL               ;Make a copy of byte
        MOV     CX,4                ;Get the upper nibble in DL
        SHR     DL,CL
        CALL    WRITE_HEX_DIGIT     ;Display first hex digit
        MOV     DL,DH               ;Get lower nibble into DL
        AND     DL,0Fh              ;Remove the upper nibble
        CALL    WRITE_HEX_DIGIT     ;Display second hex digit
        POP     DX
        POP     CX
        RET
WRITE_HEX       ENDP

        PUBLIC  WRITE_HEX_DIGIT
;-----------------------------------------------------------------;
; This procedure converts the lower 4 bits of DL to a hex digit and ;
; writes it to the screen.                                        ;
;                                                                 ;
; On Entry:    DL   Lower 4 bits contain number to be printed     ;
;                   in hex.                                       ;
;                                                                 ;
; Uses:        WRITE_CHAR                                         ;
;-----------------------------------------------------------------;
WRITE_HEX_DIGIT         PROC
        PUSH    DX                  ;Save registers used
        CMP     DL,10               ;Is this nibble <10?
        JAE     HEX_LETTER          ;No, convert to a letter
        ADD     DL,"0"              ;Yes, convert to a digit
        JMP     Short WRITE_DIGIT   ;Now write this character
HEX_LETTER:
        ADD     DL,"A"-10           ;Convert to hex letter
```

Listing 9-2. *continued*

```
WRITE_DIGIT:
            CALL        WRITE_CHAR              ;Display the letter on the screen
            POP         DX                      ;Restore old value of DX
            RET
WRITE_HEX_DIGIT         ENDP

            PUBLIC      WRITE_CHAR
;-----------------------------------------------------------------------;
; This procedure prints a character on the screen using the DOS         ;
; function call.                                                        ;
;                                                                       ;
; On Entry:    DL  Byte to print on screen.                             ;
;-----------------------------------------------------------------------;
WRITE_CHAR      PROC
            PUSH        AX
            MOV         AH,2                    ;Call for character output
            INT         21h                     ;Output character in DL register
            POP         AX                      ;Restore old value in AX
            RET                                 ;And return
WRITE_CHAR      ENDP

            END         TEST_WRITE_HEX
```

The DOS function to print characters treats some characters specially. For example, using the DOS function to output 07 results in a beep, without printing the character for 07, which is a small diamond. We'll see a new version of WRITE_CHAR that will print a diamond in Part III, where we'll learn about the ROM BIOS routines inside your IBM PC. For now, though, we'll just use the DOS function to print characters.

The new directive PUBLIC is here for future use: We'll use it in Chapter 13, when we learn about modular design. PUBLIC simply tells the assembler to generate some more information for the linker. The linker allows us to bring separate pieces of our program, assembled from different source files, together into one program. And PUBLIC informs the assembler that the procedure named after the PUBLIC directive should be made public or available to procedures in other files.

Right now, Video_io contains the three procedures to write a byte as a hex number, and a short main program to test these procedures. We'll be adding many procedures to the file as we develop Dskpatch, and by the end of this book, VIDEO_IO.ASM will be filled with many general-purpose procedures.

The procedure TEST_WRITE_HEX that we've included does just what it says: It's here to test WRITE_HEX, which, in turn, uses WRITE_HEX_DIGIT and WRITE_CHAR. As soon as we've verified that these three procedures are all correct, we'll remove TEST_WRITE_HEX from VIDEO_IO.ASM.

Create the .COM version of Video_io, and use Debug to thoroughly test WRITE_HEX. Change the 3Fh at memory location 101h to each of the boundary conditions we tried in Chapter 5, then use G to run TEST_WRITE_HEX.

We'll use many simple test programs to test new procedures we've written. In this way, we can build a program piece by piece, rather than try to build and debug it all at once. This incremental method is much faster and easier, since we can confine bugs to just the new code.

The Beginnings of Modular Design

Note that ahead of each procedure in Video_io we've included a block of comments briefly describing the function of each procedure. More important, these comments tell which registers the procedure uses to pass information back and forth, as well as what other procedures it uses. As one feature of our modular approach, the comment block allows us to use any procedure by looking at the description. There's no need to relearn how the procedure does its work. This also makes it fairly easy to rewrite one procedure without having to rewrite any of the procedures that call it.

We've also used PUSH and POP instructions to save and restore any registers we use within each procedure. We'll do this for every procedure we write, except for our test procedures. This approach, too, is part of the modular style we'll use.

Recall that we save and restore any register used so that we never have to worry about complex interactions between procedures trying to fight over the small number of registers in the 8088. Each procedure is free to use as many registers as it likes, *provided* that it restores them before the RET instruction. It's a small price to pay for the added simplicity. In addition, without saving and restoring registers, the task of rewriting procedures would be mind-rending. You'd be sure to lose much hair in the process.

We also try to use many small procedures, instead of one large one. This, too, makes our programming task simpler, although we'll sometimes write longer procedures when the design becomes particularly convoluted.

These ideas and methods will all be borne out more fully in the chapters to come. In the next chapter, for example, we'll add another procedure to Video_io: a procedure to take a word in the DX register and print the number in decimal on the screen.

A Program Skeleton

As we've seen in this and the preceding chapter, the assembler imposes a certain amount of overhead on any programs we write. In other words, we need to write a few directives that tell the assembler the basics. For future reference, here is the absolute minimum you'll need for programs you write:

```
.MODEL    SMALL
.CODE

Some_procedure PROC
        .
        .
        .

        INT  20h
Some_procedure ENDP

        END  Some_procedure
```

We'll add some new directives to this program skeleton in later chapters, but you can use it, as shown here, as the starting point for new programs you write. Or, even better, you can use some of the programs and procedures from this book as your starting point.

Summary

We're really making progress now. In this chapter, we learned how to write procedures in assembly language. From now on we'll use procedures all the time, and by using small procedures, we'll make our programs more manageable. We saw that a procedure begins with a PROC definition and ends with an ENDP directive. We rewrote PRINT_A_J to test our new knowledge of procedures, then went on to rewrite our program to write a hex number—this time with an extra procedure. Now that procedures are so easy to work with, there's little reason not to break our programs into more procedures. In fact, we've seen that there are ample reasons in favor of using many small procedures.

At the end of this chapter we talked briefly about modular design, a philosophy that will save us a great deal of time and effort. Our modular programs will be easier to write, easier to read, and easier for someone else to modify than programs created with the well-worn technique of spaghetti logic: programs written with very long procedures and many interactions.

We're now ready to build another useful procedure. Then, in Chapter 11, we'll learn about segments. And from there, we'll move on to developing larger programs, where we'll really start to use the techniques of modular design.

10

PRINTING IN DECIMAL

We promised to write a procedure to take a word and print it in decimal notation. WRITE_DECIMAL uses some new tricks—ways to save a byte here, a few microseconds there. Perhaps such tricks will hardly seem to be worth the effort. But if you memorize them, you'll find that you can use them to shorten and speed up programs. Through our tricks, we'll also learn about two new types of logical operations to add to the AND instruction we covered in Chapter 5. First, let's review the process for converting a word to decimal digits.

Recalling the Conversion

Division is the key to converting a word to decimal digits. Recall that the DIV instruction calculates both the integer answer and its remainder. So, calculating 12345/10 yields 1234 as the integer answer, and 5 as the remainder. In this example, 5 is simply the rightmost digit. And if we divide by 10 again, we'll get

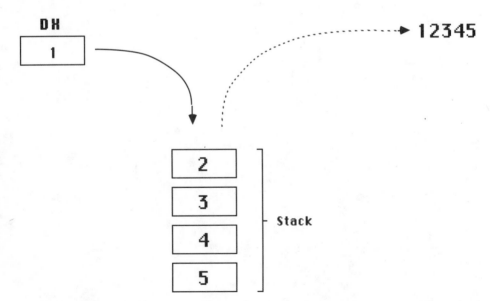

Figure 10-1. PUSHing the Digits Onto the Stack Reverses Their Order.

the next digit to the left. Repeated division by 10 *strips off* the digits from right to left, each time putting them in the remainder.

Of course, the digits come out in reverse order, but in assembly language programming, we have a fix for that. Remember the stack? It's just like a stack of lunch trays: The first one to come off the top is the last tray that was set down. If we substitute digits for trays and place the digits one on top of the other as they come out of the remainder, we'll have it. We can pull out the digits in correct order.

The top digit is the first digit in our number, and the other digits are underneath it. So, if we push the remainders as we calculate them and print them as we pop them off the stack, the digits will be in the correct order.

The following program is the complete procedure to print a number in decimal notation. As noted, there are a few tricks hiding in this procedure. We'll get to them soon enough, but let's try WRITE_DECIMAL to see if it works before we worry about how it works.

Place WRITE_DECIMAL into VIDEO_IO.ASM, along with the procedures for writing a byte in hex. Make sure you place WRITE_DECIMAL *after* TEST_WRITE_HEX, which we'll be replacing with TEST_WRITE_DECIMAL. To save some work, WRITE_DECIMAL uses WRITE_HEX_DIGIT to convert one nibble (four bits) into a digit.

Listing 10-1. Add to VIDEO_IO.ASM

```
           PUBLIC  WRITE_DECIMAL
;--------------------------------------------------------------------;
; This procedure writes a 16-bit, unsigned number in decimal notation. ;
;                                                                    ;
; On Entry:     DX      N : 16-bit, unsigned number.                 ;
;                                                                    ;
; Uses:         WRITE_HEX_DIGIT                                      ;
;--------------------------------------------------------------------;
WRITE_DECIMAL   PROC    NEAR
           PUSH    AX                      ;Save registers used here
           PUSH    CX
           PUSH    DX
           PUSH    SI
           MOV     AX,DX
           MOV     SI,10                   ;Will divide by 10 using SI
           XOR     CX,CX                   ;Count of digits placed on stack
NON_ZERO:
           XOR     DX,DX                   ;Set upper word of N to 0
           DIV     SI                      ;Calculate N/10 and (N mod 10)
           PUSH    DX                      ;Push one digit onto the stack
           INC     CX                      ;One more digit added
           OR      AX,AX                   ;N = 0 yet?
           JNE     NON_ZERO                ;Nope, continue
WRITE_DIGIT_LOOP:
           POP     DX                      ;Get the digits in reverse order
           CALL    WRITE_HEX_DIGIT
           LOOP    WRITE_DIGIT_LOOP
END_DECIMAL:
           POP     SI
```

Listing 10-1. *continued*

```
        POP     DX
        POP     CX
        POP     AX
        RET
WRITE_DECIMAL   ENDP
```

Notice that we've included a new register, the SI (*Source Index*), register. Later we'll see why it's been given that name, and we'll meet its brother, the DI, or *Destination Index*, register. Both registers have special uses, but they can also be used as if they were general-purpose registers. Since WRITE_DECIMAL needs four general-purpose registers, we used SI, even though we could have used BX, simply to show that SI (and DI) can serve as general-purpose registers if need be.

Before we try out our new procedure, we need to make two other changes to VIDEO_IO.ASM. First, we must remove the procedure TEST_WRITE_HEX and insert this test procedure in its place:

Listing 10-2. Replace TEST_WRITE_HEX in VIDEO_IO.ASM with This Procedure

```
TEST_WRITE_DECIMAL      PROC
        MOV     DX,12345
        CALL    WRITE_DECIMAL
        INT     20h                     ;Return to DOS
TEST_WRITE_DECIMAL      ENDP
```

This procedure tests WRITE_DECIMAL with the number 12345 (which the assembler converts to the word 3039h).

Second, we need to change the END statement at the end of VIDEO_IO.ASM to read END TEST_WRITE_DECIMAL, because TEST_WRITE_DECIMAL is now our main procedure.

Make these changes and give VIDEO_IO a whirl. Convert it to its .COM version and see if it works. If it doesn't, check your source file for errors (and have a look at the common errors in Appendix D). If you're adventurous, try to find your bug with Debug. After all, that's what Debug is for.

Some Tricks

Hiding in WRITE_DECIMAL are two tricks of the trade garnered from the people who wrote the ROM BIOS procedures we'll meet in Chapter 17. The first is an efficient instruction to set a register to zero. It's not much more efficient than MOV AX,0, and perhaps it's not worth the effort, but it's the sort of trick you'll find people using, so here it is. The instruction:

```
XOR     AX,AX
```

sets the AX register to zero. How? To understand that, we need to learn about the logical operation called an *Exclusive OR*, hence the name XOR.

The exclusive OR is similar to an OR (which we'll see next), but the result of XORing two trues:

```
XOR │  0    1
  0 │  0    1
  1 │  1    0
```

is true if *only* one bit is true, not if both are true. Thus, if we exclusive OR a number to itself, we get zero:

```
      1 0 1 1    0 1 0 1
XOR   1 0 1 1    0 1 0 1
      0 0 0 0    0 0 0 0
```

That's the trick. We won't find other uses for the XOR instruction in this book, but we thought you'd find it interesting.

As a short aside, you'll also find many people using another quick trick to set a register to zero. Rather than using the XOR instruction, we could have used:

```
SUB     AX,AX
```

to set the AX register to zero.

Now for the other trick. It's just about as devious as our XOR scheme to clear a register, and it uses a cousin to the Exclusive OR—the OR function.

We want to check the AX register to see if it's zero. To do this, we could use the instruction CMP AX,0. But no, we'd rather use a trick: It's more fun and a little more efficient, too. So, we write OR AX,AX and follow this instruction with a JNE (Jump if Not Equal) conditional jump. (We could also have used JNZ—Jump if Not Zero.)

The OR instruction, like any of the math instructions, sets the flags, including the zero flag. Like AND, OR is a logical concept. But here, a result is true if one *OR* the other bit is true:

```
OR │  0    1
 0 │  0    1
 1 │  1    0
```

If we take a number and OR it to itself, we get the original number back again:

```
      1 0 1 1    0 1 0 1
OR    1 0 1 1    0 1 0 1
      1 0 1 1    0 1 0 1
```

The OR instruction is also useful for setting just one bit in a byte. For example, we can set bit 3 in the number we just used:

```
      1 0 1 1   0 1 0 1
OR    0 0 0 0   1 0 0 0
      1 0 1 1   1 1 0 1
```

We'll have more tricks to play before we're through in this book, but these two are the only ones entirely for fun.

The Inner Workings

To see how WRITE_DECIMAL performs its task, study the listing; we won't cover more details here. We do need to point out a few more things.

First, the CX register is used to count how many digits we've pushed onto the stack, so that we know how many to remove. The CX register is a particularly convenient choice, because we can build a loop with the LOOP instruction and use the CX register to store the repeat count. Our choice makes the digit-output loop (WRITE_DIGIT_LOOP) almost trivial, because the LOOP instruction uses the CX register directly. We'll use CX very often when we have to store a count.

Next, be careful to check the boundary conditions here. The boundary condition at 0 isn't a problem, as you can check. The other boundary condition is 65535, or FFFFh, which you can check easily with Debug. Just load VIDEO_IO.COM into Debug by typing *DEBUG VIDEO_IO.COM* and change the 12345 (3039h) at 101h to 65535 (FFFFh). (WRITE_DECIMAL works with unsigned numbers. See if you can write a version to write signed numbers).

You may have noticed a sticky point here, having to do with the 8088, not our program. Debug works mostly with bytes (at least the E command does) but we want to change a word. We must be careful, since the 8088 stores the bytes in a different order. Here is an unassemble for the MOV instruction:

```
3985:0100 BA3930        MOV    DX,3039
```

You can tell from the *BA3930* part of this display that the byte at 101h is 39h, and the one at 102h is 30h (BA is the MOV instruction). The two bytes are the two bytes of 3039h, but seemingly in reverse order. Confusing? Actually, the order is logical, after a short explanation.

A word consists of two parts, the lower byte and the upper byte. The lower byte is the least significant byte (39h in 3039h), while the upper byte is the other part (30h). It makes sense, then, to place the lower byte at the lower address in memory. (Many other computer architectures, such as the Motorola

Figure 10-2. The 8088 stores numbers with the lower byte first in memory.

68000 in the Apple Macintosh, actually reverse these two bytes, and this can be a bit confusing if you're writing programs on several different types of computers.)

Try different numbers for the word starting at 101h, and you'll see how this storage works. Use TEST_WRITE_DECIMAL to see if you got it right, or unassemble the first instruction.

Summary

We added a few new instructions to our repertoire here, as well as a few tricks for fun. We also learned about two other registers, SI and DI, that we can use as general-purpose registers. They also have other uses, which we'll see in later chapters.

We learned about the XOR and OR logical instructions, which allow us to work between individual bits in two bytes or words. And in our WRITE_DECIMAL procedure, we used the XOR AX,AX instruction as a tricky way to set the AX register to zero. We used OR AX,AX as a devious way to write the equivalent of CMP AX,0 to test the AX register and see if it is zero.

Finally, we learned about how the 8088 stores a word in memory by checking the boundary conditions of our new procedure, WRITE_DECIMAL.

Here, at the end of this chapter, we now have another general-purpose procedure, WRITE_DECIMAL, that we'll be able to use in the future for our own programs.

Take a breather now. We have a few *different* chapters scheduled next. Chapter 11 covers segments in detail. Segments are perhaps the most complicated part of the 8088 microprocessor, so the chapter may prove to be rather heavy going. Even so, we need to cover the topic for the chapters that follow.

After that, we'll make a slight course correction and get back on track by learning about what we want to do with our program Dskpatch. We'll do a bit of probing on disks and learn about sectors, tracks, and other such things.

From there, we can plot a simple course for preliminary versions of Dskpatch. En route, you'll get a chance to see how to develop large programs. Programmers don't write an entire program, then debug it. They write sections and try each section before they move on—programming is much less work that way. We've used this approach to a limited extent by writing and testing WRITE_HEX and WRITE_DECIMAL, for which the test programs were very simple. The test programs from here on will be more complex but more interesting too.

11

SEGMENTS

In the preceding chapters, we encountered several directives that deal with segments. Now the time has come to look at segments themselves and at how the 8088 manages to address a full megabyte (1,048,576 bytes) of memory. From this, we'll begin to understand why segments need their own directives in the assembler, and in later chapters we'll begin to use different segments (thus far, we've used only one).

Let's start at the 8088 level by learning how it constructs the 20-bit addresses needed for a full megabyte of memory.

Sectioning the 8088's Memory

Segments are about the only part of the 8088 we haven't covered yet, and they are, perhaps, the most confusing part of this microprocessor to most people. In fact, segments are what we call a *kludge* in this business: computerese for a makeshift fix to a problem. (The 80386 microprocessor has additional addressing modes that are much simpler and don't use segments, but unfortunately we don't yet have an operating system from IBM or Microsoft that uses these *linear* addressing modes. OS/2, which runs on both 80286 and 80386 microprocessors, uses a slightly different type of segment to address more than 1 megabyte of memory.)

The problem, in this case, is being able to address more than 64K of memory—the limit with one word, since 65535 is the largest number a single word can hold. Intel, designers of the 8088, used segments and segment registers to "fix" this problem and in the process made the 8088 more confusing.

So far, we haven't concerned ourselves with this problem. We've been using the IP register to hold the address of the next instruction for the 8088 to execute ever since we met Debug in Chapter 2. Back then, you may recall we said the address is actually formed from both the CS register and the IP register. But we never really said how. Let's find out.

Although the complete address is formed from two registers, the 8088 doesn't form a two-word number for the address. If you were to take CS:IP as a 32-bit number (two 16-bit numbers side by side), the 8088 would be able to address about four billion bytes—far more than the one million bytes it can actually address. The 8088's method is slightly more complicated: The CS register provides the *starting* address for the code segment, where a segment is 64K of memory. Here's how it works.

As you can see in Figure 11-1, the 8088 divides memory into many overlapping segments, with a new segment starting every 16 bytes. The first segment

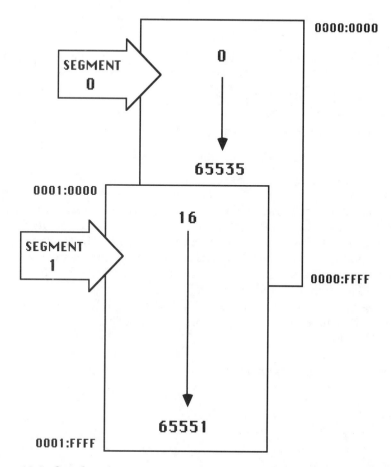

Figure 11-1. Overlapping segments start every 16 bytes, and are 65536 bytes long.

(segment 0) starts at memory location 0; the second (segment 1) starts at 10h (16); the third starts at 20h (32), and so on.

The actual address is just CS * 16 + IP. For example, if the CS register contains 3FA8 and IP contains D017, the absolute address is:

```
CS * 16  :  0 0 1 1   1 1 1 1   1 0 1 0   1 0 0 0   0 0 0 0
+  IP    :            1 1 0 1   0 0 0 0   0 0 0 1   0 1 1 1
            _____
            0 1 0 0   1 1 0 0   1 0 1 0   1 0 0 1   0 1 1 1
```

We multiplied by 16 just by shifting CS left four bits and injecting zeros at the right.

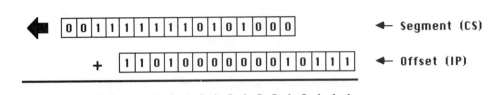

Figure 11-2. The absolute address of CS:IP is CS * 16 + IP.

Now, this may seem like a strange way to address more than 64K of memory, and it is—but it works. Soon, we'll begin to see how well it really works.

The 8088 actually has four segment registers: CS (Code Segment), DS (Data Segment), SS (Stack Segment), and ES (Extra Segment). The CS register we've been looking at is used by the 8088 for the segment where the next instruction is stored. In much the same way, DS is the segment where the 8088 looks for data, and SS is where the 8088 places the stack.

Before we go on, let's look at a short program, quite different from any we've seen before, that uses two different segments. Enter this program into the file TEST_SEG.ASM:

Listing 11-1. The Program TEST_SEG.ASM

```
DOSSEG
.MODEL    SMALL

.STACK                                  ;Allocate a 1K stack

.CODE

TEST_SEGMENT    PROC
       MOV      AH,4Ch                  ;Ask for the exit-to-dos function
       INT      21h                     ;Return to DOS
TEST_SEGMENT    ENDP

       END      TEST_SEGMENT
```

Then assemble and link Test_seg, but don't generate a .COM file for it. The result will be TEST_SEG.EXE, which is slightly different from a .COM file.

> **Note**: We have to use a method other than INT 20h to exit from .EXE files. For .COM files, INT 20h works perfectly well, but it doesn't work at all for .EXE files because the organization of segments is very different, as we'll see in this chapter; more on this difference later. From now on we'll use INT 21h, function 4Ch to exit our programs.

When we use Debug on a .COM file, Debug sets all the segment registers to the same number, with the program starting at an *offset* of 100h from the start of this segment. The first 256 bytes (100h) are used to store various pieces of information which we really aren't that interested in, but we'll take a peek at part of this area in a little bit.

Now, try loading TEST_SEG.EXE into Debug, to see what happens with segments in an .EXE file:

```
A>DEBUG TEST_SEG.EXE
-R
AX=0000  BX=0000  CX=0004  DX=0000  SP=0400  BP=0000  SI=0000  DI=0000
DS=3985  ES=3985  SS=3996  CS=3995  IP=0000   NV UP DI PL NZ NA PO NC
3995:0000 B44C          MOV     AH,4C
```

The values of the SS and CS registers are different from those for DS and ES.

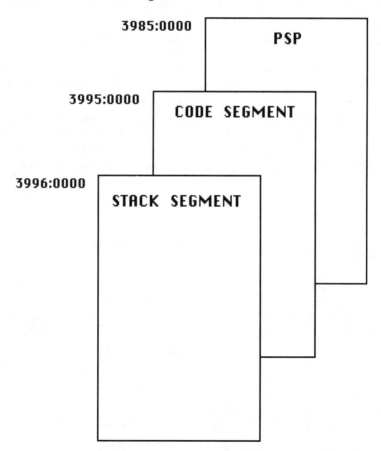

Figure 11-3. Memory Layout for TEST_SEG.EXE.

The Stack

In our program, we defined two segments. The STACK segment is where we place the stack (hence, the .STACK), and the code segment (which is actually called _TEXT) is where all our instructions are stored. The .STACK directive tells the assembler to create a 1024-byte stack. (We could create a larger or smaller stack by putting a number after .STACK. For example, .STACK 128 would create a stack 128 bytes long.)

The address for the top of the stack is given by SS:SP. SP is the Stack Pointer, like IP and CS for code, and is an offset within the current Stack Segment.

Actually, "top-of-stack" is a misnomer, because the stack grows from high memory toward low memory. Thus, the *top* of the stack is really at the bottom of the stack in memory, and new entries to the stack are placed progressively lower in memory. Here, SP is 400h, which is 1024 decimal, because we defined a stack area 1024 bytes long. We haven't placed anything on the stack as yet, so top-of-stack is still at the top of the memory we set aside for the stack: 400h.

If you think back to the .COM programs in previous chapters, we never declared a stack segment, which raises two questions: Why didn't we have to declare a stack segment for .COM programs? And where was the stack in the .COM programs? All the .COM programs we created had only one segment, and all the segment registers (CS, DS, ES, and SS) pointed to this segment. Since we had just one segment, we didn't need a separate stack segment.

As to where the stack was, if you look at the register display for WRITESTR.COM, you'll see the stack is at the very end of the segment (SP = FFEE):

```
-R
AX=0000  BX=0000  CX=0000  DX=0000  SP=FFEE  BP=0000  SI=0000 DI=0000
DS=3995  ES=3995  SS=3995  CS=3995  IP=0100     NV UP EI PL NZ NA PO NC
3995:0100 B402          MOV     AH,02
-
```

DOS always sets the stack pointer to the very end of the segment when it loads a .COM file into memory. For this reason, we don't need to declare a stack segment (with .STACK) for .COM files.

What would happen if we removed the .STACK directive from TEST_SEG.ASM?

```
A>DEBUG TEST_SEG.EXE
-R
AX=0000  BX=0000  CX=0004  DX=0000  SP=0000  BP=0000  SI=0000 DI=0000
DS=3985  ES=3985  SS=3995  CS=3995  IP=0000     NV UP EI PL NZ NA PO NC
3D90:0000 B44C          MOV     AH,4C
-
```

The stack is now at 3995:0, which is the start of our program (CS:0). This is very bad news. We don't want the stack anywhere near our program's code. Also, since the stack pointer is at SS:0, it has no room to grow (since the stack grows down in memory). For these reasons, we *must* declare a stack segment for .EXE programs.

Note: you must always declare a stack segment with .STACK in .EXE programs.

Getting back to our two-segment example, note that the Stack Segment (SS) is segment number 3996 (this will probably be different for you), while our Code Segment (CS) is at segment 3995—one less than SS, or just 16 bytes lower in memory. Since we didn't put any data into the stack segment, unassembling starting at CS:0 will show our program (MOV AH,4C and INT 21) followed by whatever happened to be in memory:

```
-U CS:0
3995:0000 B44C         MOV     AH,4C
3995:0002 CD21         INT     21
3995:0004 65           DB      65
3995:0005 2028         AND     [BX+SI],CH
3995:0007 59           POP     CX
3995:0008 2F           DAS
3995:0009 4E           DEC     SI
3995:000A 293F         SUB     [BX],DI
          .
          .
          .
```

The Program Segment Prefix (PSP)

In looking at the register display, you may have noticed that the ES and DS registers contain 3985h, 10h less than the beginning of the program at segment 3995h. Multiplying by 16 to get the number of bytes, we can see that there are 100h (or 256) bytes before our program starts. This is the same scratch area placed at the beginning of a .COM file.

Note: This "scratch area" is actually called a PSP (*Program Segment Prefix*) and contains information for use by DOS. In other words, you should not assume you can make use of this area.

Among other things, this 256-byte PSP at the start of programs contains the characters we type after the name of our program. For example:

```
A>DEBUG TEST_SEG.EXE And now for some characters we'll see in the memory dump
-D DS:80
3985:0080  39 20 41 6E 64 20 6E 6F-77 20 66 6F 72 20 73 6F   9 And now for so
3985:0090  6D 65 20 63 68 61 72 61-63 74 65 72 73 20 77 65   me characters we
3985:00A0  27 6C 6C 20 73 65 65 20-69 6E 20 74 68 65 20 6D   'll see in the m
3985:00B0  65 6D 6F 72 79 20 64 75-6D 70 0D 20 6D 65 6D 6F   emory dump. memo
3985:00C0  72 79 20 64 75 6D 70 0D-00 00 00 00 00 00 00 00   ry dump.........
              .
              .
              .
```

The first byte tells us we typed 39h (or 57) characters, including the first space after TEST_SEG.EXE. We won't use this information in this book, but it helps show why you might want such a large PSP.

The PSP also contains information that DOS uses when we exit from a program, with either the INT 20h or the INT 21h, function 4Ch, instructions. But for reasons that are not at all clear, the INT 20h instruction expects the CS register to point to the start of this PSP, which it does for a .COM program, but *not* for a .EXE program. This is an historical question. And, in fact, the exit function (INT 21h, function 4Ch) was added to DOS with the introduction of version 2.00 to make it easier to exit from .EXE programs; function 4Ch doesn't expect the CS register to point to the start of the PSP. We'll use INT 21h, function 4Ch from now on to exit from our programs.

The code for .COM files must always start at an offset of 100h in the code segment to leave room for this 256-byte PSP at the start. This is unlike the .EXE file, which had its code start at IP = 0000, because the code segment started 100h bytes after the beginning of the area in memory.

In the early days of the IBM PC, most programs were written as .COM programs because they were slightly simpler to write. But today, most programs are written as .EXE programs. So in the rest of this book, we'll be working almost entirely with .EXE programs.

The DOSSEG Directive

If you take a look again at TESTSEG.EXE, you'll notice that the stack segment is higher in memory than the code segment. Yet in our source file we defined the stack (.STACK) *before* any of the code (.CODE). So why is the stack higher in memory than the code?

The DOSSEG directive at the start of our program tells the assembler that we want the segments of our program loaded in a very specific order, with the code segment appearing first, and the stack last. In Chapter 14 we'll see more

Figure 11-4. .COM vs .EXE Programs.

about DOSSEG and the order of segments when we add another segment to hold data.

Near and Far CALLs

The rest of the information in this chapter is purely for your interest, since we won't be making use of it in this book. You can skip the next two sections and read them later if you find the going tough or you're eager to return to programming.

Let's step back for a minute and take a closer look at the CALL instructions we used in previous chapters. Specifically, let's look at the short program in

Chapter 7, where we first learned about the CALL instruction. Back then, we wrote a very short program that looked like this (without the procedure at 200h):

```
3985:0100 B241          MOV     DL,41
3985:0102 B90A00        MOV     CX,000A
3985:0105 E8F800        CALL    0200
3985:0108 E2FB          LOOP    0105
3985:010A CD20          INT     20
```

You can see by looking at the machine code on the left that the CALL instruction occupies only three bytes (E8F800). The first byte (E8h) is the CALL instruction, and the second two bytes form an offset. The 8088 calculates the address of the routine we're calling by adding this offset of 00F8h (remember that the 8088 stores the lower byte of a word in memory *before* the high byte, so we have to reverse the bytes) to the address of the next instruction (108h in our program). In this case, then, we have F8h + 108h = 200h. Just what we expected.

The fact that this instruction uses a single word for the offset means that CALLs are limited to a single segment, which is 64K bytes long. So how is it that we can write a program like Lotus 1-2-3 that is larger than 64K? We do it by using FAR, rather than NEAR, calls.

NEAR CALLs, as we've seen, are limited to a single segment. In other words, they change the IP register without affecting the CS register. And for this reason they're sometimes known as *intrasegment* CALLs.

But we can also have FAR CALLs that change both the CS *and* IP registers. Such CALLs are often known as *intersegment* CALLs because they call procedures in other segments.

Going along with these two versions of the CALL instruction are two versions of the RET instruction.

The NEAR CALL, as we saw in Chapter 7, pushes a single word onto the stack for its return address. And the corresponding RET instruction pops this word off the stack and into the IP register.

In the case of FAR CALLs and RETs, a word is not sufficient, because we're dealing with another segment. In other words, we need to save a two-word return address on the stack: one word for the instruction pointer (IP) and the other for the code segment (CS). The FAR RET, then, pops two words off the stack—one for the CS register and the other for IP.

Now we come to a sticky issue. How does the assembler know which of these two CALLs and RETs to use? When should it use the FAR CALL, and when should it use the NEAR CALL? Answer—by putting a NEAR or FAR directive after the PROC directive.

Figure 11-5. The assembler produces a FAR CALL.

By way of example, look at the following program:

```
PROC_ONE        PROC    FAR
        .
        .
        .
        RET
PROC_ONE        ENDP
PROC_TWO        PROC    NEAR
        CALL    PROC_ONE
        .
        .
        .
        RET
PROC_TWO        ENDP
```

When the assembler sees the CALL PROC_ONE instruction, it hunts in its table for the definition of PROC_ONE, which, in this case, is PROC_ONE PROC FAR. This definition tells whether the procedure is a near or far procedure.

In the case of a NEAR procedure, the assembler generates a NEAR CALL. And conversely, it generates a FAR CALL if the procedure you're calling was defined as a FAR procedure. In other words, the assembler uses the definition of the procedure that you're *calling* to determine the type of CALL instruction that's needed.

Figure 11-6. The assembler produces a FAR RET.

For the RET instruction, on the other hand, the assembler looks at the definition of the procedure that contains the RET instruction. In our program, the RET instruction for PROC_ONE will be a FAR RET, because PROC_ONE is declared to be a FAR procedure. Likewise, the RET in PROC_TWO is a NEAR RET.

What happens when we don't put a NEAR or FAR directive after the PROC? It turns out the assembler uses the information in the .MODEL directive to determine whether procedures are NEAR or FAR if you don't explicitly declare a procedure as NEAR or FAR. We're using the .MODEL SMALL directive, which tells the assembler that we only have one code segment, so all the procedures are NEAR procedures. There are other .MODEL directives (such as MEDIUM) that tell the assembler to make procedures FAR if they're not explicitly declared as NEAR.

More on the INT Instruction

The INT instruction is much like a CALL instruction, but with a minor difference. The name *INT* comes from the word *interrupt*. An interrupt is an external signal that causes the 8088 to execute a procedure and then return to what it was doing before it received the interrupt. An INT instruction doesn't interrupt the 8088, but it's treated as if it did.

When the 8088 receives an interrupt, it needs to store more information on the stack than just the two words for the return address. It has to store the values of the status flags—the carry flag, the zero flag, and so on. These values are stored in one word known as the Flag Register, and the 8088 pushes this information onto the stack before the return address. Here's why we need to save the status flags.

Your IBM PC regularly responds to a number of different interrupts. The 8088 inside your IBM PC receives an interrupt from the clock 18.2 times every second, for example. Each of these interrupts causes the 8088 to stop what it's doing and execute a procedure to count the clock pulses.

Now, envision such an interrupt occurring between these two program instructions:

```
CMP     AH,2
JNE     NOT_2
```

Let's assume AH = 2, so the zero flag will be set after the CMP instruction, which means that the JNE instruction will not branch to NOT_2.

Now, imagine that the clock interrupts the 8088 between these two instructions. That means the 8088 runs off to carry out the interrupt procedure before it checks the zero flag (with the JNE instruction). If the 8088 didn't save and restore the flag registers, the JNE instruction would use flags set by the interrupt procedure, *not* from our CMP instruction. To prevent such disasters, the 8088 *always* saves and restores the flag register for interrupts. An interrupt saves the flags, and an IRET (*Interrupt Return*) instruction restores the flags at the end of the interrupt procedure.

The same is true for an INT instruction. Thus, after executing the instruction:

```
INT     21
```

the 8088's stack will look like this:

```
Top of stack →     Old IP (return address part I)
                   Old CS (return address part II)
                   Old Flag Register
```

(The stack grows into lower memory, so the Old Flag Register is actually highest in memory).

When we place an INT instruction in a program, however, the interrupt is no surprise. Why, then, do we want to save the flags? Isn't saving the flags useful only when we have an external interrupt that comes at an unpredictable time? As it turns out, the answer is no. There is a very good reason for saving and restoring the flags for INT instructions. In fact, without this feature, Debug wouldn't be possible.

Debug uses a special flag in the flag register called the Trap Flag. This flag puts the 8088 into a special mode known as *single-step* mode, which Debug uses to trace through programs one instruction at a time. When the trap flag is set, the 8088 issues an INT 1 after it executes any instruction.

The INT 1 also clears the trap flag, so the 8088 won't be in single-step mode while we're inside Debug's INT 1 procedure. But since INT 1 saved the flags to the stack, issuing an IRET to return to the program we're debugging restores the trap flag. Then, we'll receive another INT 1 interrupt after the next instruction in our program. This is just one example of when it's useful to save the flag registers. But, as we'll see next, this restore-flag feature isn't always appropriate.

Some interrupt procedures bypass the restoration of the flag registers. For example, the INT 21h procedure in DOS sometimes changes the flag registers by short-circuiting the normal return process. Many of the INT 21h procedures that read or write disk information return with the carry flag set if there was an error of some sort (such as no disk in the drive).

Interrupt Vectors

Where do these interrupt instructions get the addresses for procedures? Each interrupt instruction has an interrupt number, such as the 21h in INT 21h. The 8088 finds addresses for interrupt procedures in a table of *interrupt vectors*, which is located at the very bottom of memory. For example, the two-word address for the INT 21h procedure is at 0000:0084. We get this address by multiplying the interrupt number by 4 (4 * 21h = 84h), since we need four bytes, two words, for each vector, or procedure address.

These vectors are exceedingly useful for adding features to DOS, because they enable us to intercept calls to interrupt procedures by changing the addresses in the vector table. We'll use exactly this trick at the end of this book to add a disk light to your computer's screen.

All these ideas and methods should become clearer as we see more examples. Most of this book from here on will be filled with examples, so there will be plenty to study. If you've been feeling a bit overwhelmed by new information, rest easy. We'll take a short breather in the next chapter and get ourselves reoriented and back on course.

Summary

As we said, this chapter contained a lot of information. We won't use it all, but we did need to learn more about segments. Chapter 13 will bring us to modular design, and we'll use some aspects of segments to make our job easier.

We began this chapter by learning how the 8088 divides memory into segments. To understand segments in more detail, we built an .EXE program with two different segments. We also learned that we need to use INT 21h, function 4Ch rather than INT 20h to exit from .EXE programs. This is important since we'll use .EXE programs from now on in this book.

We also found that the 100h (256-byte) PSP (Program Segment Prefix) at the start of our programs contains a copy of what we typed on the command line. We won't use this knowledge in this book, but it helps us see why DOS sets aside such a large chunk of memory for the purpose.

And finally we learned more about the DOSSEG, .MODEL, .CODE, .STACK, NEAR, and FAR directives. These directives help us work with segments. In this book, we'll barely use the power of these directives, because our .EXE programs will use only two segments. But for programmers who write *huge* programs in assembly language (using the MEDIUM memory model), these directives are invaluable. If you're interested, you'll find the details in your macro assembler manual.

At the very end of this chapter we learned more about the roots of our helpful INT instruction. Now, we're just about ready to slow down and learn how to *write* larger and more useful assembly language programs.

12

COURSE CORRECTIONS

W e've been poking our noses into a lot of new and interesting places, and you may at times have wondered whether we're wandering about somewhat aimlessly. We haven't been, of course. We're now familiar enough with our new surroundings to fix our sights and plot a course for the rest of this book. And that's what we'll do in this chapter: We'll take a close look at a design for our Dskpatch program. Then we'll spend the rest of this book developing Dskpatch, much as you will later develop programs of your own.

We won't present the finished version of Dskpatch all at once; that isn't the way we wrote it. Instead, we'll present short test programs to check each stage of our program as we write it. To do this, we need to know where we want to go. Hence, our course correction here.

Since Dskpatch will deal with information on disks, that's where we'll begin.

Diskettes, Sectors, and So Forth

The information on your floppy disks is divided into *sectors*, with each sector holding 512 bytes of information. A double-sided, double-density 5¼-inch disk formatted with DOS 2.0 or above has a total of 720 sectors, or 720 * 512 = 368,640 bytes (see Table 12-1 for other types of disks). If we could look directly at these sectors, we could examine the directory directly, or we could look at the files on the disk. We can't—not by ourselves—but Dskpatch will. Let's use Debug to learn more about sectors and get an idea of how we'll display a sector with Dskpatch.

Debug has a command, L (*Load*), to read sectors from disk into memory, where we can look at the data. As an example, let's look at the directory that starts at sector 5 on a double-sided disk (use Table 12-1 to determine what number to use for the directory if you have a different type of disk). Load sector 5 from the disk in drive A (that's drive 0 to Debug) by using the L command. Make sure you have a 360K (or 1.2M, 720K, or 1.44M) disk in drive A, then enter the following:

```
-L 100 0 5 1
```

Table 12-1. Starting Sector for the Root Directory

Disk Type	Sectors/disk	Directory
5¼", 360K	720	5
5¼", 1.2M	2,400	15
3½", 720K	1,440	7
3½", 1.44M	2,880	19

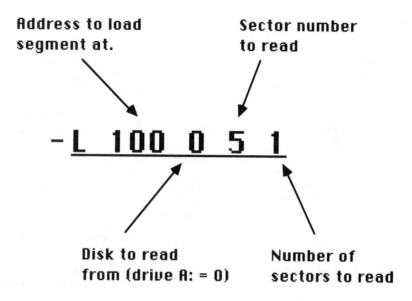

Address to load segment at.

Sector number to read

-L 100 0 5 1

Disk to read from (drive A: = 0)

Number of sectors to read

As you can see in Figure 12-1, this command loads sectors into memory, starting with sector 5 and continuing through one sector at an offset of 100 within the data segment. To display sector 5, we can use a Dump command:

```
-D 100
396F:0100  49 42 4D 42 49 4F 20 20-43 4F 4D 27 00 00 00 00   IBMBIO  COM'....
396F:0110  00 00 00 00 00 00 00 60-68 06 02 00 00 12 00 00   .......`h......
396F:0120  49 42 4D 44 4F 53 20 20-43 4F 4D 27 00 00 00 00   IBMDOS  COM'....
396F:0130  00 00 00 00 00 00 00 60-68 06 07 00 00 43 00 00   .......`h....C..
396F:0140  43 4F 4D 4D 41 4E 44 20-43 4F 4D 20 00 00 00 00   COMMAND COM ....
396F:0150  00 00 00 00 00 00 00 60-68 06 18 00 00 45 00 00   .......`h....E..
396F:0160  41 53 53 45 4D 42 4C 45-52 20 20 08 00 00 00 00   ASSEMBLER  .....
396F:0170  00 00 00 00 00 00 33 9C-B0 06 00 00 00 00 00 00   ......3.0......
-D
396F:0180  46 57 20 20 20 20 20 20-43 4F 4D 20 00 00 00 00   FW      COM ....
396F:0190  00 00 00 00 00 00 00 00-6F 05 2A 00 80 AF 00 00   ........o.*../..
396F:01A0  46 57 20 20 20 20 20 20-4F 56 4C 20 00 00 00 00   FW      OVL ....
396F:01B0  00 00 00 00 00 00 00 00-72 05 56 00 81 02 00 00   ........r.V.....
396F:01C0  46 57 20 20 20 20 20 20-53 57 50 20 00 00 00 00   FW      SWP ....
396F:01D0  00 00 00 00 00 00 9B 8A-FF 06 57 00 00 C8 00 00   ..........W..H..
396F:01E0  43 4F 4E 46 49 47 20 20-44 41 54 20 00 00 00 00   CONFIG  DAT ....
396F:01F0  00 00 00 00 00 00 1D 82-A1 06 89 00 00 28 00 00   ........!....(..
```

We'll use a format much like this for Dskpatch, but with many improvements. Dskpatch will be the equivalent of a full-screen editor for disk sectors. We'll be able to display sectors on the screen and move the cursor about the sector display, changing numbers or characters as we want. We'll also be able to write this altered sector back to the disk, and this is why we call it Disk Patch—

Disk A   Sector 0

```
        00 01 02 03 04 05 06 07 08 09 0A 0B 0C 0D 0E 0F    0123456789ABCDEF
```

Press function key, or enter character or hex byte: _

Figure 12-2. Example of Dskpatch's Display.

or rather Dskpatch, since we can't have more than eight characters in the name.

Dskpatch is the motivation for the procedures we write. It is by no means an end in itself. In using Dskpatch as an example for this book, we'll also manage to present many procedures that you'll find useful when you attempt to write your own programs. That means you'll find many general-purpose procedures for display output, display manipulation, keyboard input, and more.

Let's take a closer look at some improvements we'll make to Debug's sector dump. The display from Debug only shows the "printable" characters—96 out of the 256 different characters that an IBM PC can display. Why is that? Because MS-DOS, PC-DOS's cousin, runs on many different computers. Some of these computers display only 96 characters, so Microsoft (the author of Debug) chose to write one version of Debug that would work on all machines.

Dskpatch is for IBM Personal Computers and near cousins, so we can display all 256 different characters; to do so will require a bit of work. Using the DOS function 2 for character output, we can display almost all characters, but DOS gives special meaning to some, such as 7, which rings the bell. There are characters for special codes like 7, and in Part III we'll see how to display them.

We'll also make heavy use of the function keys so that, for example, we can display the next sector just by pressing the F4 key. And we'll be able to change any byte by moving the cursor to that byte and typing in a new number. It will be just like using a word processor, where we can change characters very easily. More of these details will appear as we slowly build Dskpatch. (Figure 12-2 shows what its normal display will look like—a vast improvement over the display from Debug.)

The Game Plan

In Chapter 13, we'll learn how to break our program into many different source files. Then, we'll begin serious work on Dskpatch in Chapter 14. At the end, we'll have nine source files for Dskpatch that have to be linked together. And even if you don't enter and run all these programs now, they'll be here when you're ready for them or when you want to borrow some of the general-purpose procedures. In any case, you'll get a better idea of how to write long programs as you read through the following chapters.

We've already created several useful procedures, such as WRITE_HEX to write a byte as a two-digit hex number and WRITE_DECIMAL to write a number in decimal. Now, we'll write some programs to display a block of memory in much the same way Debug's D command does. We'll start by displaying 16 bytes of memory, one line of Debug's display, and then work toward displaying 16 lines of 16 bytes each (half a sector). A full sector won't fit on the display at one time with the format we've chosen, so Dskpatch includes procedures for scrolling through a sector using the ROM BIOS—not DOS—interrupts. That will come much later, though, after we've built a full-screen display of half a sector.

Once we can dump 256 bytes from memory, we'll build another procedure to read a sector from the disk into our area of memory. We'll dump half a sector on the screen, and we'll be able to use Debug to alter our program, so we can dump different sectors. At that point, we'll have a functional, but not very attractive display, so making it pretty comes next.

With a bit more work and some more procedures, we'll rebuild the half-sector display to be much more pleasing aesthetically. It still won't be a full-screen display, so it will just scroll past like Debug's dump did. But the full-screen display will come next, and through it, we'll learn about the ROM BIOS routines that allow us to control the display, move the cursor—that sort of thing. Then, we'll be ready to learn how to use more ROM BIOS routines to print all 256 different characters.

Next will come the keyboard input and command procedures that will let us start interacting with Dskpatch. About that time we'll also need another course correction.

Summary

We've seen enough of the future here. You should have a better idea of where we're headed, so let's move on to the next chapter, where we'll lay the groundwork for modular design and learn how to split a program into many different source files. Then, in Chapter 14, we'll write some test procedures to display sections of memory.

13

MODULAR DESIGN

Without modular design, Dskpatch wouldn't have been much fun to write. Using a modular design greatly eases the task of writing any but the smallest program. We'll use this chapter to set some ground rules for modular design, and we'll follow those rules throughout the rest of this book. Let's begin by learning how to separate a large program into many different source files.

Separate Assembling

In Chapter 10, we added the procedure WRITE_DECIMAL to VIDEO_IO.ASM, and we also added a short test procedure called TEST_WRITE_DECIMAL. Let's take this test procedure out of VIDEO_IO.ASM and put it in a file of its own, called TEST.ASM. Then, we'll assemble these two files separately and link them together into one program. Here is the TEST.ASM file:

Listing 13-1. The File TEST.ASM

```
        DOSSEG
        .MODEL  SMALL

        .STACK

        .CODE
                EXTRN    WRITE_DECIMAL:PROC

        TEST_WRITE_DECIMAL      PROC
                MOV     DX,12345
                CALL    WRITE_DECIMAL
                MOV     AH,4Ch              ;Return to DOS
                INT     21h
        TEST_WRITE_DECIMAL      ENDP

                END     TEST_WRITE_DECIMAL
```

We've seen most of this source file before, but the EXTRN directive is new. The statement EXTRN WRITE_DECIMAL:PROC tells the assembler two things: that WRITE_DECIMAL is in another, *external,* file, and that it's a procedure. What kind of procedure (NEAR or FAR) depends on the .MODEL directive. Since we've used .MODEL SMALL, which defines procedures to be NEAR, WRITE_DECIMAL is in the same segment. The assembler thus generates a NEAR CALL for this procedure; it would generate a FAR CALL if we had placed a FAR after WRITE_DECIMAL. (We can use NEAR or FAR in place of the PROC in the EXTRN statement if we wanted to explicitly define the type of procedure, but it's better to let the .MODEL directive define the procedure types.)

These are about the only changes we need for separate source files until we begin to store data in memory. At that point, we'll introduce another segment for data. Now, let's modify VIDEO_IO.ASM and then assemble and link these two files.

Figure 13-1. LINK stitches together segments from different files.

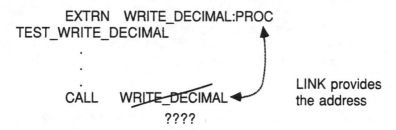

Figure 13-2. LINK assigns the addresses for external names.

Remove the procedure TEST_WRITE_DECIMAL from VIDEO_IO.ASM. We've placed this in TEST.ASM, so we don't need it in Video_io.

Finally, change END TEST_WRITE_DECIMAL at the end of VIDEO_IO.ASM to just END. Once again, we moved the main procedure to TEST.ASM. The procedures in VIDEO_IO.ASM are now *external* procedures, nothing more. That is, they have no function by themselves; they must be linked to procedures that call them from other files. We don't need a name after the END directive in VIDEO_IO.ASM, because our main program is now in TEST.ASM.

When you've finished making these changes, your VIDEO_IO.ASM source file should look something like this:

```
.MODEL   SMALL
.CODE
        PUBLIC   WRITE_HEX_DIGIT
            .
            .
            .
WRITE_HEX_DIGIT       ENDP
        PUBLIC   WRITE_HEX
            .
            .
            .
WRITE_HEX       ENDP

        PUBLIC   WRITE_CHAR
            .
            .
            .
WRITE_CHAR       ENDP

        PUBLIC   WRITE_DECIMAL
            .
            .
            .
WRITE_DECIMAL    ENDP

        END
```

Assemble these two files just as you assembled Video_io before. TEST.ASM knows all it needs to know about VIDEO_IO.ASM through the EXTRN statement. The rest will come when we link the two files.

You should now have the files TEST.OBJ and VIDEO_IO.OBJ. Use the following command to link these two files into one program named TEST.EXE:

```
A>LINK TEST VIDEO_IO;
```

LINK stitches the procedures of these two files together to create one file containing the entire program. It uses the first file name we entered as the name for the resulting .EXE file, so we now have TEST.EXE.

That's it; we created one program from two source files. The final .EXE program is identical in function to the .COM version we created in Chapter 10 from the single file VIDEO_IO.ASM, when it contained the main procedure TEST_WRITE_DECIMAL.

We'll make heavy use of separate source files from here on, and their value will become clearer as the procedures stack up. In the next chapter, we'll write a test program to dump sections of memory in hex. We'll usually write a simple test version of a procedure before we write the complete version. Doing so will allow us to see how to write a good final version, as well as saving much effort and mental turmoil in the process.

There are several other useful ways to save effort. We call them the *Three Laws of Modular Design*.

The Three Laws of Modular Design

These laws are summarized in Table 13-1. They aren't really *laws*, they're suggestions. But we'll use them throughout this book. Define your own laws if you like, but either way, stick to the same ones all the time. Your job will be much easier if you're consistent.

Table 13-1.   The Three Laws of Modular Design

---

1. Save and restore *all* registers, *unless* the procedure returns a value in that register.
2. Be consistent about which registers you use to pass information. For example:
   - DL, DX—Send byte and word values.
   - AL, AX—Return byte and word values.
   - BX:AX—Return double-word values.
   - DS:DX—Send and return addresses.
   - CX—Repeat counts and other counts.
   - CF—Set when there is an error; an error code should be returned in one of the registers, such as AL or AX.
3. Define *all* external interactions in the comment header:
   - Information needed on entry.
   - Information returned (registers changed).
   - Procedures called.
   - Variables used (read, written, and so on).

There's an obvious parallel between modular design in programming and modular design in engineering. An electrical engineer, for example, can build a very complicated piece of equipment from boxes that perform different functions, without knowing how each box works. But if each box uses different voltages and different connections, the lack of consistency creates a major headache for the poor engineer, who must somehow provide a different voltage for each box and create special connections between boxes. Not much fun, but fortunately for the engineer, there are standards providing for only a small number of standard voltages. So, perhaps only four different voltages need to be provided, instead of a different voltage for each box.

Modular design and standard interfaces are just as important in assembly language programs, and that's why we'll lay down the laws (so to speak) and use those laws from here on. As you'll see by the end of this book, these rules will make our task much simpler. Let's take a look at these laws in detail.

Save and restore *all* registers, *unless* the procedure returns a value in that register. There aren't that many registers in the 8088. By saving registers at the start of a procedure, we free them for use within that procedure. But we must be careful to restore them at the end of the procedure. You'll see us doing this in all our procedures, with PUSH instructions appearing first in each procedure, and POPs at the end.

The only exception is for procedures that must return some information to the calling procedure. For example, a procedure that reads a character from the keyboard must somehow return the character. We won't save any registers that we use to return information.

Short procedures also help the register-shortage problem. At times, we'll write a procedure that's used by only one other procedure. Not only does this help with the shortage of registers, it also makes the program easier to write and, often, easier to read. We'll see more of this as we write procedures for Dskpatch.

Be consistent about which registers you use to pass information. Our job becomes simpler if we set standards for exchanging information between procedures. We'll use one register for sending information and one for receiving information. We'll also need to send addresses for long pieces of data and for this we'll use the pair of registers DS:DX, so that our data can be anywhere in memory. You'll learn more about this when we introduce a new segment for data and begin to make use of the DS register.

We reserve the CX register for repeat counts. We'll soon write a procedure to write one character several times, so that we can write ten spaces by calling this procedure (WRITE_CHAR_N_TIMES) with CX set to 10. We'll use the CX register whenever we have a repeat count or when we want to return some count, such as the number of characters read from the keyboard (we'll do this when we write a procedure named READ_STRING).

Finally, we'll set the Carry Flag (CF) whenever there is an error, and we'll clear it whenever there isn't an error. Not all procedures use the carry flags. For example, WRITE_CHAR always works, so there's no reason to return an error report. But a procedure that writes to the disk can encounter many errors (no disk, write-protection, and so on). In this case, we'll use a register to return an error code. There's no standard here, because DOS uses different registers for different functions—its fault, not ours.

Define *all* external interactions in the comment header. There's no need to learn how a procedure works if all we want to do is use it, and this is why we place a detailed comment header before each procedure. This header contains *all* the information we need to know. It tells us what to place in each register before calling the procedure, and it tells what information the procedure returns. Most procedures use registers for their variables, but some of the procedures we'll soon see use variables in memory. The comment header should say which of these memory variables are read and which are changed. Finally, each header should list other procedures called. Here is an example of a full-blown header with much of this information:

```
;-------------------------------------------------------------------;
; This is an example of a full-blown header.  This part would normally ;
; be a brief description of what this procedure does.  For example,    ;
; this procedure will write the message "Sector    " on the first line. ;
;                                                                    ;
; On entry: DS:DX    Address of the message "Sector    "             ;
; Returns:  AX       Error code if there was an error                ;
;                                                                    ;
; Calls:    GOTO_XY, WRITE_STRING (procedures called)                ;
; Reads:    STATUS_LINE_NO        (memory variables read only)       ;
; Writes:   DUMMY                 (memory variables altered)         ;
;-------------------------------------------------------------------;
```

Whenever we want to use any procedure we've written, we can just glance at this comment header to learn how to use it. There will be no need to delve into the inner workings of the procedure to find out what it does.

These laws make assembly language programming easier, and we'll be certain to abide by them, but not necessarily on the first try—we often won't. The first version of a procedure or program is a test case. Frequently, we don't know exactly how to write the program we have in mind, so on these "rough drafts," we'll write the program without concern for the laws of modular design. We'll just plow through and get something that works. Then we can backtrack and do a good job by rewriting each procedure to conform to these laws.

Programming is a process that goes by leaps and bounds. Throughout this book we'll show much of the stuttering that went into writing Dskpatch, but we certainly can't show it all. There isn't room enough to contain all the versions we wrote before we settled on the final version. Our first tries often bore very little resemblance to the final versions you'll see, so when you write programs, don't worry about getting everything right the first time. Be prepared to rewrite each procedure as you learn more about what you really want.

In the next chapter, we'll build a simple test program to print a block of memory. It won't be the final version; we'll go through others before we're satisfied, and even then, there will be other changes we'd like to make. The moral is: A program is never done, but we must stop somewhere.

Summary

This has been a chapter for you to remember and use in the future. We began by learning how to separate a program into a number of different source files that we can assemble independently, then stitch together with the linker. We used the PUBLIC and EXTRN directives to inform the linker that there are connections between different source files. PUBLIC says that other source files can CALL the procedures named after PUBLICs, while EXTRN tells the assembler that the procedure we want to use is in another file.

Then we moved on to the Three Laws of Modular Design. These rules are meant to make your programming job simpler, so use them when you write your own programs, just as you'll see us use them in this book. You'll find it easier to write, debug, and read programs if they conform to these Three Laws.

14

DUMPING MEMORY

From here on, we'll concentrate on building Dskpatch in much the same way that we originally wrote it. Some of the instructions in procedures to come may be unfamiliar; we'll explain each briefly as we come across them, but for detailed information, you'll need a book that covers all of the instructions in detail. Most reference books that cover the 8088, 80286, or 80386 have all the information you should need. Rather than cover all the 8088 instructions, we'll concentrate on new concepts, such as the different modes of addressing memory, which we'll cover in this chapter. In Part III, we'll move even farther away from the details of instructions and begin to see information specific to the IBM Personal Computer and its near cousins.

Now, let's learn about *addressing modes* by writing a short test program to dump 16 bytes of memory in hex notation. To begin, we need to learn how to use memory as variables.

Addressing Modes

We've seen two addressing modes; they're known as the *register* and *immediate* addressing modes. The first mode we learned about was the register mode, which uses registers as variables. For example, the instruction:

```
MOV     AX,BX
```

uses the two registers AX and BX as variables.

Then, we moved on to the immediate addressing mode, in which we moved a number directly into a register, as in the example:

```
MOV     AX,2
```

This moves the byte or word of memory *immediately* following the instruction into a register. In this sense, the MOV instruction in our example is one byte long, with two more bytes for the data (0002):

```
396F:0100 B80200        MOV     AX,0002
```

The instruction is B8h, and the two bytes of data (02h and 00h) follow this (remember that the 8088 stores the low byte, 02h, first in memory).

Now, we'll learn how to use memory as a variable. The immediate mode allows us to read the piece of fixed memory immediately following that one instruction, but it doesn't allow us to change memory. For this, we'll need other addressing modes.

Let's begin with an example. The following program reads 16 bytes of memory, one byte at a time, and displays each byte in hex notation, with a single space between each of the 16 hex numbers. Enter the program into the file DISP_SEC.ASM and assemble it. Enter the following into the new file DISP_SEC.ASM:

Listing 14-1. The New File DISP_SEC.ASM

```
        DOSSEG
        .MODEL  SMALL

        .STACK

        .DATA

        PUBLIC  SECTOR
SECTOR  DB      10h, 11h, 12h, 13h, 14h, 15h, 16h, 17h  ;Test pattern
        DB      18h, 19h, 1Ah, 1Bh, 1Ch, 1Dh, 1Eh, 1Fh

        .CODE

        EXTRN   WRITE_HEX:PROC
        EXTRN   WRITE_CHAR:PROC
;-----------------------------------------------------------------;
; This is a simple test program to dump 16 bytes of memory as hex ;
; numbers, all on one line.                                       ;
;-----------------------------------------------------------------;
DISP_LINE       PROC
        MOV     AX,DGROUP       ;Put data segment into AX
        MOV     DS,AX           ;Set DS to point to data

        XOR     BX,BX           ;Set BX to 0
        MOV     CX,16           ;Dump 16 bytes
HEX_LOOP:
        MOV     DL,SECTOR[BX]   ;Get 1 byte
        CALL    WRITE_HEX       ;Dump this byte in hex
        MOV     DL,' '          ;Write a space between numbers
        CALL    WRITE_CHAR
        INC     BX
        LOOP    HEX_LOOP

        MOV     AH,4Ch          ;Return to DOS
        INT     21h
DISP_LINE ENDP

        END     DISP_LINE
```

Let's try our new program to see how it works. Assemble Disp_sec.

We're ready to link DISP_SEC.OBJ and VIDEO_IO.OBJ and create an .EXE file named DISP_SEC.EXE. LINK creates a program by putting the pieces together in the same order as the names on the command line. Since we want the main procedure to appear at the start of the program, the first file name in the LINK command needs to be the name of the file that contains the main pro-

Figure 14-1. Translation of SECTOR[BX].

cedure (Disp_sec in this case). And a semicolon must appear at the end of the
list of files, so type:

```
A>LINK DISP_SEC VIDEO_IO;
```

Linking will always be the same, with more names before the semicolon
when we have more files, but the main procedure must always be in the first
file listed.

In general, the preceding step for the files *file1*, *file2*, and so on, looks like
this:

```
LINK file1 file2 file3 ...;
```

Now, run the .EXE file. If you don't see:

```
10 11 12 13 14 15 16 17 18 19 1A 1B 1C 1D 1E 1F
```

when you run the program, go back and check carefully for a mistake.

Now, let's see how Disp_sec works. The instruction:

```
MOV     DL,SECTOR[BX]           ;Get 1 byte
```

uses a new addressing mode known as *Indirect Memory Addressing*—addressing memory through the *Base* register with *offset*, or more simply, *Base Relative*. To see what this really means, we need to first learn more about segments.

The Data Segment

Looking at Disp_sec, you'll see the label SECTOR appears after .DATA. The
.DATA directive declares a data segment that is used for memory variables.

DS,SS ——▶

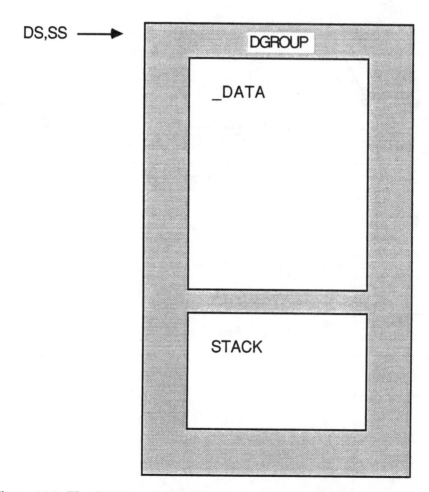

Figure 14-2. The .DATA and .STACK data are put into a single segment when we use the SMALL memory model.

(By the way, the name of the segment created by .DATA is _DATA. Any time we want to store and read data in memory, we'll set aside some space in this segment. We'll get back to memory variables in just a minute, but first let's learn a little more about segments.

The .MODEL SMALL directive creates what Microsoft calls a small memory-model program. Small programs are defined as programs that have up to 64K of code, and up to 64K of data. In other words, one segment for code and one segment for data. Since both the data (defined by .DATA) and the stack (defined by .STACK) are data, they're put into a single segment.

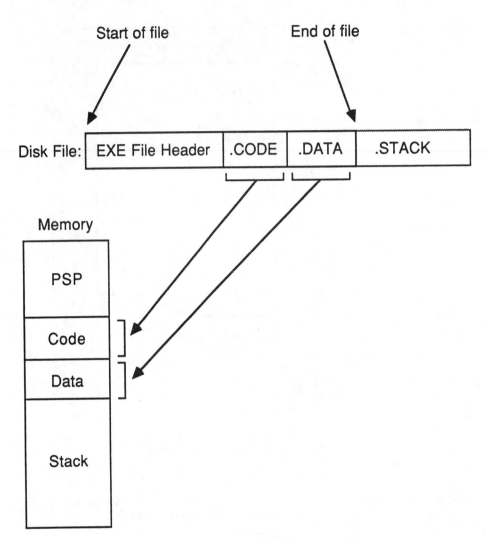

Figure 14-3. The stack doesn't require disk space.

This *grouping* of the stack and data segments into one segment is handled by a mechanism in the assembler called *groups*. In particular, the assembler creates a group called DGROUP that creates a single segment out of all the segments used for data. So far we've seen the .DATA and .STACK directive, and there are several other data directives that create segments in this group (we'll see another later in this book). Fortunately, the .MODEL, .DATA, and .STACK directives handle all of this behind the scenes. Knowing some of what happens behind the scenes, however, will come into use later when we look at memory maps to see how our programs are put together.

Another thing that happens automatically, as a result of the DOSSEG directive, is that the STACK segment is loaded into memory above the DATA segment. And there is a very good reason for this. The data segment we created has data in it (10h, 11h, 12h, and so on) that needs to be in the .EXE file so it can be copied into memory when our program is run by DOS. The stack, on the other hand, needs to take space in memory, but the stack's memory doesn't need to be initialized (only SS:SP has to be set). So by putting the stack segment after the data segment, we don't need to set aside space on the disk for the stack (see Figure 14-3).

Base-Relative Addressing

It's time to get back to our base-relative addressing mode. The two lines:

```
SECTOR   DB        10h, 11h, 12h, 13h, 14h, 15h, 16h, 17h  ;Test pattern
         DB        18h, 19h, 1Ah, 1Bh, 1Ch, 1Dh, 1Eh, 1Fh
```

set aside 16 bytes of memory in the data segment starting at SECTOR, which the assembler converts to an address. DB, you may recall, stands for *Define Byte*; the numbers after each DB are initial values. So, when we first start DISP_SEC.COM, the memory starting at SECTOR will contain 10h, 11h, 12h, and so on. If we wrote:

```
MOV      DL,SECTOR
```

the instruction would move the first byte (10h) into the DL register. This is known as *direct* memory addressing. But we didn't write that. Instead, we placed [BX] after SECTOR. This may look suspiciously like an index into an array, like the BASIC statement:

```
K = L(10)
```

which moves the 10th element of L into K.

In fact, our MOV instruction is much the same. The BX register contains an *offset* in memory from SECTOR. So if BX is 0, the MOV DL,SECTOR[BX] moves the first byte (10h here) into DL. If BX is 0Ah, this MOV instruction moves the eleventh byte (1Ah—remember, we started at 0) into DL.

On the other hand, the instruction MOV DX,SECTOR[BX] would move the sixth word into DX, since an offset of 10 bytes is the same as 5 words, and the first word is at offset zero. (For enthusiasts: This last MOV instruction isn't legal, because SECTOR is a byte label, whereas DX is a word register. We would have to write MOV DX,Word Ptr SECTOR[BX] to tell the assembler that we really want to use SECTOR as a word label in this instruction.)

There are many other addressing modes; some we'll encounter later, but most we won't. All the addressing modes are summarized in Table 14-1.

Table 14-1.   Addressing Modes

Addressing Mode	Format of Address	Segment Register Used
Register	register (such as AX)	None
Immediate	data (such as 12345)	None
Memory Addressing Modes		
Register Indirect	[BX]	DS
	[BP]	SS
	[DI]	DS
	[SI]	DS
Base Relative*	label[BX]	DS
	label[BP]	SS
Direct Indexed*	label[DI]	DS
	label[SI]	DS
Base Indexed*	label[BX + SI]	DS
	label[BX + DI]	DS
	label [BP + SI]	SS
	label[BP + DI]	SS
String Commands: (MOVSW, LODSB, *and so on*)		Read from DS:SI Write to ES:DI

* Label[...] can be replaced by [disp + ...], where *disp* is a displacement. Thus, we could write [10 + BX] and the address would be 10 + BX.

Setting Up DS

There's one minor detail we've glossed over. In Chapter 11 we noted that both the DS and ES registers point to the PSP, not to our data segment, when DOS starts our program. How do we set DS so it points to our data segment? Using the first two lines in DISP_LINE:

```
MOV   AX,DGROUP          ;Put data segment into AX
MOV   DS,AX              ;Set DS to point to data
```

These two lines set the DS register so it points to our data segment. The first line moves the segment address for our data group (called DGROUP) that contains .DATA and .STACK into the AX register. And the second line sets DS so it points to our data.

But there's one sticky point here. If you remember back to the discussions about the segment registers, we said the segment used for our programs depends on how much of our memory is already in use. In other words, we can't know the value of DGROUP until DOS loads our program in memory. How, then do we know what number to load into AX?

As it turns out, there is a small header at the start of each .EXE file that contains a list of addresses in our program that have to be calculated. DOS uses this information to calculate the value of DGROUP and update the value in the MOV AX,DGROUP instruction when it loads DISP_SEC.EXE into memory. This process is known as relocation, and we'll see exactly how it works in Chapter 28.

There is another fine point of writing programs for the 8088 family of microprocessor. You'll notice we set the value of DS with two instructions, rather than the single instruction:

```
MOV   DS,DGROUP
```

Why do we need two instructions? It turns out that you can't move a number directly into a segment register on the 8088, so we have to move the segment number first into the AX register. Requiring two instructions, rather than one, simplified the design of the 8088 microprocessor, which made it less expensive to manufacture but more difficult to program.

Adding Characters to the Dump

We're almost finished writing the procedure that creates a dump display similar to Debug's. So far, we've dumped the hex numbers for one line; in the next step, we'll add the character display following the hex display. It's not very involved, so without further delay, here's the new version of DISP_LINE (in DISP_SEC.ASM), with a second loop added to display the characters:

Listing 14-2. Changes to DISP_LINE in DISP_SEC.ASM

```
DISP_LINE       PROC
        MOV     AX,DGROUP       ;Put data segment into AX
        MOV     DS,AX           ;Set DS to point to data

        XOR     BX,BX           ;Set BX to 0
        MOV     CX,16           ;Dump 16 bytes
HEX_LOOP:
        MOV     DL,SECTOR[BX]   ;Get 1 byte
        CALL    WRITE_HEX       ;Dump this byte in hex
        MOV     DL,' '          ;Write a space between numbers
        CALL    WRITE_CHAR
        INC     BX
        LOOP    HEX_LOOP

        MOV     DL,' '          ;Add another space before characters
        CALL    WRITE_CHAR
        MOV     CX,16
        XOR     BX,BX           ;Set BX back to 0
ASCII_LOOP:
        MOV     DL,SECTOR
        CALL    WRITE_CHAR
        INC     BX
        LOOP    ASCII_LOOP

        MOV     AH,4Ch          ;Return to DOS
        INT     21h
DISP_LINE ENDP
```

Assemble this, link it to Video_io, and try it. Just the display we wanted. (See Figure 14-4.)

Try changing the data to include a 0Dh or a 0Ah. You'll see a rather strange display. Here's why: 0Ah and 0Dh are the characters for the line-feed and carriage-return characters. DOS interprets these as commands to move the cursor, but we'd like to see them as just ordinary characters for this part of the display. To do this, we'll have to change WRITE_CHAR to print *all* characters, without applying any special meaning. We'll do that in Part III, but for now, let's rewrite WRITE_CHAR slightly so that it prints a period in place of the low characters (between 0 and 1Fh):

```
A>disp_sec
10 11 12 13 14 15 16 17 18 19 1A 1B 1C 1D 1E 1F   ▶◄‼¶§▬↕↑↓→←∟↔▲▼
A>_
```

Figure 14-4. DISP_LINE's Output.

```
A>disp_sec
10 11 12 13 14 15 16 17 18 19 1A 1B 1C 1D 1E 1F   ................
A>_
```

Figure 14-5. Modified Version of DISP_Line.

Replace the WRITE_CHAR in VIDEO_IO.ASM with this new procedure:

Listing 14-3. A New WRITE_CHAR in VIDEO_IO.ASM

```
        PUBLIC    WRITE_CHAR
;-------------------------------------------------------------------;
; This procedure prints a character on the screen using the DOS     ;
; function call.  WRITE_CHAR replaces the characters 0 through 1Fh with ;
; a period.                                                         ;
;                                                                   ;
; On entry:    DL   byte to print on screen.                       ;
;-------------------------------------------------------------------;
WRITE_CHAR    PROC
        PUSH      AX
        PUSH      DX
        CMP       DL,32         ;Is character before a space?
        JAE       IS_PRINTABLE  ;No, then print as is
        MOV       DL,'.'        ;Yes, replace with a period
IS_PRINTABLE:
        MOV       AH,2          ;Call for character output
        INT       21h           ;Output character in DL register
        POP       DX            ;Restore old value in AX and DX
        POP       AX
        RET
WRITE_CHAR    ENDP
```

Try this new procedure with Disp_sec and change the data to various characters to check the boundary conditions.

Dumping 256 Bytes of Memory

Now we've managed to dump one line, or 16 bytes, of memory. The next step is to dump 256 bytes of memory. This happens to be exactly half the number of bytes in a sector, so we're working toward building a display of half a sector. We still have many more improvements to make; this is just a test version.

We'll need two new procedures here, and a modified version of DISP_LINE. The new procedures are DISP_HALF_SECTOR, which will soon evolve into a finished procedure to display half a sector, and SEND_CRLF, which just sends the cursor to the beginning of the next line (CRLF stands for *Carriage Return-Line Feed*, the pair of characters that move the cursor to the next line).

SEND_CRLF is very simple, so let's start with it. Place the following procedure into a file called CURSOR.ASM:

Listing 14-4. The New File CURSOR.ASM

```
CR      EQU    13           ;Carriage return
LF      EQU    10           ;Line feed

.MODEL  SMALL
.CODE
```

Listing 14-4. *continued*

```
         PUBLIC    SEND_CRLF
;----------------------------------------------------------------------;
; This routine just sends a carriage return-line feed pair to the      ;
; display, using the DOS routines so that scrolling will be handled    ;
; correctly.                                                           ;
;----------------------------------------------------------------------;
SEND_CRLF         PROC
         PUSH     AX
         PUSH     DX
         MOV      AH,2
         MOV      DL,CR
         INT      21h
         MOV      DL,LF
         INT      21h
         POP      DX
         POP      AX
         RET
SEND_CRLF         ENDP


         END
```

This procedure sends a Carriage Return and Line Feed pair, using the DOS function 2 to send characters. The statement:

```
   CR   EQU   13              ;Carriage return
```

uses the EQU directive to define the name CR to be equal to 13. So the instruction MOV DL,CR is equivalent to MOV DL,13. As shown in Figure 14-6, the assembler substitutes 13 whenever it sees CR. Likewise, it substitutes 10 whenever it sees LF.

> **Note:** From here on, we'll use color to show the changes in our programs so you won't have to check each line to see if it's new or different. Additions to our programs will be shown against a gray background, and text you should delete will be printed in blue with a line through the text:
> Add or change lines against a gray background.
> Delete text shown in blue

Figure 14-6. The EQU pseudo-op lets us use names in place of numbers.

The file Disp_sec now needs much work. Here's the new version of DISP_SEC.ASM:

Listing 14-5. The New Version of DISP_SEC.ASM

```
        DOSSEG
        .MODEL  SMALL

        .STACK

        .DATA
SECTOR  DB      10h, 11h, 12h, 13h, 14h, 15h, 16h, 17h  ;Test pattern
        DB      18h, 19h, 1Ah, 1Bh, 1Ch, 1Dh, 1Eh, 1Fh
SECTOR  DB      16 DUP (10h)
        DB      16 DUP (11h)
        DB      16 DUP (12h)
        DB      16 DUP (13h)
        DB      16 DUP (14h)
        DB      16 DUP (15h)
        DB      16 DUP (16h)
        DB      16 DUP (17h)
        DB      16 DUP (18h)
        DB      16 DUP (19h)
        DB      16 DUP (1Ah)
        DB      16 DUP (1Bh)
        DB      16 DUP (1Ch)
        DB      16 DUP (1Dh)
        DB      16 DUP (1Eh)
        DB      16 DUP (1Fh)

        .CODE

        PUBLIC  DISP_HALF_SECTOR
        EXTRN   SEND_CRLF:PROC
;------------------------------------------------------------------;
; This procedure displays half a sector (256 bytes)               ;
;                                                                  ;
; Uses:          DISP_LINE, SEND_CRLF                             ;
;------------------------------------------------------------------;
DISP_HALF_SECTOR        PROC
        MOV     AX,DGROUP               ;Put data segment into AX
        MOV     DS,AX                   ;Set DS to point to data

        XOR     DX,DX                   ;Start at beginning of SECTOR
        MOV     CX,16                   ;Display 16 lines
HALF_SECTOR:
        CALL    DISP_LINE
        CALL    SEND_CRLF
        ADD     DX,16
        LOOP    HALF_SECTOR

        MOV     AH,4Ch                  ;Return to DOS
        INT     21h
DISP_HALF_SECTOR        ENDP


        PUBLIC  DISP_LINE
        EXTRN   WRITE_HEX:PROC
        EXTRN   WRITE_CHAR:PROC
;------------------------------------------------------------------;
; This procedure displays one line of data, or 16 bytes, first in hex, ;
; then in ASCII.                                                  ;
;                                                                  ;
; On entry:      DS:DX    Offset into sector, in bytes.           ;
;                                                                  ;
; Uses:          WRITE_CHAR, WRITE_HEX                            ;
; Reads:         SECTOR                                           ;
;------------------------------------------------------------------;
```

Listing 14-5. *continued*

```
DISP_LINE       PROC
        MOV         AX,DGROUP          ;Put data segment into AX
        MOV         DS,AX              ;Set DS to point to data

        XOR         BX,BX
        PUSH        BX
        PUSH        CX
        PUSH        DX
        MOV         BX,DX              ;Offset is more useful in BX
        MOV         CX,16              ;Dump 16 bytes
        PUSH        BX                 ;Save the offset for ASCII_LOOP
HEX_LOOP:
        MOV         DL,SECTOR[BX]      ;Get 1 byte
        CALL        WRITE_HEX          ;Dump this byte in hex
        MOV         DL,' '             ;Write a space between numbers
        CALL        WRITE_CHAR
        INC         BX
        LOOP        HEX_LOOP

        MOV         DL,' '             ;Add another space before characters
        CALL        WRITE_CHAR
        MOV         CX,16
        POP         BX                 ;Get back offset into SECTOR
        XOR         BX,BX
ASCII_LOOP:
        MOV         DL,SECTOR[BX]
        CALL        WRITE_CHAR
        INC         BX
        LOOP        ASCII_LOOP

        POP         DX
        POP         CX
        POP         BX
        RET

        MOV         AH,4Ch             ;Return to DOS
        INT         21h
DISP_LINE       ENDP

        END         DISP_HALF_SECTOR
```

The changes are all fairly straightforward. In DISP_LINE, we've added a PUSH BX and POP BX around the HEX_LOOP, because we want to reuse the initial offset in ASCII_LOOP. We've also added PUSH and POP instructions to save and restore all the registers we use within DISP_LINE. Actually, DISP_LINE is almost done; the only changes we have left are aesthetic, to add spaces and graphics characters so we'll have an attractive display; those will come later.

When you link the files, remember that we now have three files: Disp_sec, Video_io, and Cursor. Disp_sec should be first in this list. You should see a display like the one in Figure 14-7 when you run Disp_sec.exe.

We'll have more files before we're done, but now, let's move on to the next chapter, where we'll read a sector directly from the disk before we dump half a sector.

```
A>disp_sec
10 10 10 10 10 10 10 10 10 10 10 10 10 10 10 10    ................
11 11 11 11 11 11 11 11 11 11 11 11 11 11 11 11    ................
12 12 12 12 12 12 12 12 12 12 12 12 12 12 12 12    ................
13 13 13 13 13 13 13 13 13 13 13 13 13 13 13 13    ................
14 14 14 14 14 14 14 14 14 14 14 14 14 14 14 14    ................
15 15 15 15 15 15 15 15 15 15 15 15 15 15 15 15    ................
16 16 16 16 16 16 16 16 16 16 16 16 16 16 16 16    ................
17 17 17 17 17 17 17 17 17 17 17 17 17 17 17 17    ................
18 18 18 18 18 18 18 18 18 18 18 18 18 18 18 18    ................
19 19 19 19 19 19 19 19 19 19 19 19 19 19 19 19    ................
1A 1A 1A 1A 1A 1A 1A 1A 1A 1A 1A 1A 1A 1A 1A 1A    ................
1B 1B 1B 1B 1B 1B 1B 1B 1B 1B 1B 1B 1B 1B 1B 1B    ................
1C 1C 1C 1C 1C 1C 1C 1C 1C 1C 1C 1C 1C 1C 1C 1C    ................
1D 1D 1D 1D 1D 1D 1D 1D 1D 1D 1D 1D 1D 1D 1D 1D    ................
1E 1E 1E 1E 1E 1E 1E 1E 1E 1E 1E 1E 1E 1E 1E 1E    ................
1F 1F 1F 1F 1F 1F 1F 1F 1F 1F 1F 1F 1F 1F 1F 1F    ................

A>_
```

Figure 14-7. Output From Disp_sec.

Summary

We know more about the different memory modes for addressing memory and registers in the 8088 microprocessor. We learned about indirect memory addressing, which we first used to read 16 bytes of memory.

We also used indirect memory addressing in several programs we wrote in this chapter, starting with our program to print 16 hex numbers on the screen. These 16 numbers came from an area in memory labeled SECTOR, which we expanded a bit later so we could display a memory dump for 256 bytes—half a sector.

And, at last, we've begun to see dumps of the screen, as they appear on your display, rather than as they are set in type. We'll use these screen dumps to more advantage in the following chapters.

DUMPING A DISK SECTOR

N ow that we have a program that dumps 256 bytes of memory, we can add some procedures to read a sector from the disk and place it in memory starting at SECTOR. Then, our dump procedures will dump the first half of this disk sector.

Making Life Easier

With the three source files we had in the last chapter, life becomes somewhat complicated. Did we change all three of the files we were working on, or just two? You probably assembled all three, rather than checking to see if you made any changes since the last assemble.

But assembling all our source files when we've changed only one of them is rather slow and will become even slower as Dskpatch grows in size. What we'd really like to do is assemble only the files that we've changed.

Fortunately, all the assemblers covered in this book (MASM, Turbo Assembler, and OPTASM) allow you to do just that. Borland and Microsoft provide a program called Make that does exactly what we want. (OPTASM includes a very simple Make inside its assembler, which we'll describe at the end of the next section.) To use it, we create a file (we'll call it Makefile) that tells Make how to do its work, then just type:

```
A>MAKE MAKEFILE
```

Make then assembles only the files you've changed.

> **Note:** If you're using Borland's Make, you'll type just MAKE.)

The file you create (Makefile) tells Make which files depend on which other files. Every time you change a file, DOS updates the modify time for this file (you can see this in the DIR display). Make simply looks at both the .ASM and .OBJ versions of a file. If the .ASM version has a more recent modify time than the .OBJ version, Make knows that it needs to assemble that file again.

That's all there is to it, but there is one caveat we need to point out: Make will work correctly only if you're diligent about setting DOS's date and time each time you start your computer or if your computer has a built-in clock (as most computers do these days). Without this information, Make won't always know when you've made changes to a file.

Format of the Make File

The format for our file, Makefile, that we'll use with Make is fairly simple:

Listing 15-1. The Make File MAKEFILE

```
disp_sec.obj:   disp_sec.asm
        masm disp_sec;

video_io.obj:   video_io.asm
        masm video_io;

cursor.obj:     cursor.asm
        masm cursor;

disp_sec.exe:   disp_sec.obj video_io.obj cursor.obj
        link disp_sec video_io cursor;
```

> **Note:** If you're using Borland's Make, the last two lines must be at the beginning of the file rather than at the end, as here.

Each entry has a file name on the left (before the colon) and one or more file names on the right. If any of the files on the right (such as DISP_SEC.ASM in the first line) are more recent than the first file (DISP_SEC.OBJ), Make will execute all the indented commands that appear on the following lines.

If your assembler has the Make program, enter these lines into the file Dskpatch (without an extension) and make a small change to DISP_SEC.ASM. Then type:

```
A>MAKE MAKEFILE
```

(type just MAKE if you're using Borland's Make) and you'll see something like the following:

```
Microsoft (R) Program Maintenance Utility  Version 4.06
Copyright (C) Microsoft Corp 1984-1987.  All rights reserved.


   masm disp_sec;
Microsoft (R) Macro Assembler Version 5.10
Copyright (C) Microsoft Corp 1981, 1988.  All rights reserved.

  49620 + 233303 Bytes symbol space free

      0 Warning Errors
```

```
     0 Severe  Errors

  link disp_sec video_io cursor;

Microsoft (R) Overlay Linker  Version 3.64
Copyright (C) Microsoft Corp 1983-1988.  All rights reserved.



A>
```

Make has done the minimum amount of work necessary to rebuild our program.

If you have an older version of the Microsoft Macro Assembler that doesn't include Make, you'll find this program worth the price of an upgrade. And you'll get a nice replacement for Debug, too. It's called CodeView, and we'll take a look at it later.

OPTASM's Make

SLR Systems's OPTASM includes a Make built into the assembler itself. But unlike Microsoft's, IBM's, and Borland's Make, OPTASM's Make can assemble only files that have changed: It can't run the linker to build a new .EXE file. Nonetheless, it's very convenient to use OPTASM's Make to assemble only the files we've changed.

The format for OPTASM's make file is a little different from the format for the Make program:

Listing 15-2. OPTASM's Make File MAKEFILE

```
     disp_sec.obj disp_sec.asm
disp_sec;

     video_io.obj video_io.asm
video_io;

     cursor.obj cursor.asm
cursor;
```

Each entry has the name of an object file (such as disp_sec.obj) followed by the files that affect it. If any of the files on the line after the object file are more recent (if you've changed disp_sec.asm in the first line), OPTASM will assemble the file that appears on the next line. You can see this is slightly different from the file that Make uses, but it gets the same job done.

To assemble all the files you've changed, type:

```
A>OPTASM @MAKEFILE
```

This tells OPTASM to use the information in MAKEFILE to decide which files to assemble.

You'll then need to run Link after this to create a new .EXE file:

```
A>LINK DISP_SEC VIDEO_IO CURSOR;
```

That's all there is to using OPTASM's built-in Make feature. (You'll find more information in the OPTASM manual.) Now on with Dskpatch.

Patching Up Disp_sec

Disp_sec, as we left it, included a version of DISP_HALF_SECTOR, which we used as a test procedure, and the main procedure. Now, we'll change DISP_HALF_SECTOR to an ordinary procedure so we can call it from a procedure we'll name READ_SECTOR. Our test procedure will be in Disk_io.

First, let's modify Disp_sec to make it a file of procedures, just as we did with Video_io. Change the END DISP_HALF_SECTOR to just END, since our main procedure will now be in Disk_io. Then remove the .STACK and DOSSEG directives near the top of Disp_sec.asm, again because we're moving these to a different file.

Then, since we plan to read a sector into memory starting at SECTOR, there is no need for us to supply test data. We can replace all the 16 DB statements after SECTOR with one line:

```
SECTOR   DB      8192 DUP (0)
```

which reserves 8192 bytes for storing a sector.

Recall our earlier statement that sectors are 512 bytes long. So why do we need such a large storage area? It turns out that some hard disks (300-megabyte, for example) use very large sector sizes. These large sector sizes are by no means common, but we still want to be certain that we don't read in a sector that is too large to fit into the memory we've reserved for SECTOR. So, in the interest of safety, we've reserved 8192 bytes for SECTOR. In the rest of this book, with the exception of SECTOR, which we'll cover soon, we'll assume that sectors are only 512 bytes long.

Now what we need is a new version of DISP_HALF_SECTOR. The old version is nothing more than a test procedure that we used to test DISP_LINE. In the new version, we'll want to supply an offset into the sector so that we can display 256 bytes, starting anywhere in the sector. Among other things, this means we could dump the first half, the last half, or the middle 256 bytes. Once again, we'll supply this offset in DX. Here is the new—and final—version of DISP_HALF_SECTOR in Disp_sec:

Listing 15-3. The Final Version of DISP_HALF_SECTOR in DISP_SEC.ASM

```
        PUBLIC    DISP_HALF_SECTOR
        EXTRN     SEND_CRLF:PROC
;--------------------------------------------------------------;
;   This procedure displays half a sector (256 bytes)          ;
;                                                              ;
; On entry:     DS:DX     Offset into sector, in bytes -- should be ;
;                         multiple of 16.                      ;
;                                                              ;
; Uses:   DISP_LINE, SEND_CRLF                                 ;
;--------------------------------------------------------------;
DISP_HALF_SECTOR    PROC
        MOV     AX,DGROUP            ;Put data segment into AX
        MOV     DS,AX                ;Set DS to point to data

        XOR     DX,DX                ;Start at beginning of SECTOR
        PUSH    CX
        PUSH    DX
        MOV     CX,16                ;Display 16 lines
HALF_SECTOR:
        CALL    DISP_LINE
        CALL    SEND_CRLF
        ADD     DX,16
        LOOP    HALF_SECTOR
        POP     DX
        POP     CX
        RET

        MOV     AH,4Ch               ;Return to DOS
        INT     21h
DISP_HALF_SECTOR    ENDP
```

Let's move on now to our procedure to read a sector.

Reading a Sector

In this first version of READ_SECTOR we'll deliberately ignore errors, such as having no disk in the disk drive. This is not good practice, but this isn't the final version of READ_SECTOR. We won't be able to cover error handling in this book, but you will find error-handling procedures in the version of Dskpatch on the disk that is available for this book. For now, though, we just want to read a sector from the disk. Here is the test version of the file DISK_IO.ASM:

Listing 15-4. The New File DISK_IO.ASM

```
        DOSSEG
        .MODEL  SMALL

        .STACK
```

```
        .DATA

                EXTRN       SECTOR:BYTE

        .CODE

                EXTRN       DISP_HALF_SECTOR:PROC
        ;-------------------------------------------------------------------;
        ; This procedure reads the first sector on disk A and dumps the first ;
        ; half of this sector.                                                ;
        ;-------------------------------------------------------------------;
        READ_SECTOR         PROC
                MOV         AX,DGROUP           ;Put data segment into AX
                MOV         DS,AX               ;Set DS to point to data

                MOV         AL,0                ;Disk drive A (number 0)
                MOV         CX,1                ;Read only 1 sector
                MOV         DX,0                ;Read sector number 0
                LEA         BX,SECTOR           ;Where to store this sector
                INT         25h                 ;Read the sector
                POPF                            ;Discard flags put on stack by DOS
                XOR         DX,DX               ;Set offset to 0 within SECTOR
                CALL        DISP_HALF_SECTOR    ;Dump the first half

                MOV         AH,4Ch              ;Return to DOS
                INT         21h
        READ_SECTOR         ENDP

                END  READ_SECTOR
```

There are three new instructions in this procedure. The first:

```
        LEA     BX,SECTOR
```

moves the *address*, or offset, of SECTOR (from the start of DGROUP data group created by .DATA) into the BX register; LEA stands for *Load Effective Address*. After this LEA instruction, DS:BX contains the full address of SECTOR, and DOS uses this address for the second new instruction, the INT 25h call, as we'll see after a few more words about SECTOR. (Actually, LEA loads the offset into the BX register without setting the DS register; we have to ensure that DS is pointing to the correct segment.)

SECTOR isn't in the same source file as READ_SECTOR. It's over in DISP_SEC.ASM. How do we tell the assembler where it is? We use the EXTRN directive:

```
        .DATA

                EXTRN   SECTOR:BYTE
```

This set of instructions tells the assembler that SECTOR is defined in the data segment created by .DATA, that it's defined in another source file, and that SECTOR is a variable of bytes (rather than words). We'll be using such EXTRNs often in following chapters; it's the way we use the same variables in

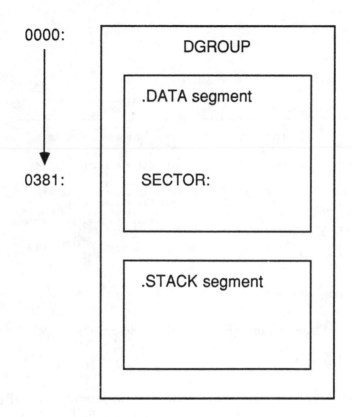

0000:

0381:

DGROUP

.DATA segment

SECTOR:

.STACK segment

LEA BX,SECTOR ◄──────► MOV BX,0381

Figure 15-1. LEA loads the effective address.

a number of source files. We just need to be careful that we define our variables in only one place.

Let's return to the INT 25h instruction. INT 25h is a special function call to DOS for reading sectors from a disk. When DOS receives a call from INT 25h, it uses the information in the registers as follows:

AL   Drive number (0 = A, 1 = B, and so on)
CX   Number of sectors to read at one time

DX   Number of the first sector to read (the first sector is 0)
DS:BX   Transfer address: where to write the sectors read

The number in the AL register determines the drive from which DOS will read sectors. If AL = 0, DOS reads from drive A.

> **Note:** Some recent versions of DOS (COMPAQ DOS 3.31 and DOS 4.0 and above) support hard disks larger than 32 megabytes by changing the way the INT 25h function call works. This isn't a problem for reading from a floppy disk, as we're doing in this book, but it can be if you want to use Dskpatch on a hard disk.

DOS can read more than one sector with a single call, and it reads the number of sectors given by CX. Here, we set CX to one so DOS will read just one sector of 512 bytes.

We set DX to zero, so DOS will read the very first sector on the disk. You can change this number if you want to read a different sector; later on, we will.

DS:BX is the full address for the area in memory where we want DOS to store the sector(s) it reads. In this case, we've set DS:BX to the address of SECTOR, so that we can call DISP_HALF_SECTOR to dump the first half of the first sector read from the disk in drive A.

Finally, you'll notice a POPF instruction immediately following the INT 25h. As noted, the 8088 has a status register that contains the various flags, like the zero and carry flags. POPF is a special POP instruction that pops a word into the status register. Why do we need this POPF instruction?

```
        .DATA

        EXTRN    SECTOR:BYTE
```

A byte variable.
LINK will provide
the address.

Figure 15-2. The EXTRN pseudo-op.

```
A>disk_io
EB 28 90 49 42 4D 20 20 33 2E 32 00 02 02 01 00   ♂(ÉIBM  3.2.....
02 70 00 D0 02 FD 02 00 09 00 02 00 00 00 00 00   .p.╨.².........
00 00 00 00 00 00 00 00 00 00 FA C4 5C 08 33 ED   ..........·─\.3ø
B8 C0 07 8E D8 33 C9 88 16 FD 01 0A D2 79 0A 89   ╕└.Ä╪3╔ê.²..╥y.ë
1E 1C 00 8C 06 1E 00 B1 02 8E C5 8E D5 BC 00 7C   ...î...▌.Ä┼ÄĤ╝.¦
FC 1E 36 C5 36 78 00 BF 2A 7C B9 0B 00 F3 A4 1F   ⁿ.6┼6x.╕*¦╣..≤ñ.
C6 06 2E 00 0F BF 78 00 B8 2A 7C AB 91 AB FB 8A   ╞...╕x.╕*¦½æ½√è
16 FD 01 CD 13 A0 10 00 98 F7 26 16 00 03 06 0E   .².=.á.ÿ≈&.....
00 E8 73 00 E8 79 00 BB 00 05 53 E8 A0 00 5F BE   .Φs.Φy.╗..SΦá._╛
74 01 B9 0B 00 90 F3 A6 75 57 83 C7 15 B1 0B 90   t.╣..É≤ªuWâ╟.▌.É
90 F3 A6 75 4C 26 8B 47 1C 99 8B 0E 0B 00 03 C1   É≤ªuL&ïG.Öï....┴
48 F7 F1 3D 14 00 7F 02 B0 14 96 A1 11 00 B1 04   H≈±.=.⌂.░.û¡..▌.
D3 E8 E8 32 00 FF 36 1C 00 C4 1E 70 01 E8 30 00   ╙ΦΦ2. 6..·.p.φ0.
E8 5B 00 2B F0 76 0D E8 1D 00 52 F7 26 0B 00 03   φ[.+≡v.♪φ..R≈&...
D8 5A EB E9 5B 8A 2E 15 00 8A 16 FD 01 FF 2E 70   ╪ZδΘ[è...è.². .p
01 BE 8B 01 EB 54 90 01 06 1C 00 11 2E 1E 00 C3   .╛ï.δT É...◄...├

A>_
```

Figure 15-3: Screen Dump from DISK_IO.COM.

The INT 25h instruction pushes first the status registers, then the return address onto the stack. When DOS returns from this INT 25h, it leaves the status register on the stack. DOS does this so that it can set the carry flag on return if there was a disk error, such as trying to read from drive A with no disk in the drive. We won't be checking for errors in this book, but we have to remove the status register from the stack—hence the POPF instruction. (Note: INT 25h, along with INT 24h which *writes* a disk sector, are the only DOS routines that leave the status register on the stack.)

Now you can assemble DISK_IO.ASM, and reassemble DISP_SEC.ASM. Then, link the four files Disk_io, Disp_sec, Video_io, and Cursor, with Disk_io listed first. Or, if you have Make, add these two lines to your Makefile:

```
disk_io.obj:    disk_io.asm
        masm disk_io;
```

(for OPTASM's Make, you'll need to indent the first line, and remove the leading spaces from the second line) and change the last two lines (first two lines for Borland's Make) to:

```
disk_io.exe:    disk_io.obj disp_sec.obj video_io.obj cursor.obj
        link disk_io disp_sec video_io cursor;
```

After you create your .EXE version of Disk_io, you should see a display something like Figure 15-3 (remember to put a disk in drive A before you run Disk_io).

The .DATA? Directive

If you look back at our definition of SECTOR in Disp_sec.asm, you'll see that we reserved 8192 bytes of zeros. Which means we have to reserve room in the DISK_IO.EXE file on your disk:

```
A>DIR DISK_IO.EXE

 Volume in drive A has no label
 Directory of  A:

DISK_IO  EXE     8922   5-16-89  10:42a
        1 File(s)    20704 bytes free

A>
```

As you can see, Disk_io.exe is 8,922 bytes long, which is mostly filled with zeros. That's a lot of space to reserve just for zeros, especially since we don't care what's in SECTOR before we read a sector into memory. So does SECTOR really need to take space on the disk? No.

There is another directive, .DATA?, that allows to define memory variables that take space in memory, but not on the disk. We can do this by telling the assembler we don't care what value a memory variable has.

Change the three lines in DISP_SEC that define SECTOR to the following:

```
.DATA?

    SECTOR    DB    8192 DUP (?)
```

There are two changes here. First, there is a ? after the .DATA directive, which tells the assembler we're about to define variables that don't have initial values and, therefore, don't need to take space in the disk file. Second there is a ? rather than a 0 for the value of each byte in SECTOR. The DUP (?) tells the assembler that we don't care what value each byte has.

> **Note:** You need to define variables in the .DATA? section with DUP (?). If you define any variables with a value (such as VAR DB 0), or if you use VAR DB ?, the assembler will reserve room in the .EXE file for *all* the variables in .DATA?. In other words, put all the variables that have initial values into .DATA, and all variables with DUP (?) in .DATA?.

After making these changes, rebuild Disk_io.exe. It should now be only 729 bytes long. The .DATA? directive allows us to keep our programs quite small on the disk.

We'll come back later to add more to Disk_io; we have enough for now. In the next chapter, we'll build a nicer sector display by adding some graphics characters to the display, and then adding a few more pieces of information.

Summary

Now that we have four different source files, Dskpatch is becoming somewhat more involved. In this chapter, we looked at the program Make, which helps make life simpler by assembling only the files we've changed.

We also wrote a new procedure, READ_SECTOR. It's in a different source file from SECTOR, so we used an EXTRN definition in DISK_IO.ASM to tell the assembler about SECTOR and let it know that SECTOR is a byte variable.

We also learned about the LEA (Load Effective Address) instruction, which we used to load the address of SECTOR into the BX register.

DISK_IO uses a new INT number, INT 25h, to read sectors from a disk to memory. We used INT 25h to read one sector into our memory variable, SECTOR, so we could dump it on the screen with DISP_HALF_SECTOR.

We also learned about the POPF instruction to pop a word off the stack and into the status register. We used this instruction to remove the flags which DOS didn't remove from the stack when it returned from INT 25h.

Our half-sector display isn't very attractive yet, in the next chapter we'll use some of the graphics characters available on the IBM PC to make it more aesthetically pleasing.

ENHANCING THE SECTOR DISPLAY

We've come to the last chapter in Part II. Everything we've done so far has been applicable to MS-DOS and the 8088 (or the 8086, 80286, and so on). In Part III, we'll begin to write procedures that work more closely with your computer's screen.

But before we move on, we'll use this chapter to add several more procedures to Video_io. We'll also modify DISP_LINE in Disp_sec. All our modifications and additions will be to the display. Most of them will be to improve the appearance of the display, but one will add new information: It will add numbers on the left that act like the addresses in Debug's dump. Let's begin with graphics.

Adding Graphics Characters

The IBM Personal Computer has a number of line-drawing characters we can use to draw boxes around various parts of our dump display. We'll draw one box around the hex dump, and another around the ASCII dump. This change requires very little thought, just work.

Enter the following definitions near the top of the file DISP_SEC.ASM, between the .MODEL directive and the .DATA? directive, leaving one or two blank lines before and after these definitions:

Listing 16-1. Add to the Top of DISP_SEC.ASM

```
;-------------------------------------------------------------------;
; Graphics characters for border of sector.                         ;
;-------------------------------------------------------------------;
VERTICAL_BAR    EQU    0BAh
HORIZONTAL_BAR  EQU    0CDh
UPPER_LEFT      EQU    0C9h
UPPER_RIGHT     EQU    0BBh
LOWER_LEFT      EQU    0C8h
LOWER_RIGHT     EQU    0BCh
TOP_T_BAR       EQU    0CBh
BOTTOM_T_BAR    EQU    0CAh
TOP_TICK        EQU    0D1h
BOTTOM_TICK     EQU    0CFh
```

These are the definitions for the graphics characters. Note that we put a zero before each hex number so the assembler will know these are numbers, rather than labels.

We could just as easily have written hex numbers instead of these definitions in our procedure, but the definitions make the procedure easier to understand. For example, compare the following two instructions:

```
MOV     DL,VERTICAL_BAR
MOV     DL,0BAh
```

Most people find the first instruction clearer.

Now, here is the new DISP_LINE procedure to separate the different parts of the display with the VERTICAL_BAR character, number 186 (0BAh). As before, additions are shown against a gray background:

Listing 16-2. Changes to DISP_LINE in DISP_SEC.ASM

```
DISP_LINE       PROC
        PUSH    BX
        PUSH    CX
        PUSH    DX
        MOV     BX,DX                   ;Offset is more useful in BX
                                        ;Write separator
        MOV     DL,' '
        CALL    WRITE_CHAR
        MOV     DL,VERTICAL_BAR         ;Draw left side of box
        CALL    WRITE_CHAR
        MOV     DL,' '
        CALL    WRITE_CHAR
                                        ;Now write out 16 bytes
        MOV     CX,16                   ;Dump 16 bytes
        PUSH    BX                      ;Save the offset for ASCII_LOOP
HEX_LOOP:
        MOV     DL,SECTOR[BX]           ;Get 1 byte
        CALL    WRITE_HEX               ;Dump this byte in hex
        MOV     DL,' '                  ;Write a space between numbers
        CALL    WRITE_CHAR
        INC     BX
        LOOP    HEX_LOOP

        MOV     DL,VERTICAL_BAR         ;Write separator
        CALL    WRITE_CHAR
        MOV     DL,' '                  ;Add another space before characters
        CALL    WRITE_CHAR

        MOV     CX,16
        POP     BX                      ;Get back offset into SECTOR
ASCII_LOOP:
        MOV     DL,SECTOR[BX]
        CALL    WRITE_CHAR
        INC     BX
        LOOP    ASCII_LOOP

        MOV     DL,' '                  ;Draw right side of box
        CALL    WRITE_CHAR
        MOV     DL,VERTICAL_BAR
        CALL    WRITE_CHAR

        POP     DX
        POP     CX
        POP     BX
        RET
DISP_LINE       ENDP
```

Assemble this new version of Disp_sec and link your four files (remember to place Disk_io first in the list of files following the LINK command). You'll see nice double bars separating the display into two parts, as you can see in Figure 16-1.

```
A>disk_io
 ║ EB 28 90 49 42 4D 20 20 33 2E 32 00 02 02 01 00 ║ ó(ÉIBM  3.2.....
 ║ 02 70 00 D0 02 FD 02 00 09 00 02 00 00 00 00 00 ║ .p.╨.².........
 ║ 00 00 00 00 00 00 00 00 00 00 FA C4 5C 08 33 ED ║ ..........·─╲.3ø
 ║ B8 C0 07 8E D8 33 C9 88 16 FD 01 0A D2 79 0A 89 ║ ╕└.Ä╪3╔ê.²..╥y.ë
 ║ 1E 1C 00 8C 06 1E 00 B1 02 8E C5 8E D5 BC 00 7C ║ ...î...▌.ÄÅÄ╣╜.╎
 ║ FC 1E 36 C5 36 78 00 BF 2A 7C B9 0B 00 F3 A4 1F ║ n.6┼6x.┐*╎╣..╙ñ.
 ║ C6 06 2E 00 0F BF 78 00 B8 2A 7C AB 91 AB FB 8A ║ ╞....┐x.┐*╎½æ½√è
 ║ 16 FD 01 CD 13 A0 10 00 98 F7 26 16 00 03 06 0E ║ .².=.á..ÿ≈&.....
 ║ 00 E8 73 00 E8 79 00 BB 00 05 53 E8 A0 00 5F BE ║ .ès.èy.╗..Sèá._╛
 ║ 74 01 B9 0B 00 90 F3 A6 75 57 83 C7 15 B1 0B 90 ║ t.╣...╙ªuWâ╟.▌.É
 ║ 90 F3 A6 75 4C 26 8B 47 1C 99 8B 0E 0B 00 03 C1 ║ É╙ªuL&ïG.Öï....┴
 ║ 48 F7 F1 3D 14 00 7F 02 B0 14 96 A1 11 00 B1 04 ║ H≈±=..▲.░í..▌.
 ║ D3 E8 E8 32 00 FF 36 1C 00 C4 1E 70 01 E8 30 00 ║ ╙èè2. 6.─.p.è0.
 ║ E8 5B 00 2B F0 76 0D E8 1D 00 52 F7 26 0B 00 03 ║ è[.+≡v.è..R≈&...
 ║ D8 5A EB E9 5B 8A 2E 15 00 8A 16 FD 01 FF 2E 70 ║ ╪Zëé[è...è.². .p
 ║ 01 BE 8B 01 EB 54 90 01 06 1C 00 11 2E 1E 00 C3 ║ .╛ï.ëTÉ.......┤
A>_
```

Figure 16-1. Adding Vertical Bars.

Adding Addresses to the Display

Now let's try something a bit more challenging: Let's add the hex addresses down the left side of the display. These numbers will be the offset from the beginning of the sector, so the first number will be 00, the next 10, then 20, and so on.

The process is fairly simple, since we already have the procedure WRITE_HEX for writing a number in hex. But we do have a problem in dealing with a sector 512 bytes long: WRITE_HEX prints only two-digit hex numbers, whereas we need three hex digits for numbers greater than 255.

Here's the solution. Since our numbers will be between zero and 511 (0h to 1FFh), the first digit will either be a space, if the number (such as BCh) is below 100h, or it will be a 1. So, if the number is larger than 255, we'll simply print a 1, followed by the hex number for the lower byte. Otherwise, we'll print a space first. These are the additions to DISP_LINE that will print this leading three-digit hex number:

Listing 16-3. Additions to DISP_LINE in DISP_SEC.ASM

```
DISP_LINE       PROC
       PUSH     BX
       PUSH     CX
       PUSH     DX
       MOV      BX,DX              ;Offset is more useful in BX
       MOV      DL,' '
```

```
            CMP      BX,100h              ;Write offset in hex
            JB       WRITE_ONE            ;Is the first digit a 1?
            MOV      DL,'1'               ;No, white space already in DL
WRITE_ONE:                               ;Yes, then place '1' into DL for output
            CALL     WRITE_CHAR
            MOV      DL,BL
            CALL     WRITE_HEX            ;Copy lower byte into DL for hex output

            MOV      DL,' '               ;Write separator
            CALL     WRITE_CHAR
            MOV      DL,VERTICAL_BAR      ;Draw left side of box
                       .
                       .
                       .
```

```
A>disk_io
 00 ║ EB 28 90 49 42 4D 20 20 33 2E 32 00 02 02 01 00 ║ δ(ÉIBM  3.2.....
 10 ║ 02 70 00 D0 02 FD 02 00 09 00 02 00 00 00 00 00 ║ .p.╨.²..........
 20 ║ 00 00 00 00 00 00 00 00 00 00 00 FA C4 5C 08 33 ED ║ ...........-\.3ø
 30 ║ B8 C0 07 8E D8 33 C9 88 16 FD 01 0A D2 79 0A 89 ║ ╕└.Ä╪3É�ê.²..╥y.ë
 40 ║ 1E 1C 00 8C 06 1E 00 B1 02 8E C5 8E D5 BC 00 7C ║ ...î...±.Ä┼Ä╒╝.¦
 50 ║ FC 1E 36 C5 36 78 00 BF 2A 7C B9 00 00 F3 A4 1F ║ ⁿ.6┼6x.┐*¦┤..≤ñ.
 60 ║ C6 06 2E 00 0F BF 78 00 B8 2A 7C AB 91 AB FB 8A ║ ╞....┐x.╕*¦½æ½√è
 70 ║ 16 FD 01 CD 13 A0 10 00 98 F7 26 16 00 03 06 0E ║ .².=.á.÷&.....
 80 ║ 00 E8 73 00 E8 79 00 BB 00 05 53 E8 A0 00 5F BE ║ .φs.φy.╗..Sφá._╛
 90 ║ 74 01 B9 0B 00 90 F3 A6 75 57 83 C7 15 B1 0B 90 ║ t.╣...≤ªuWâ╟.±..É
 A0 ║ 90 F3 A6 75 4C 26 8B 47 1C 99 8B 0E 0B 00 03 C1 ║ É≤ªuL&ïG.öï....┴
 B0 ║ 48 F7 F1 3D 14 00 7F 02 B0 14 96 A1 11 00 B1 04 ║ H≈±=..⌂.░.û í..±
 C0 ║ D3 E8 E8 32 00 FF 36 1C 00 C4 1E 70 01 E8 30 00 ║ ╙φφ2. 6.─.p.φ0.
 D0 ║ E8 5B 00 2B F0 76 0D E8 1D 00 52 F7 26 0B 00 03 ║ φ[.+≡v.φ..R÷&...
 E0 ║ D8 5A EB E9 5B 8A 2E 15 00 8A 16 FD 01 FF 2E 70 ║ ╪ZδΘ[è...è.². .p
 F0 ║ 01 BE 8B 01 EB 54 90 01 06 1C 00 11 2E 1E 00 C3 ║ .╛ï.δTÉ...ÉTÉ...├
A>_
```

Figure 16-2. Adding Numbers on the Left.

You can see the result in Figure 16-2.

We're getting closer to our full display. But on the screen, our display isn't quite centered. We need to move it to the right by about three spaces. Let's make this one last change; then we'll have our finished version of DISP_LINE.

We could make the change by calling WRITE_CHAR three times with a space character, but we won't. Instead, we'll add another procedure, called WRITE_CHAR_N_TIMES, to Video_io. As its name implies, this procedure writes one character N times. That is, we place the number N into the CX register and the character code into DL, and we call WRITE_CHAR_N_TIMES to write N copies of the character whose ASCII code we placed in DL. Thus, we'll be able to write three spaces by placing 3 into CX and 20h (the ASCII code for a space) into DL.

Here's the procedure to add to VIDEO_IO.ASM:

Listing 16-4. Add this Procedure to VIDEO_IO.ASM

```
        PUBLIC   WRITE_CHAR_N_TIMES
;-------------------------------------------------------------------;
; This procedure writes more than one copy of a character          ;
;                                                                   ;
; On entry:    DL        Character code                            ;
;              CX        Number of times to write the character    ;
;                                                                   ;
; Uses:        WRITE_CHAR                                           ;
;-------------------------------------------------------------------;
WRITE_CHAR_N_TIMES      PROC
        PUSH    CX
N_TIMES:
        CALL    WRITE_CHAR
        LOOP    N_TIMES
        POP     CX
        RET
WRITE_CHAR_N_TIMES      ENDP
```

You can see how simple this procedure is, since we already have WRITE_CHAR. If you're wondering why we bothered to write a procedure for something so simple, it's because our program Dskpatch is much clearer when we call WRITE_CHAR_N_TIMES, rather than write a short loop to print multiple copies of a character. Besides, we'll find use for this procedure several times again.

Here are the changes to DISP_LINE to add three spaces on the left of our display. Make the changes to DISP_SEC.ASM:

Listing 16-5. Changes to DISP_LINE in DISP_SEC.ASM

```
        PUBLIC   DISP_LINE
        EXTRN    WRITE_HEX:PROC
        EXTRN    WRITE_CHAR:PROC
        EXTRN    WRITE_CHAR_N_TIMES:PROC
;-------------------------------------------------------------------;
; This procedure displays one line of data, or 16 bytes, first in hex, ;
; then in ASCII.                                                    ;
;                                                                   ;
; On entry:    DS:DX   Offset into sector, in bytes                 ;
;                                                                   ;
; Uses:        WRITE_CHAR, WRITE_HEX, WRITE_CHAR_N_TIMES            ;
; Reads:       SECTOR                                               ;
;-------------------------------------------------------------------;
DISP_LINE       PROC
        PUSH    BX
        PUSH    CX
        PUSH    DX
        MOV     BX,DX                   ;Offset is more useful in BX
        MOV     DL,' '
        MOV     CX,3                    ;Write 3 spaces before line
        CALL    WRITE_CHAR_N_TIMES
                                        ;Write offset in hex
        CMP     BX,100h                 ;Is the first digit a 1?
        JB      WRITE_ONE               ;No, white space already in DL
        MOV     DL,'1'                  ;Yes, then place '1' into DL for output
WRITE_ONE:
                .
                .
                .
```

We made changes in three places. First, we had to add an EXTRN statement for WRITE_CHAR_N_TIMES, because the procedure is in Video_io, and not in this file. We also changed the comment block, to show that we use this new procedure. Our third change, the two lines that use WRITE_CHAR_N_TIMES, is quite straightforward and needs no explanation.

Try this new version of our program to see how the display is now centered. Next we'll move on to add more features to our display—the top and bottom lines of our boxes.

Adding Horizontal Lines

Adding horizontal lines to our display is not quite as simple as it sounds, because we have a few special cases to think about. We have the ends, where the lines must go around corners, and we also have T-shaped junctions at the top and bottom of the division between the hex and ASCII windows.

We could write a long list of instructions (with WRITE_CHAR_N_TIMES) to create our horizontal lines, but we won't. We have a shorter way. We'll introduce another procedure, called WRITE_PATTERN, which will write a pattern on the screen. Then, all we'll need is a small area of memory to hold a description of each pattern. Using this new procedure, we can also easily add tick marks to subdivide the hex window, as you'll see when we finish this section.

WRITE_PATTERN uses two entirely new instructions, LODSB and CLD. We'll describe them after we see more about WRITE_PATTERN and how we describe a pattern. Right now, enter this procedure into the file VIDEO_IO.ASM:

Listing 16-6. Add This Procedure to VIDEO_IO.ASM

```
        PUBLIC  WRITE_PATTERN
;------------------------------------------------------------------;
; This procedure writes a line to the screen, based on data in the ;
; form                                                             ;
;                                                                  ;
;       DB      (character, number of times to write character), 0 ;
; Where (x) means that x can be repeated any number of times        ;
;                                                                  ;
; On entry:      DS:DX   Address of the pattern to draw            ;
;                                                                  ;
; Uses:          WRITE_CHAR_N_TIMES                                ;
;------------------------------------------------------------------;
WRITE_PATTERN   PROC
        PUSH    AX
        PUSH    CX
        PUSH    DX
        PUSH    SI
        PUSHF                           ;Save the direction flag
        CLD                             ;Set direction flag for increment
        MOV     SI,DX                   ;Move offset into SI register for LODSB
PATTERN_LOOP:
```

Listing 16-6. *continued*

```
        LODSB                               ;Get character data into AL
        OR          AL,AL                   ;Is it the end of data (0h)?
        JZ          END_PATTERN             ;Yes, return
        MOV         DL,AL                   ;No, set up to write character N times
        LODSB                               ;Get the repeat count into AL
        MOV         CL,AL                   ;And put in CX for WRITE_CHAR_N_TIMES
        XOR         CH,CH                   ;Zero upper byte of CX
        CALL        WRITE_CHAR_N_TIMES
        JMP         PATTERN_LOOP
END_PATTERN:
        POPF                                ;Restore direction flag
        POP         SI
        POP         DX
        POP         CX
        POP         AX
        RET
WRITE_PATTERN   ENDP
```

Before we see how this procedure works, let's see how to write data for patterns. We'll place the data for the top-line pattern into the file Disp_sec, which is where we'll use it. To this end, we'll add another procedure, called INIT_SEC_DISP, to initialize the sector display by writing the half-sector display, then we'll modify READ_SECTOR to call our INIT_SEC_DISP procedure.

First, place the following data before the .DATA? where we defined SECTOR (in DISP_SEC.ASM):

Listing 16-7. Additions to DISP_SEC.ASM

```
.DATA

TOP_LINE_PATTERN        LABEL   BYTE
        DB          ' ',7
        DB          UPPER_LEFT,1
        DB          HORIZONTAL_BAR,12
        DB          TOP_TICK,1
        DB          HORIZONTAL_BAR,11
        DB          TOP_TICK,1
        DB          HORIZONTAL_BAR,11
        DB          TOP_TICK,1
        DB          HORIZONTAL_BAR,12
        DB          TOP_T_BAR,1
        DB          HORIZONTAL_BAR,18
        DB          UPPER_RIGHT,1
        DB          0
BOTTOM_LINE_PATTERN     LABEL   BYTE
        DB          ' ',7
        DB          LOWER_LEFT,1
        DB          HORIZONTAL_BAR,12
        DB          BOTTOM_TICK,1
        DB          HORIZONTAL_BAR,11
        DB          BOTTOM_TICK,1
        DB          HORIZONTAL_BAR,11
        DB          BOTTOM_TICK,1
        DB          HORIZONTAL_BAR,12
        DB          BOTTOM_T_BAR,1
        DB          HORIZONTAL_BAR,18
        DB          LOWER_RIGHT,1
        DB          0

.DATA?

SECTOR  DB      8192 DUP (?)
```

(Note that we put all the new data into .DATA rather than .DATA? because we need to set values for all these variables.)

Each DB statement contains part of the data for one line. The first byte is the character to print; the second byte tells WRITE_PATTERN how many times to repeat that character. For example, we start the top line with seven blank spaces, followed by one upper-left corner character, followed by twelve horizontal-bar characters, and so on. The last DB is a solitary hex zero, which marks the end of the pattern.

Let's continue our modifications and see the result before we discuss the inner workings of WRITE_PATTERN. Here is the test version of INIT_SEC_DISP. This procedure writes the top-line pattern, the half-sector display, and finally the bottom-line pattern. Place it in the file DISP_SEC.ASM, just before DISP_HALF_SECTOR:

Listing 16-8. Add This Procedure to DISP_SEC.ASM

```
        PUBLIC  INIT_SEC_DISP
        EXTRN   WRITE_PATTERN:PROC, SEND_CRLF:PROC
;-------------------------------------------------------------------;
;  This procedure initializes the half-sector display.              ;
;                                                                   ;
; Uses:          WRITE_PATTERN, SEND_CRLF, DISP_HALF_SECTOR         ;
; Reads:         TOP_LINE_PATTERN, BOTTOM_LINE_PATTERN              ;
;-------------------------------------------------------------------;
INIT_SEC_DISP   PROC
        PUSH    DX
        LEA     DX,TOP_LINE_PATTERN
        CALL    WRITE_PATTERN
        CALL    SEND_CRLF
        XOR     DX,DX                   ;Start at the beginning of the sector
        CALL    DISP_HALF_SECTOR
        LEA     DX,BOTTOM_LINE_PATTERN
        CALL    WRITE_PATTERN
        POP     DX
        RET
INIT_SEC_DISP   ENDP
```

We used the LEA instruction to load an address into the DX register, thus WRITE_PATTERN knows where to find the pattern data.

Finally, we need to make a small change to READ_SECTOR in the file DISK_IO.ASM, to call INIT_SECTOR_DISP, rather than WRITE_HALF_SECTOR_DISP, so that a full box will be drawn around our half-sector display:

Listing 16-9. Changes to READ_SECTOR in DISK_IO.ASM

```
        EXTRN   INIT_SEC_DISP:PROC
;-------------------------------------------------------------------;
; This procedure reads the first sector on disk A and dumps the first ;
; half of this sector.                                              ;
;-------------------------------------------------------------------;
```

Listing 16-9. *continued*

```
READ_SECTOR     PROC
        MOV     AX,DGROUP               ;Put data segment into AX
        MOV     DS,AX                   ;Set DS to point to data

        MOV     AL,0                    ;Disk drive A (number 0)
        MOV     CX,1                    ;Read only 1 sector
        MOV     DX,0                    ;Read sector number 0
        LEA     BX,SECTOR               ;Where to store this sector
        INT     25h                     ;Read the sector
        POPF                            ;Discard flags put on stack by DOS
        XOR     DX,DX                   ;Set offset to 0 within SECTOR
        CALL    INIT_SEC_DISP           ;Dump the first half

        MOV     AH,4Ch                  ;Return to DOS
        INT     21h
READ_SECTOR     ENDP
```

That's all we need to write the top and bottom lines for our sector display. Assemble and link all these files (remember to assemble the three files we changed), and give it a try. Figure 16-3 shows the output we now have.

Let's see how WRITE_PATTERN works. As mentioned, it uses two new instructions. LODSB stands for *Load String Byte*, and it is one of the string instructions: specially designed instructions that work with strings of characters. That's not quite what we're doing here, but the 8088 doesn't care whether we're dealing with a string of characters or just numbers, so LODSB suits our purposes just fine.

LODSB moves (loads) a single byte into the AL register from the memory location given by DS:SI, a register pair we haven't used before. (We already set

```
A>disk_io

00 ║ EB 28 90 49 42 4D 20 20 33 2E 32 00 02 02 01 00 ║ δ(ÉIBM  3.2.....
10 ║ 02 70 00 D0 02 FD 02 90 09 00 02 00 00 00 00 00 ║ .p.⊥.².........
20 ║ 00 00 00 00 00 00 00 00 00 00 FA C4 5C 08 33 ED ║ ..........·─\.3ø
30 ║ B8 C0 07 8E D8 33 C9 88 16 FD 01 0A D2 79 0A 89 ║ ¸└.Ä┌3╔ê.².╥y.ë
40 ║ 1E 1C 00 8C 06 1E 00 B1 02 8E C5 8E D5 BC 00 7C ║ ...î..▌.ÄÅÄ┘.¦
50 ║ FC 1E 36 C5 36 78 00 BF 2A 7C B9 0B 00 F3 A4 1F ║ n.6┼6x.¬*¦¦..Ññ.
60 ║ C6 06 2E 00 0F BF 78 00 B8 2A 7C AB 91 AB FB 8A ║ ╞...¬x.¬*¦½æ½┘è
70 ║ 16 FD 01 CD 13 A0 10 60 98 F7 26 16 00 03 06 0E ║ .².=.á..ÿ≈&.....
80 ║ 00 E8 73 00 E8 79 00 BB 00 05 53 E8 A0 00 5F BE ║ .Φs.Φy.╗..SΦá._¥
90 ║ 74 01 B9 0B 00 90 F3 A6 75 57 83 C7 15 B1 0B 90 ║ t.¦..É≤ªuWâ╟.¦..É
A0 ║ 90 F3 A6 75 4C 26 8B 47 1C 99 8B 0E 0B 00 03 C1 ║ É≤ªuL&ïG.Öï....┴
B0 ║ 48 F7 F1 3D 14 00 7F 02 B0 14 96 A1 11 00 B1 04 ║ H≈±=...⌂.░.û¡..¦.
C0 ║ D3 E8 E8 32 00 FF 36 1C 00 C4 1E 70 01 E8 30 00 ║ ⌂ΦΦ2. 6..·.p.Φ0.
D0 ║ E8 5B 00 2B F0 76 0D E8 1D 00 52 F7 26 0B 00 03 ║ Φ[.+≡v.Φ..R≈&...
E0 ║ D8 5A EB E9 5B 8A 2E 15 00 8A 16 FD 01 FF 2E 70 ║ ╪ZδΘ[è...è.². .p
F0 ║ 01 BE 8B 01 EB 54 90 01 06 1C 00 11 2E 1E 00 C3 ║ .¦ï.δT É..... ┤

A>_
```

Figure 16-3. The Display with Closed Boxes.

DS in READ_SECTOR to point to our data.) And, before the LODSB instruction, we moved the offset into the SI register with the instruction MOV SI,DX.

The LODSB instruction is somewhat like the MOV instruction, but more powerful. With one LODSB instruction, the 8088 moves one byte into the AL register and then either increments or decrements the SI register. Incrementing the SI register points to the following byte in memory; decrementing the register points to the previous byte in memory.

The former (incrementing) is exactly what we want to do. We want to go through the pattern, one byte at a time, starting at the beginning, and that is what our LODSB instruction does, because we used the other new instruction, CLD (*Clear Direction Flag*) to clear the direction flag. If we had set the direction flag, the LODSB instruction would decrement the SI register, instead. We'll use the LODSB instruction in a few other places in Dskpatch, always with the direction flag cleared, to increment.

Aside from LODSB and CLD, note that we also used the PUSHF and POPF instructions to save and restore the flag register. We did this just in case we later decide to use the direction flag in a procedure that calls WRITE_PATTERN.

Adding Numbers to the Display

We're almost through with Part II of this book now. We'll create one more procedure, then we'll move on to Part III, and bigger and better things.

Right now, notice that our display lacks a row of numbers across the top. Such numbers—00 01 02 03 and so forth—would allow us to sight down the columns to find the address for any byte. So, let's write a procedure to print this row of numbers. Add this procedure, WRITE_TOP_HEX_NUMBERS, to DISP_SEC.ASM, just after INIT_SEC_DISP:

Listing 16-10. Add This Procedure to DISP_SEC.ASM

```
        EXTRN   WRITE_CHAR_N_TIMES:PROC, WRITE_HEX:PROC, WRITE_CHAR:PROC
        EXTRN   WRITE_HEX_DIGIT:PROC, SEND_CRLF:PROC
;-------------------------------------------------------------------------;
; This procedure writes the index numbers (0 through F) at the top of     ;
; the half-sector display.                                                ;
;                                                                         ;
; Uses:           WRITE_CHAR_N_TIMES, WRITE_HEX, WRITE_CHAR               ;
;                 WRITE_HEX_DIGIT, SEND_CRLF                              ;
;-------------------------------------------------------------------------;
WRITE_TOP_HEX_NUMBERS    PROC
        PUSH    CX
        PUSH    DX
        MOV     DL,' '                  ;Write 9 spaces for left side
        MOV     CX,9
        CALL    WRITE_CHAR_N_TIMES
        XOR     DH,DH                   ;Start with 0
```

Listing 16-10. *continued*

```
HEX_NUMBER_LOOP:
        MOV     DL,DH
        CALL    WRITE_HEX
        MOV     DL,' '
        CALL    WRITE_CHAR
        INC     DH
        CMP     DH,10h                  ;Done yet?
        JB      HEX_NUMBER_LOOP

        MOV     DL,' '                  ;Write hex numbers over ASCII window
        MOV     CX,2
        CALL    WRITE_CHAR_N_TIMES
        XOR     DL,DL
HEX_DIGIT_LOOP:
        CALL    WRITE_HEX_DIGIT
        INC     DL
        CMP     DL,10h
        JB      HEX_DIGIT_LOOP
        CALL    SEND_CRLF
        POP     DX
        POP     CX
        RET
WRITE_TOP_HEX_NUMBERS   ENDP
```

Modify INIT_SEC_DISP (also in DISP_SEC.ASM) as follows, so it calls WRITE_TOP_HEX_NUMBERS before it writes the rest of the half-sector display:

Listing 16-11. Changes to INIT_SEC_DISP in DISP_SEC.ASM

```
;---------------------------------------------------------------;
; Uses:         WRITE_PATTERN, SEND_CRLF, DISP_HALF_SECTOR      ;
;               WRITE_TOP_HEX_NUMBERS                           ;
; Reads:        TOP_LINE_PATTERN, BOTTOM_LINE_PATTERN           ;
;---------------------------------------------------------------;
INIT_SEC_DISP   PROC
        PUSH    DX
        CALL    WRITE_TOP_HEX_NUMBERS
        LEA     DX,TOP_LINE_PATTERN
        CALL    WRITE_PATTERN
        CALL    SEND_CRLF
        XOR     DX,DX                   ;Start at the beginning of the sector
        CALL    DISP_HALF_SECTOR
        LEA     DX,BOTTOM_LINE_PATTERN
        CALL    WRITE_PATTERN
        POP     DX
        RET
INIT_SEC_DISP   ENDP
```

Now we have a complete half-sector display, as you can see in Figure 16-4.

There are still some differences between this display and the final version. We'll change WRITE_CHAR so it will print all 256 characters the IBM PC can display, and then we'll clear the screen and center this display vertically, using the ROM BIOS routines inside the IBM Personal Computer. We'll do that next.

```
A>disk_io
         00 01 02 03 04 05 06 07 08 09 0A 0B 0C 0D 0E 0F  0123456789ABCDEF

   00   EB 28 90 49 42 4D 20 20 33 2E 32 00 02 02 01 00   ó(ÉIBM  3.2.....
   10   02 70 00 D0 02 FD 02 00 09 00 02 00 00 00 00 00   .p.⊥.².........
   20   00 00 00 00 00 00 00 00 00 FA C4 5C 08 33 ED   ..........·─\.3ø
   30   B8 C0 07 8E D8 33 C9 88 16 FD 01 0A D2 79 0A 89   ˥ ˪.Ä┼3┌ê.²..┬ψ.ë
   40   1E 1C 00 8C 06 1E 00 B1 02 8E C5 8E D5 BC 00 7C   ...î...█.Ä┤Ä┘..¦
   50   FC 1E 36 C5 36 78 00 BF 2A 7C B9 0B 00 F3 A4 1F   ⁿ.6┼6x.┐*¦‖..ⓢñ.
   60   C6 06 2E 00 0F BF 78 00 B8 2A 7C AB 91 AB FB 8A   ╞....┐x.┐*½æ½╛ê
   70   16 FD 01 CD 13 A0 10 00 98 F7 26 16 00 03 06 0E   .².=.á..ÿ≈&.....
   80   00 E8 73 00 E8 79 00 BB 00 05 53 E8 A0 00 5F BE   .ŏs.ŏy.┐..Sŏá._
   90   74 01 B9 0B 00 90 F3 A6 75 57 83 C7 15 B1 0B 90   t.‖..É<ƏuŴâ‖.█.É
   A0   90 F3 A6 75 4C 26 8B 47 1C 99 8B 0E 0B 00 03 C1   É<ƏuL&ïG.öï....⊥
   B0   48 F7 F1 3D 14 00 7F 02 B0 14 96 A1 11 00 B1 04   H≈±=..▵.█.ûí..█.
   C0   D3 E8 E8 32 00 FF 36 1C 00 C4 1E 70 01 E8 30 00   ⁴ⓢ½2. 6..─.p.ŏ0.
   D0   E8 5B 00 2B F0 76 0D E8 1D 00 52 F7 26 0B 00 03   ŏ[ .+≈v.ⓢ..R≈&...
   E0   D8 5A EB E9 5B 8A 2E 15 00 8A 16 FD 01 FF 2E 70   ┼Zŏⓔè...è.². .p
   F0   01 BE 8B 01 EB 54 90 01 06 1C 00 11 2E 1E 00 C3   .┘ï.óTÉ.......╞
```

Figure 16-4. A Complete Half Sector Display.

Summary

We've done a lot of building on our Dskpatch program, adding new procedures, changing old ones, and moving from one source file to another. From now on, if you find yourself losing track of what you're doing, refer to the complete listing of Dskpatch in Appendix B. The listing there is the final version, but you'll probably see enough resemblances to help you along.

Most of our changes in this chapter didn't rely on tricks, just hard work. But we did learn two new instructions: LODSB and CLD. LODSB is one of the string instructions that allows us to use one instruction to do the work of several. We used LODSB in WRITE_PATTERN to read consecutive bytes from the pattern table, always loading a new byte into the AL register. CLD clears the direction flag, which sets the direction for increment. Each following LODSB instruction loads the next byte from memory.

In the next part of this book, we'll learn about the IBM PC's ROM BIOS routines. They will save us a lot of time.

PART III

The IBM PC's ROM BIOS

17

THE ROM BIOS ROUTINES

Inside your IBM Personal Computer are some computer chips, or ICs (*Integrated Circuits*), known as ROMs (*Read-Only Memory*). One of these ROMs contains a number of routines, very much like procedures, that provide all the basic routines for doing input and output to several different parts of your IBM PC. Because this ROM provides routines for performing input and output at a very low level, it is frequently referred to as the BIOS, for Basic Input Output System. DOS uses the ROM BIOS for such activities as sending characters to the screen and reading and writing to the disk, and we're free to use the ROM BIOS routines in our programs.

We'll concentrate on the BIOS routines we need for Dskpatch. Among them is a set for video display, which includes a number of functions we couldn't otherwise reach without working directly with the hardware—a very difficult job.

VIDEO_IO, the ROM BIOS Routines

We refer to the elements of the ROM BIOS as routines to distinguish them from procedures. We use procedures with a CALL instruction, whereas we call routines with INT instructions, not CALLs. We'll use an INT 10h instruction, for example, to call the video I/O routines, just as we used an INT 21h instruction to call routines in DOS.

Specifically, INT 10h calls the routine VIDEO_IO in the ROM BIOS. Other numbers call other routines, but we won't see any of them; VIDEO_IO provides all the functions we need outside of DOS. (Just for your information, however, DOS calls one of the other ROM BIOS routines when we ask for a sector from the disk.)

In this chapter, we'll use ROM BIOS routines to add two new procedures to Dskpatch: one to clear the screen, and the other to move the cursor to any screen location we choose. Both are very useful functions, but neither is available directly through DOS. Hence, we'll use the ROM BIOS routines to do the job. Later, we'll see even more interesting things we can do with these ROM routines, but let's begin by using INT 10h to clear the screen before we display our half sector.

The INT 10h instruction is our entry to a number of different functions. Recall that, when we used the DOS INT 21h instruction, we selected a particular function by placing its function number in the AH register. We select a VIDEO_IO function in just the same way: by placing the appropriate function number in the AH register (a full list of these functions is given in Table 17-1).

Table 17-1. INT 10h Functions

(AH) = 0   **Set the display mode.** The AL register contains the mode number.

TEXT MODES

(AL) = 0	40 by 25, black and white mode
(AL) = 1	40 by 25, color
(AL) = 2	80 by 25, black and white
(AL) = 3	80 by 25, color
(AL) = 7	80 by 25, monochrome display adapter

GRAPHICS MODE

(AL) = 4	320 by 200, color
(AL) = 5	320 by 200, black and white
(AL) = 6	640 by 200, black and white

(AH) = 1   **Set the cursor size.**

(CH)	Starting scan line of the cursor. The top line is 0 on both the monochrome and color graphics displays, while the bottom line is 7 for the color graphics adapter and 13 for the monochrome adapter. Valid range: 0 to 31.
(CL)	Last scan line of the cursor.

The power-on setting for the color graphics adapter is CH = 6 and CL = 7. For the monochrome display: CH = 11 and CL = 12.

(AH) = 2   **Set the cursor position.**

(DH,DL)	Row, column of new cursor position; the upper left corner is (0,0).

Table 17-1. *continued*

(BH)	Page number. This is the number of the display page. The color-graphics adapter has room for several display pages, but most programs use page 0.

(AH) = 3 **Read the cursor position.**

(BH)	Page number	
On exit	(DH,DL)	Row, column of cursor
	(CH,CL)	Cursor size

(AH) = 4 **Read light pen position** (see Tech. Ref. Man.).

(AH) = 5 **Select active display page.**

(AL)	New page number (from 0 to 7 for modes 0 and 1; from 0 to 3 for modes 2 and 3)

(AH) = 6 **Scroll up.**

(AL)	Number of lines to blank at the bottom of the window. Normal scrolling blanks one line. Set to zero to blank entire window.
(CH,CL)	Row, column of upper, left corner of window
(DH,DL)	Row, column of lower, right corner of window
(BH)	Display attribute to use for blank lines

(AH) = 7 **Scroll down.**

Same as scroll up (function 6), but lines are left blank at the top of the window instead of the bottom

(AH) = 8   **Read attribute and character under the cursor.**

(BH)	Display page (text modes only)
(AL)	Character read
(AH)	Attribute of character read (text modes only)

(AH) = 9   **Write attribute and character under the cursor.**

(BH)	Display page (text modes only)
(CX)	Number of times to write character and attribute on screen
(AL)	Character to write
(BL)	Attribute to write

(AH) = 10   **Write character under cursor** (with normal attribute).

(BH)	Display page
(CX)	Number of times to write character
(AL)	Character to write

(AH) = 11 to 13   **Various graphics functions.** (See Tech. Ref. Man. for the details)

(AH) = 14   **Write teletype.** Write one character to the screen and move the cursor to the next position.

(AL)	Character to write
(BL)	Color of character (graphics mode only)
(BH)	Display page (text mode)

(AH) = 15   **Return current video state.**

(AL)	Display mode currently set
(AH)	Number of characters per line
(BH)	Active display pages

Clearing the Screen

We'll use the INT 10h function number 6, *SCROLL ACTIVE PAGE UP*, to clear the screen. We don't actually want to scroll the screen, but this function also doubles as a clear-screen function. Here is the procedure; enter it into the file CURSOR.ASM:

Listing 17-1. Add This Procedure to CURSOR.ASM

```
        PUBLIC  CLEAR_SCREEN
;---------------------------------------------------------------;
; This procedure clears the entire screen.                      ;
;---------------------------------------------------------------;
CLEAR_SCREEN    PROC
        PUSH    AX
        PUSH    BX
        PUSH    CX
        PUSH    DX
        XOR     AL,AL               ;Blank entire window
        XOR     CX,CX               ;Upper left corner is at (0,0)
        MOV     DH,24               ;Bottom line of screen is line 24
        MOV     DL,79               ;Right side is at column 79
        MOV     BH,7                ;Use normal attribute for blanks
        MOV     AH,6                ;Call for SCROLL-UP function
        INT     10h                 ;Clear the window
        POP     DX
        POP     CX
        POP     BX
        POP     AX
        RET
CLEAR_SCREEN    ENDP
```

It appears that INT 10h function number 6 needs quite a lot of information, even though all we want to do is clear the display. This function is rather powerful: It can actually clear any rectangular part of the screen—window, as it's called. We have to set the window to the entire screen by setting the first and last lines to 0 and 24, and setting the columns to 0 and 79. The routines we are using here can also clear the screen to all white (for use with black characters), or all black (for use with white characters). We want the latter, and that is what is specified with the instruction MOV BH,7. Then, too, setting AL to 0, the number of lines to scroll, tells this routine to clear the window, rather than to scroll it.

Now we need to modify our test procedure, READ_SECTOR, to call CLEAR_SCREEN just before it starts to write the sector display. We didn't place this CALL in INIT_SEC_DISP, because we'll want to use INIT_SEC_DISP to rewrite just the half-sector display, without affecting the rest of the screen.

To modify READ_SECTOR, add an EXTRN declaration for CLEAR_SCREEN and insert the CALL to CLEAR_SCREEN. Make the following changes in the file DISK_IO.ASM:

Listing 17-2. Changes to READ_SECTOR in DISK_IO.ASM

```
        EXTRN   INIT_SEC_DISP:PROC, CLEAR_SCREEN:PROC
;-------------------------------------------------------------------;
; This procedure reads the first sector on disk A and dumps the first ;
; half of this sector.                                               ;
;-------------------------------------------------------------------;
READ_SECTOR     PROC
        MOV     AX,DGROUP               ;Put data segment into AX
        MOV     DS,AX                   ;Set DS to point to data
        MOV     AL,0                    ;Disk drive A (number 0)
        MOV     CX,1                    ;Read only 1 sector
        MOV     DX,0                    ;Read sector number 0
        LEA     BX,SECTOR               ;Where to store this sector
        INT     25h                     ;Read the sector
        POPF                            ;Discard flags put on stack by DOS
        CALL    CLEAR_SCREEN
        CALL    INIT_SEC_DISP           ;Dump the first half

        MOV     AH,4Ch                  ;Return to DOS
        INT     21h
READ_SECTOR     ENDP
```

Just before you run the new version of Disk_io, note where the cursor is located. Then, run Disk_io. The screen will clear, and Disk_io will start writing the half sector display wherever the cursor happened to be before you ran the program—probably at the bottom of the screen.

Even though we cleared the screen, we didn't mention anything about moving the cursor back to the top. In BASIC, the CLS command clears the screen in two steps: It clears the screen, then it moves the cursor to the top of the screen. Our procedure doesn't do that; we'll have to move the cursor ourselves.

Moving the Cursor

The INT 10h function number 2 sets the cursor position in much the same way BASIC's LOCATE statement does. We can use GOTO_XY to move the cursor anywhere on the screen (such as to the top after a clear). Enter this procedure into the file CURSOR.ASM:

Listing 17-3. Add This Procedure to CURSOR.ASM

```
        PUBLIC  GOTO_XY
;-------------------------------------------------------------------;
;   This procedure moves the cursor                                 ;
;                                                                   ;
; On entry: DH      Row (Y)                                         ;
;           DL      Column (X)                                      ;
;-------------------------------------------------------------------;
GOTO_XY PROC
        PUSH    AX
        PUSH    BX
        MOV     BH,0                    ;Display page 0
        MOV     AH,2                    ;Call for SET CURSOR POSITION
        INT     10h
```

Listing 17-3. *continued*

```
                POP     BX
                POP     AX
                RET
    GOTO_XY     ENDP
```

We'll use GOTO_XY in a revised version of INIT_SEC_DISP to move the cursor to the second line just before we write the half-sector display. Here are the modifications to INIT_SEC_DISP in DISP_SEC.ASM:

Listing 17-4. Changes to INIT_SEC_DISP in DISP_SEC.ASM

```
        PUBLIC  INIT_SEC_DISP
        EXTRN   WRITE_PATTERN:PROC, SEND_CRLF:PROC
        EXTRN   GOTO_XY:PROC
;-----------------------------------------------------------------;
;  This procedure initializes the half-sector display.            ;
;                                                                 ;
; Uses:          WRITE_PATTERN, SEND_CRLF, DISP_HALF_SECTOR        ;
;                WRITE_TOP_HEX_NUMBERS, GOTO_XY                    ;
; Reads:         TOP_LINE_PATTERN, BOTTOM_LINE_PATTERN             ;
;-----------------------------------------------------------------;
INIT_SEC_DISP   PROC
        PUSH    DX
        XOR     DL,DL           ;Move cursor into position at beginning
        MOV     DH,2            ;of 3rd line
        CALL    GOTO_XY
        CALL    WRITE_TOP_HEX_NUMBERS
        LEA     DX,TOP_LINE_PATTERN
                .
                .
                .
```

If you try it now, you'll see that the half-sector display is nicely centered.

As you can see now, it's easy to work with the screen when we have the ROM BIOS routines. In the next chapter, we'll use another routine in the ROM BIOS to improve WRITE_CHAR, so that it will write any character to the screen. But before we continue, let's make some other changes to our program, then finish up with a procedure called WRITE_HEADER, which will write a status line at the top of the screen, to show the current disk drive and sector number.

Rewiring Variable Usage

There is much that we need to revamp before we create WRITE_HEADER. Many of our procedures, as they are now, have numbers hard-wired into them; for example, READ_SECTOR reads sector 0 on drive A. We want to place the disk-drive and sector numbers into memory variables, so more than one procedure can read them.

We'll need to change these procedures so they'll use memory variables, but let's begin by putting all memory variables into one file, DSKPATCH.ASM, to make our work simpler. Dskpatch.asm will be the first file in our program Dskpatch, so the memory variables will be easy to find there. Here is DSKPATCH.ASM, complete with a long list of memory variables:

Listing 17-5. The New File DSKPATCH.ASM

```
DOSSEG
.MODEL  SMALL

.STACK

.DATA

        PUBLIC  SECTOR_OFFSET
;------------------------------------------------;
; SECTOR_OFFSET is the offset of the half-       ;
; sector display into the full sector.  It must  ;
; be a multiple of 16, and not greater than 256  ;
;------------------------------------------------;
SECTOR_OFFSET   DW       0

        PUBLIC  CURRENT_SECTOR_NO, DISK_DRIVE_NO
CURRENT_SECTOR_NO       DW       0              ;Initially sector 0
DISK_DRIVE_NO           DB       0              ;Initially Drive A:

        PUBLIC  LINES_BEFORE_SECTOR, HEADER_LINE_NO
        PUBLIC  HEADER_PART_1, HEADER_PART_2
;------------------------------------------------;
; LINES_BEFORE_SECTOR is the number of lines     ;
; at the top of the screen before the half-      ;
; sector display.                                ;
;------------------------------------------------;
LINES_BEFORE_SECTOR     DB       2
HEADER_LINE_NO          DB       0
HEADER_PART_1           DB       'Disk ',0
HEADER_PART_2           DB       '         Sector ',0

.DATA?

        PUBLIC  SECTOR
;------------------------------------------------;
; The entire sector (up to 8192 bytes) is        ;
; stored in this part of memory.                 ;
;------------------------------------------------;
SECTOR  DB      8192 DUP (?)

.CODE

    EXTRN     CLEAR_SCREEN:PROC, READ_SECTOR:PROC
    EXTRN     INIT_SEC_DISP:PROC
DISK_PATCH      PROC
    MOV   AX,DGROUP           ;Put data segment into AX
    MOV   DS,AX               ;Set DS to point to data

    CALL CLEAR_SCREEN
    CALL READ_SECTOR
    CALL INIT_SEC_DISP

    MOV   AH,4Ch              ;Return to DOS
    INT   21h
DISK_PATCH      ENDP

    END  DISK_PATCH
```

The main procedure, DISK_PATCH, calls three other procedures. We've seen them all before, soon we'll rewrite both READ_SECTOR and INIT_SEC_DISP to use the variables just placed into the data segment.

Before we can use Dskpatch, we need to modify Disp_sec, to replace the definition of SECTOR with an EXTRN. We also need to alter Disk_io, to change READ_SECTOR into an ordinary procedure we can call from Dskpatch.

Let's take SECTOR first. Since we've placed it in DSKPATCH.ASM as a memory variable, we need to change the definition of SECTOR in Disp_sec to an EXTRN declaration. Make these changes in DISP_SEC.ASM:

Listing 17-6. Changes to DISP_SEC.ASM

```
.DATA?
        EXTRN    SECTOR:BYTE
        PUBLIC   SECTOR
SECTOR  DB       8192 DUP(?)
```

Let's rewrite the file DISK_IO.ASM so that it contains only procedures, and READ_SECTOR uses memory variables (not hard-wired numbers) for the sector and disk-drive numbers. Here is the new version of DISK_IO.ASM:

Listing 17-7. Changes to DISK_IO.ASM

```
        DOSSEG
        .MODEL  SMALL

        .STACK

        .DATA

        EXTRN    SECTOR:BYTE
        EXTRN    DISK_DRIVE_NO:BYTE
        EXTRN    CURRENT_SECTOR_NO:WORD

        PUBLIC   READ_SECTOR
        EXTRN    INIT_SEC_DISP:PROC, CLEAR_SCREEN:PROC
;---------------------------------------------------------------------;
; This procedure reads one sector (512 bytes) into SECTOR.            ;
;                                                                     ;
; Reads:        CURRENT_SECTOR_NO, DISK_DRIVE_NO                      ;
; Writes:       SECTOR                                                ;
;---------------------------------------------------------------------;
READ_SECTOR     PROC
        MOV      AX,DGROUP             ;Put data segment into AX
        MOV      DS,AX                 ;Set DS to point to data
        PUSH     AX
        PUSH     BX
        PUSH     CX
        PUSH     DX
        MOV      AL,DISK_DRIVE_NO      ;Drive number
        MOV      CX,1                  ;Read only 1 sector
        MOV      DX,CURRENT_SECTOR_NO  ;Logical sector number
        LEA      BX,SECTOR             ;Where to store this sector
        INT      25h                   ;Read the sector
        POPF                           ;Discard flags put on stack by DOS
        POP      DX
        POP      CX
        POP      BX
```

```
        POP     AX
        RET
        CALL    CLEAR_SCREEN
        CALL    INIT_SEC_DISP           ;Dump the first half

        MOV     AH,4Ch                  ;Return to DOS
        INT     21h
READ_SECTOR     ENDP

        END
```

This new version of Disk_io uses the memory variables DISK_DRIVE_NO and CURRENT_SECTOR_NO as the disk drive and sector numbers for the sector to read. Since these variables are already defined in DSKPATCH.ASM, we won't have to change Disk_io when we start reading different sectors from other disk drives.

If you're using the Make program to rebuild DSKPATCH.COM, you'll need to make some additions to your Make file named Makefile:

Listing 17-8. The New Version of MAKEFILE

```
dskpatch.obj:    dskpatch.asm
        masm dskpatch;

disk_io.obj:     disk_io.asm
        masm disk_io;

disp_sec.obj:    disp_sec.asm
        masm disp_sec;

video_io.obj:    video_io.asm
        masm video_io;

cursor.obj:      cursor.asm
        masm cursor;

dskpatch.exe:    dskpatch.obj disk_io.obj disp_sec.obj video_io.obj cursor.obj
        link dskpatch disk_io disp_sec video_io cursor;
```

(Remember that if you're using Borland's Make, the last two lines shown here must be at the start of your Makefile. And if you're using OPTASM, you'll just add the first two lines, with the first line indented, and the second line flush left.) If you're not using Make, be sure to reassemble all three files we've changed (Dskpatch, Disk_io, and Disp_sec) and to link our five files, with Dskpatch listed first:

```
LINK DSKPATCH DISK_IO DISP_SEC VIDEO_IO CURSOR;
```

We've made quite a few changes, so test Dskpatch and make sure it works correctly before you move on.

Writing the Header

Now that we've converted the hard-wired numbers into direct references to memory variables, we can write the procedure WRITE_HEADER to write a status line, or header, at the top of the screen. Our header will look like this:

```
Disk A              Sector 0
```

WRITE_HEADER will use WRITE_DECIMAL to write the current sector number in decimal. It will also write two strings of characters, *Disk* and *Sector* (each followed by a blank space), and a disk letter, such as A. We'll place the procedure in the file DISP_SEC.ASM.

To begin, place the following procedure in DISP_SEC.ASM.

Listing 17-9. Add This Procedure to DISP_SEC.ASM.

```
            PUBLIC    WRITE_HEADER
.DATA
            EXTRN     HEADER_LINE_NO:BYTE
            EXTRN     HEADER_PART_1:BYTE
            EXTRN     HEADER_PART_2:BYTE
            EXTRN     DISK_DRIVE_NO:BYTE
            EXTRN     CURRENT_SECTOR_NO:WORD
.CODE
            EXTRN     WRITE_STRING:PROC, WRITE_DECIMAL:PROC
            EXTRN     GOTO_XY:PROC
;-------------------------------------------------------------------;
; This procedure writes the header with disk-drive and sector number. ;
;                                                                   ;
; Uses:       GOTO_XY, WRITE_STRING, WRITE_CHAR, WRITE_DECIMAL      ;
; Reads:      HEADER_LINE_NO, HEADER_PART_1, HEADER_PART_2          ;
;             DISK_DRIVE_NO, CURRENT_SECTOR_NO                      ;
;-------------------------------------------------------------------;
WRITE_HEADER    PROC
            PUSH      DX
            XOR       DL,DL                  ;Move cursor to header line number
            MOV       DH,HEADER_LINE_NO
            CALL      GOTO_XY
            LEA       DX,HEADER_PART_1
            CALL      WRITE_STRING
            MOV       DL,DISK_DRIVE_NO
            ADD       DL,'A'                 ;Print drives A, B, ...
            CALL      WRITE_CHAR
            LEA       DX,HEADER_PART_2
            CALL      WRITE_STRING
            MOV       DX,CURRENT_SECTOR_NO
            CALL      WRITE_DECIMAL
            POP       DX
            RET
WRITE_HEADER    ENDP
```

The procedure WRITE_STRING doesn't exist yet. As you can see, we plan to use it to write a string of characters to the screen. The two strings, HEADER_PART_1 and HEADER_PART_2, are already defined in DSKPATCH.ASM. WRITE_STRING will use DS:DX as the address for the string.

We've chosen to supply our own string-output procedure so that our strings can contain any character, including the $, which we couldn't print with the DOS function 9. Where DOS uses a $ to mark the end of a string, we'll use a hex 0. Here is the procedure. Enter it into VIDEO_IO.ASM:

Listing 17-10. Add This Procedure to VIDEO_IO.ASM

```
               PUBLIC  WRITE_STRING
;----------------------------------------------------------------;
; This procedure writes a string of characters to the screen.  The  ;
; string must end with          DB      0                          ;
;                                                                    ;
; On entry:     DS:DX   Address of the string                       ;
;                                                                    ;
; Uses:         WRITE_CHAR                                          ;
;----------------------------------------------------------------;
WRITE_STRING    PROC
        PUSH    AX
        PUSH    DX
        PUSH    SI
        PUSHF                           ;Save direction flag
        CLD                             ;Set direction for increment (forward)
        MOV     SI,DX                   ;Place address into SI for LODSB
STRING_LOOP:
        LODSB                           ;Get a character into the AL register
        OR      AL,AL                   ;Have we found the 0 yet?
        JZ      END_OF_STRING           ;Yes, we are done with the string
        MOV     DL,AL                   ;No, write character
        CALL    WRITE_CHAR
        JMP     STRING_LOOP
END_OF_STRING:
        POPF                            ;Restore direction flag
        POP     SI
        POP     DX
        POP     AX
        RET
WRITE_STRING    ENDP
```

As it stands now, WRITE_STRING will write characters with ASCII codes below 32 (the space character) as a period (.), because we don't have a version of WRITE_CHAR that will write *any* character. We'll take care of that detail in the next chapter, and—here's the advantage of modular design—we won't have to change WRITE_STRING in the process.

After all our work in this chapter, let's put the icing on the cake. Change DISK_PATCH in DSKPATCH.ASM to include the CALL to WRITE_HEADER:

Listing 17-11. Changes to DISK_PATCH in DSKPATCH.ASM

```
        EXTRN   CLEAR_SCREEN:PROC, READ_SECTOR:PROC
        EXTRN   INIT_SEC_DISP:PROC, WRITE_HEADER:PROC
DISK_PATCH      PROC
        MOV     AX,DGROUP               ;Put data segment into AX
        MOV     DS,AX                   ;Set DS to point to data

        CALL    CLEAR_SCREEN
        CALL    WRITE_HEADER
        CALL    READ_SECTOR
```

Listing 17-11. *continued*

```
        CALL    INIT_SEC_DISP

        MOV     AH,4Ch                        ;Return to DOS
        INT     21h
DISK_PATCH      ENDP
```

Dskpatch should now produce a display like this one:

Figure 17-1. **Dskpatch with the Header at the Top.**

Summary

At last, we've met the ROM BIOS routines inside our IBM PCs and already used two of these routines to help us toward our goal of a full Dskpatch program.

First we learned about INT 10h, function number 6, which we used to clear the screen. We also saw (though very briefly) that this function has more uses than we'll take advantage of in this book. For example, you may eventually find it helpful for scrolling portions of the screen—in Dskpatch or in your own programs.

We then used function 2 of INT 10h to move the cursor to the third line on the screen (line number 2), where we started writing our sector dump.

To make our programs easier to work with, we also rewrote several procedures so they would use memory variables, rather than hard-wired numbers. Now, we'll be able to read other sectors and change the way our program works in other ways, just by changing a few central numbers in DSKPATCH.ASM.

Finally, we wrote the procedures WRITE_HEADER and WRITE_STRING, so we could write a header at the top of the screen. As noted we'll write an improved version of WRITE_CHAR in the next chapter, replacing the dots in the ASCII window of our display with graphics characters. And thanks to modular design, we'll do this without changing any of the procedures that use WRITE_CHAR.

18

THE ULTIMATE WRITE_CHAR

W e made good use of the ROM BIOS routines in the last chapter to clear the screen and move the cursor. But there are many more uses for the ROM BIOS, and we'll see some of them in this chapter.

Using DOS alone, we haven't been able to display all 256 of the characters that the IBM PC can display. So, in this chapter, we'll present a new version of WRITE_CHAR that displays any character, thanks to another VIDEO_IO function.

Then, we'll add another useful procedure, called CLEAR_TO_END_OF_LINE, that clears the line from the cursor to the right edge of the screen. We'll put this to use in WRITE_HEADER, so that it will clear the rest of the line.

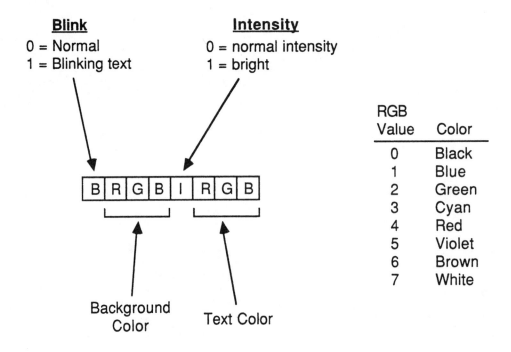

Attribute = background color * 16 + text color

Figure 18-1. Color Table.

Suppose we go from sector number 10 (two digits) to sector number 9. A zero would be left over from the 10 after we call WRITE_HEADER with the sector set to 9. CLEAR_TO_END_OF_LINE will clear this zero, as well as anything else on the remainder of the line.

A New WRITE_CHAR

The ROM BIOS function 9 for INT 10h writes a character and its *attribute* at the current cursor position. The attribute controls such features as underlining, blinking, and color (See Figure 18-1). We'll use only two attributes for Dskpatch: attribute 7, which is the normal attribute, and attribute 70h, which is a foreground color of zero and background of 7 and produces inverse video (black characters on a white background). We can set the attributes individually for each character, and we'll do this later to create a block cursor in inverse video—known as a *phantom* cursor. For now, though, we'll just use the normal attribute when we write a character.

INT 10h, function 9 writes the character and attribute at the current cursor position. Unlike DOS, it doesn't advance the cursor to the next character position unless it writes more than one copy of the character. We'll use this fact later, in a different procedure, but now we only want one copy of each character, so we'll move the cursor ourselves.

Here is the new version of WRITE_CHAR, which writes a character and then moves the cursor right one character. Enter it into the file VIDEO_IO.ASM:

Listing 18-1. Changes to WRITE_CHAR in VIDEO_IO.ASM

```
            PUBLIC   WRITE_CHAR
            EXTRN    CURSOR_RIGHT:PROC
;-------------------------------------------------------------;
; This procedure outputs a character to the screen using the ROM BIOS ;
; routines, so characters such as the backspace are treated as ;
; any other character and are displayed.                      ;
;                                                             ;
; This procedure must do a bit of work to update the cursor position. ;
;                                                             ;
; On entry:   DL      Byte to print on screen                ;
;                                                             ;
; Uses:       CURSOR_RIGHT                                    ;
;-------------------------------------------------------------;
WRITE_CHAR  PROC
            PUSH     AX
            PUSH     BX
            PUSH     CX
            PUSH     DX
            CMP      DL,32                   ;Is character before a space?
            JAE      IS_PRINTABLE            ;No, then print as is
            MOV      DL,'.'                  ;Yes, replace with a period
IS_PRINTABLE:
            MOV      AH,2                    ;Call for character output
            INT      21h                     ;Output character in DL register
```

Listing 18-1. *continued*

```
        MOV     AH,9            ;Call for output of character/attribute
        MOV     BH,0            ;Set to display page 0
        MOV     CX,1            ;Write only one character
        MOV     AL,DL           ;Character to write
        MOV     BL,7            ;Normal attribute
        INT     10h             ;Write character and attribute
        CALL    CURSOR_RIGHT    ;Now move to next cursor position
        POP     DX
        POP     CX
        POP     BX
        POP     AX
        RET
WRITE_CHAR      ENDP
```

In reading through this procedure, you may have wondered why we included the instruction MOV BH,0. If you have a graphics display adapter, your adapter has four text pages in normal text mode. We'll only use the first page, page 0; hence, the instruction.

As for the cursor, WRITE_CHAR uses the procedure CURSOR_RIGHT to move the cursor right one character position or to the beginning of the next line if the movement would take the cursor past column 79. Place the following procedure into CURSOR.ASM:

Listing 18-2. Add This Procedure to CURSOR.ASM

```
        PUBLIC  CURSOR_RIGHT
;-------------------------------------------------------------------;
; This procedure moves the cursor one position to the right or to the ;
; next line if the cursor was at the end of a line.                   ;
;                                                                     ;
; Uses:          SEND_CRLF                                            ;
;-------------------------------------------------------------------;
CURSOR_RIGHT    PROC
        PUSH    AX
        PUSH    BX
        PUSH    CX
        PUSH    DX
        MOV     AH,3            ;Read the current cursor position
        MOV     BH,0            ;On page 0
        INT     10h             ;Read cursor position
        MOV     AH,2            ;Set new cursor position
        INC     DL              ;Set column to next position
        CMP     DL,79           ;Make sure column <= 79
        JBE     OK
        CALL    SEND_CRLF       ;Go to next line
        JMP     DONE
OK:     INT     10h
DONE:   POP     DX
        POP     CX
        POP     BX
        POP     AX
        RET
CURSOR_RIGHT    ENDP
```

CURSOR_RIGHT uses two new INT 10h functions. Function 3 reads the position of the cursor, and function 2 changes the cursor position. The procedure first uses function 3 to find the cursor position, which is returned in two

Disk A   Sector 0

```
        00 01 02 03 04 05 06 07 08 09 0A 0B 0C 0D 0E 0F   0123456789ABCDEF

00 ║  EB 28 90 49 42 4D 20 20 33 2E 32 00 02 02 01 00   δ(ÉIBM  3.2 ☻☻☻
10 ║  02 70 00 D0 02 FD 02 00 09 00 02 00 00 00 00 00   ☻p ╜☻²☻ ☻ ☻ ☻
20 ║  00 00 00 00 00 00 00 00 00 00 FA C4 5C 08 33 ED    .-\□3φ
30 ║  B8 C0 07 8E D8 33 C9 88 16 FD 01 0A D2 79 0A 89   ┐ ╰•Å╫3 ┌ê-²☻ô¬ymÿ☻ë
40 ║  1E 1C 00 8C 06 1E 00 B1 02 8E C5 8E D5 BC 00 7C   ▲└ î♠▲ ░☻à┼à╒╝ |
50 ║  FC 1E 36 C5 36 78 00 BF 2A 7C B9 00 00 F3 A4 1F   ⁿ▲6╫6x ┐*¦│δ Σñ▼
60 ║  C6 06 2E 00 0F BF 78 00 B8 2A 7C AB 91 AB FB 8A   ╞♠. ☼┐x ┐*│½æ½√è
70 ║  16 FD 01 CD 13 A0 10 00 98 F7 26 16 00 03 06 0E   ▬²☻=!¦á► ÿ≈&▬ ♥♠♫
80 ║  00 E8 73 00 E8 79 00 BB 00 05 53 E8 A0 00 5F BE    δs δy ┐ ♦Sδá _²
90 ║  74 01 B9 0B 00 90 F3 A6 75 57 83 C7 15 B1 0B 90   t☻│♂  δªuWâ╟§░♂É
A0 ║  90 F3 A6 75 4C 26 8B 47 1C 99 8B 0E 0B 00 03 C1    δªuL&ïG-Öï♂♂  ♥┴
B0 ║  48 F7 F1 3D 14 00 7F 02 B0 14 96 A1 11 00 B1 04   H≈±=¶ ▲░ûí◄ ░♦
C0 ║  D3 E8 E8 32 00 FF 36 1C 00 C4 1E 70 01 E8 30 00   ╙δδ2  6└ ─♠pδδ♥
D0 ║  E8 5B 00 2B F0 76 0D E8 1D 00 52 F7 26 0B 00 03   δ[ +≡v♪δ♦ R≈&♂ ♥
E0 ║  D8 5A EB E9 5B 8A 2E 15 00 8A 16 FD 01 FF 2E 70   ╪ZδΘ[è.§ è²☻ .p
F0 ║  01 BE 8B 01 EB 54 90 01 06 1C 00 11 2E 1E 00 C3   ☻┐ï☻δT ☻♠└ ◄.▲ ├
```

A>_

Figure 18-2. Dskpatch with the New WRITE_CHAR.

bytes, the column number in DL, and the line number in DH. Then, CUR-SOR_RIGHT increments the column number (in DL) and moves the cursor. If DL was at the last column (79), the procedure sends a carriage-return/line-feed pair to move the cursor to the next line. We don't need this column 79 check in Dskpatch, but including it makes CURSOR_RIGHT a general-purpose proce-dure you can use in any of your own programs.

With these changes, Dskpatch should now display all 256 characters as shown in Figure 18.2.

You can verify that it does by searching for a byte with a value less than 20h and seeing whether some strange character has replaced the period that value formerly produced in the ASCII window.

Now let's do something perhaps even more interesting: Let's write a proce-dure to clear a line from the cursor position to the end.

Clearing to the End of a Line

In the last chapter, we used INT 10h, function 6, to clear the screen in the CLEAR_SCREEN procedure. At that time, we mentioned that function 6 could be used to clear any rectangular window. That capability applies even if a window is only one line high and less than one line long, so we can use function 6 to clear part of a line—to the end of the line.

The left side of the window, in this case, is the column number of the cursor, which we get with a function 3 call (also used by CURSOR_RIGHT). The right side of the window is always at column 79. You can see the details in CLEAR_TO_END_OF_LINE; place the procedure in CURSOR.ASM:

Listing 18-3. Add This Procedure to CURSOR.ASM

```
        PUBLIC  CLEAR_TO_END_OF_LINE
;-------------------------------------------------------------------------;
; This procedure clears the line from the current cursor position to      ;
; the end of that line.                                                   ;
;-------------------------------------------------------------------------;
CLEAR_TO_END_OF_LINE    PROC
        PUSH    AX
        PUSH    BX
        PUSH    CX
        PUSH    DX
        MOV     AH,3            ;Read current cursor position
        XOR     BH,BH           ; on page 0
        INT     10h             ;Now have (X,Y) in DL, DH
        MOV     AH,6            ;Set up to clear to end of line
        XOR     AL,AL           ;Clear window
        MOV     CH,DH           ;All on same line
        MOV     CL,DL           ;Start at the cursor position
        MOV     DL,79           ;And stop at the end of the line
        MOV     BH,7            ;Use normal attribute
        INT     10h
        POP     DX
        POP     CX
        POP     BX
        POP     AX
        RET
CLEAR_TO_END_OF_LINE    ENDP
```

We'll use this procedure in WRITE_HEADER, to clear the rest of the line when we start reading other sectors (we'll do that very soon). There isn't any way for you to see CLEAR_TO_END_OF_LINE work with WRITE_HEADER until we add the procedures that allow us to read a different sector and update the display, but let's revise WRITE_HEADER now, just to get it out of the way. Make the following changes to WRITE_HEADER in VIDEO_IO.ASM, to call CLEAR_TO_END_OF_LINE at the end of the procedure:

Listing 18-4. Changes to WRITE_HEADER in VIDEO_IO.ASM

```
        PUBLIC  WRITE_HEADER
DATA_SEG        SEGMENT PUBLIC
        EXTRN   HEADER_LINE_NO:BYTE
        EXTRN   HEADER_PART_1:BYTE
        EXTRN   HEADER_PART_2:BYTE
        EXTRN   DISK_DRIVE_NO:BYTE
        EXTRN   CURRENT_SECTOR_NO:WORD
DATA_SEG        ENDS
        EXTRN   GOTO_XY:NEAR, CLEAR_TO_END_OF_LINE:NEAR
```

```
;--------------------------------------------------------------------;
;   This procedure writes the header with disk-drive and sector number. ;
;                                                                    ;
; Uses:          GOTO_XY, WRITE_STRING, WRITE_CHAR, WRITE_DECIMAL    ;
;                CLEAR_TO_END_OF_LINE                                ;
; Reads:         HEADER_LINE_NO, HEADER_PART_1, HEADER_PART_2        ;
;                DISK_DRIVE_NO, CURRENT_SECTOR_NO                    ;
;--------------------------------------------------------------------;
WRITE_HEADER    PROC    NEAR
        PUSH    DX
        XOR     DL,DL                   ;Move cursor to header line number
        MOV     DH,HEADER_LINE_NO
        CALL    GOTO_XY
        LEA     DX,HEADER_PART_1
        CALL    WRITE_STRING
        MOV     DL,DISK_DRIVE_NO
        ADD     DL,'A'                  ;Print drives A, B, ...
        CALL    WRITE_CHAR
        LEA     DX,HEADER_PART_2
        CALL    WRITE_STRING
        MOV     DX,CURRENT_SECTOR_NO
        CALL    WRITE_DECIMAL
        CALL    CLEAR_TO_END_OF_LINE    ;Clear rest of sector number
        POP     DX
        RET
WRITE_HEADER    ENDP
```

This revision marks both the final version of WRITE_HEADER and the completion of the file CURSOR.ASM. We are still missing several important parts of Dskpatch, though. In the next chapter, we'll continue on and add the central dispatcher for keyboard commands, we'll be able to press F3 and F4 to read other sectors on the disk.

Summary

This chapter has been relatively easy, without much in the way of new information or tricks. We did learn how to use INT 10h, function number 9, in the ROM BIOS to write any character to the screen.

In the process, we also saw how to read the cursor position with INT 10h function 3, so we could move the cursor right one position after we wrote a character. The reason: INT 10h function 9 doesn't move the cursor after it writes just one character, unless it writes more than one copy of the character. Finally, we put INT 10h function 6 to work clearing part of just one line.

In the next chapter, we'll get down to business again as we build the central dispatcher.

19

THE DISPATCHER

In any language it's nice to have a well-written program that does something, but to really bring a program to life we need to make it interactive. It's human nature to say, "If I do this, you do that," so we'll use this chapter to add some interactivity to Dskpatch.

We'll write a simple keyboard-input procedure and a central dispatcher. The dispatcher's job will be to call the correct procedure for each key pushed. For example, when we press the F3 key to read and display the previous sector, the dispatcher will call a procedure called PREVIOUS_SECTOR. To do this, we'll be making many changes to Dskpatch. We'll start by creating DISPATCHER, the central dispatcher, and some other procedures for display formatting. Next, we'll add two new procedures, PREVIOUS_SECTOR and NEXT_SECTOR, which we'll call through DISPATCHER.

The Dispatcher

The Dispatcher will be the central control for Dskpatch, so all keyboard input and editing will be done through it. DISPATCHER's job will be to read characters and call other procedures to do the work. You'll soon see how the dispatcher does its work, but first let's see how it fits into Dskpatch.

DISPATCHER will have its own prompt line, just under the half-sector display where the cursor waits for keyboard input. You won't be able to enter hex numbers in our first version of the keyboard-input procedure, but later on you will. Here are our first modifications to DSKPATCH.ASM; these add the data for a prompt line:

Listing 19-1. Additions to DATA_SEG in DSKPATCH.ASM

```
HEADER_LINE_NO          DB      0
HEADER_PART_1           DB      'Disk ',0
HEADER_PART_2           DB      '       Sector ',0
        PUBLIC  PROMPT_LINE_NO, EDITOR_PROMPT
PROMPT_LINE_NO          DB      21
EDITOR_PROMPT           DB      'Press function key, or enter'
                        DB      ' character or hex byte: ',0
```

We'll add more prompts later to take care of such matters as inputting a new sector number, so we'll make our job simpler by using a common procedure, WRITE_PROMPT_LINE, to write each prompt line. Each procedure that uses WRITE_PROMPT_LINE will supply it with the address of the prompt (here, the address of EDITOR_PROMPT), and then write the prompt on line 21 (because PROMPT_LINE_NO is 21). For example, this new version of

DISK_PATCH (in DSKPATCH.ASM) uses WRITE_PROMPT_LINE just before it calls DISPATCHER:

Listing 19-2. Additions to DISK_PATCH in DSKPATCH.ASM

```
            EXTRN   CLEAR_SCREEN:PROC, READ_SECTOR:PROC
            EXTRN   INIT_SEC_DISP:PROC, WRITE_HEADER:PROC
            EXTRN   WRITE_PROMPT_LINE:PROC, DISPATCHER:PROC
DISK_PATCH  PROC
            MOV     AX,DGROUP               ;Put data segment into AX
            MOV     DS,AX                   ;Set DS to point to data

            CALL    CLEAR_SCREEN
            CALL    WRITE_HEADER
            CALL    READ_SECTOR
            CALL    INIT_SEC_DISP
            LEA     DX,EDITOR_PROMPT
            CALL    WRITE_PROMPT_LINE
            CALL    DISPATCHER

            MOV     AH,4C                   ;Return to DOS
            INT     21h
DISK_PATCH  ENDP
```

The dispatcher itself is a fairly simple program, but we do use some new tricks in it. The following listing is our first version of the file DIS-PATCH.ASM:

Listing 19-3. The New File DISPATCH.ASM.

```
.MODEL  SMALL

.CODE
            EXTRN   NEXT_SECTOR:PROC        ;In DISK_IO.ASM
            EXTRN   PREVIOUS_SECTOR:PROC    ;In DISK_IO.ASM
.DATA
;-----------------------------------------------------------------------;
; This table contains the legal extended ASCII keys and the addresses   ;
; of the procedures that should be called when each key is pressed.      ;
;                                                                       ;
; The format of the table is                                            ;
;               DB      72                      ;Extended code for cursor up ;
;               DW      OFFSET_TEXT:PHANTOM_UP                          ;
;-----------------------------------------------------------------------;
DISPATCH_TABLE  LABEL   BYTE
                DB      61                      ;F3
                DW      OFFSET_TEXT:PREVIOUS_SECTOR
                DB      62                      ;F4
                DW      OFFSET_TEXT:NEXT_SECTOR
                DB      0                       ;End of the table


.CODE
            PUBLIC  DISPATCHER
            EXTRN   READ_BYTE:PROC
;-----------------------------------------------------------------------;
; This is the central dispatcher. During normal editing and viewing,    ;
; this procedure reads characters from the keyboard and, if the char    ;
; is a command key (such as a cursor key), DISPATCHER calls the          ;
; procedures that do the actual work.  This dispatching is done for      ;
; special keys listed in the table DISPATCH_TABLE, where the procedure   ;
```

Listing 19-3. *continued*

```
; addresses are stored just after the key names.                        ;
;                                                                        ;
; If the character is not a special key, then it should be placed       ;
; directly into the sector buffer--this is the editing mode.            ;
;                                                                        ;
; Uses:          READ_BYTE                                              ;
;------------------------------------------------------------------------;
DISPATCHER      PROC
        PUSH    AX
        PUSH    BX
DISPATCH_LOOP:
        CALL    READ_BYTE               ;Read character into AX
        OR      AH,AH                   ;AX = -10 if no character read, 1
                                        ; for an extended code.
        JS      DISPATCH_LOOP           ;No character read, try again
        JNZ     SPECIAL_KEY             ;Read extended code
; do nothing with the character for now
        JMP     DISPATCH_LOOP           ;Read another character
SPECIAL_KEY:
        CMP     AL,68                   ;F10--exit?
        JE      END_DISPATCH            ;Yes, leave
                                        ;Use BX to look through table
        LEA     BX,DISPATCH_TABLE
SPECIAL_LOOP:
        CMP     BYTE PTR [BX],0         ;End of table?
        JE      NOT_IN_TABLE            ;Yes, key was not in the table
        CMP     AL,[BX]                 ;Is it this table entry?
        JE      DISPATCH                ;Yes, then dispatch
        ADD     BX,3                    ;No, try next entry
        JMP     SPECIAL_LOOP            ;Check next table entry

DISPATCH:
        INC     BX                      ;Point to address of procedure
        CALL    WORD PTR [BX]           ;Call procedure
        JMP     DISPATCH_LOOP           ;Wait for another key

NOT_IN_TABLE:                           ;Do nothing, just read next character
        JMP     DISPATCH_LOOP

END_DISPATCH:
        POP     BX
        POP     AX
        RET
DISPATCHER      ENDP

        END
```

DISPATCH_TABLE holds the extended ASCII codes for the F3 and F4 keys. Each code is followed by the address of the procedure DISPATCHER should call when it reads that particular extended code. For example, when READ_BYTE, which is called by DISPATCHER, reads an F3 key (extended code 61), DIS-PATCHER calls the procedure PREVIOUS_SECTOR.

The addresses of the procedures we want DISPATCHER to call are in the dispatch table, so we used a new directive, OFFSET, to obtain them. The line

```
DW      OFFSET _TEXT:PREVIOUS_SECTOR
```

for example, tells the assembler to use the *offset* of our PREVIOUS_SECTOR procedure. This offset is calculated relative to the start of our code segment

_TEXT, which is why we put the _TEXT: in front of the procedure name. (As it turns out here, this _TEXT: isn't absolutely necessary. Still, in the interest of clarity, we'll write OFFSET _TEXT: anyway.)

Notice that DISPATCH_TABLE contains both byte and word data. This raises a few considerations. In the past, we've always dealt with tables of one type or the other: either all words, or all bytes. But here, we have both, so we have to tell the assembler which type of data to expect when we use a CMP or CALL instruction. In the case of an instruction written like this:

```
CMP     [BX],0
```

the assembler doesn't know whether we want to compare words or bytes. But by writing the instruction like this:

```
CMP     BYTE PTR [BX],0
```

we tell the assembler that BX points to a byte and that we want a byte compare. Similarly, the instruction CMP WORD PTR [BX],0 would compare words. On the other hand, an instruction like CMP AL,[BX] doesn't cause any problems, because AL is a byte register, and the assembler knows without being told that we want a byte compare.

Then, too, remember that a CALL instruction can be either a NEAR or a FAR CALL. A NEAR CALL needs one word for the address, while the FAR CALL needs two. Here, the instruction:

```
CALL    WORD PTR [BX]
```

tells the assembler, with WORD PTR, that [BX] points to one word, so it should generate a NEAR CALL and use the word pointed to by [BX] as the address, that being the address we stored in DISPATCH_TABLE. (For a FAR CALL, which uses a two-word address, we would use the instruction CALL DWORD PTR [BX]. DWORD stands for *Double Word*, or two words.)

As you'll see in Chapter 22, we can easily add more key commands to Dskpatch simply by adding more procedures and placing new entries in DIS-PATCH_TABLE. Right now, however, we still need to add four procedures before we can test this new version of Dskpatch. We're missing READ_BYTE, WRITE_PROMPT_LINE, PREVIOUS_SECTOR, and NEXT_SECTOR.

READ_BYTE is a procedure to read characters and extended ASCII codes from the keyboard. The final version will be able to read special keys (such as the function and cursor keys), ASCII characters, and two-digit hex numbers. At this point, we'll write a simple version of READ_BYTE—to read either a character or a special key. Here is the first version of KBD_IO.ASM, which is the file in which we'll store all our procedures to read from the keyboard:

Listing 19-4. The New File KBD_IO.ASM

```
.MODEL   SMALL
.CODE

         PUBLIC   READ_BYTE
;---------------------------------------------------------------;
; This procedure reads a single ASCII character.  This is just  ;
; a test version of READ_BYTE.                                  ;
;                                                               ;
; Returns:       AL       Character code (unless AH = 1)        ;
;                AH       0 if read ASCII char                  ;
;                         1 if read a special key               ;
;---------------------------------------------------------------;
READ_BYTE        PROC
         XOR     AH,AH                    ;Ask for keyboard read function
         INT     16h                      ;Read character/scan code from keyboard
         OR      AL,AL                    ;Is it an extended code?
         JZ      EXTENDED_CODE            ;Yes
NOT_EXTENDED:
         XOR     AH,AH                    ;Return just the ASCII code
DONE_READING:
         RET

EXTENDED_CODE:
         MOV     AL,AH                    ;Put scan code into AL
         MOV     AH,1                     ;Signal extended code
         JMP     DONE_READING
READ_BYTE        ENDP

         END
```

READ_BYTE uses a new interrupt, INT 16h, which is an interrupt that gives us access to the keyboard services in the ROM BIOS. Function 0 reads a character from the keyboard without echoing it to the screen. It returns the character code in AL, and the *scan code* in the AH register.

The scan code is the code assigned to each key on the keyboard. Some keys, such as F3 haven't been assigned ASCII codes (which means AL will be 0), but they do have scan codes (you'll find a table of scan codes in Appendix D). READ_BYTE puts this scan code into the AL register for special keys, and sets AH to 1.

Next, add the new procedure WRITE_PROMPT_LINE to DISP_SEC.ASM:

Listing 19-5. Add This Procedure to VIDEO_IO.ASM

```
         PUBLIC   WRITE_PROMPT_LINE
         EXTRN    CLEAR_TO_END_OF_LINE:PROC, WRITE_STRING:PROC
         EXTRN    GOTO_XY:PROC
.DATA
         EXTRN    PROMPT_LINE_NO:BYTE
.CODE
;---------------------------------------------------------------;
; This procedure writes the prompt line to the screen and clears the ;
; end of the line.                                              ;
;                                                               ;
```

```
; On entry       DS:DX    Address of the prompt-line message      ;
;                                                                 ;
; Uses:          WRITE_STRING, CLEAR_TO_END_OF_LINE, GOTO_XY      ;
; Reads:         PROMPT_LINE_NO                                   ;
;-----------------------------------------------------------------;
WRITE_PROMPT_LINE       PROC
        PUSH    DX
        XOR     DL,DL                   ;Write the prompt line and
        MOV     DH,PROMPT_LINE_NO       ; move the cursor there
        CALL    GOTO_XY
        POP     DX
        CALL    WRITE_STRING
        CALL    CLEAR_TO_END_OF_LINE
        RET
WRITE_PROMPT_LINE       ENDP
```

There really isn't much to this procedure. It moves the cursor to the beginning of the prompt line, which we set (in DSKPATCH.ASM) to line 21. Then, it
writes the prompt line and clears the rest of the line. The cursor is at the end of
the prompt when WRITE_PROMPT_LINE is done, and the rest of the line is
cleared by CLEAR_TO_END_OF_LINE.

Reading Other Sectors

Finally, we need the two procedures PREVIOUS_SECTOR and
NEXT_SECTOR, to read and redisplay the previous and next disk sectors. Add
these two procedures to DISK_IO.ASM:

Listing 19-6. Add These Procedures to DISK_IO.ASM

```
        PUBLIC  PREVIOUS_SECTOR
        EXTRN   INIT_SEC_DISP:PROC, WRITE_HEADER:PROC
        EXTRN   WRITE_PROMPT_LINE:PROC
.DATA
        EXTRN   CURRENT_SECTOR_NO:WORD, EDITOR_PROMPT:BYTE
.CODE
;-----------------------------------------------------------------;
; This procedure reads the previous sector, if possible.          ;
;                                                                 ;
; Uses:          WRITE_HEADER, READ_SECTOR, INIT_SEC_DISP         ;
;                WRITE_PROMPT_LINE                                ;
; Reads:         CURRENT_SECTOR_NO, EDITOR_PROMPT                 ;
; Writes:        CURRENT_SECTOR_NO                                ;
;-----------------------------------------------------------------;
PREVIOUS_SECTOR         PROC
        PUSH    AX
        PUSH    DX
        MOV     AX,CURRENT_SECTOR_NO    ;Get current sector number
        OR      AX,AX                   ;Don't decrement if already 0
        JZ      DONT_DECREMENT_SECTOR
        DEC     AX
        MOV     CURRENT_SECTOR_NO,AX    ;Save new sector number
        CALL    WRITE_HEADER
        CALL    READ_SECTOR
        CALL    INIT_SEC_DISP           ;Display new sector
        LEA     DX,EDITOR_PROMPT
        CALL    WRITE_PROMPT_LINE
DONT_DECREMENT_SECTOR:
        POP     DX
        POP     AX
```

Listing 19-6. *continued*

```
        RET
PREVIOUS_SECTOR        ENDP

        PUBLIC   NEXT_SECTOR
        EXTRN    INIT_SEC_DISP:PROC, WRITE_HEADER:PROC
        EXTRN    WRITE_PROMPT_LINE:PROC
.DATA
        EXTRN    CURRENT_SECTOR_NO:WORD, EDITOR_PROMPT:BYTE
.CODE
;-----------------------------------------------------------------------;
;                                                                       ;
; Reads the next sector.                                                ;
;                                                                       ;
; Uses:         WRITE_HEADER, READ_SECTOR, INIT_SEC_DISP                ;
;               WRITE_PROMPT_LINE                                       ;
; Reads:        CURRENT_SECTOR_NO, EDITOR_PROMPT                        ;
; Writes:       CURRENT_SECTOR_NO                                       ;
;-----------------------------------------------------------------------;
NEXT_SECTOR     PROC
        PUSH     AX
        PUSH     DX
        MOV      AX,CURRENT_SECTOR_NO
        INC      AX                     ;Move to next sector
        MOV      CURRENT_SECTOR_NO,AX
        CALL     WRITE_HEADER
        CALL     READ_SECTOR
        CALL     INIT_SEC_DISP          ;Display new sector
        LEA      DX,EDITOR_PROMPT
        CALL     WRITE_PROMPT_LINE
        POP      DX
        POP      AX
        RET
NEXT_SECTOR     ENDP
```

Now, you're ready to assembly all the files we created or changed: Dskpatch, Video_io, Kbd_io, Dispatch, and Disk_io. When you link the Dskpatch files, remember there are now seven of them: Dskpatch, Disp_sec, Disk_io, Video_io, Kbd_io, Dispatch, and Cursor.

If you are using Make, here are the additions you need to make to the Makefile Dskpatch (the backslash at the end of the fourth line from the bottom tells Make we're continuing the list of files onto the next line):

Listing 19-7. Changes to the Make File MAKEFILE

```
                .
                .
                .
cursor.obj:     cursor.asm
        masm cursor;

dispatch.obj:   dispatch.asm
        masm dispatch;

kbd_io.obj:     kbd_io.asm
        masm kbd_io;

dskpatch.exe:   dskpatch.obj disk_io.obj disp_sec.obj video_io.obj cursor.obj \
                dispatch.obj kbd_io.obj
        link dskpatch disk_io disp_sec video_io cursor dispatch kbd_io;
```

Disk A   Sector 0

```
        00 01 02 03 04 05 06 07 08 09 0A 0B 0C 0D 0E 0F   0123456789ABCDEF

00 ║ EB 28 90 49 42 4D 20 20 33 2E 32 00 02 02 01 00 │ δ(ÉIBM   3.2 ☺☻⌂
10 ║ 02 70 00 D0 02 FD 02 00 09 00 02 00 00 00 00 00 │ ☻p  ╜⌐☻☺ ○ ☺
20 ║ 00 00 00 00 00 00 00 00 00 00 FA C4 5C 08 33 ED │           .─╢3φ
30 ║ B8 C0 07 8E D8 33 C9 88 16 FD 01 0A D2 79 0A 89 │ ╕ └•Ä┼3┌ê·²☺☺╥y◘ë
40 ║ 1E 1C 00 8C 06 1E 00 B1 02 8E C5 8E D5 BC 00 7C │ ▲∟ î♠▲ ▒☻Ä┼Ä╒╝ |
50 ║ FC 1E 36 C5 36 78 00 BF 2A 7C B9 0B 00 F3 A4 1F │ ⁿ▲6╞6x ╕*|╣♂ ≤ñ▼
60 ║ C6 06 2E 00 0F BF 78 00 B8 2A 7C AB 91 AB FB 8A │ ╞♠. ☼╕x ╕*|½æ½√è
70 ║ 16 FD 01 CD 13 A0 10 00 98 F7 26 16 00 03 06 0E │ ▬²☺═‼á►  ÿ≈&▬ ♥♠♫
80 ║ 00 E8 73 00 E8 79 00 BB 00 05 53 E8 A0 00 5F BE │  ╚s ╚y ╗ ♣S╚á _╛
90 ║ 74 01 B9 0B 00 90 F3 A6 75 57 83 C7 15 B1 0B 90 │ t☺╣♂  ≤ªuWâ╟§▒♂
A0 ║ 90 F3 A6 75 4C 26 8B 47 1C 99 8B 0E 0B 00 03 C1 │ ≤ªuL&ïG∟Öï♂♂  ┴
B0 ║ 48 F7 F1 3D 14 00 7F 02 B0 14 96 A1 11 00 B1 04 │ H≈±=¶ ⌂☻░¶û í◄ ▒♦
C0 ║ D3 E8 E8 32 00 FF 36 1C 00 C4 1E 70 01 E8 30 00 │ ╙╚╚2  6∟ ─▲p☺╚0
D0 ║ E8 5B 00 2B F0 76 0D E8 1D 00 52 F7 26 0B 00 03 │ ╚[ +≡v♪╚↔ R≈&♂  ♥
E0 ║ D8 5A E8 E9 5B 8A 2E 15 00 8A 16 FD 01 FF 2E 70 │ ┼Z♦è.§ è·²☺ .p
F0 ║ 01 BE 8B 01 EB 54 90 01 06 1C 00 11 2E 1E 00 C3 │ ☺╛ï☺ïT ☺♠∟ ◄.▲ ├
```

Press function key, or enter character or hex byte: _

Figure 19-1. Dskpatch with the Prompt Line.

(Remember that the last three lines need to be at the top of your file if you're using Borland's Make. If you're using OPTASM, you need to add four lines to assemble dispatch and kbd_io.) If you do not have Make, you may wish to write the following short batch file to link and create your .EXE file:

```
LINK DSKPATCH DISK_IO DISP_SEC VIDEO_IO CURSOR DISPATCH KBD_IO;
```

As we add more files, you'll only need to change this batch file, rather than type this long link list each time you rebuild the .EXE program.

This version of Dskpatch has three active keys: F3 reads and displays the previous sector, stopping at sector 0; F4 reads the next sector; F10 exits from Dskpatch. Give these keys a try. Your display should now look something like Figure 19-1.

Philosophy of the Following Chapters

We covered far more ground than usual in this chapter, and in that respect you've had a taste of the philosophy we'll be following in Chapters 20 through 27. From now on, we'll clip along at a fairly rapid pace, so that we can get through more examples of how to write large programs. You'll also find more procedures that you can use in your own programs.

These chapters are here for you to learn from, hence the rather high density of new procedures. But in the chapters in Part IV of the book, we'll come back to learning new subjects, so hang on, or (if you wish) skip the remaining chapters on Dskpatch until you're ready to write your own programs. When you're ready to come back again, you'll find many useful tidbits for programming.

Of course, if you're champing at the bit and eager to write your own procedures, read the next chapter. There, you'll find a number of hints, and we'll give you a chance to write the procedures in following chapters by giving you enough details to forge ahead.

From Chapter 21 on, we'll present many different procedures and let you discover how they work. Why? There are two reasons, both related to setting you on your feet and on your way to assembly language programming. First, we want you to have a library of procedures you can use in your own programs; to use them comfortably, you need to exercise your own skills. Second, by presenting this large programming example, we want to show you not only how to write a large program, but to give you a feel for it as well.

So take the rest of this book in the way that suits you best. Chapter 20 is for those of you eager to write your own programs. In Chapter 21, we'll return to Dskpatch and build the procedures to write and move what we call a phantom cursor: a reverse-video cursor for the hex and ASCII displays.

20

A PROGRAMMING CHALLENGE

This book contains six more chapters of procedures. If you want to try navigating on your own, read this chapter. We'll chart a course for you here, and plot your way through Chapters 21 and 22. Then you can try to write the procedures in each chapter before you read it. If you don't wish to try writing pieces of Dskpatch just yet, skip this chapter for now. It's very brief and leaves many details to your imagination.

If you decide to read through this chapter, here's a suggestion on how to proceed: Read one section and then try to make your own corresponding changes to Dskpatch. When you feel you've made enough progress, read the chapter with the same name as the section title. After you've read the corresponding chapter, then you can go on to read the next section.

> **Note**: You may want to make a copy of all your files before you start making changes. Then when you get to Chapter 21, you'll have the choice of following along with the changes, or using your own version.

The Phantom Cursors

In Chapter 21 we'll place two phantom cursors on the screen: one in the hex window and one in the ASCII window. A phantom cursor is similar to a normal cursor, but it doesn't blink and the background turns white, with the characters black, as you can see in Figure 20-1.

The phantom cursor in the hex window is four characters wide, while the one in the ASCII window is only one character wide.

How do we create a phantom cursor? Each character on the screen has an *attribute* byte. This byte tells your IBM PC how to display each character. An attribute code of 7h displays a normal character, while 70h displays a character in inverse video. The latter is exactly what we want for the phantom cursor, so the question is: How can we change the attribute of our characters to 70h?

INT 10h function 9 writes both a character and an attribute to the screen, and INT 10h function 8 reads the character code at the current cursor position. We can create a phantom cursor in the hex window with the following steps:

- Save the position of the real cursor (use INT 10h function 3 to read the cursor position and save this in variables).
- Move the real cursor to the start of the phantom cursor in the hex window.

- For the next four characters, read the character code (function 8) and write both the character and its attribute (setting the attribute to 70h).
- Finally, restore the old cursor position.

```
Disk A          Sector 0

      00 01 02 03 04 05 06 07 08 09 0A 0B 0C 0D 0E 0F   0123456789ABCDEF

00    EB 21 90 49 42 4D 20 20 33 2E 31 00 02 02 01 00   Ƌ!ÉIBM   3.1 ⌂⌂Ɗ
10    02 70 00 D0 02 FD 02 00 09 00 02 00 00 00 00 00   Ɗp ⌐Ɗ²Ɗ ○ Ɗ
20    00 00 00 C4 5C 08 33 ED B8 C0 07 8E D8 33 C9 0A   ─\3↓┐L•Ȧ‡3┌⌐
30    D2 79 0E 89 1E 1E 00 8C 06 20 00 88 16 22 00 B1   ┬уñë▲▲ î↕ ê¸"▐
40    02 8E C5 8E D5 BC 00 7C 51 FC 1E 36 C5 36 78 00   ƋȦ┤Ȧ┘ !Q▐▲6┼6x
50    BF 23 7C B9 0B 00 F3 A4 1F 88 8E 2C 00 A0 18 00   ┐#!┘δ ⌐ñvêñ, át
60    A2 27 00 BF 78 00 B8 23 7C AB 91 AB A1 16 00 D1   ó' ┐x ¶!¼₪½í¸ ┬
70    E0 40 E8 00 00 E8 86 00 BB 00 05 53 B0 01 E8 AB   «∅δÇ δå ┐ ↕S░∅δ½
80    00 5F BE 73 01 B9 0B 00 90 F3 A6 75 62 83 C7 15   ┘ s∅▐δ É≤ªubâ┃§
90    B1 0B 90 90 F3 A6 75 57 26 8B 47 1C 99 8B 0E 0B   ┃δÉÉ≤ªuW&ïG¬öïñδ
A0    00 03 C1 48 F7 F1 80 3E 71 01 60 75 02 B0 14 96   ♦┴H≡±Ç)q∅`u∅░ûû
B0    A1 11 00 B1 04 D3 E8 E8 3B 00 FF 36 1E 00 C4 1E   í◄ ┃♦┘δδ; 6▲ ─▲
C0    6F 01 E8 39 00 E8 64 00 2B F0 76 0D E8 26 00 52   o∅δ9 δd +≡v♪8& R
D0    F7 26 0B 00 03 D8 5A EB E9 CD 11 B9 02 00 D3 E0   ≈&δ ♥Ƶδ=◄∥∅ ┗«
E0    00 E4 03 74 04 FE C4 8A CC 5B 58 FF 2E 6F 01 BE   ÇΣ♥t•─èⱢ[X .o∅▐
F0    89 01 EB 55 90 01 06 1E 00 11 2E 20 00 C3 A1 18   ê∅δUÉ∅♠▲ ◄. ⌐ít
```

Press function key, or enter character or hex byte:

Figure 20-1. A Display with Phantom Cursors.

We write a phantom cursor in the ASCII window in much the same way. Once you have a working phantom cursor in the hex window, you can add the extra code for the ASCII window.

Keep in mind that your first try is only temporary. Once you have a working program with phantom cursors, you can go back and rewrite your changes, so you have a number of small procedures to do the work. Look at the procedures in Chapter 21 when you're done, to see one way of doing this.

Simple Editing

Once we have our phantom cursors, we'll want to move them around on the screen. We have to pay attention here to boundary conditions to keep the phantom cursors inside each of the two windows. We also want our two phantom cursors to move together, since they represent the hex and ASCII representations of the same thing.

How can we move each phantom cursor? Each of the four cursor keys on the keypad sends out a special function number: 72 for cursor up, 80 for cursor down, 75 for cursor left, and 77 for cursor right. These are the numbers we need to add to DISPATCH_TABLE, along with the addresses of the four procedures to move the phantom cursors in each of these four directions.

To actually move each phantom cursor, erase it, then change its two coordinates and write it again. If you've been careful about how you wrote the phantom cursors, the four procedures to move them should be fairly simple.

Whenever you type a character on the keyboard, Dskpatch should read this character and replace the byte under the phantom cursor with the character just read. Here are the steps for simple editing:

- Read a character from the keyboard.
- Change the hex number in the hex window and the character in the ASCII window to match the character just read.
- Change the byte in the sector buffer, SECTOR.

Here's a simple hint: You don't have to make many changes to add editing. Dispatch requires little more than calling a new procedure (we've called it EDIT_BYTE) that does most of the work. EDIT_BYTE is responsible for changing both the screen and SECTOR.

Other Additions and Changes to Dskpatch

From Chapter 23 through Chapter 27, the changes start to become somewhat trickier and more involved. If you're still interested in writing your own version, consider this: What more would you like to see Dskpatch do than it does right now? We've used the following ideas in the remaining chapters.

We want a new version of READ_BYTE that will read either one character or a two-digit hex number and wait for us to press the Enter key before it returns a character to Dispatch. This part of our "wish list" isn't as simple as it sounds, and we'll spend two chapters (Chapters 23 and 24) working on this problem.

In Chapter 25, we'll go bug hunting, then in Chapter 26 we'll learn how to write modified sectors back to the disk using the DOS INT 26h function, which is analogous to the INT 25h that we used to read a sector from the disk. (In

Chapter 26 we won't check for read errors, but you'll find such checks in the disk version of Dskpatch that is available with this book.)

Finally, in Chapter 27, we'll make some changes to Dskpatch so we can see the other half of our sector display. These changes won't allow us to scroll through the sector display as freely as we'd like but, again, those changes are on the disk version of Dskpatch.

21

THE PHANTOM CURSORS

In this chapter we'll build the procedures to write and erase a phantom cursor in the hex window, and another in the ASCII window. A phantom cursor is so called because it's not the PC's hardware cursor; it's a shadow—albeit a rather unusual shadow, since it inverts the character, turning the background to white and the character to black. In the hex window, we have the room to make this cursor four characters wide so it will be easy to read. In the ASCII window, our phantom cursor will be just one character wide, because there is no room between characters.

We have a lot of procedures and code to cover here, so we'll describe these procedures only briefly.

The Phantom Cursors

INIT_SEC_DISP is the only procedure we have that changes the sector display. A new display appears when we start Dskpatch, and each time we read a new sector. Since our phantom cursors will be in the sector display, we'll begin our work here by placing a call to WRITE_PHANTOM in INIT_SEC_DISP. That way, we'll write the phantom cursors every time we write a new sector display.

Here is the revised—and final—version of INIT_SEC_DISP in DISP_SEC.ASM:

Listing 21-1. Changes to INIT_SEC_DISP in DISP_SEC.ASM

```
        PUBLIC    INIT_SEC_DISP
        EXTRN     WRITE_PATTERN:PROC, SEND_CRLF:PROC
        EXTRN     GOTO_XY:PROC, WRITE_PHANTOM:PROC
.DATA
        EXTRN     LINES_BEFORE_SECTOR:BYTE
        EXTRN     SECTOR_OFFSET:WORD
.CODE
;---------------------------------------------------------------;
;   This procedure initializes the half-sector display.         ;
;                                                               ;
; Uses:   WRITE_PATTERN, SEND_CRLF, DISP_HALF_SECTOR            ;
;         WRITE_TOP_HEX_NUMBERS, GOTO_XY, WRITE_PHANTOM         ;
; Reads:  TOP_LINE_PATTERN, BOTTOM_LINE_PATTERN                 ;
;         LINES_BEFORE_SECTOR                                   ;
; Writes: SECTOR_OFFSET                                         ;
;---------------------------------------------------------------;
INIT_SEC_DISP   PROC
        PUSH      DX
        XOR       DL,DL                   ;Move cursor into position
        MOV       DH,LINES_BEFORE_SECTOR
        CALL      GOTO_XY
        CALL      WRITE_TOP_HEX_NUMBERS
        LEA       DX,TOP_LINE_PATTERN
        CALL      WRITE_PATTERN
        CALL      SEND_CRLF
        XOR       DX,DX                   ;Start at the beginning of the sector
```

```
        MOV         SECTOR_OFFSET,DX        ;Set sector offset to 0
        CALL        DISP_HALF_SECTOR
        LEA         DX,BOTTOM_LINE_PATTERN
        CALL        WRITE_PATTERN
        CALL        WRITE_PHANTOM           ;Display the phantom cursor
        POP         DX
        RET
INIT_SEC_DISP ENDP
```

Note that we've also updated INIT_SEC_DISP to use and initialize variables. It now sets SECTOR_OFFSET to zero to display the first half of a sector.

Let's move on to WRITE_PHANTOM itself. This will take quite a bit of work. Altogether, we have to write six procedures, including WRITE_PHANTOM. The idea is fairly simple, though. First, we move the real cursor to the position of the phantom cursor in the hex window and change the attribute of the next four characters to inverse video (attribute 70h). This creates a block of white, four characters wide, with the hex number in black. Then we do the same in the ASCII window, but for a single character. Finally, we move the real cursor back to where it was when we started. All the procedures for the phantom cursors will be in PHANTOM.ASM, with the exception of WRITE_ATTRIBUTE_N_ TIMES, the procedure that will set the attribute of characters.

Enter the following procedures into the file PHANTOM.ASM:

Listing 21-2. The New File PHANTOM.ASM

```
    .MODEL      SMALL

    .DATA

REAL_CURSOR_X           DB  0
REAL_CURSOR_Y           DB  0
        PUBLIC      PHANTOM_CURSOR_X, PHANTOM_CURSOR_Y
PHANTOM_CURSOR_X        DB  0
PHANTOM_CURSOR_Y        DB  0

    .CODE

        PUBLIC      MOV_TO_HEX_POSITION
        EXTRN       GOTO_XY:PROC
    .DATA
        EXTRN       LINES_BEFORE_SECTOR:BYTE
    .CODE
;-------------------------------------------------------------------;
; This procedure moves the real cursor to the position of the phantom ;
; cursor in the hex window.                                          ;
;                                                                    ;
; Uses:       GOTO_XY                                                ;
; Reads:      LINES_BEFORE_SECTOR, PHANTOM_CURSOR_X,PHANTOM_CURSOR_Y  ;
;-------------------------------------------------------------------;
MOV_TO_HEX_POSITION PROC
        PUSH        AX
        PUSH        CX
        PUSH        DX
        MOV         DH,LINES_BEFORE_SECTOR  ;Find row of phantom (0,0)
        ADD         DH,2                    ;Plus row of hex and horizontal bar
        ADD         DH,PHANTOM_CURSOR_Y     ;DH = row of phantom cursor
        MOV         DL,8                    ;Indent on left side
        MOV         CL,3                    ;Each column uses 3 characters, so
        MOV         AL,PHANTOM_CURSOR_X     ; we must multiply CURSOR_X by 3
```

Listing 21-2. *continued*

```
        MUL     CL
        ADD     DL,AL                   ;And add to the indent, to get column
        CALL    GOTO_XY                 ; for phantom cursor
        POP     DX
        POP     CX
        POP     AX
        RET
MOV_TO_HEX_POSITION ENDP

        PUBLIC  MOV_TO_ASCII_POSITION
        EXTRN   GOTO_XY:PROC
.DATA
        EXTRN   LINES_BEFORE_SECTOR:BYTE
.CODE
;-------------------------------------------------------------------;
; This procedure moves the real cursor to the beginning of the phantom ;
; cursor in the ASCII window.                                       ;
;                                                                   ;
; Uses:       GOTO_XY                                               ;
; Reads:      LINES_BEFORE_SECTOR, PHANTOM_CURSOR_X, PHANTOM_CURSOR_Y ;
;-------------------------------------------------------------------;
MOV_TO_ASCII_POSITION   PROC
        PUSH    AX
        PUSH    DX
        MOV     DH,LINES_BEFORE_SECTOR  ;Find row of phantom (0,0)
        ADD     DH,2                    ;Plus row of hex and horizontal bar
        ADD     DH,PHANTOM_CURSOR_Y     ;DH = row of phantom cursor
        MOV     DL,59                   ;Indent on left side
        ADD     DL,PHANTOM_CURSOR_X     ;Add CURSOR_X to get X position
        CALL    GOTO_XY                 ; for phantom cursor
        POP     DX
        POP     AX
        RET
MOV_TO_ASCII_POSITION   ENDP

        PUBLIC  SAVE_REAL_CURSOR
;-------------------------------------------------------------------;
; This procedure saves the position of the real cursor in the two   ;
; variables REAL_CURSOR_X and REAL_CURSOR_Y.                        ;
;                                                                   ;
; Writes:     REAL_CURSOR_X, REAL_CURSOR_Y                          ;
;-------------------------------------------------------------------;
SAVE_REAL_CURSOR        PROC
        PUSH    AX
        PUSH    BX
        PUSH    CX
        PUSH    DX
        MOV     AH,3                    ;Read cursor position
        XOR     BH,BH                   ; on page 0
        INT     10h                     ;And return in DL,DH
        MOV     REAL_CURSOR_Y,DL        ;Save position
        MOV     REAL_CURSOR_X,DH
        POP     DX
        POP     CX
        POP     BX
        POP     AX
        RET
SAVE_REAL_CURSOR        ENDP

        PUBLIC  RESTORE_REAL_CURSOR
        EXTRN   GOTO_XY:PROC
;-------------------------------------------------------------------;
; This procedure restores the real cursor to its old position, saved in ;
; REAL_CURSOR_X and REAL_CURSOR_Y.                                  ;
;                                                                   ;
; Uses:       GOTO_XY                                               ;
; Reads:      REAL_CURSOR_X, REAL_CURSOR_Y                          ;
;-------------------------------------------------------------------;
```

```
RESTORE_REAL_CURSOR PROC
     PUSH    DX
     MOV     DL,REAL_CURSOR_Y
     MOV     DH,REAL_CURSOR_X
     CALL    GOTO_XY
     POP     DX
     RET
RESTORE_REAL_CURSOR ENDP

     PUBLIC  WRITE_PHANTOM
     EXTRN   WRITE_ATTRIBUTE_N_TIMES:PROC
;---------------------------------------------------------------------;
; This procedure uses CURSOR_X and CURSOR_Y, through MOV_TO_..., as the ;
; coordinates for the phantom cursor.  WRITE_PHANTOM writes this        ;
; phantom cursor.                                                       ;
;                                                                       ;
; Uses:        WRITE_ATTRIBUTE_N_TIMES, SAVE_REAL_CURSOR                ;
;              RESTORE_REAL_CURSOR, MOV_TO_HEX_POSITION                 ;
;              MOV_TO_ASCII_POSITION                                    ;
;---------------------------------------------------------------------;
WRITE_PHANTOM  PROC
     PUSH    CX
     PUSH    DX
     CALL    SAVE_REAL_CURSOR
     CALL    MOV_TO_HEX_POSITION       ;Coord. of cursor in hex window
     MOV     CX,4                      ;Make phantom cursor four chars wide
     MOV     DL,70h
     CALL    WRITE_ATTRIBUTE_N_TIMES
     CALL    MOV_TO_ASCII_POSITION     ;Coord. of cursor in ASCII window
     MOV     CX,1                      ;Cursor is one character wide here
     CALL    WRITE_ATTRIBUTE_N_TIMES
     CALL    RESTORE_REAL_CURSOR
     POP     DX
     POP     CX
     RET
WRITE_PHANTOM  ENDP

     PUBLIC  ERASE_PHANTOM
     EXTRN   WRITE_ATTRIBUTE_N_TIMES:PROC
;---------------------------------------------------------------------;
; This procedure erases the phantom cursor, just the opposite of        ;
; WRITE_PHANTOM.                                                        ;
;                                                                       ;
; Uses:        WRITE_ATTRIBUTE_N_TIMES, SAVE_REAL_CURSOR                ;
;              RESTORE_REAL_CURSOR, MOV_TO_HEX_POSITION                 ;
;              MOV_TO_ASCII_POSITION                                    ;
;---------------------------------------------------------------------;
ERASE_PHANTOM  PROC
     PUSH    CX
     PUSH    DX
     CALL    SAVE_REAL_CURSOR
     CALL    MOV_TO_HEX_POSITION       ;Coord. of cursor in hex window
     MOV     CX,4                      ;Change back to white on black
     MOV     DL,7
     CALL    WRITE_ATTRIBUTE_N_TIMES
     CALL    MOV_TO_ASCII_POSITION
     MOV     CX,1
     CALL    WRITE_ATTRIBUTE_N_TIMES
     CALL    RESTORE_REAL_CURSOR
     POP     DX
     POP     CX
     RET
ERASE_PHANTOM  ENDP


     END
```

WRITE_PHANTOM and ERASE_PHANTOM are much the same. In fact, the only difference is in the attribute used: WRITE_PHANTOM sets the attribute to 70h for inverse video, while ERASE_PHANTOM sets to attribute back to the normal attribute (7).

Both of these procedures save the old position of the real cursor with SAVE_REAL_CURSOR, which uses the INT 10h function number 3 to read the position of the cursor and then saves this position in the two bytes REAL_CURSOR_X and REAL_CURSOR_Y.

After saving the real cursor position, both WRITE_PHANTOM and ERASE_PHANTOM then call MOV_TO_HEX_POSITION, which moves the cursor to the start of the phantom cursor in the hex window. Next, WRITE_ATTRIBUTE_N_TIMES writes the inverse-video attribute for four characters, starting at the cursor and moving to the right. This writes the phantom cursor in the hex window. In much the same way, WRITE_PHANTOM then writes a phantom cursor one character wide in the ASCII window. Finally, RESTORE_REAL_CURSOR restores the position of the real cursor to the position it was in before the call to WRITE_PHANTOM.

The only procedure we have left unwritten is WRITE_ATTRIBUTE_N_TIMES, so let's take care of it now.

Changing Character Attributes

We're going to use WRITE_ATTRIBUTE_N_TIMES to do three things. First, it will read the character under the cursor position. We'll do this because the INT 10h function we use to set a character's attribute, function number 9, writes both the character *and* the attribute under the cursor. Thus, WRITE_ATTRIBUTE_N_TIMES will change the attribute by writing the new attribute along with the character just read. Finally, the procedure will move the cursor right to the next character position, so we can repeat the whole process N times. You can see the details in the procedure itself; place WRITE_ATTRIBUTE_N_TIMES in the file VIDEO_IO.ASM:

Listing 21-3. Add This Procedure to VIDEO_IO.ASM

```
        PUBLIC    WRITE_ATTRIBUTE_N_TIMES
        EXTRN     CURSOR_RIGHT:PROC
;-----------------------------------------------------------------------;
; This procedure sets the attribute for N characters, starting at the   ;
; current cursor position.                                              ;
;                                                                       ;
; On entry:    CX   Number of characters to set attribute for           ;
;              DL   New attribute for characters                        ;
;                                                                       ;
; Uses:        CURSOR_RIGHT                                             ;
```

Disk A   Sector 0

```
        00 01 02 03 04 05 06 07 08 09 0A 0B 0C 0D 0E 0F   0123456789ABCDEF
00    EB 28 90 49 42 4D 20 20 33 2E 32 00 02 02 01 00   )(ÉIBM  3.2 ☻☻☺
10    02 70 00 D0 02 FD 02 00 09 00 02 00 00 00 00 00   ☻p @ ▌² ☐ o ☺
20    00 00 00 00 00 00 00 00 00 00 FA C4 5C 08 33 ED      ·-\■3ø
30    B8 C0 07 8E D8 33 C9 88 16 FD 01 0A D2 79 0A 89   ┐ └•Ä┼3┌ê.²☺╥y∎ë
40    1E 1C 00 8C 06 1E 00 B1 02 8E C5 8E D5 BC 00 7C   ▲└ î♠▲ ▌êÄ┤∎▌ !
50    FC 1E 36 C5 36 78 00 BF 2A 7C B9 0B 00 F3 A4 1F   n▲6┼6x ┐*!↓δ ñ▼
60    C6 06 2E 00 0F BF 78 00 B8 2A 7C AB 91 AB FB 8A   ╞♠. ☼┐x ┐*↓½æ½√è
70    16 FD 01 CD 13 A0 10 00 98 F7 26 16 00 03 06 0E   _²☐=‼á) ÿ≈& ♥♠♫
80    00 E8 73 00 E8 79 00 BB 00 05 53 E8 A0 00 5F BE   δs δy ┐ ♦S§á _
90    74 01 B9 0B 00 90 F3 A6 75 57 83 C7 15 B1 0B 90   t☺↓ É<êuⁿè ║S█é
A0    90 F3 A6 75 4C 26 8B 47 1C 99 8B 0E 0B 00 03 C1   É<êuL&ïG-Öï∎♥ ♥┴
B0    48 F7 F1 3D 14 00 7F 02 B0 14 96 A1 11 00 B1 04   H≈±=¶ ▲░¶Öí◄ ▌♦
C0    D3 E8 E8 32 00 FF 36 1C 00 C4 1E 70 01 E8 30 00   ╙δδ2 6∟ ╥▲p☺δ0
D0    E8 5B 00 2B F0 76 0D E8 1D 00 52 F7 26 0B 00 03   δ[ +≡v♪δ↔ R≈& ♥
E0    D8 5A EB E9 5B 8A 2E 15 00 8A 16 FD 01 FF 2E 70   ↓Zδé[è.§ è.²☐ .p
F0    01 BE 8B 01 EB 54 90 01 06 1C 00 11 2E 1E 00 C3   ☐╛ï☺δTÉ☺♠∟ ◄.▲ ├
```

Press function key, or enter character or hex byte: _

Figure 21-1. Screen Display with Phantom Cursors.

```
;---------------------------------------------------------------;
WRITE_ATTRIBUTE_N_TIMES    PROC
        PUSH    AX
        PUSH    BX
        PUSH    CX
        PUSH    DX
        MOV     BL,DL           ;Set attribute to new attribute
        XOR     BH,BH           ;Set display page to 0
        MOV     DX,CX           ;CX is used by the BIOS routines
        MOV     CX,1            ;Set attribute for one character
ATTR_LOOP:
        MOV     AH,8            ;Read character under cursor
        INT     10h
        MOV     AH,9            ;Write attribute/character
        INT     10h
        CALL    CURSOR_RIGHT
        DEC     DX              ;Set attribute for N characters?
        JNZ     ATTR_LOOP       ;No, continue
        POP     DX
        POP     CX
        POP     BX
        POP     AX
        RET
WRITE_ATTRIBUTE_N_TIMES    ENDP
```

This is both the first and final version of WRITE_ATTRIBUTE_N_TIMES. With it, we've also created the final version of VIDEO_IO.ASM, so you won't need to change or assemble it again.

Summary

We now have eight files to link, with the main procedure still in Dskpatch. Of these, we've changed two files, Disp_sec and Video_io, and created one, Phantom. If you're using Make or the short batch file we suggested in Chapter 20, remember to add your new file, Phantom, to the list.

When you run Dskpatch now, you'll see it write the sector display, just as before, but Dskpatch will also write in the two phantom cursors. (See Figure 21-1.) Notice that the real cursor is back where it should be at the very end.

In the next chapter, we'll add procedures to move our newly formed phantom cursors, and we'll add a simple editing procedure to allow us to change the byte under the phantom cursor.

22

SIMPLE EDITING

W e've almost reached the point at which we can begin to edit our sector display—change numbers in our half sector display. We'll soon add simple versions of the procedures for editing bytes in our display, but before we do, we need some way to move the phantom cursors to different bytes within the half sector display. This task turns out to be fairly simple, now that we have the two procedures ERASE_PHANTOM and WRITE_PHANTOM.

Moving the Phantom Cursors

Moving the phantom cursors in any direction depends on three basic steps: Erasing the phantom cursor at its current position; changing the cursor position by changing one of the variables, PHANTOM_CURSOR_X or PHANTOM_CURSOR_Y; and using WRITE_PHANTOM to write the phantom cursor at this new position. In the process, however, we must be careful not to let the cursor move outside the window, which is 16 bytes wide and 16 bytes high.

To move the phantom cursors, we'll need four new procedures, one for each of the arrow keys on the keyboard. DISPATCHER needs no changes, because all the information on procedures and extended codes is in the table DISPATCH_TABLE. We just need to add the extended ASCII codes and addresses of the procedures for each of the arrow keys. Here are the additions to DISPATCH.ASM that will bring the cursor keys to life:

Listing 22-1. Changes to DISPATCH.ASM

```
.MODEL    SMALL

.CODE
    EXTRN    NEXT_SECTOR:PROC                        ;In DISK_IO.ASM
    EXTRN    PREVIOUS_SECTOR:PROC                    ;In DISK_IO.ASM
    EXTRN    PHANTOM_UP:PROC, PHANTOM_DOWN:PROC      ;In PHANTOM.ASM
    EXTRN    PHANTOM_LEFT:PROC, PHANTOM_RIGHT:PROC
.DATA
;-------------------------------------------------------------------;
; This table contains the legal extended ASCII keys and the addresses ;
; of the procedures that should be called when each key is pressed.   ;
;                                                                     ;
; The format of the table is                                          ;
;           DB    72        ;Extended code for cursor up              ;
;           DW    OFFSET _TEXT:PHANTOM_UP                             ;
;-------------------------------------------------------------------;
DISPATCH_TABLE LABEL    BYTE
    DB    61                              ;F3
    DW    OFFSET _TEXT:PREVIOUS_SECTOR
    DB    62                              ;F4
    DW    OFFSET _TEXT:NEXT_SECTOR
```

```
DB      72                                        ;Cursor up
DW      OFFSET _TEXT:PHANTOM_UP
DB      80                                        ;Cursor down
DW      OFFSET _TEXT:PHANTOM_DOWN
DB      75                                        ;Cursor left
DW      OFFSET _TEXT:PHANTOM_LEFT
DB      77                                        ;Cursor right
DW      OFFSET _TEXT:PHANTOM_RIGHT
DB      0                                         ;End of the table
```

As you can see, it's simple to add commands to Dskpatch: We merely place the procedure names in DISPATCH_TABLE and write the procedures.

Speaking of writing procedures, the procedures PHANTOM_UP, PHANTOM_DOWN, and so on are fairly simple. They're also quite similar to one another, differing only in the boundary conditions used for each. We've already described how they work; see if you can write them yourself, in the file PHANTOM.ASM, before you read on.

Here are our versions of the procedures to move the phantom cursors:

Listing 22-2. Add These Procedures to PHANTOM.ASM

```
;--------------------------------------------------------------------;
; These four procedures move the phantom cursors.                    ;
;                                                                    ;
; Uses:           ERASE_PHANTOM, WRITE_PHANTOM                       ;
; Reads:          PHANTOM_CURSOR_X, PHANTOM_CURSOR_Y                 ;
; Writes:         PHANTOM_CURSOR_X, PHANTOM_CURSOR_Y                 ;
;--------------------------------------------------------------------;

            PUBLIC  PHANTOM_UP
PHANTOM_UP  PROC
            CALL    ERASE_PHANTOM             ;Erase at current position
            DEC     PHANTOM_CURSOR_Y          ;Move cursor up one line
            JNS     WASNT_AT_TOP              ;Was not at the top, write cursor
            MOV     PHANTOM_CURSOR_Y,0        ;Was at the top, so put back there
WASNT_AT_TOP:
            CALL    WRITE_PHANTOM             ;Write the phantom at new position
            RET
PHANTOM_UP  ENDP

            PUBLIC  PHANTOM_DOWN
PHANTOM_DOWN PROC
            CALL    ERASE_PHANTOM             ;Erase at current position
            INC     PHANTOM_CURSOR_Y          ;Move cursor down one line
            CMP     PHANTOM_CURSOR_Y,16       ;Was it at the bottom?
            JB      WASNT_AT_BOTTOM           ;No, so write phantom
            MOV     PHANTOM_CURSOR_Y,15       ;Was at bottom, so put back there
WASNT_AT_BOTTOM:
            CALL    WRITE_PHANTOM             ;Write the phantom cursor
            RET
PHANTOM_DOWN ENDP

            PUBLIC  PHANTOM_LEFT
PHANTOM_LEFT PROC
            CALL    ERASE_PHANTOM             ;Erase at current position
            DEC     PHANTOM_CURSOR_X          ;Move cursor left one column
            JNS     WASNT_AT_LEFT            ;Was not at the left side, write cursor
            MOV     PHANTOM_CURSOR_X,0        ;Was at left, so put back there
WASNT_AT_LEFT:
            CALL    WRITE_PHANTOM             ;Write the phantom cursor
            RET
PHANTOM_LEFT ENDP
```

Listing 22-2. *continued*

```
          PUBLIC    PHANTOM_RIGHT
PHANTOM_RIGHT  PROC    NEAR
          CALL      ERASE_PHANTOM         ;Erase at current position
          INC       PHANTOM_CURSOR_X      ;Move cursor right one column
          CMP       PHANTOM_CURSOR_X,16   ;Was it already at the right side?
          JB        WASNT_AT_RIGHT
          MOV       PHANTOM_CURSOR_X,15   ;Was at right, so put back there
WASNT_AT_RIGHT:
          CALL      WRITE_PHANTOM         ;Write the phantom cursor
          RET
PHANTOM_RIGHT  ENDP
```

PHANTOM_LEFT and PHANTOM_RIGHT are the final versions, but we'll have to change PHANTOM_UP and PHANTOM_DOWN when we begin to scroll the display.

Test Dskpatch now to see if you can move the phantom cursors around on the screen. They should move together, and they should stay within their own windows.

As Dskpatch stands now, we can see only the first half of a sector. In Chapter 27, we'll make some additions and changes to Dskpatch so we can scroll the display to see other parts of the sector. At that time, we'll change both PHANTOM_UP and PHANTOM_DOWN to scroll the screen when we try to move the cursor beyond the top or bottom of the screen. For example, when the cursor is at the bottom of the half-sector display, pushing the cursor-down key again should scroll the display up one line, adding another line at the bottom, so that we see the next 16 bytes. Scrolling is rather messy, however, so we'll keep these procedures until almost last. Through Chapter 26, we'll develop the editing and keyboard-input sections of Dskpatch by using only the first half sector. Now, we'll go on to add editing, so we can change bytes on our display.

Simple Editing

We already have a simple keyboard-input procedure, READ_BYTE, which reads just one character from the keyboard without waiting for you to press the Enter key. We'll use this old, test version of READ_BYTE to develop editing. Then, in the next chapter, we'll write a more sophisticated version of the procedure that will wait until we press either the Enter key or a special key, such as a function or cursor key.

Our editing procedure will be called EDIT_BYTE, and it will change one byte both on the screen and in memory (SECTOR). EDIT_BYTE will take the character in the DL register, write it to the memory location within SECTOR that is currently pointed to by the phantom cursor, and then change the display.

DISPATCHER already has a nice niche where we can place a CALL to EDIT_BYTE. Here is the new version of DISPATCHER in DISPATCH.ASM, with the CALL to EDIT_BYTE and the changes to go along with it:

Listing 22-3. Changes to DISPATCHER in DISPATCH.ASM

```
        PUBLIC  DISPATCHER
        EXTRN   READ_BYTE:PROC, EDIT_BYTE:PROC
;------------------------------------------------------------------;
; This is the central dispatcher.  During normal editing and viewing,  ;
; this procedure reads characters from the keyboard and, if the character;
; is a command key (such as a cursor key), DISPATCHER calls the    ;
; procedures that do the actual work.  This dispatching is done for ;
; special keys listed in the table DISPATCH_TABLE, where the procedure  ;
; addresses are stored just after the key names.                   ;
;                                                                  ;
; If the character is not a special key, then it should be placed  ;
; directly into the sector buffer--this is the editing mode.       ;
;                                                                  ;
; Uses:          READ_BYTE, EDIT_BYTE                              ;
;------------------------------------------------------------------;
DISPATCHER      PROC
        PUSH    AX
        PUSH    BX
        PUSH    DX
DISPATCH_LOOP:
        CALL    READ_BYTE       ;Read character into AL
        OR      AH,AH           ;AX = -1 if no character read, 1
                                ; for an extended code.
        JS      DISPATCH_LOOP   ;No character read, try again
        JNZ     SPECIAL_KEY     ;Read extended code
; do nothing with the character for now
        MOV     DL,AL
        CALL    EDIT_BYTE       ;Was normal character, edit byte
        JMP     DISPATCH_LOOP   ;Read another character

SPECIAL_KEY:
        CMP     AL,68           ;F10--exit?
        JE      END_DISPATCH    ;Yes, leave
                                ;Use BX to look through table
        LEA     BX,DISPATCH_TABLE
SPECIAL_LOOP:
        CMP     BYTE PTR [BX],0 ;End of table?
        JE      NOT_IN_TABLE    ;Yes, key was not in the table
        CMP     AL,[BX]         ;Is it this table entry?
        JE      DISPATCH        ;Yes, then dispatch
        ADD     BX,3            ;No, try next entry
        JMP     SPECIAL_LOOP    ;Check next table entry

DISPATCH:
        INC     BX              ;Point to address of procedure
        CALL    WORD PTR [BX]   ;Call procedure
        JMP     DISPATCH_LOOP   ;Wait for another key

NOT_IN_TABLE:                   ;Do nothing, just read next character
        JMP     DISPATCH_LOOP

END_DISPATCH:
        POP     DX
        POP     BX
        POP     AX
        RET
DISPATCHER      ENDP
```

The EDIT_BYTE procedure itself does a lot of work, almost entirely by calling other procedures, and this is one feature of modular design. With modular design, we can often write rather complex procedures simply by giving a list of CALLs to other procedures that do the work. Many of the procedures in EDIT_BYTE work with a character in the DL register, but this is already set when we call EDIT_BYTE, so the only instruction other than a CALL (or PUSH, POP) is the LEA instruction to set the address of the prompt for WRITE_PROMPT_LINE. Most of the procedure calls in EDIT_BYTE are for updating the display when we edit a byte. You'll see the other details of EDIT_BYTE when we come to the procedure listing in a moment.

Since EDIT_BYTE changes the byte on screen, we need another procedure, WRITE_TO_MEMORY, to change the byte in SECTOR. WRITE_TO_MEMORY uses the coordinates in PHANTOM_CURSOR_X and PHANTOM_CURSOR_Y to calculate the offset into SECTOR of the phantom cursor, then it writes the character (byte) in the DL register to the correct byte within SECTOR.

Here is the new file, EDITOR.ASM, which contains the final versions of both EDIT_BYTE and WRITE_TO_MEMORY:

Listing 22-4. The New File EDITOR.ASM

```
.MODEL   SMALL

.CODE

.DATA
        EXTRN    SECTOR:BYTE
        EXTRN    SECTOR_OFFSET:WORD
        EXTRN    PHANTOM_CURSOR_X:BYTE
        EXTRN    PHANTOM_CURSOR_Y:BYTE
.CODE
;-----------------------------------------------------------------;
; This procedure writes one byte to SECTOR, at the memory location ;
; pointed to by the phantom cursor.                                ;
;                                                                  ;
; On entry:      DL   Byte to write to SECTOR                      ;
;                                                                  ;
; The offset is calculated by                                     ;
;   OFFSET = SECTOR_OFFSET + (16 * PHANTOM_CURSOR_Y) + PHANTOM_CURSOR_X ;
;                                                                  ;
; Reads:         PHANTOM_CURSOR_X, PHANTOM_CURSOR_Y, SECTOR_OFFSET ;
; Writes:        SECTOR                                            ;
;-----------------------------------------------------------------;
WRITE_TO_MEMORY      PROC
        PUSH     AX
        PUSH     BX
        PUSH     CX
        MOV      BX,SECTOR_OFFSET
        MOV      AL,PHANTOM_CURSOR_Y
        XOR      AH,AH
        MOV      CL,4              ;Multiply PHANTOM_CURSOR_Y by 16
        SHL      AX,CL
        ADD      BX,AX             ;BX = SECTOR_OFFSET + (16 * Y)
        MOV      AL,PHANTOM_CURSOR_X
        XOR      AH,AH
        ADD      BX,AX             ;That's the address!
```

```
          MOV       SECTOR[BX],DL          ;Now, store the byte
          POP       CX
          POP       BX
          POP       AX
          RET
WRITE_TO_MEMORY      ENDP


          PUBLIC    EDIT_BYTE
          EXTRN     SAVE_REAL_CURSOR:PROC, RESTORE_REAL_CURSOR:PROC
          EXTRN     MOV_TO_HEX_POSITION:PROC, MOV_TO_ASCII_POSITION:PROC
          EXTRN     WRITE_PHANTOM:PROC, WRITE_PROMPT_LINE:PROC
          EXTRN     CURSOR_RIGHT:PROC, WRITE_HEX:PROC, WRITE_CHAR:PROC
.DATA
          EXTRN     EDITOR_PROMPT:BYTE
.CODE
;-----------------------------------------------------------------;
; This procedure changes a byte in memory and on the screen.      ;
;                                                                 ;
; On entry:      DL   Byte to write into SECTOR, and change on screen ;
;                                                                 ;
; Uses:          SAVE_REAL_CURSOR, RESTORE_REAL_CURSOR            ;
;                MOV_TO_HEX_POSITION, MOV_TO_ASCII_POSITION       ;
;                WRITE_PHANTOM, WRITE_PROMPT_LINE, CURSOR_RIGHT   ;
;                WRITE_HEX, WRITE_CHAR, WRITE_TO_MEMORY           ;
; Reads:         EDITOR_PROMPT                                    ;
;-----------------------------------------------------------------;
EDIT_BYTE           PROC
          PUSH      DX
          CALL      SAVE_REAL_CURSOR
          CALL      MOV_TO_HEX_POSITION      ;Move to the hex number in the
          CALL      CURSOR_RIGHT             ; hex window
          CALL      WRITE_HEX                ;Write the new number
          CALL      MOV_TO_ASCII_POSITION    ;Move to the char. in the ASCII window
          CALL      WRITE_CHAR               ;Write the new character
          CALL      RESTORE_REAL_CURSOR      ;Move cursor back where it belongs
          CALL      WRITE_PHANTOM            ;Rewrite the phantom cursor
          CALL      WRITE_TO_MEMORY          ;Save this new byte in SECTOR
          LEA       DX,EDITOR_PROMPT
          CALL      WRITE_PROMPT_LINE
          POP       DX
          RET
EDIT_BYTE           ENDP


          END
```

Summary

Dskpatch now consists of nine files: Dskpatch, Dispatch, Disp_sec, Disk_io, Video_io, Kbd_io, Phantom, Cursor, and Editor. In this chapter, we changed Dispatch and added Editor. None of these files is very long, so none takes very long to assemble. Furthermore, we can make changes fairly quickly by editing just one of these files, reassembling it, and then linking all the files together again.

In terms of our current version of Dskpatch, when you push any key, you'll see a change in the number and character under the phantom cursor. Our editing works, but it's not very safe as yet, since we can change a byte by hitting any key. We need to build in some type of safeguard, such as pressing Enter to change a byte, so we don't make an accidental change by leaning on the keyboard unintentionally.

In addition, the current version of READ_BYTE doesn't allow us to enter a hex number to change a byte. In Chapter 24, we'll rewrite READ_BYTE, both so we'll have to push the Enter key before it will accept a new character, and to allow us to enter a two-digit hex number. First, we need to write a hex input procedure; in the next chapter, we'll write input procedures for both hex and decimal.

HEX AND DECIMAL INPUT

We'll encounter two new procedures for keyboard input in this chapter: one procedure for reading a byte by reading either a two-digit hex number or a single character, and another for reading a word by reading the characters of a decimal number. These will be our hex and decimal input procedures.Both procedures are sufficiently tricky that we need to use a test program with them before we even consider linking them into Dskpatch. We'll be working with READ_BYTE, and a test procedure will be particularly important here, because this procedure will (temporarily) lose its ability to read special function keys. Since Dskpatch relies on the function keys, we won't be able to use our new READ_BYTE with Dskpatch. We'll also find out why we can't read special function keys with the READ_BYTE developed here, and in the next chapter we'll modify the file to make our function-key problems go away.

Hex Input

Let's begin by rewriting READ_BYTE. In the last chapter, READ_BYTE would read either an ordinary character or a special function key and return one byte to Dispatch. Dispatch then called the Editor if READ_BYTE read an ordinary character, and EDIT_BYTE modified the byte pointed to by the phantom cursor. Otherwise, Dispatch looked for special function keys in DISPATCH_TABLE to see if the byte was there; if so, Dispatch called the procedure named in the table.

But, as mentioned in the last chapter, the old version of READ_BYTE makes it much too easy to change a byte by accident. If you unintentionally hit any key on the keyboard (other than special keys), EDIT_BYTE will change the byte under the phantom cursor. All of us are sometimes clumsy, and such an inadvertent change in a sector can lead to disaster.

We'll change READ_BYTE so that, henceforth, it won't return the character we type until we press the Enter key. We'll provide this feature by using the DOS INT 21h function 0Ah to read a string of characters. DOS returns this string only when we press Enter, so we get our fix for clumsiness. But along the way, we lose special function keys, for reasons you'll see later.

To see exactly how our changes affect READ_BYTE, we need to write a test program to test READ_BYTE in isolation. That way, if anything strange happens, we'll know it's READ_BYTE and not some other part of Dskpatch. Our job of writing a test procedure will be simpler if we use a few procedures from Kbd_io, Video_io, and Cursor to print information on the progress of READ_BYTE. We'll use such procedures as WRITE_HEX and WRITE_DECI-

MAL to print the character code returned and the number of characters read. The details are here, in TEST.ASM:

Listing 23-1. The Test Program TEST.ASM

```
        .MODEL     SMALL

        .STACK

        .DATA
ENTER_PROMPT                    DB    'Enter characters: ',0
CHARACTER_PROMPT                DB    'Character code: ',0
SPECIAL_CHAR_PROMPT             DB    'Special character read: ',0

        .CODE
                EXTRN     WRITE_HEX:PROC, WRITE_DECIMAL:PROC
                EXTRN     WRITE_STRING:PROC, SEND_CRLF:PROC
                EXTRN     READ_BYTE:PROC

TEST_READ_BYTE PROC
                MOV       AX,DGROUP
                MOV       DS,AX

                LEA       DX,ENTER_PROMPT
                CALL      WRITE_STRING
                CALL      READ_BYTE
                CALL      SEND_CRLF
                LEA       DX,CHARACTER_PROMPT
                CALL      WRITE_STRING
                MOV       DL,AL
                CALL      WRITE_HEX
                CALL      SEND_CRLF
                LEA       DX,SPECIAL_CHAR_PROMPT
                CALL      WRITE_STRING
                MOV       DL,AH
                XOR       DH,DH
                CALL      WRITE_DECIMAL
                CALL      SEND_CRLF

                MOV       AH,4Ch                 ;Return to DOS
                INT       21h
TEST_READ_BYTE ENDP

                END       TEST_READ_BYTE
```

Try linking this with your current versions of Kbd_io, Video_io, and Cursor (place Test first in the LINK list). If you press any special function key, Test will display the scan code, and a 1 to tell you that you typed a special character. Otherwise it will display 0 (no special key).

The bulk of the instructions in TEST.ASM are for formatting—making the display look nice. One thing you may have noticed is that we've used some of the procedures in kbd_io, video_io, and cursor without regard to the other files in our project. We could do this because we were careful to place only general-purpose procedures into these files. In other words, kbd_io, video_io, and cursor are designed to be used by any program you write. In general, it's a good idea to separate your procedures by source file into general-purpose and specific procedures so that you can easily reuse general-purpose procedures in new programs you write.

Let's move on to rewriting READ_BYTE to accept a string of characters. Not only will this save us from our clumsiness when we use Dskpatch, it will also allow us to use the Backspace key to delete characters if we change our mind about what we want to type in—another nice feature since it's easy to make mistakes. READ_BYTE will use the procedure READ_STRING to read a string of characters.

READ_STRING is very simple, almost trivial, but we've placed it in a separate procedure so you can rewrite it in the next chapter to read special function keys without having to press the Enter key. To save time, we'll also add three other procedures that READ_BYTE uses: STRING_TO_UPPER, CONVERT_HEX_DIGIT, and HEX_TO_BYTE.

STRING_TO_UPPER and HEX_TO_BYTE both work on strings. STRING_TO_UPPER converts all the lowercase letters in a string to uppercase. That means we can type either f3 or F3 for the hex number F3h. By allowing hex numbers to be typed in either lower- or uppercase letters, we add user-friendliness to Dskpatch.

HEX_TO_BYTE takes the string read by DOS, after we call STRING_TO_UPPER, and converts the two-digit hex string to a single-byte number. HEX_TO_BYTE makes use of CONVERT_HEX_DIGIT to convert each hex digit to a four-bit number.

How do we ensure that DOS won't read more than two hex digits? The DOS function 0Ah reads an entire string of characters into an area of memory defined like this:

```
CHAR_NUM_LIMIT   DB      0
NUM_CHARS_READ   DB      0
STRING           DB      80 DUP (0)
```

The first byte ensures that we don't read too many characters. CHAR_NUM_LIMIT tells DOS how many characters, at most, to read. If we set this to three, DOS will read up to two characters, plus the carriage-return character (DOS always counts the carriage return). Any characters we type after that will be discarded—thrown away—and for each extra character, DOS will beep to let us know we've passed the limit. When we press the Enter key, DOS sets the second byte, NUM_CHARS_READ, to the number of characters it actually read, not including the carriage return.

STRING_TO_UPPER, READ_BYTE, and STRING_TO_UPPER all use NUM_CHARS_READ. For example, READ_BYTE checks NUM_CHARS_READ to find out whether you typed a single character or a two-digit hex number. If NUM_CHARS_READ was set to one, READ_BYTE returns a single character in the AL register. If NUM_CHARS_READ was set to two, READ_BYTE uses HEX_TO_BYTE to convert the two-digit hex string to a byte.

Without further ado, here is the new file KBD_IO.ASM, with all four new procedures (note that we kept the old READ_BYTE by renaming it to READ_KEY, which we'll use in the next chapter):

Listing 23-2. The New Version of KBD_IO.ASM

```
        .MODEL  SMALL

        .DATA

KEYBOARD_INPUT  LABEL   BYTE
CHAR_NUM_LIMIT  DB      0               ;Length of input buffer
NUM_CHARS_READ  DB      0               ;Number of characters read
CHARS           DB      80 DUP (0)      ;A buffer for keyboard input

        .CODE
        PUBLIC  STRING_TO_UPPER
;----------------------------------------------------------------;
; This procedure converts the string, using the DOS format for strings, ;
; to all uppercase letters.                                      ;
;                                                                ;
; On entry:     DS:DX   Address of string buffer                 ;
;----------------------------------------------------------------;
STRING_TO_UPPER         PROC
        PUSH    AX
        PUSH    BX
        PUSH    CX
        MOV     BX,DX
        INC     BX                      ;Point to character count
        MOV     CL,[BX]                 ;Character count in 2nd byte of buffer
        XOR     CH,CH                   ;Clear upper byte of count
UPPER_LOOP:
        INC     BX                      ;Point to next character in buffer
        MOV     AL,[BX]
        CMP     AL,'a'                  ;See if it is a lowercase letter
        JB      NOT_LOWER               ;Nope
        CMP     AL,'z'
        JA      NOT_LOWER
        ADD     AL,'A'-'a'              ;Convert to uppercase letter
        MOV     [BX],AL
NOT_LOWER:
        LOOP    UPPER_LOOP
        POP     CX
        POP     BX
        POP     AX
        RET
STRING_TO_UPPER        ENDP


;----------------------------------------------------------------;
; This procedure converts a character from ASCII (hex) to a nibble (4 ;
; bits).                                                         ;
;                                                                ;
; On entry:     AL    Character to convert                       ;
; Returns:      AL    Nibble                                     ;
;               CF    Set for error, cleared otherwise           ;
;----------------------------------------------------------------;
CONVERT_HEX_DIGIT      PROC
        CMP     AL,'0'                  ;Is it a legal digit?
        JB      BAD_DIGIT               ;Nope
        CMP     AL,'9'                  ;Not sure yet
```

Listing 23-2. *continued*

```
          JA       TRY_HEX               ;Might be hex digit
          SUB      AL,'0'                ;Is decimal digit, convert to nibble
          CLC                            ;Clear the carry, no error
          RET
TRY_HEX:
          CMP      AL,'A'                ;Not sure yet
          JB       BAD_DIGIT             ;Not hex
          CMP      AL,'F'                ;Not sure yet
          JA       BAD_DIGIT             ;Not hex
          SUB      AL,'A'-10             ;Is hex, convert to nibble
          CLC                            ;Clear the carry, no error
          RET
BAD_DIGIT:
          STC                            ;Set the carry, error
          RET
CONVERT_HEX_DIGIT   ENDP


          PUBLIC   HEX_TO_BYTE
;------------------------------------------------------------------------;
; This procedure converts the two characters at DS:DX from hex to one    ;
; byte.                                                                   ;
;                                                                         ;
; On entry:     DS:DX    Address of two characters for hex number         ;
; Returns:      AL       Byte                                             ;
;               CF       Set for error, clear if no error                 ;
;                                                                         ;
; Uses:         CONVERT_HEX_DIGIT                                         ;
;------------------------------------------------------------------------;
HEX_TO_BYTE   PROC
          PUSH     BX
          PUSH     CX
          MOV      BX,DX                 ;Put address in BX for indirect addr
          MOV      AL,[BX]               ;Get first digit
          CALL     CONVERT_HEX_DIGIT
          JC       BAD_HEX               ;Bad hex digit if carry set
          MOV      CX,4                  ;Now multiply by 16
          SHL      AL,CL
          MOV      AH,AL                 ;Retain a copy
          INC      BX                    ;Get second digit
          MOV      AL,[BX]
          CALL     CONVERT_HEX_DIGIT
          JC       BAD_HEX               ;Bad hex digit if carry set
          OR       AL,AH                 ;Combine two nibbles
          CLC                            ;Clear carry for no error
DONE_HEX:
          POP      CX
          POP      BX
          RET
BAD_HEX:
          STC                            ;Set carry for error
          JMP      DONE_HEX
HEX_TO_BYTE   ENDP



;------------------------------------------------------------------------;
; This is a simple version of READ_STRING.                               ;
;                                                                         ;
; On entry:     DS:DX    Address of string area                          ;
;------------------------------------------------------------------------;
READ_STRING   PROC
          PUSH     AX
          MOV      AH,0Ah                ;Call for buffered keyboard input
          INT      21h                   ;Call DOS function for buffered input
          POP      AX
          RET
READ_STRING   ENDP

          PUBLIC   READ_BYTE
```

```
;-----------------------------------------------------------------;
; This procedure reads either a single ASCII character or a two-digit ;
; hex number.  This is just a test version of READ_BYTE.          ;
;                                                                 ;
; Returns:       AL       Character code (unless AH = 0)          ;
;                AH       0 if read ASCII char                    ;
;                         1 if read a special key                ;
;                         -1 if no characters read               ;
;                                                                 ;
; Uses:          HEX_TO_BYTE, STRING_TO_UPPER, READ_STRING        ;
; Reads:         KEYBOARD_INPUT, etc.                             ;
; Writes:        KEYBOARD_INPUT, etc.                             ;
;-----------------------------------------------------------------;
READ_BYTE       PROC
        PUSH    DX
        MOV     CHAR_NUM_LIMIT,3        ;Allow only two characters (plus Enter)
        LEA     DX,KEYBOARD_INPUT
        CALL    READ_STRING
        CMP     NUM_CHARS_READ,1       ;See how many characters
        JE      ASCII_INPUT            ;Just one, treat as ASCII character
        JB      NO_CHARACTERS          ;Only Enter key hit
        CALL    STRING_TO_UPPER        ;No, convert string to uppercase
        LEA     DX,CHARS               ;Address of string to convert
        CALL    HEX_TO_BYTE            ;Convert string from hex to byte
        JC      NO_CHARACTERS          ;Error, so return 'no characters read'
        XOR     AH,AH                  ;Signal read one character
DONE_READ:
        POP     DX
        RET
NO_CHARACTERS:
        XOR     AH,AH                  ;Set to 'no characters read'
        NOT     AH                     ;Return -1 in AH          JMP
DONE_READ
ASCII_INPUT:
        MOV     AL,CHARS               ;Load character read
        XOR     AH,AH                  ;Signal read one byte
        JMP     DONE_READ
READ_BYTE       ENDP


        PUBLIC  READ_KEY
;-----------------------------------------------------------------;
; This procedure reads one key from the keyboard.                 ;
;                                                                 ;
; Returns:       AL       Character code (unless AH = 1)          ;
;                AH       0 if read ASCII char                    ;
;                         1 if read a special key                ;
;-----------------------------------------------------------------;
READ_KEY        PROC
        XOR     AH,AH                  ;Ask for keyboard read function
        INT     16h                    ;Read character/scan code from keyboard
        OR      AL,AL                  ;Is it an extended code?
        JZ      EXTENDED_CODE          ;Yes
NOT_EXTENDED:
        XOR     AH,AH                  ;Return just the ASCII code
DONE_READING:
        RET

EXTENDED_CODE:
        MOV     AL,AH                  ;Put scan code into AL
        MOV     AH,1                   ;Signal extended code
        JMP     DONE_READING
READ_KEY        ENDP


        END
```

Reassemble Kbd_io and link the four files Test, Kbd_io, Video_io, and Cursor to try this version of READ_BYTE.

At this point, we have two problems with READ_BYTE. Remember the special function keys? We can't read them with DOS function 0Ah; it just doesn't work. Try pressing a function key when you run Test. DOS doesn't return two bytes, with the first set to zero as you might expect. Instead, our test program reports 255 for the special key (1 in AH), which means READ_BYTE didn't read any characters.

We have no way to read extended codes with DOS's buffered input, using function 0Ah. We used this function so that we could use the Backspace key to delete characters before we press the Enter key. But now, since we can't read special function keys, we have to write our own READ_STRING procedure. We'll have to replace function 0Ah to ensure that we can press a special function key without pressing Enter.

The other problem with DOS's function 0Ah for keyboard input has to do with the line-feed character. Press Control-Enter (line feed) after you type one character and then try the Backspace key. You'll find that you're on the next line, with no way to return to the one above. Our new version of Kbd_io in the next chapter will treat the line-feed character (Control-Enter) as an ordinary character; then, pressing line feed won't move the cursor to the next line.

But before we move on to fix the problems with READ_BYTE and READ_STRING, let's write a procedure to read an unsigned decimal number. We won't use the procedure in this book, but the version of Dskpatch on the companion disk does use it so that we can, for example, ask Dskpatch to display sector number 567.

Decimal Input

Recall that the largest unsigned decimal number we can put into a single word is 65536. When we use READ_STRING to read a string of decimal digits, we'll tell DOS to read no more than six characters (five digits and a carriage return at the end). Of course, that means READ_DECIMAL will still be able to read numbers from 65536 to 99999, even though these numbers don't fit into one word. We'll have to keep watch for such numbers and return an error code if READ_DECIMAL tries to read a number larger than 65535, or if it tries to read a character that is not between zero and nine.

To convert our string of up to five digits into a word, we'll use multiplication as we did in Chapter 1: We'll take the first (leftmost) digit, multiply it by ten, tack on the second digit, multiply it by ten, and so on. Using this method, we could, for example, write 49856 as:

$$4*10^4 + 9*10^3 + 8*10^2 + 5*10^1 + 6*10^0$$

or, as we'll do the calculation:

$$10*(\ 10*(\ 10*(10*4+9) \ +8) \ +5) \ +6$$

Of course, we must watch for errors as we do these multiplications and return with the carry flag set whenever an error occurs. How do we know when we try to read a number larger than 65535? With larger numbers, the last MUL will overflow into the DX register. The CF flag is set when DX is not zero after a word MUL, so we can use a JC (*Jump if Carry set*) instruction to handle an error. Here is READ_DECIMAL, which also checks each digit for an error (a digit that is not between 0 and 9). Place this procedure in the file KBD_IO.ASM:

Listing 23-3. Add This Procedure to KBD_IO.ASM

```
         PUBLIC  READ_DECIMAL
;----------------------------------------------------------------------;
; This procedure takes the output buffer of READ_STRING and converts   ;
; the string of decimal digits to a word.                              ;
;                                                                      ;
; Returns:      AX        Word converted from decimal                  ;
;               CF        Set if error, clear if no error              ;
;                                                                      ;
; Uses:         READ_STRING                                            ;
; Reads:        KEYBOARD_INPUT, etc.                                   ;
; Writes:       KEYBOARD_INPUT, etc.                                   ;
;----------------------------------------------------------------------;
READ_DECIMAL    PROC
         PUSH   BX
         PUSH   CX
         PUSH   DX
         MOV    CHAR_NUM_LIMIT,6        ;Max number is 5 digits (65535)
         LEA    DX,KEYBOARD_INPUT
         CALL   READ_STRING
         MOV    CL,NUM_CHARS_READ       ;Get number of characters read
         XOR    CH,CH                   ;Set upper byte of count to 0
         CMP    CL,0                    ;Return error if no characters read
         JLE    BAD_DECIMAL_DIGIT       ;No chars read, signal error
         XOR    AX,AX                   ;Start with number set to 0
         XOR    BX,BX                   ;Start at beginning of string
CONVERT_DIGIT:
         MOV    DX,10                   ;Multiply number by 10
         MUL    DX                      ;Multiply AX by 10
         JC     BAD_DECIMAL_DIGIT       ;CF set if MUL overflowed one word
         MOV    DL,CHARS[BX]            ;Get the next digit
         SUB    DL,'0'                  ;And convert to a nibble (4 bits)
         JS     BAD_DECIMAL_DIGIT       ;Bad digit if < 0
         CMP    DL,9                    ;Is this a bad digit?
         JA     BAD_DECIMAL_DIGIT       ;Yes
         ADD    AX,DX                   ;No, so add it to number
         INC    BX                      ;Point to next character
         LOOP   CONVERT_DIGIT           ;Get the next digit
DONE_DECIMAL:
         POP    DX
         POP    CX
         POP    BX
         RET
```

Listing 23-3. *continued*

```
BAD_DECIMAL_DIGIT:
        STC                             ;Set carry to signal error
        JMP     DONE_DECIMAL
READ_DECIMAL    ENDP
```

To make certain it works properly, we need to test this procedure with all the boundary conditions. Here is a simple test program for READ_DECIMAL that uses much the same approach we used to test READ_BYTE:

Listing 23-4. Changes to TEST.ASM

```
.MODEL  SMALL

.STACK

.DATA
ENTER_PROMPT            DB      'Enter decimal number: ',0
NUMBER_READ_PROMPT      DB      'Number read: ',0
CHARACTER_PROMPT        DB      'Character code: ',0
SPECIAL_CHAR_PROMPT     DB      'Special character read: ',0

.CODE
        EXTRN   WRITE_HEX:PROC, WRITE_DECIMAL:PROC
        EXTRN   WRITE_STRING:PROC, SEND_CRLF:PROC
        EXTRN   READ_DECIMAL:PROC

TEST_READ_DECIMAL       PROC
        MOV     AX,DGROUP
        MOV     DS,AX

        LEA     DX,ENTER_PROMPT
        CALL    WRITE_STRING
        CALL    READ_DECIMAL
        JC      ERROR
        CALL    SEND_CRLF
        LEA     DX,NUMBER_READ_PROMPT
        CALL    WRITE_STRING
        MOV     DX,AX
        CALL    WRITE_DECIMAL
ERROR:  CALL    SEND_CRLF
        LEA     DX,SPECIAL_CHAR_PROMPT
        CALL    WRITE_STRING
        MOV     DL,AH
        XOR     DH,DH
        CALL    WRITE_DECIMAL
        CALL    SEND_CRLF

        MOV     AH,4Ch                  ;Return to DOS
        INT     21h
TEST_READ_DECIMAL       ENDP

        END     TEST_READ_DECIMAL
```

Again, we need to link four files: Test (the preceding file), Kbd_io, Video_io, and Cursor. Try the boundary conditions, using both valid digits and invalid ones (such as A, which is not a valid decimal digit), and with such numbers as 0, 65535, and 65536.

Summary

We'll return to the two simple test procedures later on, when we discuss ways you can write your own programs. Then, we'll see how you can use a slightly more advanced version of TEST.ASM to write a program that will convert numbers between hex and decimal.

But now, we're ready to move on to the next chapter, where we'll write improved versions of READ_BYTE and READ_STRING.

24

IMPROVED KEYBOARD INPUT

We mentioned we would present the development of Dskpatch just as we first wrote it—including bugs and clumsily designed procedures, some of which you've already seen. In this chapter, we'll write a new version of READ_BYTE, and it will place a subtle bug into Dskpatch. In the next chapter, we'll find a can of insecticide to exorcise this small bug, but see if you can find it yourself first. (Hint: Carefully check all the boundary conditions for READ_BYTE when it's attached to Dskpatch.)

A New READ_STRING

Our modular-design philosophy calls for short procedures so that no single procedure is too difficult to understand. The new version of READ_STRING will be an example of a clumsy procedure: much too long. It should be rewritten with more procedures, but we'll leave this rewrite to you. This book is quickly drawing to an end, and we still have a few more procedures left to write before Dskpatch is a useful program. Right now, we can still edit only the first half of any sector, and we can't write this sector back to the disk yet.

In this chapter, we'll give READ_STRING a new procedure, BACK_SPACE, to emulate the function of the Backspace key found in the DOS function 0Ah. When we push the Backspace key, BACK_SPACE will erase the last character typed, from both the screen and the string in memory.

On screen, BACK_SPACE will erase the character by moving the cursor left one character, writing a space over it, and then moving right one character again. This sequence will perform the same backspace deletion provided by DOS.

In the buffer, BACK_SPACE will erase a character by changing the buffer pointer, DS:SI + BX, so it points to the next lower byte in memory. In other words, BACK_SPACE will simply decrement BX: (BX = BX − 1). The character will still be in the buffer, but our program won't see it. Why not? READ_STRING tells us how many characters it's read. If we try to read more than this number from the buffer, we'll see characters we erased. Otherwise, we won't.

We have to be careful not to erase any characters when the buffer is empty. Remember that our string-data area looked something like this:

```
CHAR_NUM_LIMIT   DB      0
NUM_CHARS_READ   DB      0
STRING           DB      80 DUP (0)
```

The string buffer starts at the second byte of this data area or at an *offset* of 2 from the start. So, BACK_SPACE won't erase a character if BX is set to 2, the start of the string buffer, because the buffer is empty when BX equals 2.

Here is BACK_SPACE; place it into KBD_IO.ASM:

Listing 24-1. Add This Procedure to KBD_IO.ASM

```
            PUBLIC   BACK_SPACE
            EXTRN    WRITE_CHAR:PROC
;------------------------------------------------------------------;
; This procedure deletes characters, one at a time, from the buffer and ;
; the screen when the buffer is not empty.  BACK_SPACE simply returns  ;
; when the buffer is empty.                                          ;
;                                                                    ;
; On entry:      DS:SI+BX      Most recent character still in buffer ;
; Returns:       DS:SI+BX      Points to next most recent character  ;
;                                                                    ;
; Uses:          WRITE_CHAR                                          ;
;------------------------------------------------------------------;
BACK_SPACE      PROC                    ;Delete one character
            PUSH    AX
            PUSH    DX
            CMP     BX,2                ;Is buffer empty?
            JE      END_BS              ;Yes, read the next character
            DEC     BX                  ;Remove one character from buffer
            MOV     AH,2                ;Remove character from screen
            MOV     DL,BS
            INT     21h
            MOV     DL,20h              ;Write space there
            CALL    WRITE_CHAR
            MOV     DL,BS               ;Back up again
            INT     21h
END_BS:     POP     DX
            POP     AX
            RET
BACK_SPACE      ENDP
```

Let's move on to the new version of READ_STRING. It will be a large mouthful; the listing you'll see is for only one procedure. By far the longest procedure we've written, READ_STRING is, as we said, too large. That's because it's complicated by so many possible conditions.

Why does READ_STRING do so many things? We added a few more features. If you press the Escape key, READ_STRING will clear the string buffer and remove all the characters from the screen. DOS also erases all the characters in the string buffer when you press Escape, but it doesn't erase any characters from the screen. Instead, it simply writes a backslash (\) character at the end of the line and moves to the next line. Our version of READ_STRING will be more versatile than the DOS READ_STRING function.

READ_STRING uses three special keys: the Backspace, Escape, and Enter keys. We could write the ASCII codes for each of these keys in READ_STRING whenever we need them, but instead we'll add a few definitions to the beginning of KBD_IO.ASM to make READ_STRING more readable. Here are the definitions:

Listing 24-2. Additions to KBD_IO.ASM

```
.MODEL   SMALL

BS       EQU      8                      ;Backspace character
CR       EQU      13                     ;Carriage-return character
ESCAPE   EQU      27                     ;Escape character

.DATA
                  .
                  .
                  .
```

Here is READ_STRING. Although it's rather long, you can see from the listing that it's not very complicated—just long. Replace the old version of READ_STRING in KBD_IO.ASM with this new version:

Listing 24-3. The New READ_STRING in KBD_IO.ASM

```
         PUBLIC   READ_STRING
         EXTRN    WRITE_CHAR:NEAR
;-------------------------------------------------------------------;
; This procedure performs a function very similar to the DOS 0Ah    ;
; function.  But this function will return a special character if a ;
; function or keyboard key is pressed--no return for these keys.  And ;
; ESCAPE will erase the input and start over again.                 ;
;                                                                   ;
;         DS:DX   Address for keyboard buffer.  The first byte must ;
;                 contain the maximum number of characters to read (plus ;
;                 one for the return).  And the second byte will be used ;
;                 by this procedure to return the number of characters ;
;                 actually read.                                    ;
;                         0      No characters read                 ;
;                         -1     One special character read         ;
;                 otherwise number actually read (not including     ;
;                         Enter key)                                ;
;                                                                   ;
; Uses:          BACK_SPACE, WRITE_CHAR, READ_KEY                   ;
;-------------------------------------------------------------------;
READ_STRING    PROC      PROC
         PUSH     AX
         PUSH     BX
         PUSH     SI
         MOV      SI,DX                   ;Use SI for index register and
START_OVER:
         MOV      BX,2                    ;BX for offset to beginning of buffer
         CALL     READ_KEY                ;Read one key from the keyboard
         OR       AH,AH                   ;Is character extended ASCII?
         JNZ      EXTENDED                ;Yes, the process it.
STRING_NOT_EXTENDED:                      ;Extnd char is error unless buf empty
         CMP      AL,CR                   ;Is this a carriage return?
         JE       END_INPUT               ;Yes, we are done with input
         CMP      AL,BS                   ;Is it a backspace character?
         JNE      NOT_BS                  ;Nope
         CALL     BACK_SPACE              ;Yes, delete character
         CMP      BL,2                    ;Is buffer empty?
         JE       START_OVER              ;Yes, can now read extended ASCII again
         JMP      SHORT READ_NEXT_CHAR    ;No, continue reading normal characters
NOT_BS:  CMP      AL,ESCAPE               ;Is it an ESC--purge buffer?
         JE       PURGE_BUFFER            ;Yes, then purge the buffer
         CMP      BL,[SI]                 ;Check to see if buffer is full
         JA       BUFFER_FULL             ;Buffer is full
         MOV      [SI+BX],AL              ;Else save char in buffer
```

```
                INC     BX                              ;Point to next free character in buffer
                PUSH    DX
                MOV     DL,AL                   ;Echo character to screen
                CALL    WRITE_CHAR
                POP     DX
READ_NEXT_CHAR:
                CALL    READ_KEY
                OR      AH,AH                   ;An extended ASCII char is not valid
                                                ; when the buffer is not empty
                JZ      STRING_NOT_EXTENDED     ;Char is valid

;------------------------------------------------;
; Signal an error condition by sending a beep    ;
; character to the display: chr$(7).             ;
;------------------------------------------------;
SIGNAL_ERROR:
                PUSH    DX
                MOV     DL,7                    ;Sound the bell by writing chr$(7)
                MOV     AH,2
                INT     21h
                POP     DX
                JMP     SHORT READ_NEXT_CHAR    ;Now read next character

;------------------------------------------------;
; Empty the string buffer and erase all the      ;
; characters displayed on the screen.            ;
;------------------------------------------------;
PURGE_BUFFER:
                PUSH    CX
                MOV     CL,[SI]                 ;Backspace over maximum number of
                XOR     CH,CH
PURGE_LOOP:                                     ; characters in buffer.  BACK_SPACE
                CALL    BACK_SPACE              ; will keep the cursor from moving too
                LOOP    PURGE_LOOP              ; far back
                POP     CX
                JMP     START_OVER              ;Can now read extended ASCII characters
                                                ; since the buffer is empty

;------------------------------------------------;
; The buffer was full, so can't read another     ;
; character.  Send a beep to alert user of       ;
; buffer-full condition.                         ;
;------------------------------------------------;
BUFFER_FULL:
                JMP     SHORT SIGNAL_ERROR      ;If buffer full, just beep

;------------------------------------------------;
; Read the extended ASCII code and place this    ;
; in the buffer as the only character, then      ;
; return -1 as the number of characters read.    ;
;------------------------------------------------;
EXTENDED:                                       ;Read an extended ASCII code
                MOV     [SI+2],AL               ;Place just this char in buffer
                MOV     BL,0FFh                 ;Num chars read = -1 for special
                JMP     SHORT END_STRING

;------------------------------------------------;
; Save the count of the number of characters     ;
; read and return.                               ;
;------------------------------------------------;
END_INPUT:                                      ;Done with input
                SUB     BL,2                    ;Count of characters read
END_STRING:
                MOV     [SI+1],BL               ;Return number of chars read
                POP     SI
                POP     BX
                POP     AX
                RET
READ_STRING     ENDP
```

Stepping through the procedure, we can see that READ_STRING first checks to see if we pressed a special function key. It allows us to do so only when the string is empty. For example, if we press the F3 key after we press the *a* key, READ_STRING will ignore the F3 key and beep to tell us we pressed a special key at the wrong time (we'll come back to this later in this chapter). We can, however, press Escape, then F3, because the Escape key causes READ_STRING to clear the string buffer.

If READ_STRING reads a carriage-return character, it places the number of characters it read into the second byte of the string area and returns. Our new version of READ_BYTE looks at this byte to see how many characters READ_STRING actually read.

Next, READ_STRING checks to see if we typed a backspace character. If so, it CALLs BACK_SPACE to erase one character. If the string buffer becomes empty (BX becomes equal to 2—the start of the string buffer), then READ_STRING goes back to the start, where it can read a special key. Otherwise, it just reads the next character.

Finally, READ_STRING checks for the ESC character. BACK_SPACE erases characters only when there are characters in the buffer, so we can clear the string buffer by calling the BACK_SPACE procedure CHAR_NUM_LIMIT times, because READ_STRING can never read more than CHAR_NUM_LIMIT characters. Any other character is stored in the string buffer and echoed to the screen with WRITE_CHAR. Unless, that is, the buffer is full.

In the last chapter, we changed READ_BYTE in such a way that it couldn't read special function keys. We need only add a few lines here to allow READ_BYTE to work with our new version of READ_STRING, which can read special function keys. Here are the changes to make to READ_BYTE in KBD_IO.ASM:

Listing 24-4. Changes to READ_BYTE in KBD_IO.ASM

```
          PUBLIC   READ_BYTE
;------------------------------------------------------------------;
; This procedure reads a single ASCII character of a hex number.   ;
;                                                                  ;
; Returns:      AL         Character code (unless AH = 0)          ;
;               AH         0 if read ASCII char or hex number      ;
;                          1 if read a special key                 ;
;                          -1 if no characters read                ;
;                                                                  ;
; Uses:         HEX_TO_BYTE, STRING_TO_UPPER, READ_STRING          ;
; Reads:        KEYBOARD_INPUT, etc.                               ;
; Writes:       KEYBOARD_INPUT, etc.                               ;
;------------------------------------------------------------------;
READ_BYTE       PROC
        PUSH    DX
        MOV     CHAR_NUM_LIMIT,3        ;Allow only two characters (plus Enter)
        LEA     DX,KEYBOARD_INPUT
        CALL    READ_STRING
        CMP     NUM_CHARS_READ,1       ;See how many characters
        JE      ASCII_INPUT            ;Just one, treat as ASCII character
        JB      NO_CHARACTERS          ;Only Enter key hit
```

```
        CMP         BYTE PTR NUM_CHARS_READ,0FFh     ;Special function key?
        JE          SPECIAL_KEY              ;Yes
        CALL        STRING_TO_UPPER          ;No, convert string to uppercase
        LEA         DX,CHARS                 ;Address of string to convert
        CALL        HEX_TO_BYTE              ;Convert string from hex to byte
        JC          NO_CHARACTERS            ;Error, so return 'no characters read'
        XOR         AH,AH                    ;Signal read one byte
DONE_READ:
        POP         DX
        RET
NO_CHARACTERS:
        XOR         AH,AH                    ;Set to 'no characters read'
        NOT         AH                       ;Return -1 in AH
        JMP         DONE_READ
ASCII_INPUT:
        MOV         AL,CHARS                 ;Load character read
        XOR         AH,AH                    ;Signal read one character
        JMP         DONE_READ
SPECIAL_KEY:
        MOV         AL,CHARS[0]              ;Return the scan code
        MOV         AH,1                     ;Signal special key with 1
        JMP         DONE_READ
READ_BYTE   ENDP
```

Dskpatch, with the new versions of READ_BYTE and READ_STRING, should be much nicer to use. But there is a bug here, as we said. To try to find it, run Dskpatch and try all the boundary conditions for READ_BYTE and HEX_TO_BYTE. (Remember there are nine files that must be linked and converted to a .EXE program: Dskpatch, Dispatch, Disp_sec, Disk_io, Video_io, Kbd_io, Phantom, Cursor, and Editor.)

User *vs* Programmer Friendly

We made a design decision in READ_STRING that made Dskpatch easier to write, but isn't very friendly to the user. Run Dskpatch and try the following: Type a letter, such as *f*, then press one of the cursor keys. Dskpatch will beep at you. Why?

As the programmers of Dskpatch, we know exactly why: Our READ_STRING procedure doesn't return control once you've started entering a hex number until you press either the Escape or the Enter keys. But will the user know why Dskpatch is beeping at them? Probably not, which is problem number one. Problem number two is that users tend to become rather irritated and ornery when programs beep at them for no apparent reason. After all, they know that they should be able to move the cursor before they've finished entering a hex number—and they should!

Cases like this we call *Programmer Friendly* since they're simple for the programmer to write. User-Friendly programs, on the other hand, often require a considerable effort in programming to make them feel simple and natural. Here are a few words of advice on writing user-friendly programs:

- Avoid beeps except to alert the user of a critical error condition (such as a disk error). There is almost never cause to beep when you press a key that isn't allowed.
- Try to keep in mind what users will want, rather than what is simple to write. Sometimes they will be one and the same, but more often than not, you'll find you have to expend additional effort and development time to write user-friendly programs.
- Try to write modeless programs. By doing so, you'll eliminate many error conditions such as the one we placed (artificially) into READ_STRING.
- And above all, try out your ideas on real users, not just on other programmers, who can easily figure out how your program really works. Users don't want to understand your assumptions; they want your programs to be "obvious." And if a user has trouble running your program, try to understand why so you can make it easier to use.

Of course, these words of advice just scratch the surface on the issue of writing user-friendly programs. There are a number of books devoted entirely to design; we've recommended a few books in the bibliography that you'll find in the last chapter of this book (Chapter 32).

Summary

We wrote a new version of READ_STRING in this chapter that allowed us to read special characters again, in addition to strings. And with the exception of the small bug that we'll find and fix in the next chapter, READ_STRING works as advertised.

We then looked at several problems with READ_STRING. First of all, it is too long and complicated. We should rewrite it to be more modular.

Finally, we saw that READ_STRING isn't very user friendly since it beeps when you try to move the cursor after you've started to type a hex number. We won't fix this problem in this book, but you might want to try your hand at making Dskpatch less modal and therefore more user friendly.

Now its time to go on a little bug hunt to see if we can find and remove a small bug that lurks in Dskaptch.

IN SEARCH OF BUGS

If you try the new version of Dskpatch with *ag*, which isn't a valid hex number, you'll notice that Dskpatch doesn't do anything when you press the Enter key. Since the string *ag* isn't a hex number, there is nothing wrong with Dskpatch ignoring it, but the program should, at least, erase it from the screen.

This error is the sort we can find only by thoroughly checking the boundary conditions of a program. Not just the pieces, but the entire program. The bug here isn't the fault of READ_BYTE, even though it appeared when we rewrote that procedure. Rather, the problem is in the way we wrote DISPATCHER and EDIT_BYTE.

EDIT_BYTE is designed so it calls WRITE_PROMPT_LINE to rewrite the editor prompt line and clear the rest of the line. This will remove any character we typed. But if we type a string like *ag*, READ_BYTE reports that it read a string of zero length, and DISPATCH doesn't call EDIT_BYTE. What's the solution?

Fixing DISPATCHER

There are actually two ways to solve this problem. The best solution would be to rewrite Dskpatch to be more modular and to redesign DISPATCHER. We won't do that. Remember: Programs are never complete, but we have to stop somewhere. Instead, we'll add a fix to DISPATCHER so it will rewrite the prompt line whenever READ_BYTE reads a string of zero length.

Here are the modifications to DISPATCHER (in DISPATCH.ASM) to fix the bug:

Listing 25-1. Changes to DISPATCHER in DISPATCH.ASM

```
        PUBLIC  DISPATCHER
        EXTRN   READ_BYTE:PROC, EDIT_BYTE:PROC
        EXTRN   WRITE_PROMPT_LINE:PROC
.DATA
        EXTRN   EDITOR_PROMPT:BYTE
.CODE
;-------------------------------------------------------------------;
; This is the central dispatcher.  During normal editing and viewing,  ;
; this procedure reads characters from the keyboard and, if the character;
; is a command key (such as a cursor key), DISPATCHER calls the       ;
; procedures that do the actual work.  This dispatching is done for   ;
; special keys listed in the table DISPATCH_TABLE, where the procedure ;
; addresses are stored just after the key names.                      ;
;   If the character is not a special key, then it should be placed   ;
; directly into the sector buffer--this is the editing mode.          ;
;                                                                     ;
; Uses:         READ_BYTE, EDIT_BYTE, WRITE_PROMPT_LINE               ;
; Reads:        EDITOR_PROMPT                                         ;
;-------------------------------------------------------------------;
```

```
DISPATCHER          PROC
        PUSH        AX
        PUSH        BX
        PUSH        DX
DISPATCH_LOOP:
        CALL        READ_BYTE               ;Read character into AX
        OR          AH,AH                   ;AX = -1 if no character read, 1
                                            ; for an extended code.
        JS          NO_CHARS_READ           ;No character read, try again
        JNZ         SPECIAL_KEY             ;Read extended code
        MOV         DL,AL
        CALL        EDIT_BYTE               ;Was normal character, edit byte
        JMP         DISPATCH_LOOP           ;Read another character

SPECIAL_KEY:
        CMP         AL,68                   ;F10--exit?
        JE          END_DISPATCH            ;Yes, leave
                                            ;Use BX to look through table
        LEA         BX,DISPATCH_TABLE
SPECIAL_LOOP:
        CMP         BYTE PTR [BX],0         ;End of table?
        JE          NOT_IN_TABLE            ;Yes, key was not in the table
        CMP         AL,[BX]                 ;Is it this table entry?
        JE          DISPATCH                ;Yes, then dispatch
        ADD         BX,3                    ;No, try next entry
        JMP         SPECIAL_LOOP            ;Check next table entry

DISPATCH:
        INC         BX                      ;Point to address of procedure
        CALL        WORD PTR [BX]           ;Call procedure
        JMP         DISPATCH_LOOP           ;Wait for another key

NOT_IN_TABLE:
        JMP         DISPATCH_LOOP           ;Do nothing, just read next character

NO_CHARS_READ:
        LEA         DX,EDITOR_PROMPT
        CALL        WRITE_PROMPT_LINE       ;Erase any invalid characters typed
        JMP         DISPATCH_LOOP           ;Try again

END_DISPATCH:
        POP         DX
        POP         BX
        POP         AX
        RET
DISPATCHER          ENDP
```

This bug fix doesn't create any great problems, but it does make DIS-PATCHER slightly less elegant. Elegance is a virtue to strive for. Elegance and clarity often go hand in hand, and our rules of modular design are aimed at increasing elegance.

Summary

DISPATCHER is elegant because it's such a simple solution to a problem. Rather than using many comparisons for each special character we might type, we built a table we can search. Doing so made DISPATCHER simpler, and hence more reliable, than a program containing different instructions for each possible condition that might arise. By adding our small fix, we complicated

DISPATCHER—not by much in this case, but some bugs might require us to really complicate a procedure.

If you find yourself adding fixes that make a procedure too complicated, rewrite whichever procedures you must to remove this complexity. And always check the boundary conditions both before and after you add a procedure to your main program. You'll save yourself a lot of debugging effort if you do.

We can't overemphasize the importance of testing procedures with boundary conditions and of following the rules of modular design. Both techniques lead to better and more reliable programs. In the next chapter, we'll look at another method for debugging programs.

WRITING MODIFIED SECTORS

W e almost have a usable Dskpatch program. In this chapter, we'll build the procedure to write a modified sector back to disk, and in the next chapter, we'll write a procedure to show the second half of a sector.

Writing to the Disk

Writing a modified sector back to the disk can be disastrous if it's not done intentionally. All of Dskpatch's functions so far depend on the function keys F3, F4, and F10, and on the cursor keys. But any of these keys could be pressed quite by accident. Fortunately, the same doesn't hold true for the shifted function keys, so we'll use the shifted F2 key for writing a disk sector (we've chosen Shift F2 because F2 is often used in programs to save changes). This will prevent us from writing a sector back to disk unless we really want to.

Make the following changes to DISPATCH.ASM, to add WRITE_SECTOR to the table:

Listing 26-1. Changes to DISPATCH.ASM

```
      .CODE
            EXTRN    NEXT_SECTOR:PROC                          ;In DISK_IO.ASM
            EXTRN    PREVIOUS_SECTOR:PROC                      ;In DISK_IO.ASM
            EXTRN    PHANTOM_UP:PROC, PHANTOM_DOWN:PROC        ;In PHANTOM.ASM
            EXTRN    PHANTOM_LEFT:PROC, PHANTOM_RIGHT:PROC
            EXTRN    WRITE_SECTOR:PROC                         ;In DISK_IO.ASM
      .DATA
      ;----------------------------------------------------------------------;
      ; This table contains the legal extended ASCII keys and the addresses  ;
      ; of the procedures that should be called when each key is pressed.     ;
      ;                                                                       ;
      ;        The format of the table is                                     ;
      ;                DB      72              ;Extended code for cursor up    ;
      ;                DW      OFFSET PHANTOM_UP                               ;
      ;----------------------------------------------------------------------;
      DISPATCH_TABLE  LABEL    BYTE
            DB       61                       ;F3
            DW       OFFSET _TEXT:PREVIOUS_SECTOR
            DB       62                       ;F4
            DW       OFFSET _TEXT:NEXT_SECTOR
            DB       72                       ;Cursor up
            DW       OFFSET _TEXT:PHANTOM_UP
            DB       80                       ;Cursor down
            DW       OFFSET _TEXT:PHANTOM_DOWN
            DB       75                       ;Cursor left
            DW       OFFSET _TEXT:PHANTOM_LEFT
            DB       77                       ;Cursor right
            DW       OFFSET _TEXT:PHANTOM_RIGHT
            DB       85                       ;Shift F2
            DW       OFFSET _TEXT:WRITE_SECTOR
            DB       0                        ;End of the table
```

WRITE_SECTOR itself is almost identical to READ_SECTOR. The only change is that we wish to write, rather than read, a sector. Whereas the INT 25h asks DOS to read one sector, its companion function, INT 26h, asks DOS to write a sector to the disk. Here is WRITE_SECTOR; place it into DISK_IO.ASM:

Listing 26-2. Add This Procedure to DISK_IO.ASM

```
        PUBLIC  WRITE_SECTOR
;-----------------------------------------------------------------;
; This procedure writes the sector back to the disk.              ;
;                                                                 ;
; Reads:        DISK_DRIVE_NO, CURRENT_SECTOR_NO, SECTOR          ;
;-----------------------------------------------------------------;
WRITE_SECTOR    PROC
        PUSH    AX
        PUSH    BX
        PUSH    CX
        PUSH    DX
        MOV     AL,DISK_DRIVE_NO        ;Drive number
        MOV     CX,1                    ;Write 1 sector
        MOV     DX,CURRENT_SECTOR_NO    ;Logical sector
        LEA     BX,SECTOR
        INT     26h                     ;Write the sector to disk
        POPF                            ;Discard the flag information
        POP     DX
        POP     CX
        POP     BX
        POP     AX
        RET
WRITE_SECTOR    ENDP
```

Now, reassemble both Dispatch and Disk_io, but don't try Dskpatch's write function just yet. Find an old disk you don't care much about and put it in drive A, with your program disk in another drive, such as C. Run Dskpatch from drive C (or whatever drive you choose), so that Dskpatch reads the first sector from your scratch disk in drive A. Before you go on, make sure this is a scratch disk you have no qualms about destroying.

Change one byte in your sector display and make a note of the one you changed. Then, press the shifted F5 key. You'll see the red drive light come on: You've just written a modified sector back to drive A.

Next, press F4 to read the next sector (sector 1), then F3 to read the previous sector (your original sector, number 0). You should see the modified sector back again. Restore this sector and write it back to Drive A to restore the integrity of your scratch disk.

More Debugging Techniques

What would happen if we had made a small error in our program? Dskpatch is sufficiently large that we'd expect to have problems using Debug to find the bug. Besides, Dskpatch is composed of nine different files we must link to form DSKPATCH.EXE. How do we find any one procedure in this large program without tracing slowly through much of the program? As you'll see in this chapter, there are two ways to find procedures: by using a road map we can get from LINK, or by using a source-level debugger, such as Microsoft's CodeView or Borland's Turbo Debugger.

When we, the authors, originally wrote Dskpatch, something went wrong when we added WRITE_SECTOR; pressing the Shift-F2 key caused our machine to hang. But we couldn't find anything wrong with WRITE_SECTOR and the only other changes were to DISPATCH_TABLE. Everything appeared to be correct.

Finally, we traced the bug to a faulty definition in the dispatcher. The bug turned out to be an error in the DISPATCH_TABLE entry for WRITE_SECTOR. Somehow, we had typed a DW rather than a DB in the table, so WRITE_SECTOR's address was stored one byte higher in memory than it should have been. You can see the bug shown against a gray background here:

```
DISPATCH_TABLE   LABEL     BYTE
                   .
                   .
                   .
          DB      77                              ;Cursor right
          DW      OFFSET _TEXT:PHANTOM_RIGHT
          DW      85                              ;Shift F2
          DW      OFFSET _TEXT:WRITE_SECTOR
          DB      0                               ;End of the table
DATA_SEG         ENDS
```

As an exercise in debugging, make this change to your file DISPATCH.ASM, then follow the directions in the next section.

Building a Road Map

Let's learn how to use LINK to build a map of Dskpatch. This map will help us find procedures and variables in memory.

The LINK command we've used so far has grown to be fairly long:

```
LINK DSKPATCH DISK_IO DISP_SEC VIDEO_IO CURSOR DISPATCH KBD_IO PHANTOM EDITOR;
```

and we'll want to add even more to it. Does that mean we'll have to keep typing file after file after file? No, there is a much easier way. LINK allows us to supply an *automatic response* file containing all the information. With such a file, which we'll call linkinfo, we can simply type:

```
LINK @LINKINFO
```

and LINK will read all of its information from this file.

With the file names that we've used so far, linkinfo looks like this:

```
DSKPATCH DISK_IO DISP_SEC VIDEO_IO CURSOR +
DISPATCH KBD_IO PHANTOM EDITOR
```

The plus (+) at the end of the first line tells LINK to continue reading file names from the next line.

We can also add some more information that tells LINK to create a map of the procedures and variables in our program to this simple linkinfo file. Here is the entire linkinfo file:

```
DSKPATCH DISK_IO DISP_SEC VIDEO_IO CURSOR +
DISPATCH KBD_IO PHANTOM EDITOR
DSKPATCH
DSKPATCH /MAP;
```

The last two lines are new parameters. The first, *dskpatch*, tells LINK we want the .EXE file to be named DSKPATCH.EXE; the second new line tells LINK to create a listing file called DSKPATCH.MAP—to create our road map. The */map* switch tells LINK to provide a list of all the procedures and variables that we've declared to be public.

Create the map file by relinking Dskpatch with this linkinfo response file. The map file produced by the linker is about 130 lines long. That's a bit too long for us to reproduce in its entirety, so we'll reproduce the parts that are of particular interest. Here is our partial listing of the map file, DSKPATCH.MAP:

```
Start   Stop    Length  Name            Class
00000H  005C9H  005CAH  _TEXT           CODE
005CAH  006BBH  000F2H  _DATA           DATA
006BCH  026BBH  02000H  _BSS            BSS
026C0H  02ABFH  00400H  STACK           STACK

Origin  Group
005C:0  DGROUP

 Address         Publics by Name

 0000:03EA       BACK_SPACE
 0000:027E       CLEAR_SCREEN
 0000:02C0       CLEAR_TO_END_OF_LINE
 005C:000C       CURRENT_SECTOR_NO
 0000:02A0       CURSOR_RIGHT
 005C:000E       DISK_DRIVE_NO
 0000:02EC       DISPATCHER
 0000:0131       DISP_HALF_SECTOR
                      .
                      .
                      .
```

```
0000:01EB          WRITE_HEX_DIGIT
0000:025F          WRITE_PATTERN
0000:0546          WRITE_PHANTOM
0000:01A9          WRITE_PROMPT_LINE
0000:0086          WRITE_SECTOR
0000:01BC          WRITE_STRING
005C:00FC          _edata
005C:2100          _end

  Address          Publics by Value

0000:0030          PREVIOUS_SECTOR
0000:0050          NEXT_SECTOR
0000:006C          READ_SECTOR
0000:0086          WRITE_SECTOR
0000:00A0          INIT_SEC_DISP
0000:00CC          WRITE_HEADER
0000:0131          DISP_HALF_SECTOR
                      .
                      .
                      .

005C:000F          LINES_BEFORE_SECTOR
005C:0010          HEADER_LINE_NO
005C:0011          HEADER_PART_1
005C:0017          HEADER_PART_2
005C:0028          PROMPT_LINE_NO
005C:0029          EDITOR_PROMPT
005C:00FA          PHANTOM_CURSOR_X
005C:00FB          PHANTOM_CURSOR_Y
005C:00FC          _edata
005C:00FC          SECTOR
005C:2100          _end

Program entry point at 0000:0010
```

There are three main parts to this *load map* (so called because it tells us where our procedures are loaded in memory). The first shows a list of segments in our program. Dskpatch has several segments: _TEXT (which contains all our code) and _DATA, _BSS, and STACK, which are grouped together into the group DGROUP, and contain all our data. For those of you interested in more detail, _DATA contains all the memory variables defined in the .DATA segment (such as HEADER_LINE_NO), _BSS contains variables defined in the .DATA? segment (such as SECTOR), and STACK contains the stack defined by .STACK.

> **Note:** You may see slightly different numbers here if your procedures are in a different order than our procedures (you can check the order in Appendix B).

The next part of the load map shows our public procedures and variables, listed in alphabetical order. LINK lists only those procedures and variables you've declared to be PUBLIC—visible to the outside world. If you're debugging a long program, you may want to declare *all* procedures and variables to be public, just so you can find them in this map.

The final section of the map lists all the procedures and memory variables again, but this time in the order they appear in memory.

Both these lists include the memory address for each PUBLIC procedure or variable. If you check this list, you'll find that our procedure DISPATCHER starts at address 2ECh. We'll use this address now, to track down the bug in Dskpatch.

Tracking Down Bugs

If you were to try running the version of Dskpatch with the bug in it, you'd find that everything works, with the exception of Shift-F2, which on our machine caused Dskpatch to hang. You probably don't want to try Shift-F2; there's no telling what it will do on your machine.

Since everything worked (and works now) except for Shift-F2, our first guess when we wrote the program was that we had introduced a bug into WRITE_SECTOR. To find this bug, we could start debugging Dskpatch by tracing through WRITE_SECTOR. Instead, we'll take a somewhat different tack.

We know that DISPATCHER works correctly, because everything else (the cursor keys, F3, F4, and F10) all work correctly. That means DISPATCHER is a good starting point to search for the bug in Dskpatch. In other words, start your bug search with code you *know* works properly.

If you look at the program listing for DISPATCHER (in Chapter 25), you'll see that the instruction:

```
CALL WORD PTR [BX]
```

is the heart of DISPATCHER, because it calls all the other routines. In particular, this CALL instruction will call WRITE_SECTOR when we press Shift-F2. Let's start our search here.

We'll use Debug to start Dskpatch with a breakpoint set on this instruction. Of course, that means we need the address of this instruction, and we can find that by unassembling DISPATCHER, which starts at 2ECh. After a U 2EC, followed by another U command, you should see the CALL command:

```
               .
               .
               .
3E05:0313 EBF2      JMP      0307
3E05:0315 43        INC      BX
3E05:0316 FF17      CALL     [BX]
3E05:0318 EBD5      JMP      02EF
               .
               .
               .
```

Now that we know the CALL instruction is at location 316h, we can set a breakpoint at this address, then single-step into and through WRITE_SECTOR.

First, use the command G 316 to execute Dskpatch up to this instruction. You'll see Dskpatch start up, then wait for you to type a command. Press Shift-F2, since this is the command that is causing problems, and you'll see the following:

```
-G 316

AX=0155  BX=00A3  CX=06BC  DX=0029  SP=03F8  BP=75F0  SI=0000  DI=0F8A
DS=3E61  ES=3DF5  SS=4071  CS=3E05  IP=0316   NV UP EI PL NZ NA PE NC
3E05:0316 FF17         CALL    [BX]                        DS:00A3=0086
```

At this point the BX register is pointing to a word that should contain the address of WRITE_SECTOR. Let's see if it does:

```
-D A3 L 2
3E61:00A0          00 86
-
```

In other words, we're trying to CALL a procedure located at 8600h (remember the lower byte is displayed first). But if we look at our memory map, we can see that WRITE_SECTOR should be at 86h. In fact, we can also tell from this load map that we don't have *any* procedures at 8600h. The address is totally wrong!

In our original bug-hunting, once we discovered that this address was wrong, it didn't take us very long to find the error. We knew that DISPATCHER and the table were basically sound, because all the other keys worked, so we took a closer look at the data for Shift-F2 and found the DW where we should have had a DB. Having a road map makes debugging much simpler. Now let's take a look at some more powerful tools.

Source-Level Debugging

Both Microsoft and Borland have been hard at work providing the *ultimate* in programming tools. Microsoft's CodeView and Borland's Turbo Debugger are both debuggers of a type called *Source-Level* Debuggers. In other words, whereas Debug shows you just addresses in CALLs and JMPs, these two debuggers show you the actual source code.

You may only want to read one of the next two sections, since one section covers Microsoft's CodeView and the other Borland's Turbo Debugger, and there is some repetition of material between the two sections. (Those of you using

OPTASM need not despair: it also has a source-level debugger, which wasn't available in time for us to write about it in this edition.

Microsoft's CodeView

CodeView, the older of the two debuggers, was introduced in 1986, about two years before Borland's Turbo Debugger. It is now included with every Microsoft Macro Assembler package (we're using version 5.1) as well as most of the company's other language products. As you'll see in this section, CodeView is so useful that you may want to consider upgrading your macro assembler if you don't already have the latest version.

CodeView shares some similarities with Debug, since Microsoft wrote both programs. But there are more differences than similarities. We'll use two of the new features here: source-level debugging and screen swapping.

Source-level debugging lets us see the actual source code complete with comments, rather than just instructions and addresses, in our display. For example, if we use Debug to unassemble the first line in Dskpatch, we see:

```
2C14:0100 E88C03     CALL     048F
```

With CodeView, on the other hand, we see the following (as you can also see in Figure 26-1):

```
CALL     CLEAR_SCREEN
```

Which of these is easier to read? We rest our case.

The second new feature, screen swapping, is handy for debugging Dskpatch. Dskpatch moves the cursor around the screen, writing in different places. In the last section, where we used Debug, Debug started writing to this same screen and we eventually lost the Dskpatch screen.

CodeView, however, maintains two separate screens: one for Dskpatch and one for itself. Whenever Dskpatch is active, we see its screen; whenever CodeView is active, we see *its* screen. You'll get a clearer idea of screen swapping as we run through the following examples.

Before we can use CodeView's symbolic debugging features, we need to tell both the assembler and the linker to save debugging information, which we do with the /Zi switch in the assembler and the /CO (COdeview) switch in the linker.

Modify each line in your Makefile (or reassemble each file by hand) so it has the /Zi switch before the semicolon, and so we use a response file for LINK:

Listing 26-3. Make These Changes to MAKEFILE

```
dskpatch.obj:  dskpatch.asm
        masm dskpatch /Zi;

disk_io.obj:   disk_io.asm
        masm disk_io /Zi;
                .
                .
                .
dskpatch.exe:  dskpatch.obj disk_io.obj disp_sec.obj video_io.obj cursor.obj \
               dispatch.obj kbd_io.obj phantom.obj editor.obj
        link @linkinfo
```

Then change the linker response file LINKINFO as follows:

Listing 26-4. Changes to the Response File LINKINFO

```
dskpatch disk_io disp_sec video_io cursor +
dispatch kbd_io phantom editor
dskpatch
dskpatch /map /CO;
```

Finally, delete all the *.obj files and remake Dskpatch.exe.

We're now ready to start CodeView. Type:

```
C>CV DSKPATCH
```

and you should see a display like the one in Figure 26-1. Notice that you're viewing the *actual source file!* This is why CodeView is known as a source-level debugger.

Now that we have CodeView up and running, we can look at the procedure DISPATCHER without knowing where it is. Press Alt-S (to pull down the Search menu), then L (Label. . .) to search for a label. Next, type *dispatcher* into the dialog box that pops up and press Enter to see the code for DISPATCHER. Finally, use the cursor keys to scroll the CALL WORD PTR [BX] instruction on the second page.

Once you have the cursor on the line with CALL WORD PTR [BX] instruction, press F7 (which will run the program until it reaches the CALL). You'll see Dskpatch draw its screen. Then, you'll be returned to CodeView after you push Shift-F2. This time, though, we won't see any of Dskpatch's screen because CodeView swapped screens. To flip back to the Dskpatch screen, press the F4 key. Once you're looking at Dskpatch's screen, pressing any key will return you to CodeView's screen.

If you look on the lower, right part of the screen in Figure 26-2, you'll see two short lines that say:

```
DS:00A3
8600
```

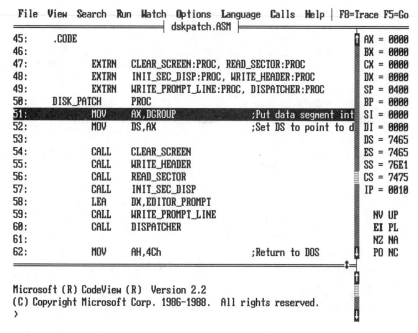

Figure 26-1. The Initial View of Dskpatch.exe Inside CodeView.

This area of the display is used to show the value in memory pointed to by the current instruction, which is the CALL instruction under the inverse-video cursor bar. In this case, it is the value at memory location [BX]. As you can clearly see, 8600 is exactly the value we found using Debug with the help of Link's memory map. But here we found this value much more quickly.

Type Alt-F (to pull down the File menu) and X (eXit) to exit from CodeView. You may want to skip the next section and go directly to the Summary. Don't forget to change the DW back to a DB in Dispatch.asm.

You may also want to change back the linkinfo file. We added the /CO switch so Link would add the debugging information to the .EXE file. But this debugging information makes the .EXE file quite a bit larger. In any case, you will probably want to remove the /CO switch before you give your programs to other people.

Borland's Turbo Debugger

Turbo Debugger shares few similarities with Debug. As you'll see in this section, Turbo Debugger's uses Borland's multiple-window style of user interface,

```
  File  View  Search  Run  Watch  Options  Language  Calls  Help │ F8=Trace F5=Go
                          ┤ dispatch.ASM ├
80:              JE       DISPATCH              ;Yes, then dispatch    ▯ AX = 0155
81:              ADD      BX,3                  ;No, try next entry      BX = 00A3
82:              JMP      SPECIAL_LOOP          ;Check next table ent    CX = 0000
83:                                                                     DX = 0029
84:    DISPATCH:                                                        SP = 03F8
85:              INC      BX                    ;Point to address of     BP = 75F0
86:              CALL     WORD PTR [BX]         ;Call procedure          SI = 0000
87:              JMP      DISPATCH_LOOP         ;Wait for another key    DI = 0F8A
88:                                                                     DS = 7463
89:    NOT_IN_TABLE:                            ;Do nothing, just rea    ES = 73F7
90:              JMP      DISPATCH_LOOP                                  SS = 7673
91:                                                                     CS = 7407
92:    NO_CHARS_READ:                                                   IP = 0316
93:              LEA      DX,EDITOR_PROMPT
94:              CALL     WRITE_PROMPT_LINE     ;Erase any invalid ch    NV UP
95:              JMP      DISPATCH_LOOP         ;Try again               EI PL
96:                                                                     NZ NA
97:    END_DISPATCH:                                                    PE NC
═══════════════════════════════════════════════════════════════════
                                                                      DS:00A3
Microsoft (R) CodeView (R)  Version 2.2                                 8600
(C) Copyright Microsoft Corp. 1986-1988.  All rights reserved.
>
```

Figure 26-2. CodeView After the F7 (Go) Command.

as opposed to Debug's command-line interface. Borland has also added many debugging features not present in Debug. We'll use two of the new features here: source-level debugging and screen swapping.

Source level debugging lets us see the actual source code complete with comments, rather than just instructions and addresses, in our display. For example, if we use Debug to unassemble the first line in Dskpatch, we see:

```
2C14:0100 E88C03        CALL    048F
```

With Turbo Debugger, on the other hand, we see the following (as you can also see in Figure 26-3):

```
CALL    CLEAR_SCREEN
```

Which of these is easier to read? We rest our case.

The second new feature, screen swapping, is handy for debugging Dskpatch. Dskpatch moves the cursor around the screen, writing in different places. In the last section, where we used Debug, Debug started writing to this same screen, and we eventually lost the Dskpatch screen.

Turbo Debugger, however, maintains two separate screens: one for Dskpatch and one for itself. Whenever Dskpatch is active, we see its screen; whenever Turbo Debugger is active, we see *its* screen. You'll get a clearer idea of screen swapping as we run through the following examples.

Before we can use Turbo Debugger's symbolic debugging features, we need to tell both the assembler and the linker to save debugging information, which we do with the -zi switch in the assembler and the /z switch in the linker.

Modify each line in your Makefile (or reassemble each file by hand) so that it has the -zi switch before the semicolon, and so we use a response file for TLINK (note that we're using TLINK):

Listing 26-5. Make These Changes to Makefile

```
dskpatch.exe:   dskpatch.obj disk_io.obj disp_sec.obj video_io.obj cursor.obj \
                dispatch.obj kbd_io.obj phantom.obj editor.obj
        tlink @linkinfo

dskpatch.obj:   dskpatch.asm
        tasm dskpatch -zi;

disk_io.obj:    disk_io.asm
        tasm disk_io -zi;
                .
                .
                .
```

Then change the linker response file LINKINFO as follows:

Listing 26-6. Changes to the Response File LINKINFO

```
dskpatch disk_io disp_sec video_io cursor +
dispatch kbd_io phantom editor
dskpatch
dskpatch /map /v;
```

Finally, delete all the *.obj files and remake Dskpatch.exe.

We're now ready to start Turbo Debugger. Type:

```
C>TD DSKPATCH.EXE
```

and you should see a display like the one in Figure 26-3. Notice that you're viewing the *actual source file*! This is why Turbo Debugger is known as a source-level debugger.

Now that we have Turbo Debugger up and running, we can look at the procedure DISPATCHER without knowing where it is. Press Alt-V to pulldown the View menu, followed by V to show the variable window (Figure 26-5). Then use the cursor up and down keys to move the cursor to dispatcher, and press Enter

```
 File   View   Run   Breakpoints   Data   Window   Options              READY
┌Module: dskpatch  File: dskpatch.asm 51────────────────────────────────1┐
│          EXTRN    CLEAR_SCREEN:PROC, READ_SECTOR:PROC                   │
│          EXTRN    INIT_SEC_DISP:PROC, WRITE_HEADER:PROC                 │
│          EXTRN    WRITE_PROMPT_LINE:PROC, DISPATCHER:PROC               │
│   DISK_PATCH    PROC                                                    │
│►         MOV      AX,DGROUP              ;Put data segment into AX       │
│          MOV      DS,AX                  ;Set DS to point to data        │
│                                                                         │
│          CALL     CLEAR_SCREEN                                          │
│          CALL     WRITE_HEADER                                          │
│          CALL     READ_SECTOR                                           │
│          CALL     INIT_SEC_DISP                                         │
│          LEA      DX,EDITOR_PROMPT                                      │
│          CALL     WRITE_PROMPT_LINE                                     │
│          CALL     DISPATCHER                                            │
│                                                                         │
│          MOV      AH,4Ch                 ;Return to DOS                  │
│          INT      21h                                                   │
│   DISK_PATCH    ENDP                                                    │
└─────────────────────────────────────────────────────────────────────────┘
┌Watches───────────────────────────────────────────────────────────────2┐
│                                                                         │
│                                                                         │
└─────────────────────────────────────────────────────────────────────────┘
F2-Bkpt F3-Close F4-Here F5-Zoom F6-Next F7-Trace F8-Step F9-Run F10-Menu
```

Figure 26-3. The Initial View of Dskpatch.exe Inside Turbo Debugger.

```
┌Variables──────────────────────────────────────────────3┐
│disp_line           @6F4F:0134│disk_patch          @6F4F:0000│
│dispatcher          @6F4F:02DC│sector_offset            0 (0h)│
│edit_byte           @6F4F:0595│current_sector_no        0 (0h)│
│editor_prompt  "Press function k│disk_drive_no        ' ' 0 (00h)│
│erase_phantom       @6F4F:0555│lines_before_sector  '0' 2 (02h)│
│goto_xy             @6F4F:0285│header_line_no       ' ' 0 (00h)│
│header_line_no    ' ' 0 (00h)│header_part_1          "Disk "│
│header_part_1        "Disk "│header_part_2 "        Sector "│
└──────────────────────────────────────────────────────┘
```

Figure 26-4. Turbo Debugger's variable window allows us to jump to a procedure.

to show the code for DISPATCHER. You can then use the cursor keys to scroll to the CALL Word Ptr [BX] instruction on the second page.

Once you have the cursor on the line with the CALL WORD PTR [BX] instruction, press F4, and follow that with Shift-F2. You'll see Dskpatch draw its screen. Then, you'll be returned to Turbo Debugger after you push Shift-F2.

```
 File   View   Run   Breakpoints   Data   Window   Options          READY
┌Module: dispatch  File: dispatch.asm 86───────────────────────────────1┐
│         CMP     AL,68                 ;F10--exit?                       │
│         JE      END_DISPATCH          ;Yes, leave                       │
│                                       ;Use BX to look through table     │
│         LEA     BX,DISPATCH_TABLE                                       │
│ SPECIAL_LOOP:                                                           │
│         CMP     BYTE PTR [BX],0       ;End of table?                    │
│         JE      NOT_IN_TABLE          ;Yes, key was not in the table    │
│         CMP     AL,[BX]               ;Is it this table entry?          │
│         JE      DISPATCH              ;Yes, then dispatch               │
│         ADD     BX,3                  ;No, try next entry               │
│         JMP     SPECIAL_LOOP          ;Check next table entry           │
│                                                                         │
│ DISPATCH:                                                               │
│         INC     BX                    ;Point to address of procedure    │
│▶        CALL    WORD PTR [BX]         ;Call procedure                   │
│         JMP     DISPATCH_LOOP         ;Wait for another key             │
│                                                                         │
│ NOT_IN_TABLE:                         ;Do nothing, just read next characte│
└─────────────────────────────────────────────────────────────────────┘
┌Watches──────────────────────────────────────────────────────────────2┐
│ [bx]                          word 38288 (7600h)                       │
└─────────────────────────────────────────────────────────────────────┘
 F2-Bkpt F3-Close F4-Here F5-Zoom F6-Next F7-Trace F8-Step F9-Run F10-Menu
```

**Figure 26-5. Turbo Debugger After Executing Dskpatch up to the CALL
       Instruction.**

This time, though, we won't see any of Dskpatch's screen because Turbo Debugger swapped screens. To flip back to the Dskpatch screen, press the Alt-F5 key. Once you're looking at Dskpatch's screen, pressing any key will return you to Turbo Debugger's screen.

At this point we want to see the value of [BX] so we'll know which procedure Dskpatch is about to call. For this we'll add a *watch*, which allows us to watch a value. Press Ctrl-W to bring up a dialog box that asks for an expression and type in [BX]. As you can see in the Watches window, 8600 is exactly the value we found using Debug with the help of Link's memory map. But here we found this value much more quickly.

Type Alt-X to exit from Turbo Debugger. Don't forget to change the DW back to a DB in Dispatch.asm.

You may also want to change back the linkinfo file. We added the /v switch so Link would add the debugging information to the .EXE file. But this debugging information makes the .EXE file quite a bit larger. In any case, you will probably want to remove the /v switch before you give your programs to other people.

Summary

That ends our discussion of debugging techniques. In the next chapter, we'll add the procedures to scroll the screen between the two half sectors. Then, in the final part of this book we'll cover a number of advanced topics.

By the way: Don't forget to fix the bug we placed in DISPATCH_TABLE.

27

THE OTHER HALF SECTOR

Ideally, Dskpatch should behave like a word processor when you try to move the cursor below the bottom of the half-sector display: The display should move up one line, with a new line appearing at the bottom. The version of Dskpatch on the disk available with this book does just that, but we won't get quite so sophisticated here. In this chapter, we'll add skeletal versions of the two procedures, SCROLL_UP and SCROLL_DOWN, that scroll the screen. In the disk version of Dskpatch, SCROLL_UP and SCROLL_DOWN can scroll by any number of lines from one to sixteen (there are sixteen lines in our half-sector display). The versions of SCROLL_UP and SCROLL_DOWN that we'll add to Dskpatch here scroll by full half sectors, so we'll see either the first or second half of the sector.

Scrolling by Half a Sector

Our old versions of PHANTOM_UP and PHANTOM_DOWN restore the cursor to the top or bottom of the half-sector display whenever we try to move the cursor off the top or bottom of the display. We'll change PHANTOM_UP and PHANTOM_DOWN so that we call either SCROLL_UP or SCROLL_DOWN when the cursor moves off the top or bottom of the display. These two new procedures will scroll the display and place the cursor at its new position.

Here are the modified versions of PHANTOM_UP and PHANTOM_DOWN (in PHANTOM.ASM):

Listing 27-1. Changes to PHANTOM.ASM

```
PHANTOM_UP          PROC
        CALL        ERASE_PHANTOM           ;Erase at current position
        DEC         PHANTOM_CURSOR_Y        ;Move cursor up one line
        JNS         WASNT_AT_TOP            ;Was not at the top, write cursor
        MOV         PHANTOM_CURSOR_Y,0      ;Was at the top, so put back there
        CALL        SCROLL_DOWN             ;Was at the top, scroll
WASNT_AT_TOP:
        CALL        WRITE_PHANTOM           ;Write the phantom at new position
        RET
PHANTOM_UP          ENDP


PHANTOM_DOWN        PROC
        CALL        ERASE_PHANTOM           ;Erase at current position
        INC         PHANTOM_CURSOR_Y        ;Move cursor up one line
        CMP         PHANTOM_CURSOR_Y,16     ;Was it at the bottom?
        JB          WASNT_AT_BOTTOM         ;No, so write phantom
        MOV         PHANTOM_CURSOR_Y,15     ;Was at bottom, so put back there
        CALL        SCROLL_UP               ;Was at bottom, scroll
WASNT_AT_BOTTOM:
        CALL        WRITE_PHANTOM           ;Write the phantom cursor
        RET
PHANTOM_DOWN        ENDP
```

Don't forget to change the comment header for PHANTOM_UP and PHANTOM_DOWN, to mention that these procedures now use SCROLL_UP and SCROLL_DOWN:

Listing 27-2. Changes to PHANTOM.ASM

```
;-------------------------------------------------------------------;
; These four procedures move the phantom cursors.                   ;
;                                                                   ;
; Uses:        ERASE_PHANTOM, WRITE_PHANTOM                         ;
;              SCROLL_DOWN, SCROLL_UP                               ;
; Reads:       PHANTOM_CURSOR_X, PHANTOM_CURSOR_Y                   ;
; Writes:      PHANTOM_CURSOR_X, PHANTOM_CURSOR_Y                   ;
;-------------------------------------------------------------------;
```

SCROLL_UP and SCROLL_DOWN are both fairly simple procedures, since they switch the display to the other half sector. For example, if we're looking at the first half sector, and PHANTOM_DOWN calls SCROLL_UP, we'll see the second half sector. SCROLL_UP changes SECTOR_OFFSET to 256, the start of the second half sector, moves the cursor to the start of the sector display, writes the half sector display for the second half, and finally writes the phantom cursor at the top of this display.

You can see all the details for both SCROLL_UP and SCROLL_DOWN in the following listing. Add these two procedures to PHANTOM.ASM.

Listing 27-3. Add These Procedures to PHANTOM.ASM

```
          EXTRN   DISP_HALF_SECTOR:PROC, GOTO_XY:PROC
     .DATA
          EXTRN   SECTOR_OFFSET:WORD
          EXTRN   LINES_BEFORE_SECTOR:BYTE
     .CODE
     ;-------------------------------------------------------------------;
     ; These two procedures move between the two half-sector displays.   ;
     ;                                                                   ;
     ; Uses:        WRITE_PHANTOM, DISP_HALF_SECTOR, ERASE_PHANTOM, GOTO_XY ;
     ;              SAVE_REAL_CURSOR, RESTORE_REAL_CURSOR                ;
     ; Reads:       LINES_BEFORE_SECTOR                                 ;
     ; Writes:      SECTOR_OFFSET, PHANTOM_CURSOR_Y                     ;
     ;-------------------------------------------------------------------;
     SCROLL_UP          PROC
          PUSH    DX
          CALL    ERASE_PHANTOM           ;Remove the phantom cursor
          CALL    SAVE_REAL_CURSOR        ;Save the real cursor position
          XOR     DL,DL                   ;Set cursor for half-sector display
          MOV     DH,LINES_BEFORE_SECTOR
          ADD     DH,2
          CALL    GOTO_XY
          MOV     DX,256                  ;Display the second half sector
          MOV     SECTOR_OFFSET,DX
          CALL    DISP_HALF_SECTOR
          CALL    RESTORE_REAL_CURSOR     ;Restore the real cursor position
          MOV     PHANTOM_CURSOR_Y,0      ;Cursor at top of second half sector
          CALL    WRITE_PHANTOM           ;Restore the phantom cursor
          POP     DX
          RET
     SCROLL_UP          ENDP
```

Listing 27-3. *continued*

```
SCROLL_DOWN     PROC
        PUSH    DX
        CALL    ERASE_PHANTOM           ;Remove the phantom cursor
        CALL    SAVE_REAL_CURSOR        ;Save the real cursor position
        XOR     DL,DL                   ;Set cursor for half-sector display
        MOV     DH,LINES_BEFORE_SECTOR
        ADD     DH,2
        CALL    GOTO_XY
        XOR     DX,DX                   ;Display the first half sector
        MOV     SECTOR_OFFSET,DX
        CALL    DISP_HALF_SECTOR
        CALL    RESTORE_REAL_CURSOR     ;Restore the real cursor position
        MOV     PHANTOM_CURSOR_Y,15     ;Cursor at bottom of first half sector
        CALL    WRITE_PHANTOM           ;Restore the phantom cursor
        POP     DX
        RET
SCROLL_DOWN     ENDP
```

SCROLL_UP and SCROLL_DOWN both work nicely, although there is one minor problem with them as Dskpatch stands now. Start Dskpatch and leave the cursor at the top of the screen. Press the cursor-up key, and you'll see Dskpatch rewrite the first half-sector display. Why? We didn't check for this boundary condition. Dskpatch rewrites the screen whenever you try to move the cursor off the top or bottom of the half-sector display.

Here's a challenge for you: Modify Dskpatch so that it checks for two boundary conditions. If the phantom cursor is at the top of the first half-sector display and you press the cursor-up key, Dskpatch should do nothing. If you're at the bottom of the second half-sector display and press the cursor-down key, again Dskpatch should do nothing.

Summary

This ends our work on Dskpatch in this book (with the exception of Chapter 30, where we'll modify Dskpatch for faster screen writing). Our intent was to use Dskpatch as a "live" example of the evolution of an assembly language program, at the same time provide you with a usable program, and a set of procedures you'll find helpful in your own programming. But the Dskpatch you've developed here isn't as finished as it could be. You'll find more features in the disk version of Dskpatch available with this book. And you may find yourself changing that disk version, for "a program is never done . . . but there comes a time when it has to be shipped to users."

We'll wrap up this book with a number of advanced topics: relocation, writing .COM programs, writing directly to the screen, writing C procedures in assembly language, and TSR or RAM-resident programs.

PART IV

Advanced Topics

28

RELOCATION

Most of the programs in Parts II and III of this book have been .EXE programs with two segments, one for code and one for data. There is one point in dealing with such programs that we've glossed over: relocation. In this chapter, we'll take a closer look at the relocation process, and we'll look at the steps DOS takes when it loads an .EXE program into memory.

To show something of the relocation process, we'll build a .COM program that does its own relocation (since DOS provides no relocation support for .COM programs). Because we haven't dealt yet with using the assembler to build .COM programs, we'll start with a short look at some new directives that we'll need to write .COM programs.

.COM Programs

Throughout this book we've been using the assembler to build .EXE programs, which is what you'll probably write most of the time. Some programs, however, need to be .COM programs (such as RAM-resident programs like the one we'll write in Chapter 32 and our example program in this chapter). For such programs, we can't use the simplified segment definitions (such as .CODE) since these directives support only .EXE programs. Instead, we have to use full segment definitions.

Full segment directives look very much like procedure definitions, as you can see in this example that defines the code segment:

```
_TEXT    SEGMENT
           .
           .
           .
_TEXT    ENDS
```

Rather than start a code segment with .CODE, we need to bracket the code with a SEGMENT and an ENDS (END Segment) directive. We also have to provide the name of the segment (_TEXT in this example).

Besides the segment definitions, we need to use another directive called the ASSUME directive. When we're using the simplified segment directives, the assembler knows from the .MODEL directive which segments the segment registers will point to. With full segment directives, however, we need to provide this information to the assembler ourselves (since we can't use the .MODEL directive). For this we use a new directive, ASSUME, as in this example:

```
ASSUME   CS:_TEXT, DS:_DATA, SS:STACK
```

This statement tells the assembler that the CS register will be pointing to our code (which is certainly the case when our program starts to run), that the DS register points to the data segment, and that SS points to the stack segment. The .MODEL directive automatically provides this information to the assembler (the last two we'll have to set up ourselves).

Finally, a .COM program, being contained entirely in a single segment, begins with the 256-byte PSP. To reserve room for the PSP, .COM programs must begin with ORG 100h. The ORG tells the assembler to start the program code at 100h (or 256) bytes into the segment. You'll see all these details in the next section, as well as in Chapter 32.

Relocation

Each of our .EXE programs begins with the following code that sets the DS register so it points to the data segment (which actually consists of a group of segments called DGROUP):

```
MOV   AX,DGROUP
MOV   DS,AX
```

The question is, where does the value for DGROUP come from? If you think about it, our programs can be loaded anywhere into memory, which means the value of DGROUP won't be known until we know where our program is loaded into memory. As it turns out, DOS performs an operation known as *relocation* when it loads an .EXE program into memory. This relocation processes patches numbers such as DGROUP so they reflect the actual location of the program in memory.

To understand this process, we'll write a .COM program that does its own relocation. Our goal is to set the DS register to the beginning of the _DATA segment, and the SS register to the beginning of the STACK segment. We can do this with a bit of trickery. First, we need to ensure that our three segments are loaded into memory in the correct order:

```
Code segment (_TEXT)
Data segment (_DATA)
Stack segment (STACK)
```

Fortunately, we've already taken care of this. When we're using the full segment directives, segments are loaded in the order in which they appear in our source file. A word of warning though: If you ever use the following technique to set segment registers, make sure you know the order in which LINK loads your segments (you can use the .MAP file to check the segment order).

How do we calculate the value for DS? Let's begin by looking at three labels we've placed into various segments in the following listing. Those labels are END_OF_CODE_SEG, END_OF_DATA_SEG, and END_OF_STACK_SEG. They aren't exactly where you might have expected them to be. Why not? Well, when we define a segment like this:

```
_TEXT    SEGMENT
```

(we need to use full segment definitions for .COM programs), we don't really tell the linker how to stitch together various segments. So, it starts each new segment on a paragraph boundary—at a hex address that ends with a zero, such as 32C40h. Because the Linker skips to the next paragraph boundary to start each segment, there will very often be a short, blank area between segments. By placing the label END_OF_CODE_SEG at the beginning of _DATA, we include this blank area. If we had put END_OF_CODE_SEG at the end of _TEXT, we wouldn't include the blank area between segments. (Look at the unassemble listing of our program on page 295. You'll see a blank area filled with zeros that is nine bytes long.)

As for the value of the DS register, _DATA starts at 39AF:0130, or 39C2:0000. The instruction OFFSET _TEXT:END_OF_CODE_SEG will return 130h, which is the number of bytes used by _TEXT. Divide this number by 16 to get the number we need to add to DS so that DS points to _DATA. We use the same technique to set SS.

Here's the listing for our program, including the relocation instructions needed for a .COM file:

```
              ASSUME  CS:_TEXT, DS:_DATA, SS:STACK


_TEXT    SEGMENT
         ORG     100h                      ;Reserve data area for .COM program
WRITE_STRING  PROC FAR
         MOV     AX,OFFSET _TEXT:END_OF_CODE_SEG
         MOV     CL,4                      ;Calculate number of paragraphs
         SHR     AX,CL                     ; (16 bytes) used by the code segment

         MOV     BX,CS
         ADD     AX,BX                     ;Add CS to this
         MOV     DS,AX                     ;Set the DS register to _DATA

         MOV     BX,OFFSET _DATA:END_OF_DATA_SEG
         SHR     BX,CL                     ;Calculate paras used by data segment
         ADD     AX,BX                     ;Add to value used for data segment
         MOV     SS,AX                     ;Set the SS register for STACK
         MOV     AX,OFFSET STACK:END_OF_STACK_SEG
         MOV     SP,AX                     ;Set SP to end of stack area

         MOV     AH,9                      ;Call for string output
         LEA     DX,STRING                 ;Load address of string
         INT     21h                       ;Write string

         MOV     AH,4Ch                    ;Ask to Exit back to DOS
         INT     21h                       ;Return to DOS
```

```
WRITE_STRING      ENDP

_TEXT      ENDS


_DATA    SEGMENT
END_OF_CODE_SEG            LABEL      BYTE
STRING   DB         "Hello, DOS here.$"
_DATA    ENDS


STACK    SEGMENT
END_OF_DATA_SEG            LABEL      BYTE
         DB         10 DUP ('STACK   ')     ;'STACK' followed by three spaces
END_OF_STACK_SEG    LABEL      BYTE
STACK    ENDS


         END      WRITE_STRING
```

Assemble and link this program, just as you would a .EXE program, and then type:

```
EXE2BIN WRITESTR WRITESTR.COM
```

to convert writestr.exe into a .COM program. EXE2BIN stands for convert an EXE file into (2) a BINary (.COM) file; in other words, EXE to BINary.

You can see the results of all this work in the following Debug session:

```
A>DEBUG WRITESTR.COM
-U
3E05:0100 B83001        MOV     AX,0130
3E05:0103 B104          MOV     CL,04
3E05:0105 D3E8          SHR     AX,CL
3E05:0107 8CCB          MOV     BX,CS
3E05:0109 03C3          ADD     AX,BX
3E05:010B 8ED8          MOV     DS,AX
3E05:010D BB2000        MOV     BX,0020
3E05:0110 D3EB          SHR     BX,CL
3E05:0112 03C3          ADD     AX,BX
3E05:0114 8ED0          MOV     SS,AX
3E05:0116 B85000        MOV     AX,0050
3E05:0119 8BE0          MOV     SP,AX
3E05:011B B409          MOV     AH,09
3E05:011D 8D160000      LEA     DX,[1000]
-U
3E05:0121 CD21          INT     21
3E05:0123 B44C          MOV     AH,4C
3E05:0125 CD21          INT     21
3E05:0127 0000          ADD     [BX+SI],AL
3E05:0129 0000          ADD     [BX+SI],AL
3E05:012B 0000          ADD     [BX+SI],AL
3E05:012D 0000          ADD     [BX+SI],AL
3E05:012F 004865        ADD     [BX+SI+65],CL
3E05:0132 6C            DB      6C
3E05:0133 6C            DB      6C
3E05:0134 6F            DB      6F
3E05:0135 2C20          SUB     AL,20
3E05:0137 44            INC     SP
3E05:0138 4F            DEC     DI
3E05:0139 53            PUSH    BX
3E05:013A 206865        AND     [BX+SI+65],CH
3E05:013D 7265          JB      01A4
3E05:013F 2E            CS:
```

```
3E05:0140 2400          AND     AL,00
-G 121

AX=0950  BX=0002  CX=0104  DX=0000  SP=0050  BP=0000  SI=0000  DI=0000
DS=3E18  ES=3DF5  SS=3E1A  CS=3E05  IP=0121   NV UP EI PL NZ NA PO NC
3E05:0121 CD21          INT     21
```

You'll rarely need to do this type of relocation yourself since DOS handles this automatically for .EXE programs. But it helps to understand what's happening behind the scenes.

.COM versus .EXE Programs

We'll finish this chapter by summarizing the difference between .COM and .EXE files and how DOS loads both types of programs into memory.

A .COM program stored on disk is essentially a memory image of the program. Because of this, a .COM program is restricted to a single segment, unless it does its own relocation, as we did in this chapter.

An .EXE program, on the other hand, lets DOS take care of the relocation. This delegating makes it very easy for .EXE programs to use multiple segments. For this reason, most large programs are .EXE rather than .COM programs.

For our final look at .COM versus .EXE programs, let's take a closer look at how DOS loads and starts both of them. This should make the differences between these types of program clearer and more concrete. We'll begin with .COM programs.

When DOS loads a .COM program into memory, it follows these steps:

- First, DOS creates the program segment prefix (PSP), which is the 256-byte area we saw in Chapter 11. Among other things, this PSP contains the command line typed.
- DOS next copies the entire .COM file from the disk into memory, immediately after the 256-byte PSP.
- DOS then sets the three segment registers DS, ES, and SS to the start of the PSP.
- DOS sets the SP register to the end of the segment—usually FFFE, which is the last word in the segment.
- Finally, DOS jumps to the start of the program, which sets the CS register to the start of the PSP and the IP register to 100h (the start of the .COM program).

In contrast, the steps involved in loading an .EXE file are somewhat more involved, because DOS does the relocation. Where does DOS finds the information it needs to do the relocation?

As it turns out, every .EXE file has a header that's stored at the start of the file. This header, or *relocation table*, is always at least 512 bytes long, and contains all the information DOS needs to do the relocation. With recent releases of its macro assembler, Microsoft has included a program called EXEMOD that we can use to look at some of the information in this header. For example, here is the header we get for an .EXE version of WRITESTR:

```
A>EXEMOD WRITESTR
Microsoft (R) EXE File Header Utility   Version 4.02
Copyright (C) Microsoft Corp 1985-1987.  All rights reserved.

WRITESTR                        (hex)           (dec)

.EXE size (bytes)                290             656
Minimum load size (bytes)         90             144
Overlay number                     0               0
Initial CS:IP               0000:0000
Initial SS:SP               0004:0050              80
Minimum allocation (para)          0               0
Maximum allocation (para)       FFFF           65535
Header size (para)                20              32
Relocation table offset           1E              30
Relocation entries                 1               1

A>
```

At the bottom of this table, you can see that we have a single relocation entry for the MOV AX,DGROUP instruction. Anytime we make a reference to a segment address, as with 'MOV AX,DGROUP, LINK' will add a relocation entry to the table. The segment address isn't known until DOS loads our program into memory, so we must let DOS supply the segment number.

There are also some other interesting pieces of information in the table; for example, the initial CS:IP and SS:SP values. These pairs tell us the initial values for IP and SP. The table also tells DOS how much memory our program needs before it can run: the Minimum load size.

Because DOS uses this relocation table to supply absolute addresses for such locations as segment addresses, there are a few extra steps it takes when loading a program into memory. Here are the steps DOS follows in loading an .EXE program:

- DOS creates the program-segment prefix (PSP), just as it does for a .COM program.
- Second, DOS checks the .EXE header to find where the header ends and the program starts. It then loads the rest of the program into memory after the PSP.

- Next, using the header information, DOS finds and patches all the references in the program that need to be relocated, such as references to segment addresses.
- DOS then sets the ES and DS registers so they point to the start of the PSP. If your program has its own data segment, your program needs to change DS and/or ES so they point to your data segment.
- DOS sets SS:SP according to the information in the .EXE header. In the case illustrated, the header states that SS:SP will be placed at 0004:0050. That means DOS will set SP to 0050, and set SS so it is four paragraphs higher in memory than the end of the PSP.
- Finally, DOS jumps to the start of the program using the address provided in the .EXE header. This sets the CS register to the start of the code segment, and IP to the offset given in the .EXE header.

29

MORE ON SEGMENTS AND ASSUME

In this chapter we'll learn about a feature called *segment overrides*, which we'll use in the next chapter when we write directly to the screen. In the process, we'll also take a closer look at ASSUME statements and full segment definitions.

Segment Override

So far we've always read and written data located in the data segment. We've been dealing with a single data segment in this book (which is actually several segments grouped into a single segment called DGROUP), so we've had no reason to read or write data in other segments.

But, in some cases, we'll need more than one data segment. A classic example is writing directly to the screen: Many commercial programs write to the screen by moving the data directly into screen memory and completely bypassing the ROM BIOS routines in the interest of speed. Screen memory on the IBM PC is located at segment B800h for a color/graphics adapter and at segment B000h for monochrome display adapters. To write directly to the screen means we'd want to write in different segments.

In this section, we'll write a short program showing how we can write to two different segments, using the DS and ES registers to point to the two segments. In fact, many programs that write directly to screen memory do use the ES register to point to screen memory, as we'll do in the next chapter.

In this example, we use full segment definitions to give us more control over segments than the simplified segment definitions give us. Most of the time you'll be able to use the simplified segment definitions (as we will when we write directly to the screen in the next chapter). But we chose to use the full segment definitions in this chapter to give you more examples of how to use them and to give you a better understanding of the ASSUME statement that you'll need along with the full segment definitions.

Here is our program. It's very short, and you can see that it has two data segments, along with one variable in each data segment:

```
DOSSEG

_DATA       SEGMENT
DS_VAR              DW    1
_DATA       ENDS

EXTRA_SEG           SEGMENT PUBLIC
ES_VAR              DW    2
EXTRA_SEG           ENDS
```

```
STACK         SEGMENT STACK
              DB       10 DUP ('STACK    ') ;'STACK' followed by three spaces
STACK         ENDS

_TEXT         SEGMENT
              ASSUME  CS:_TEXT, DS:_DATA, ES:EXTRA_SEG, SS:STACK

TEST_SEG              PROC
              MOV      AX,_DATA               ;Segment address for _DATA
              MOV      DS,AX                  ;Set up DS register for _DATA
              MOV      AX,EXTRA_SEG           ;Segment address for EXTRA_SEG
              MOV      ES,AX                  ;Set up ES register for EXTRA_SEG

              MOV      AX,DS_VAR              ;Read a variable from data segment
              MOV      BX,ES:ES_VAR           ;Read a variable from extra segment

              MOV      AH,4Ch                 ;Ask to Exit back to DOS
              INT      21h                    ;Return to DOS
TEST_SEG             ENDP

_TEXT         ENDS


              END    TEST_SEG
```

We'll use this program to learn about both segment overrides and the ASSUME directive.

Note that we've put both data segments and the stack segment *before* our code segment, and that we've also put the ASSUME directive after all the segment declarations. As we'll see in this section, this arrangement is a direct result of using two data segments.

Let's take a look at the two MOV instructions in this program:

```
MOV  AX,DS_VAR
MOV  BX,ES:ES_VAR
```

The ES: in front of the second instruction tells the 8088 to use the ES, rather than the DS, register for this operation (to read the data from our extra segment). Every instruction has a default segment register it uses when it refers to data. But, as we've done with the ES register here, we can also tell the 8088 we want to use some other segment register for data.

Here's how it works: The 8088 has four special instructions, one for each of the four segment registers. These instructions are the *segment-override* instructions, and they tell the 8088 to use a specific segment register, rather than the default, when the instruction following the segment override tries to read or write memory.

For example, the instruction MOV AX,ES:ES_VAR is actually encoded as two instructions. You'll see the following if you unassemble our test program:

```
2CF4:000D              ES:
2CF4:000E 8B1E0000     MOV     BX,[0000]
```

This shows that the assembler translated our instruction into a segment-override instruction, followed by the MOV instruction. Now the MOV instruction will read its data from the ES, rather than the DS, segment.

If you trace through this program, you'll see that the first MOV instruction sets AX equal to 1 (DS_VAR) and the second MOV sets BX equal to 2 (ES_VAR). In other words: We've read data from two different segments.

Another Look at ASSUME

Let's take a look at what happens when we remove the ES: from our program. Change the line:

```
MOV  BX,ES:ES_VAR
```

so it reads:

```
MOV  BX,ES_VAR
```

We're no longer telling the assembler we want to use the ES register when we read from memory, so it should go back to using the default segment (DS), right? Wrong. Use Debug to look at the result of this change. You'll see that we still have the ES: segment override in front of our MOV instruction. How could the assembler possibly have known that our variable is in the extra, rather than the data, segment? By using the information we gave it in the ASSUME directive.

Our ASSUME statement tells the assembler that the DS register points to the segment DATA_SEG, while ES points to EXTRA_SEG. Each time we write an instruction that uses a memory variable, the assembler searches for a declaration of this variable to see which segment it's declared in. Then, it searches through the ASSUME list to find out which segment register is pointing to this segment. The assembler uses this segment register when it generates the instruction.

In the case of our MOV BX,ES_VAR instruction, the assembler noticed ES_VAR was in the segment called EXTRA_SEG and that the ES register was pointing to that segment, so it generated an ES: segment-override instruction on its own. If we were to move ES_VAR into STACK_SEG, the assembler would generate an SS: segment-override instruction. The assembler automatically generates any segment-override instructions we need, provided, of course, that our ASSUME directives reflect the actual contents of the segment registers.

Summary

In this chapter we learned more about segments and how the assembler works with them. First we learned about segment overrides, which allow us to read and write data in other segments. We'll use such overrides in the next chapter when we write characters directly to the screen. Finally, we learned more about the ASSUME directive.

The next chapter covers writing directly to screen memory. We'll do this to dramatically increase the speed of writing characters to the screen.

A VERY FAST WRITE_CHAR

At the very start of this book, we mentioned that many people who write programs in assembly language often do so for speed. Assembly language programs are almost always faster than programs written in other languages. But you may have noticed that our Dskpatch program doesn't draw the screen as quickly as many commercial programs. Why is it so much slower?

So far we've been using the ROM BIOS routines to display characters on the screen. But as we'll see in this chapter, the ROM BIOS routines can be quite slow. Most programs these days bypass the ROM BIOS and write characters directly to screen memory in favor of raw speed.

In this chapter we'll modify Dskpatch so it writes characters very quickly to the screen. Unfortunately, we'll have to make a number of changes to Dskpatch to obtain faster screen display: We can't just write a new WRITE_CHAR for reasons we'll cover soon.

Screen Segment

Before we can write characters directly to screen memory, we need a few pieces of information, like: Where is the display memory and how are characters stored in display memory?

The first question has a simple, two-part answer. Screen memory has its own segment, which is either B800h or B000h. Why do we have two different segments? There are two classes of display adapters, monochrome display adapters and color graphics adapters (CGA, EGA, and VGA), and you can have one adapter of each class in your computer at the same time (but few people do). So IBM gave them non-overlapping screen segments.

Monochrome refers to IBM's monochrome display adapter, Hercules graphics cards, and EGA and VGA cards attached to an IBM monochrome display. Monochrome cards display characters on the screen in green, white, or amber (it depends on the display), and have only a limited set of "colors" they can display: normal, bright, inverse, and underlined. Monochrome cards have their screen segment at B000h.

Color graphics adapters, on the other hand, can display 16 different text colors at one time, and they can also be switched into graphics mode (which we won't talk about in this book). The most common color graphics adapters are EGA and VGA cards, although there are still CGA cards from the earlier days. Color graphics adapters have their screen memory at B800h.

Many users these days don't know which type of display adapter they have and they shouldn't need to know. It is up to our program to determine which

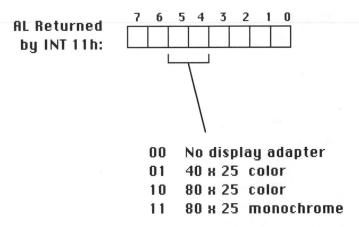

Figure 30-1. The INT 11h Equipment Flags.

display adapter is active. For this we can use INT 11h, which returns a list of equipment that we have installed. As you can see from Figure 30-1, bits 4 and 5 tell us if the display is a monochrome or color display. In other words, the screen segment will be at B000h (monochrome) if both bits are 1, and B800h (color) otherwise (we'll ignore the case when no display adapter is installed).

Since we won't know which screen segment to use until we run our program, we'll need to call a procedure, INIT_WRITE_CHAR, that determines the screen segment before we make any calls to WRITE_CHAR. We'll place this call at the start of Disk_patch to make sure we call it before writing any characters on the screen. Here are the changes to DSKPATCH.ASM to add this call:

Listing 30-1. Changes to DSKPATCH.ASM

```
            EXTRN       WRITE_PROMPT_LINE:PROC, DISPATCHER:PROC
            EXTRN       INIT_WRITE_CHAR:PROC
DISK_PATCH      PROC
            MOV         AX,DGROUP               ;Put data segment into AX
            MOV         DS,AX                   ;Set DS to point to data

            CALL        INIT_WRITE_CHAR
            CALL        CLEAR_SCREEN
            CALL        WRITE_HEADER
                          .
                          .
                          .
```

Then add INIT_WRITE_CHAR to VIDEO_IO.ASM:

Listing 30-2. Add This Procedure to VIDEO_IO.ASM

```
            PUBLIC  INIT_WRITE_CHAR
```

Listing 30-2. *continued*

```
;----------------------------------------------------------------;
; You need to call this procedure before you call WRITE_CHAR since ;
; WRITE_CHAR uses information set by this procedure.               ;
;                                                                 ;
; Writes:      SCREEN_SEG                                         ;
;----------------------------------------------------------------;
INIT_WRITE_CHAR          PROC
        PUSH    AX
        PUSH    BX
        MOV     BX,0B800h              ;Set for color graphics display
        INT     11h                    ;Get equipment information
        AND     AL,30h                 ;Keep just the video display type
        CMP     AL,30h                 ;Is this a monochrome display adapter?
        JNE     SET_BASE               ;No, it's color, so use B800
        MOV     BX,0B000h              ;Yes, it's monochrome, so use B000
SET_BASE:
        MOV     SCREEN_SEG,BX          ;Save the screen segment
        POP     BX
        POP     AX
        RET
INIT_WRITE_CHAR          ENDP
```

Note that we're saving the screen segment in SCREEN_SEG (which we'll add below). WRITE_CHAR will use this variable when we modify it to write directly to screen memory.

Now that we know how to find the screen memory, we need to know how the characters and their attributes are stored.

Organization of Screen Memory

If you were to use Debug to look at screen memory when the first line of the screen is:

```
DSKPATCH ASM
```

you would see the following (for a color graphics card):

```
-B800:0
B800:0000   44 07 53 07 4B 07 50 07-41 07 54 07 43 07 48 07   D.S.K.P.A.T.C.H.
B800:0010   20 07 41 07 53 07 4D 07-20 07 20 07 20 07 20 07   .A.S.M. . . . .
                                    .
                                    .
                                    .
```

In other words, there is a 07 between each character on the screen. As you'll recall from Chapter 18, 7 is the character attribute for normal text (and 70h is the attribute for inverse text). Each 7 in the debug display is the attribute for one character, with the character lower in memory. In other words, every character on the screen uses one word of screen memory, with the character code in the lower byte and the attribute in the upper byte. Let's write a new version of

WRITE_CHAR that writes characters directly to screen memory. Make these changes to Video_io.asm:

Listing 30-3. Changes to VIDEO_IO.ASM

```
        PUBLIC  WRITE_CHAR
        EXTRN   CURSOR_RIGHT:PROC
;---------------------------------------------------------------------;
; This procedure outputs a character to the screen by writing directly ;
; into screen memory, so that characters such as the backspace are      ;
; treated as any other characters and are displayed.                    ;
;                                                                        ;
; This procedure must do a bit of work to update the cursor position.   ;
;                                                                        ;
; On entry:     DL      Byte to print on screen                          ;
;                                                                        ;
; Uses:         CURSOR_RIGHT                                             ;
; Reads:        SCREEN_SEG                                               ;
;---------------------------------------------------------------------;
WRITE_CHAR      PROC
        PUSH    AX
        PUSH    BX
        PUSH    CX
        PUSH    DX
        PUSH    ES

        MOV     AX,SCREEN_SEG           ;Get segment for screen memory
        MOV     ES,AX                   ;Point ES to screen memory

        PUSH    DX                      ;Save the character to write
        MOV     AH,3                    ;Ask for the cursor position
        XOR     BH,BH                   ;On page 0
        INT     10h                     ;Get row, column
        MOV     AL,DH                   ;Put row into AL
        MOV     BL,80                   ;There are 80 characters per line
        MUL     BL                      ;AX = row * 80
        ADD     AL,DL                   ;Add the column
        ADC     AH,0                    ;Propagate carry into AH
        SHL     AX,1                    ;Convert to byte offset
        MOV     BX,AX                   ;Put byte offset of cursor into BX
        POP     DX                      ;Restore the character

        MOV     DH,7                    ;Use the normal attribute
        MOV     ES:[BX],DX              ;Write character/attribute to screen
        CALL    CURSOR_RIGHT            ;Now move to next cursor position

        POP     ES
        POP     DX
        POP     CX
        POP     BX
        POP     AX
        RET
WRITE_CHAR      ENDP
```

Finally, we need to add a memory variable to VIDEO_IO.ASM:

Listing 30-4. Add DATA_SEG to the Start of VIDEO_IO.ASM

```
.MODEL SMALL

.DATA
SCREEN_SEG      DW      0B800h          ;Segment of the screen buffer

.CODE
```

After you've made these changes, rebuild Dskpatch (you'll need to assemble DSKPATCH and VIDEO_IO) and try the new version. What you'll find is that Dskpatch doesn't write to the screen any faster than before. And for a very simple reason. We're moving the cursor after we write each character, which is a slow process.

High Speed

The solution is to rewrite the routines in VIDEO_IO and CURSOR to keep track of where the cursor should be instead of moving the cursor; we'll move the cursor only when we need to. For this we'll introduce two new memory variables: SCREEN_X and SCREEN_Y. Now this may sound simple, but as you'll see here, we'll have to change a number of procedures and write a few new ones.

There is another optimization we can make while we're at it. Right now WRITE_CHAR calculates the offset of the cursor into the screen buffer each time you call it. But since we'll be keeping track of where the cursor should be, we can also keep track of this offset in the variable SCREEN_PTR:

Listing 30-5. Changes to WRITE_CHAR in VIDEO_IO.ASM

```
; Uses:         CURSOR_RIGHT                                          ;
; Reads:        SCREEN_SEG, SCREEN_PTR                                ;
;----------------------------------------------------------------------;
WRITE_CHAR      PROC
        PUSH    AX
        PUSH    BX
        PUSH    CX
        PUSH    DX
        PUSH    ES

        MOV     AX,SCREEN_SEG         ;Get segment for screen memory
        MOV     ES,AX                 ;Point ES to screen memory
        MOV     BX,SCREEN_PTR         ;Pointer to character in screen memory

        PUSH    DX                    ;Save the character to write
        MOV     AH,3                  ;Ask for the cursor position
        XOR     BH,BH                 ;On page 0
        INT     10h                   ;Get row, column
        MOV     AL,DH                 ;Put row into AL
        MOV     BL,80                 ;There are 80 characters per line
        MUL     BL                    ;AX = row * 80
        ADD     AL,DL                 ;Add the column
        ADC     AH,0                  ;Propagate carry into AH
        SHL     AX,1                  ;Convert to byte offset
        MOV     BX,AX                 ;Put byte offset of cursor into BX
        POP     DX                    ;Restore the character

        MOV     DH,7                  ;Use the normal attribute
        MOV     ES:[BX],DX            ;Write character/attribute to screen
        CALL    CURSOR_RIGHT          ;Now move to next cursor position

        POP     ES
        POP     DX
        POP     CX
```

```
            POP    BX
            POP    AX
            RET
WRITE_CHAR  ENDP
```

You can see that WRITE_CHAR has become quite simple.

You'll also need to add our three new memory variables to the DATA_SEG in VIDEO_IO.ASM:

Listing 30-6. Changes to .DATA in VIDEO_IO.ASM

```
.DATA
            PUBLIC    SCREEN_PTR
            PUBLIC    SCREEN_X, SCREEN_Y
SCREEN_SEG          DW    0B800h        ;Segment of the screen buffer
SCREEN_PTR          DW    0             ;Offset into screen memory of cursor
SCREEN_X            DB    0             ;Position of the screen cursor
SCREEN_Y            DB    0

.CODE
```

And finally (in VIDEO_IO.ASM, that is) here are the changes to WRITE_ATTRIBUTE_N_TIMES so it will write directly to the screen:

Listing 30-7. Changes to WRITE_ATTRIBUTE_N_TIMES in VIDEO_IO.ASM

```
; Uses:        CURSOR_RIGHT                                           ;
; Reads:       SCREEN_SEG, SCREEN_PTR                                 ;
;----------------------------------------------------------------------;
WRITE_ATTRIBUTE_N]TIMES              PROC
        PUSH    AX
        PUSH    BX
        PUSH    CX
        PUSH    DX
        PUSH    DI
        PUSH    ES

        MOV     AX,SCREEN_SEG        ;Set ES to point to screen segment
        MOV     ES,AX
        MOV     DI,SCREEN_PTR        ;Character under cursor
        INC     DI                   ;Point to the attribute under cursor
        MOV     AL,DL                ;Put attribute into AL
ATTR_LOOP:
        STOSB                        ;Save one attribute
        INC     DI                   ;Move to next attribute
        INC     SCREEN_X             ;Move to next column
        LOOP    ATTR_LOOP            ;Write N attributes

        DEC     DI                   ;Point to start of next character
        MOV     SCREEN_PTR,DI        ;Remember where we are

        POP     ES
        POP     DI
        POP     DX
        POP     CX
        POP     BX
        POP     AX
        RET
WRITE_ATTRIBUTE_N_TIMES      ENDP
```

Most of this procedure should be fairly clear, with the exception of a new instruction: STOSB (*STOre String Byte*). STOSB is basically the opposite of the LODSB string instruction that loaded a byte from DS:SI and incremented the SI register. STOSB, on the other hand, stores the byte from AL into the address at ES:DI, then increments DI.

All the other changes we need to make (with the exception of a simple fix in KBD_IO) are to procedures in CURSOR.ASM. First, we'll need to change GOTO_XY so it sets SCREEN_X and SCREEN_Y and calculates the value of SCREEN_PTR:

Listing 30-8. Changes to GOTO_XY in CURSOR.ASM

```
        PUBLIC  GOTO_XY
.DATA
        EXTRN   SCREEN_PTR:WORD        ;Pointer to character under cursor
        EXTRN   SCREEN_X:BYTE, SCREEN_Y:BYTE
.CODE
;---------------------------------------------------------------;
; This procedure moves the cursor                               ;
;                                                               ;
; On entry:    DH   Row (Y)                                     ;
;              DL   Column (X)                                  ;
;---------------------------------------------------------------;
GOTO_XY       PROC
        PUSH    AX
        PUSH    BX
        MOV     BH,0                   ;Display page 0
        MOV     AH,2                   ;Call for SET CURSOR POSITION
        INT     10h

        MOV     AL,DH                  ;Get the row number
        MOV     BL,80                  ;Multiply by 80 chars per line
        MUL     BL                     ;AX = row * 80
        ADD     AL,DL                  ;Add column
        ADC     AH,0                   ;AX = row * 80 + column
        SHL     AX,1                   ;Convert to a byte offset
        MOV     SCREEN_PTR,AX          ;Save the cursor offset
        MOV     SCREEN_X,DL            ;Save the cursor position
        MOV     SCREEN_Y,DH

        POP     BX
        POP     AX
        RET
GOTO_XY ENDP
```

As you can see, we've moved the calculation of the offset to the character under the cursor from WRITE_CHAR, where it was before, to here.

We also need to modify CURSOR_RIGHT so it updates these memory variables:

Listing 30-9. Changes to CURSOR_RIGHT in CURSOR.ASM

```
        PUBLIC  CURSOR_RIGHT
.DATA
        EXTRN   SCREEN_PTR:WORD        ;Pointer to character under cursor
        EXTRN   SCREEN_X:BYTE, SCREEN_Y:BYTE
.CODE
```

```
;------------------------------------------------------------------;
; This procedure moves the cursor one position to the right or to the  ;
; next line if the cursor was at the end of a line.                ;
;                                                                  ;
; Uses:          SEND_CRLF                                         ;
; Writes:        SCREEN_PTR, SCREEN_X, SCREEN_Y                    ;
;------------------------------------------------------------------;
CURSOR_RIGHT    PROC
        INC     SCREEN_PTR              ;Move to next character position (word)
        INC     SCREEN_PTR
        INC     SCREEN_X                ;Move to next column
        CMP     SCREEN_X,79             ;Make sure column <= 79
        JBE     OK
        CALL    SEND_CRLF               ;Go to next line
OK:
        RET
CURSOR_RIGHT    ENDP
```

We'll also need to change CLEAR_TO_END_OF_LINE so it uses SCREEN_X and SCREEN_Y rather than the location of the real cursor:

Listing 30-10. Changes to CLEAR_TO_END_OF_LINE in CURSOR.ASM

```
        PUSH    CX
        PUSH    DX
        MOV     AH,3                    ;Read current cursor position
        XOR     BH,BH                   ; on page 0
        INT     10h                     ;Now have (X,Y) in DL, DH
        MOV     DL,SCREEN_X
        MOV     DH,SCREEN_Y
        MOV     AH,6                    ;Set up to clear to end of line
        XOR     AL,AL                   ;Clear window
```

The next few steps need some explaining. Because we're no longer updating the position of the real cursor, the real and virtual cursors will often be out of synchronization. Most of the time this isn't a problem. But there are a few cases when we have to synchronize both cursors; sometimes we'll want to move the real cursor to where we think the cursor is, and sometimes we'll want to move our virtual cursor. For example, before we ask the user for input, we need to move the cursor to where we think the cursor should be. We'll perform this with the procedure UPDATE_REAL_CURSOR, which moves the real cursor.

On the other hand, SEND_CRLF moves the real cursor, so we'll need to call UPDATE_VIRTUAL_CURSOR to move the virtual cursor to where the real cursor is after SEND_CRLF.

Here are the two procedures you'll need to add to CURSOR.ASM:

Listing 30-11. Add These Procedures to CURSOR.ASM

```
        PUBLIC  UPDATE_REAL_CURSOR
;------------------------------------------------------------------;
; This procedure moves the real cursor to the current virtual cursor  ;
; position.  You'll want to call it just before you wait for keyboard ;
; input.                                                           ;
;------------------------------------------------------------------;
UPDATE_REAL_CURSOR  PROC
        PUSH    DX
```

Listing 30-11. *continued*

```
            MOV     DL,SCREEN_X              ;Get position of the virtual cursor
            MOV     DH,SCREEN_Y
            CALL    GOTO_XY                  ;Move real cursor to this position
            POP     DX
            RET
UPDATE_REAL_CURSOR  ENDP


            PUBLIC  UPDATE_VIRTUAL_CURSOR
;-------------------------------------------------------------------;
; This procedure updates the position of our virtual cursor to agree;
; with the position of the real cursor.                             ;
;-------------------------------------------------------------------;
UPDATE_VIRTUAL_CURSOR      PROC
            PUSH    AX
            PUSH    BX
            PUSH    CX
            PUSH    DX
            MOV     AH,3                     ;Ask for the cursor position
            XOR     BH,BH                    ;On page 0
            INT     10h                      ;Get cursor position into DH, DL
            CALL    GOTO_XY                  ;Move virtual cursor to this position
            POP     DX
            POP     CX
            POP     BX
            POP     AX
            RET
UPDATE_VIRTUAL_CURSOR      ENDP
```

Note that we're using GOTO_XY to update the three variables SCREEN_X, SCREEN_Y, and SCREEN_PTR.

Finally, we need to modify several procedures to use the preceding two procedures. Here are the changes to SEND_CRLF:

Listing 30-12. Changes to SEND_CRLF in CURSOR.ASM

```
;                                                                   ;
; Uses:          UPDATE_VIRTUAL_CURSOR                              ;
;-------------------------------------------------------------------;
SEND_CRLF       PROC
            PUSH    AX
            PUSH    DX
            MOV     AH,2
            MOV     DL,CR
            INT     21h
            MOV     DL,LF
            INT     21h
            CALL    UPDATE_VIRTUAL_CURSOR    ;Update position of virtual cursor
            POP     DX
            POP     AX
            RET
SEND_CRLF ENDP
```

This makes sure we know where the cursor is once we've moved the real cursor to the next line.

Finally, here are the changes to READ_STRING that keep the virtual and real cursors in synchronization during keyboard input:

Listing 30-13. Changes to READ_STRING in KBD_IO.ASM

```
        EXTRN   UPDATE_REAL_CURSOR:PROC
;--------------------------------------------------------------------;
;               .                                                    ;
;               .                                                    ;
;               .                                                    ;
; Uses:         BACK_SPACE, WRITE_CHAR, UPDATE_REAL_CURSOR           ;
;--------------------------------------------------------------------;
READ_STRING     PROC
        PUSH    AX
        PUSH    BX
        PUSH    SI
        MOV     SI,DX                   ;Use SI for index register and
START_OVER:
        CALL    UPDATE_REAL_CURSOR      ;Move to position of virtual cursor
        MOV     BX,2                    ;BX for offset to beginning of buffer
             .
             .
             .
READ_NEXT_CHAR:
        CALL    UPDATE_REAL_CURSOR      ;Move real cursor to virtual cursor
        MOV     AH,7
        INT     21h
```

That should do it. Reassemble all three files that we changed this time (VIDEO_IO, CURSOR, and KBD_IO), then link Dskpatch. You'll notice that screen output is much faster than before.

Summary

Speeding up WRITE_CHAR turned out to be quite a bit of work since we had to change a number of procedures, but the results were well worth the effort. Programs that have snappy screen updates feel much nicer to work with than programs that take longer to paint the screen. When speed comes at this low a price, it's almost always worth the effort.

The next chapter moves on to another advanced subject that will probably interest many of you: writing procedures and functions for the C language in assembly language. For those of you using another language, the next chapter should be a useful starting point as well.

31

C PROCEDURES IN ASSEMBLY

In this chapter we'll show you how to write assembly language procedures you can use in your C programs. We're concentrating on C because C is one of the most popular high-level programming languages (most of our programs here at Norton Computing are written in both C and assembly language). (If you want to write procedures for other languages, such as Pascal or BASIC, you'll probably find the procedures in this chapter work without change; you need change only the .MODEL statement.)

Originally written by Dennis Ritchie at Bell Laboratories, C has become quite popular because it is a modern high-level language that nonetheless provides many assembly language type functions (such as the + + increment operator). But because it is a general-purpose programming language, there are times you'll want to write parts of your program in assembly language, whether for speed, low-level access to your machine, or other reasons.

A Clear Screen for C

We'll start by rewriting a fairly simple procedure, CLEAR_SCREEN, so we can call it directly from C. As you'll see, writing assembly language programs for use in C programs is actually quite simple.

> **Note:** To assemble the programs in this chapter, you'll need Microsoft MASM version 5.1 or later, Turbo Assembler, or the latest version of OPTASM (which wasn't available when we wrote this book) that supports the MASM 5.1 mixed language programming extensions. We're also using the Microsoft C compiler for the examples in this chapter.

The .MODEL directive we've been using so far allows us to define the memory model of the program we're building. (We've only used the SMALL memory model in this book.) Starting with version 5.1 of MASM, Microsoft added an extension to the .MODEL directive that allows us to write programs to attach to a number of different languages (including C and Pascal). To tell MASM that we're writing a C procedure, we simply append a ",C" to the end:

```
.MODEL   SMALL,C
```

Let's start our rewrite of CLEAR_SCREEN by taking another look at the assembly language version we wrote in Part II of this book:

```
          PUBLIC  CLEAR_SCREEN
;---------------------------------------------------------------------;
; This procedure clears the entire screen.                            ;
;---------------------------------------------------------------------;
CLEAR_SCREEN    PROC
          PUSH    AX
          PUSH    BX
          PUSH    CX
          PUSH    DX
          XOR     AL,AL             ;Blank entire window
          XOR     CX,CX             ;Upper left corner is at (0,0)
          MOV     DH,24             ;Bottom line of screen is line 24
          MOV     DL,79             ;Right side is at column 79
          MOV     BH,7              ;Use normal attribute for blanks
          MOV     AH,6              ;Call for SCROLL-UP function
          INT     10h               ;Clear the window
          POP     DX
          POP     CX
          POP     BX
          POP     AX
          RET
CLEAR_SCREEN    ENDP
```

This is a fairly simple assembly language procedure, as far as assembly language procedures are concerned. All we have to do to convert this into a C procedure, as you can see from the following, is remove a number of instructions. Here is the new file, CLIB.ASM, that we'll use to hold all our C procedures written in assembly language:

Listing 31-1. The New File CLIB.ASM

```
     .MODEL  SMALL,C

     .CODE

;---------------------------------------------------------------------;
; This procedure clears the entire screen.                            ;
;---------------------------------------------------------------------;
CLEAR_SCREEN    PROC
          XOR     AL,AL             ;Blank entire window
          XOR     CX,CX             ;Upper left corner is at (0,0)
          MOV     DH,24             ;Bottom line of screen is line 24
          MOV     DL,79             ;Right side is at column 79
          MOV     BH,7              ;Use normal attribute for blanks
          MOV     AH,6              ;Call for SCROLL-UP function
          INT     10h               ;Clear the window
          RET
CLEAR_SCREEN    ENDP

          END
```

(If you're using Turbo Assembler, you'll need to add two lines after .MODEL with MASM51 on the first line, and QUIRKS on the second line.) You'll note that we've removed all the PUSH and POP instructions we used to save and restore registers. We used these instructions in our assembly language programs so we wouldn't have to keep track of which registers were changed by procedures we called. This made programming in assembly language much simpler. C procedures, on the other hand, don't need to save the AX, BX, CX, or DX registers at all since the C compiler always assumes procedures change these four registers or use them to return values, as we'll see later. So we're free to use these four procedures for anything we want without having to save and restore them.

Note: You don't need to save and restore the AX, BX, CX, or DX registers in any C procedures you write in assembly language. You do, however, need to save and restore the SI, DI, BP, and segment registers if you change them in your procedures.

Can Change: AX, BX, CX, DX, ES
Must Preserve: SI, DI, BP, SP, CS, DS, SS

Here is a very short C program that uses clear_screen(). In fact, that's all this program does.

Listing 31-2. The File test.c

```
main()
{
    clear_screen()
}
```

Use the following steps to assemble CLIB.ASM, compile test.c, and link both files together to form test.exe:

```
MASM CLIB;
CL -C TEST.C
LINK TEST+CLIB,TEST,TEST/MAP;
```

(The CL -C command compiles a file without linking it.) The last line is a bit more complicated than normal because we've asked Link to create a map file so that we'll know where to find clear_screen() in Debug. Even though test.exe is a fairly small program, the memory map (test.map) turns out to be rather long because of some extra overhead present in all C programs. Here is an abbreviated version of this map that shows the pieces of information we're interested in:

```
          .
          .
          .
  Address       Publics by Name
```

```
0054:00EC        STKHQQ
0000:001A        _clear_screen
0054:01D8        _edata
0054:01E0        _end
0054:00DA        _environ
0054:00B3        _errno
0000:01A2        _exit
0000:0010        _main
                    .
                    .
                    .

Program entry point at 0000:002A
```

As you can see, our procedure is actually called _clear_screen instead of clear_screen. Most C compilers put an underscore in front of all procedure names for historical reasons we've long since forgotten (C compilers also put an underscore in front of variable names).

You may have noticed also that we didn't include a PUBLIC CLEAR_SCREEN to make CLEAR_SCREEN available to other files. This is another change that ",C" makes for us. The ",C" addition to .MODEL changes the PROC directive so it automatically defines every procedure as a PUBLIC procedure. In other words, if you're writing a C procedure in assembly language (using .MODEL SMALL,C), all your procedures will be declared PUBLIC for you, automatically.

Let's load test.exe into Debug to see if MASM made any other changes for us. Using the address in the load map above (1A), here is the code for _clear_screen:

```
A>DEBUG TEST.EXE
-U 1A
4A8A:001A 32C0        XOR     AL,AL
4A8A:001C 33C9        XOR     CX,CX
4A8A:001E B618        MOV     DH,18
4A8A:0020 B24F        MOV     DL,4F
4A8A:0022 B707        MOV     BH,07
4A8A:0024 B406        MOV     AH,06
4A8A:0026 CD10        INT     10
4A8A:0028 C3          RET
             .
             .
             .
```

This is exactly what we've written in CLIB.ASM. In other words, the ",C" at the end of the .MODEL directive only changed the name of our procedure from clear_screen to _clear_screen and declared it as PUBLIC. If this were the only help we got from ",C", we wouldn't be very impressed. Fortunately, there are a number of other areas where MASM helps writing C procedures in assembly language, all having to do with passing parameters to procedures.

Parameter Passing

Throughout this book we've used registers to pass parameters to procedures, which worked well since we never had more than six parameters (which would require the six registers—AX, BX, CX, DX, SI, and DI). C programs, however, use the stack to pass parameters to procedures. And this is where the MASM 5.1 .MODEL extensions really come into play. MASM automatically generates much of the code we'll need to work with parameters passed on the stack.

To see how this all works, we'll convert several procedures into C procedures. We'll start with a procedure to write a string of characters on the screen. We could simply convert WRITE_STRING, but since write string actually uses a number of other procedures (WRITE_CHAR, CURSOR_RIGHT, INIT_WRITE_CHAR, and so on), we'll write a new WRITE_STRING that uses the ROM BIOS to write each character to the screen. This new WRITE_STRING uses INT 10h, function 14 to write each character on the screen. This certainly won't be as fast as our WRITE_STRING is now, but it is simple enough so that we won't get lost in a lot of code.

Here is our slow, C version of WRITE_STRING that you should add to CLIB.ASM:

Listing 31-3. Add This Procedure to CLIB.ASM

```
;-------------------------------------------------------------------;
; This procedure writes a string of characters to the screen.  The  ;
; string must end with        DB    0                               ;
;                                                                   ;
;       write_string(string);                                      ;
;       char   *string;                                            ;
;-------------------------------------------------------------------;
WRITE_STRING    PROC USES SI, STRING:PTR BYTE
        PUSHF                           ;Save the direction flag
        CLD                             ;Set direction for increment (forward)
        MOV     SI,STRING               ;Place address into SI for LODSB

STRING_LOOP:
        LODSB                           ;Get a character into the AL register
        OR      AL,AL                   ;Have we found the 0 yet?
        JZ      END_OF_STRING           ;Yes, we are done with the string
        MOV     AH,14                   ;Ask for write character function
        XOR     BH,BH                   ;Write to page 0
        INT     10h                     ;Write one character to the screen
        JMP     STRING_LOOP

END_OF_STRING:
        POPF                            ;Restore direction flag
        RET
WRITE_STRING            ENDP
```

Most of this code should be familiar since we lifted it mostly verbatim from our fast WRITE_STRING. One line, however, is quite different. You'll note that we've added two pieces of information onto the end of the PROC statement.

The first piece, USES SI, tells MASM we're using the SI register in our procedure. As we mentioned above, C procedures must save and restore the SI and DI registers if they modify them. As we'll see soon, the USES SI causes MASM to generate code to save and restore the SI register—automatically!

The second piece is used to pass one parameter to our program, which is a pointer to a string, or bytes of characters. STRING:PTR BYTE simply says that we want to call the parameter STRING and that it's a pointer (PTR) to a character (BYTE), which is the first character in the string. By giving this parameter a name, we can use the parameter's value simply by writing its name, as in MOV SI,STRING.

The magic of all this will become clear as soon as we look at the code generated by MASM. Assemble the new CLIB.ASM, then make the following change to test.c:

```
main()
{
    clear_screen();
    write_string("This is a string!");
}
```

Recompile test.c (with cl -c test.c) and link again (with LINK TEST+ CLIB,TEST,TEST/MAP;).

Looking at the new map file we see that _write_string is at 33h (you may see a different number since this number will depend on the compiler you use):

```
0000:0024        _clear_screen
0056:01EA        _edata
0056:01F0        _end
0056:00DA        _environ
0056:00B3        _errno
0000:01C6        _exit
0000:0010        _main
0000:0033        _write_string
```

Here is the code actually generated by MASM for the write_string we just added to CLIB.ASM (the instructions added by MASM are against a gray background):

```
-U 33
4A8A:0033 55        PUSH    BP
4A8A:0034 8BEC      MOV     BP,SP
4A8A:0036 56        PUSH    SI
4A8A:0037 9C        PUSHF
4A8A:0038 FC        CLD
4A8A:0039 8B7604    MOV     SI,[BP+04]
4A8A:003C AC        LODSB
4A8A:003D 0AC0      OR      AL,AL
4A8A:003F 7408      JZ      0049
4A8A:0041 B40E      MOV     AH,0E
4A8A:0043 32FF      XOR     BH,BH
4A8A:0045 CD10      INT     10
4A8A:0047 EBF3      JMP     003C
4A8A:0049 9D        POPF
```

```
4A8A:004A 5E          POP   SI
4A8A:004B 5D          POP   BP
4A8A:004C C3          RET
```

As you can see, MASM added quite a few instructions to the ones we wrote. The PUSH SI and POP SI instructions should be clear since we said that MASM would save and restore the SI register in response to USES SI. The other instructions, on the other hand, take some explanation.

The BP register is a special-purpose register we haven't said much about. If you look at the table of addressing modes in Appendix D, however, you'll notice that BP is a little different from other registers in that the default segment for [BP] is the SS register rather than the DS register. This is of interest here because, as we said earlier, C programs pass parameters on the stack rather than in registers. So the instruction:

```
MOV  SI,[BP+04]
```

will always read from the stack, even if SS isn't the same as DS or ES (which it often won't be for memory models other than SMALL). Because the BP register is so convenient for working with the stack, C procedures use the BP register to access the parameters passed to them on the stack.

To use the BP register, we need to set it to the current value of SP, which the MOV BP,SP instruction does for us. But since the C procedure that called us also uses the BP register to access its parameters, we need to save and restore the BP register. So the assembler automatically generates these instructions (without the comments, of course) that allow us to use the BP register to read parameters from the stack:

```
PUSH BP                ;Save the current BP register
MOV  BP,SP             ;Set BP to point to our parameters
     .
     .
     .
POP  BP                ;Restore the old value of BP
```

Figure 31-1 shows how the stack would look for a procedure, with two parameters, that uses the SI register. The C call, c_call(param1, param2), pushes the parameters onto the stack, from right to left. By pushing the rightmost parameter first, and the leftmost parameter last, the first parameter will always be closest to the "top of the stack," in other words, closest to SP.

Next the CALL instruction created by the c_call(param1, param2) statement pushes the return address onto the stack, at which point our procedure gains control. You'll notice at this point that the PUSH SI instruction appears *after* the MOV BP,SP instruction. Once we've set the value of BP, we're free to change the stack as much as we want by PUSHing and POPing registers and by

c_call(param1, param2)

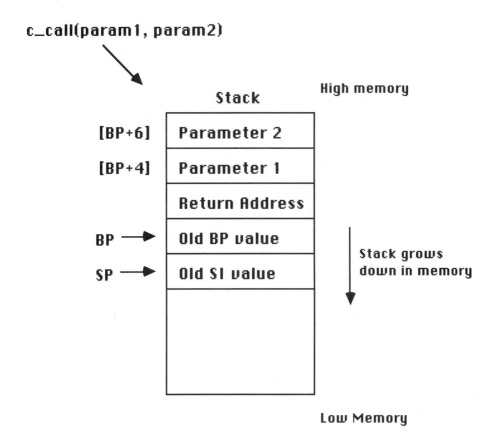

Figure 31-1. How C Passes Parameters on the Stack.

calling other procedures. Because MASM generates all the needed instructions, we need not concern ourselves with writing these instructions in the correct order.

The first parameter will always be at the same offset from BP, which is 4 for the SMALL memory model (it would be 6 for memory models that require a FAR return address, since a FAR return requires both the old CS and IP values to be on the stack). Looking at the preceding unassemble listing, you'll note that the assembler translated the MOV SI,STRING instruction into MOV SI,[BP + 4]. If we had used a memory model with FAR procedures, this would be translated into MOV SI,[BP + 6].

Just for your interest, C passes parameters on the stack in the opposite order from most other high-level languages. Pascal, BASIC, and FORTRAN, for example, push the first parameter onto the stack first, with the last parameter last,

Figure 31-2. The assembler knows where to find the parameter.

which means the last parameter would be closest to the top of the stack (SP). If you think about this for a moment, you'll realize the offset from BP to the first parameter will depend on the number of parameters we pushed onto the stack. This isn't a problem in Pascal, BASIC, or FORTRAN where procedure calls *must* have the same number of parameters as defined in the procedure.

In C procedures, however, you can pass more parameters on the stack than are defined in the procedure. The C printf() function is a very good example. The number of parameters you pass to printf() depends entirely on how many % arguments you have in the string. And to allow C procedures to have a variable number of parameters, we need to push the parameters in reverse order so the first parameter will always be closest to SP and won't depend on the number of parameters we actually pushed onto the stack.

A Two-Parameter Example

Before we move on, here's another short procedure you'll find useful in your C programs:

Listing 31-4. Add this Procedure to CLIB.ASM.

```
;-----------------------------------------------------------------;
; This procedure moves the cursor                                 ;
;                                                                 ;
;     goto_xy(x, y);                                              ;
;     int    x, y;                                                ;
;-----------------------------------------------------------------;
```

```
GOTO_XY         PROC X:WORD, Y:WORD
        MOV     AH,2                    ;Call for SET CURSOR POSITION
        MOV     BH,0                    ;Display page 0
        MOV     DH,BYTE PTR (Y)         ;Get the line number (0..N)
        MOV     DL,BYTE PTR (X)         ;Get the column number (0..79)
        INT     10h                     ;Move the cursor
        RET
GOTO_XY         ENDP
```

And here is the change to make in test.c to use goto_xy():

```
main()
{
    clear_screen();
    goto_xy(35,10);
    write_string("This is a string!");
}
```

There are two items of interest in goto_xy(). First, you'll note that we declared the two parameters (X and Y) in the order we write them in the procedure call: goto_xy(x, y). We would write these parameters in the same order for a language, like Pascal, that pushes parameters in a different order: MASM handles the differences in order on the stack so we don't have to change our code or know in what order parameters are pushed onto the stack.

The other change is a bit more subtle. You'll notice that we defined X and Y to be words, rather than bytes. We did this because C (and other high-level languages) never push a byte onto the stack: they always push words onto the stack. And there is a very good reason for this: The PUSH instructions push words, and not bytes, onto the stack. In goto_xy, this isn't a problem except that we want to move a byte into the DH and DL registers. Writing:

```
    MOV  DL,X
```

won't work because the assembler would report an error. Instead, we have to use BYTE PTR X to access X as a byte. But this also doesn't work because of how the MASM 5.1 extensions are written inside the assembler.

As it turns out, the X:WORD, Y:WORD definitions in the PROC statement are implemented inside the assembler as macros. Macros, which we won't cover in this book, are a way to add *features* to the assembler. The parameters X and Y are actually macros, so when we write MOV DL,X, X is expanded into the text defined by MASM:

```
X       -->     WORD PTR [BP+4]
```

If we then put BYTE PTR in front of this, we get something the assembler doesn't know how to handle:

```
BYTE PTR X      -->     BYTE PTR WORD PTR [BP+4]
```

We fix this problem by putting parentheses around the X and Y, which tells the assembler that [BP + 4] refers to a word, but we wish to treat it as a byte:

```
BYTE PTR (X)       -->      BYTE PTR (WORD PTR [BP+4])
```

The parentheses simply tell the assembler to process everything between the (and) first.

Returning Function Values

Besides writing C procedures in assembly language, you'll probably also want to write C functions in assembly, which is quite simple. C functions return values in the following registers: bytes in AL, words in AX, and long words (two bytes) in DX:AX, with the low word in AX. (If you want to return types with three bytes or more than four bytes, you'll need to consult the *Microsoft Mixed-Language Programming Guide* or the *Turbo Assembler User's Guide* for details.)

> **Note:** Here are the registers to use to return values to C programs:
>
> Byte AL
> Word AX
> Long DX:AX

The following procedure, which you should add to CLIB.ASM, is a rewrite of READ_KEY that returns the extended key code to C programs:

Listing 31-5. Add this Procedure to CLIB.ASM.

```
;------------------------------------------------------------------;
; This procedure reads on key from the keyboard.                   ;
;                                                                  ;
;       key = read_key();                                          ;
;------------------------------------------------------------------;
READ_KEY        PROC
        XOR     AH,AH                   ;Ask for keyboard read function
        INT     16h                     ;Read character/scan code from keyboard
        OR      AL,AL                   ;Is it an extended code?
        JZ      EXTENDED_CODE           ;Yes
NOT_EXTENDED:
        XOR     AH,AH                   ;Return just the ASCII code
        JMP     DONE_READING

EXTENDED_CODE:
        MOV     AL,AH                   ;Put scan code into AL
        MOV     AH,1                    ;Signal extended code
DONE_READING:
```

```
        RET
READ_KEY      ENDP
```

Here is a version of test.c that will clear the screen, display a string near the center, and wait until you press the space bar before exiting back to DOS:

```
main()
{
    clear_screen();
    goto_xy(35,10);
    write_string("This is a string!");
    while (read_key() != ' ')
        ;
}
```

Summary

That wraps up our discussion of writing C procedures in assembly language. If you want to write procedures for other languages, you'll need to consult the documentation on your language, or in the assembler that you're using. Not all compilers for the same language (such as Pascal) use the same conventions. So even though MASM (and Turbo Assembler) support the Pascal conventions, there may be differences if you're not using both an assembler and a compiler from the same company.

The next chapter, our last technical chapter, covers perhaps the most advanced material in this book: writing RAM-resident programs.

DISKLITE, A RAM-RESIDENT PROGRAM

In this, our final chapter of programming, we're going to cover a fairly advanced topic: writing RAM-resident programs. In doing so we'll use much of what we've learned in this book, and you'll have a nice little program as well.

RAM-Resident Programs

RAM-resident programs are almost always written in assembly language to allow maximum access to the ROM BIOS and memory, and to make them compact. The Disklite program we'll build here, for example, weighs in at just 247 bytes. Since RAM-resident programs stay in memory until you restart your computer and more and more programs need 512K or more of memory to run, keeping RAM-resident programs compact is very important. For if a program is too large, users won't be willing to keep a copy in memory, and that's the whole point.

RAM-resident programs usually need to work very closely with the ROM BIOS or with your computer's hardware to change how existing functions work or to add new functions. Disklite, for example, watches the ROM BIOS routines that read from and write to disks so it can display a disk drive "light" on the screen. Why would we want to do this?

Many programmers like to watch the disk drive light during compiles to keep track of the compiler's progress. When a compile takes 30 seconds or a minute, there isn't much else you can do. We also like to watch the disk drive light when we're testing programs that read from or write to a disk to see if they're actually accessing the disk. Fair enough. But what happens if you place your computer on its side by your desk (or you have an IBM PS/2 Model 60)? Or you have a hard disk card, which doesn't have a drive light? In either case, Disklite provides an on-screen drive light that *lights up* whenever you read to or write from a disk. And it also tells you which disk you're accessing.

Intercepting Interrupts

As we mentioned above, Disklite displays the drive light by watching the ROM BIOS routines that read to and write from disk. How can Disklite do that?

All disk reading and writing is performed by the INT 13h ROM BIOS routine. DOS uses this service by issuing an INT 13h instruction. Interrupts, as we saw in Chapter 11, use a vector table at the start of memory to determine what routine to call. Each interrupt vector in this table is two words long since it

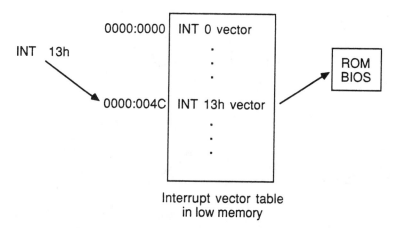

Figure 32-1. INT 13h uses the interrupt vector at 4Ch to determine the address of the routine to call.

holds the FAR address of the routine that will handle the interrupt. So the INT 13h instruction will use the address at 0:4Ch (13h times 4) in memory as the address of the routine that will handle the INT 13h function. In other words, we could change this address to point to our routine instead of the ROM BIOS's routine. In fact, this is precisely what we'll do.

Figure 32-1 shows how INT 13h calls the routine in the ROM BIOS. Now imagine that we change the interrupt vector to point to our procedure. Then the vector will point to us instead of the ROM BIOS. We've now taken control of the INT 13h function. But this isn't quite what we want. If we completely take over INT 13h, we have to write a program that will do everything INT 13h did, as well as the new functions we want to add. We'd really like to use the ROM BIOS INT 13h routines to do most of the work. As it turns out, this is very simple.

Instead of blindly replacing the INT 13h vector, we'll first save the vector in our own program. Then we can use the ROM BIOS INT 13h routines by simulating an INT call to the ROM routines. Recall that an INT is like a CALL instruction, but it saves the flags on the stack so they'll be restored by an IRET (Interrupt RETurn) instruction. All we need to do, then, is save the address of the INT 13h routines in the variable ROM_DISKETTE_INT, so we can pass control on to the ROM BIOS INT 13h routines with this pair of instructions:

```
PUSHF
CALL ROM_DISKETTE_INT
```

When the ROM finishes accessing the disk, we'll receive control again. This means we can execute some code before as well as after we call the ROM's disk

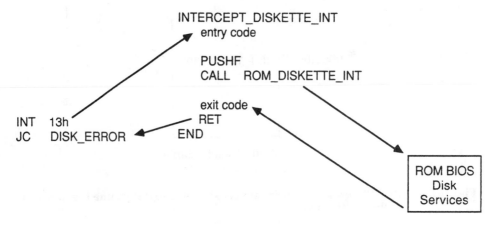

Figure 32-2. Intercepting INT 13h.

functions, which is exactly what we need if we're going to display, then remove a drive letter. Figure 32-2 shows these steps in more detail.

> **Note:** The technique we've presented here will work with most ROM BIOS routines. But there is a major caveat. Since DOS is not a multitasking operating system, you can't make DOS function calls from within an interrupt service routine unless you can be can be absolutely certain DOS wasn't in the middle of processing a function request. There are ways to ensure this, but they're rather difficult, so we won't cover them in this book. You'll find some references to this kind of information in the bibliography at the end of the last chapter.

Disklite

Most of the other details of Disklite should either be familiar or well enough documented that you can figure them out. There are a few details, however, that are new or a bit out of the ordinary.

First of all, note that we're not saving or restoring registers in the procedures of Disklite. Instead, we clearly mark which registers are altered. Then we save

all the registers that can be altered at the start of INTER-
CEPT_DISKETTE_INT and nowhere else. We save them only once so we keep
the stack usage to a minimum.

Interrupt service routines generally need to be written so they don't use
much of the stack since they're borrowing someone else's stack, and there may
not be much space left on the stack. We never worried about stack space in our
own programs because we gave ourselves a large enough stack. We can't guar-
antee that everyone will give us a large stack when we get an INT 13h request.
For these reasons, many RAM-resident programs set up their own stack.

The two procedures GET_DISPLAY_BASE, SAVE_SCREEN and
WRITE_TO_SCREEN should be fairly clear. GET_DISPLAY_BASE we've
seen before, and the other two should be clear from the last chapter:
SAVE_SCREEN saves the two characters in the upper-right corner, and
WRITE_TO_SCREEN writes two characters in the upper-right corner.
WRITE_TO_SCREEN is used both to display the drive letter and to restore the
two characters that were on the screen before we displayed the drive letter.

DISPLAY_DRIVE_LETTER is also fairly simple. INT 13h takes a drive
number in the DL register. For floppy disk drives, DL will contain 0 for drive A,
1 for drive B, and so on. For hard disks, on the other hand, DL starts at 80h. So
to get the actual drive letter for a hard disk we subtract 80h, then add the
number of floppy disk drives since the first hard disk appears after the last
floppy disk.

That leaves us with INIT_VECTORS and GET_NUM_FLOPPIES.
INIT_VECTORS shows the details of installing a procedure to intercept an
interrupt vector and to keep such a program in memory after we've returned to
DOS. First we display an author message. Then we call
GET_NUM_FLOPPIES to set NUM_FLOPPIES to the number of floppy disk
drives attached to your computer. Next we read and set the INT 13h vector with
the INT 21h functions 35h and 25h that read and set interrupt vectors.

Note that we put both initialization routines at the very end of Disklite. As it
turns out, both these procedures are used only once, when we first load Disklite
into memory, so we don't need to keep them in memory after we load Disklite.
This is exactly why we've put them at the end. The DOS function call INT 27h
called *Terminate but Stay Resident* exits our program and keeps most of the
program in memory. This function call takes an offset in DX to the first byte we
don't want to keep in memory. So by setting DX so it points to INIT_VECTORS,
we tell DOS to keep all of Disklite in memory *except* for INIT_VECTORS and
GET_NUM_FLOPPIES. You could place as much initialization code here as
you want without it consuming any memory after Disklite's been installed; this
is a very handy feature.

Enter the following program into DISKLITE.ASM. Then assemble, link, and convert it into a .COM program (by typing EXE2BIN DISKLITE DIS-KLITE.COM). After you run this program, an inverse X: (where X can be any drive letter) will appear on the very right side of the first line whenever you access a disk drive. To test it, run CHKDSK on any drive.

Listing 32-1. DISKLITE.ASM Program.

```
;---------------------------------------------------------------------;
; Disklite creates an on-screen version of the disk light that is     ;
; usually on disk drives.  The difference, however, is that this light ;
; will only be on as long as it takes to read or write to the disk.  In ;
; other words, it does not stay on while the disk spins without any    ;
; activity.                                                            ;
;                                                                      ;
; This program intercepts the INT 13h vector, which is the entry point ;
; for the ROM BIOS's diskette routine.  On entry, Disklite displays    ;
; the drive letter in the upper-right corner of the screen, and        ;
; restores this section of the screen on exit.                         ;
;---------------------------------------------------------------------;


;---------------------------------------------------------------------;
; Here is the DISKLITE's entry point.  It jumps to the initialization  ;
; routine which is at the very end so we can throw it out of memory     ;
; after we've used it.                                                 ;
;---------------------------------------------------------------------;
CODE_SEG        SEGMENT
        ASSUME  CS:CODE_SEG, DS:CODE_SEG
        ORG     100h                    ;Reserve for DOS Program Segment Prefix
BEGIN:  JMP     INIT_VECTORS

AUTHOR_STRING           DB      "Installed Disklite, by John Socha"
                        DB      0Dh, 0Ah, '$'


ROM_DISKETTE_INT        DD      ?

DISPLAY_BASE            DW      ?
OLD_DISPLAY_CHARS       DB      4 DUP (?)
DISPLAY_CHARS           DB      'A', 70h, ':', 70h
NUM_FLOPPIES            DB      ?       ;Number of floppy drives

UPPER_LEFT      EQU     (80 - 2) * 2    ;Offset to drive light

;---------------------------------------------------------------------;
; This procedure intercepts calls to the ROM BIOS's diskette I/O       ;
; vector, and it does several things:                                  ;
;                                                                      ;
;            1. Checks to see if the screen is in an 80 column text mode ;
;               so we can write to the screen.  Disklite won't write any ;
;               characters to the screen if it's not in an 80 column mode. ;
;            2. Displays the disk drive letter, "A:" for example, in the ;
;               upper-right corner of the screen.                      ;
;            3. Calls the old ROM BIOS routine to do the actual work.  ;
;            4. Restores the two characters in the upper-right corner of the ;
;               screen.                                                ;
;---------------------------------------------------------------------;
INTERCEPT_DISKETTE_INT  PROC    FAR
        Assume  CS:CODE_SEG, DS:Nothing
        PUSHF                           ;Save the old flags
        PUSH    AX
        PUSH    SI
        PUSH    DI
        PUSH    DS
```

```
            PUSH    ES
            CALL    GET_DISPLAY_BASE            ;Calculates the screen's display base
            CALL    SAVE_SCREEN                 ;Save two chars in upper right
            CALL    DISPLAY_DRIVE_LETTER        ;Display the drive letter
            POP     ES
            POP     DS
            POP     DI
            POP     SI
            POP     AX
            POPF                                ;Restore the old flags

            PUSHF                               ;Simulate an INT call
            CALL    ROM_DISKETTE_INT            ; to the old ROM BIOS routine

            PUSHF                               ;Save the returned flags
            PUSH    AX
            PUSH    SI
            PUSH    DI
            PUSH    DS
            PUSH    ES
            LEA     SI,OLD_DISPLAY_CHARS        ;Point to the old screen image
            CALL    WRITE_TO_SCREEN             ;Restore two chars in upper right
            POP     ES
            POP     DS
            POP     DI
            POP     SI
            POP     AX
            POPF                                ;Recover the returned flags
            RET     2                           ;Leave the status flags intact
INTERCEPT_DISKETTE_INT  ENDP


;--------------------------------------------------------------------------;
; This procedure calculates the segment address for the display adapter    ;
; that we're using.                                                        ;
;                                                                          ;
; Destroys:    AX                                                          ;
;--------------------------------------------------------------------------;
GET_DISPLAY_BASE        PROC    NEAR
            Assume  CS:CODE_SEG, DS:Nothing
            INT     11h                         ;Get the current equipment flag
            AND     AX,30h                      ;Isolate the display flags
            CMP     AX,30h                      ;Is this a monochrome display?
            MOV     AX,0B800h                   ;Set for a color graphics adapter
            JNE     DONE_GET_BASE               ;Color graphics, base already set
            MOV     AX,0B000h                   ;Set for monochrome display
DONE_GET_BASE:
            MOV     DISPLAY_BASE,AX             ;Save this display base
            RET
GET_DISPLAY_BASE        ENDP


;--------------------------------------------------------------------------;
; This procedure saves the two characters in the upper right corner of     ;
; the screen so that we can restore them later.                            ;
;                                                                          ;
; Destroys:    AX, SI, DI, DS, ES                                          ;
;--------------------------------------------------------------------------;
SAVE_SCREEN     PROC    NEAR
            Assume  CS:CODE_SEG, DS:Nothing
            MOV     SI,UPPER_LEFT               ;Read chars from the screen
            LEA     DI,OLD_DISPLAY_CHARS        ;Write chars to local memory
            MOV     AX,DISPLAY_BASE             ;Get segment address of screen
            MOV     DS,AX
            MOV     AX,CS                       ;Point to the local data
            MOV     ES,AX
            CLD                                 ;Set for auto-increment
            MOVSW                               ;Move two characters
            MOVSW
            RET
SAVE_SCREEN     ENDP
```

Listing 32-1. *continued*

```
;--------------------------------------------------------------;
; This procedure displays the drive letter in the upper-right corner of ;
; the screen.                                                   ;
;                                                               ;
; Destroys:    AX, SI                                           ;
;--------------------------------------------------------------;
DISPLAY_DRIVE_LETTER    PROC    NEAR
        Assume  CS:CODE_SEG, DS:Nothing
        MOV     AL,DL                   ;Get the drive number
        CMP     AL,80h                  ;Is this a hard disk drive?
        JB      DISPLAY_LETTER          ;No, then continue
        SUB     AL,80h                  ;Convert to hard disk number
        ADD     AL,NUM_FLOPPIES         ;Convert to correct disk number
DISPLAY_LETTER:
        ADD     AL,'A'                  ;Convert this into a drive letter
        LEA     SI,DISPLAY_CHARS        ;Point to new char image
        MOV     CS:[SI],AL              ;Save this character
        CALL    WRITE_TO_SCREEN
        RET
DISPLAY_DRIVE_LETTER    ENDP


;--------------------------------------------------------------;
; This procedure writes two characters in the upper-right corner of the ;
; screen.                                                       ;
;                                                               ;
; On entry:    CS:SI   Screen image for two characters          ;
; Destroys:    AX, SI, DI, DS, ES                               ;
;--------------------------------------------------------------;
WRITE_TO_SCREEN         PROC    NEAR
        Assume  CS:CODE_SEG, DS:Nothing
        MOV     DI,UPPER_LEFT           ;Write chars to the screen
        MOV     AX,DISPLAY_BASE         ;Get segment address of screen
        MOV     ES,AX
        MOV     AX,CS                   ;Point to the local data
        MOV     DS,AX
        CLD                             ;Set for auto-increment
        MOVSW                           ;Move two characters
        MOVSW
        RET
WRITE_TO_SCREEN         ENDP


;--------------------------------------------------------------;
; This procedure daisy-chains Disklite onto the diskette I/O vector ;
; so that we can monitor the disk activity.                     ;
;--------------------------------------------------------------;
INIT_VECTORS    PROC    NEAR
        Assume  CS:CODE_SEG, DS:CODE_SEG
        LEA     DX,AUTHOR_STRING        ;Print out the author notice
        MOV     AH,9                    ;Display this string
        INT     21h

        CALL    GET_NUM_FLOPPIES        ;See how many floppy drives installed

        MOV     AH,35h                  ;Ask for an interrupt vector
        MOV     AL,13h                  ;Get the vector for INT 13h
        INT     21h                     ;Put vector in ES:BX
        MOV     Word Ptr ROM_DISKETTE_INT,BX
        MOV     Word Ptr ROM_DISKETTE_INT[2],ES

        MOV     AH,25h                  ;Ask to set an interrupt vector
        MOV     AL,13h                  ;Set the INT 13h vector to DS:DX
        MOV     DX,Offset INTERCEPT_DISKETTE_INT
        INT     21h                     ;Set INT 13h to point to our procedure

        MOV     DX,Offset INIT_VECTORS  ;End of resident portion
        INT     27h                     ;Terminate but stay resident
INIT_VECTORS    ENDP
```

```
;-------------------------------------------------------------------;
; This procedure determines how many logical floppy disk drives are in  ;
; the system.  The next drive letter will be used for hard disk drives. ;
;-------------------------------------------------------------------;
GET_NUM_FLOPPIES          PROC    NEAR
        Assume  CS:CODE_SEG, DS:CODE_SEG
        INT     11h                     ;Get the equipment flag
        MOV     CL,6
        SHR     AX,CL                   ;Right justify num of floppies
        AND     AL,3                    ;Strip all the other flags
        INC     AL                      ;Returns 0 for 1 floppy
        CMP     AL,1                    ;Is this a one floppy system?
        JA      DONE_GET_FLOPPIES       ;No, then this is the correct number

        MOV     AL,2                    ;Yes, there are 2 logical drives
DONE_GET_FLOPPIES:
        MOV     NUM_FLOPPIES,AL         ;Save this number
        RET
GET_NUM_FLOPPIES          ENDP

CODE_SEG        ENDS

        END     BEGIN
```

33

CLOSING WORDS AND BIBLIOGRAPHY

 B y now you've seen many examples of assembly language programs. Throughout this book, we've constantly emphasized programming, rather than the details of the 8088 microprocessor inside your IBM Personal Computer. As a result, you haven't seen all the 8088 instructions, nor all the assembler directives. But most assembly language programs can be written with what you've learned here and no more. Your best approach to learning more about writing assembly language programs is to take the programs in this book and modify them.

If you think of a better way to write any part of Dskpatch, by all means do so. This is how we first learned to write programs. Back then the programs were in BASIC, but the idea still holds. We found programs written in BASIC, and began to learn about the language itself by rewriting bits and pieces of those programs. You can do the same with Dskpatch.

After you've tried some of these examples, you'll be ready to write your own programs. Don't start from scratch here, either; that's rather difficult for your first time out. To begin with, use the programs in this book as a framework. Don't build a completely new structure or technique (your equivalent of modular design) until you feel comfortable with writing assembly language programs.

If you really become enthralled by assembly language, you'll also need a more complete book for use as a reference to the 8088 instruction set. What follows is a list of books we've read and liked that you'll find useful as references or further reading. This list is by no means complete, as the books listed here are only ones we've read. Also, some of these references are older than you might expect since we learned assembly language programming several years ago (more than we'd like to admit).

80x86 Reference Books

The following three books are good programmers' references:

iAPX 88 Book. Intel, 1981. This is the definitive sourcebook and a very good reference.
iAPX 286 Programmer's Reference Manual. Intel, 1984. The definitive sourcebook for the 80286 microprocessor.
Rector, Russel, and Alexy, George, *The 8086 Book*. Osborne/McGraw-Hill, 1980. This is another good reference, but rather thick and dense.

The next three books were all written for the IBM PC. Much of the information in each of these is generic; only the examples in the latter part of these books are specific to the IBM PC. We recommend that you look at all three books in a bookstore to see which one you find most interesting:

Scanlon, Leo J. *IBM PC & XT Assembly Language: A Guide for Programmers, Enhanced and Enlarged.* Brady Communication Co., 1985. This book is easy reading. It's a complete introduction to 8088 assembly language, but it's not very useful as a reference. If you're still feeling somewhat shaky about assembly language, this might be a good book for you. Otherwise, look at Morse's book.

Willen, David C., and Krantz, Jeffrey I. *8088 Assembler Language Programming: The IBM PC.* Howard W. Sams & Co., 1983. This is another good second book on the 8088 microprocessor, written for the IBM PC.

Bradley, David J. *Assembly Language Programming for the IBM Personal Computer.* Prentice-Hall, 1984. The author helped design the IBM PC, and he's included many examples for the IBM PC. These examples aren't complete, but they may give you ideas of programs to work on. He also talks more about advanced subjects, such as the 8087 numeric processor, than do the authors of the preceding two books.

The next recommendation is neither a reference book, nor an introduction for the IBM PC. It's an introduction to the 8088 microprocessor, written by a member of the design team at Intel:

Morse, Stephen P. *The 8086/8088 Primer.* Hayden, 1982. This is a delightful book. As one of the designers at Intel, Morse provides many insights into the design of the 8088 and also talks about some of the design flaws and bugs in the 8088. While not very good as a reference, this book is complete, and it's very readable and informative.

DOS and ROM BIOS Programming

The references in this section are useful to anyone programming the IBM PC.

Norton, Peter. *Programmer's Guide to the IBM PC,* Microsoft Press, 1985. Includes a complete reference to all DOS and BIOS functions, descriptions of important memory locations, a summary of 8086 instructions, and a host of other useful (or at least interesting) information.

Duncan, Ray. *Advanced MS-DOS.* Microsoft Press, 1986. Covers almost everything you'll want to know about using the DOS services in your programs. It also includes a number of sample programs. A nice companion to Peter's *Programmer's Guide*.

RAM-Resident Programs

There aren't many good references for people who want to write RAM-resident programs since much of the material hasn't been published in a single place. But there are two good sources for information:

The MS-DOS Encyclopedia, edited by Ray Duncan. Microsoft Press, 1988. This book has a wealth of information. It has a nice article that covers many of the aspects of writing RAM-resident programs.

PC Magazine, published by Ziff-Davis, New York, N.Y. often prints information on RAM-resident programs, as well as example programs. A subscription to this magazine will provide you with many good assembly language programs.

Software Design

We have a few favorite books when it comes to software design. The books we recommend are a bit out of the ordinary, enjoyable, and well worth the read.

Brooks, Frederick P., Jr. *The Mythical Man-Month: Essays on Software Engineering*. Addison-Wesley, 1982. Everyone connected with a software project should read this book, especially your manager. A classic.

Normal, Donald A. *The Psychology of Everyday Things*. Basic Books, 1988. This book provides a lot of useful insight into what does and doesn't create problems with programs that interact with people.

Heckel, Paul. *The Elements of Friendly Software Design*. Warner Books, 1984.

APPENDIX A

GUIDE TO THE DISK

The companion disk to this book contains most of the Dskpatch examples you've seen in the preceding chapters, as well as an advanced version of the program that includes many improvements. The files are in two groups: the chapter examples and the advanced Dskpatch program. This appendix will explain what's on the disk and why.

Chapter Examples

All the chapter examples are from Chapters 9 through 27, 30, and 32. The examples in earlier chapters are short enough that you can type them in quickly. But starting in Chapter 9, we began to build Dskpatch, which, by the end of this book, had grown to nine different files.

In any one chapter, only a few of these nine files changed. Since they do evolve throughout each chapter, however, there wasn't enough room on the disk to store each version of each example. So you will find the examples on the disk, as they stand after each chapter. Thus, if we modify a program several times in, say, Chapter 19, the disk contains the final version.

The table in the following guide shows when each file changes. It also shows the name of the disk file for that chapter. If you want to make sure you're still on course or don't feel like typing in the changes for some chapter, just look at this table to find the names of the new files. Then you can either check your work or copy the file(s) to your disk.

Here's the complete list of all the files on the companion disk (not including the advanced version of Dskpatch):

```
VIDEO_9.ASM    VIDEO_16.ASM    DISP_S19.ASM    KBD_IO24.ASM
VIDEO_10.ASM   DISK_I16.ASM    KBD_IO19.ASM    DISPAT25.ASM
VIDEO_13.ASM   DSKPAT17.ASM    DISK_I19.ASM    DISPAT26.ASM
TEST13.ASM     DISP_S17.ASM    DISP_S21.ASM    DISK_I26.ASM
DISP_S14.ASM   CURSOR17.ASM    PHANTO21.ASM    PHANTO27.ASM
CURSOR14.ASM   VIDEO_17.ASM    VIDEO_21.ASM    DSKPAT30.ASM
VIDEO_14.ASM   DISK_I17.ASM    DISPAT22.ASM    KBD_IO30.ASM
DISP_S15.ASM   DISP_S18.ASM    EDITOR22.ASM    CURSOR30.ASM
DISK_I15.ASM   CURSOR18.ASM    PHANTO22.ASM    VIDEO_30.ASM
DISP_S16.ASM   VIDEO_18.ASM    KBD_IO23.ASM    CLIB.ASM
DSKPAT19.ASM   DISPAT19.ASM    TEST23.ASM      DISKLITE.ASM
```

Advanced Version of Dskpatch

As we said, the disk contains more than just the examples in this book. We didn't really finish Dskpatch by the end of Chapter 27, and there are many things we should have put into Dskpatch to make it a usable program. The disk contains an almost-finished version. Here's a quick overview of what you'll find there.

As it stands (in this book), Dskpatch can only read the next or previous sector. Thus, if you wanted to read sector 576, you'd have to push the F4 key 575 times. That's too much work. And what if you wanted to look at sectors within a file? Right now, you'd have to look at the directory sector and figure out where to look for the sectors of that file. Again, not much fun. The disk version of Dskpatch can read either absolute sectors, just as the book version can, or it can read sectors within a file. In its advanced form, Dskpatch is a very usable program.

The advanced version of Dskpatch has too many changes to describe in detail here, so we'll take just a quick look at the new functions we added to the disk version. You'll find many of the changes by exploring Dskpatch and making your own changes.

The advanced Dskpatch still has nine files, all of which you'll find on the disk:

```
DSKPATCH.ASM   DISPATCH.ASM   DISP_SEC.ASM   KBD_IO.ASM
CURSOR.ASM     EDITOR.ASM     PHANTOM.ASM    VIDEO_IO.ASM
DISK_IO.ASM    DSKPATCH.COM
```

You'll also find an assembled and linked .COM version ready to run, so you can try out the new version without assembling it.

When you do, you'll be able to tell that there are several improvements just by looking at the screen display. The advanced Dskpatch now uses eight function keys. That's more than you can remember, if you don't use Dskpatch very often, so the advanced Dskpatch has a "key line" at the bottom of the display. Here's a description of the function keys:

F2 we've seen in this book. Press the Shift key and F2 to write a sector back to the disk.

F3, F4 We already know about F2 and F3, because we used them in this book. F2 reads the previous sector, and F3 reads the next sector.

F5 changes the disk-drive number or letter. Just press F5 and enter a letter, such as A (without a colon, :), or enter a drive number, such as 0. When you press the Enter key, Dskpatch will change drives and read a sector from the new disk drive. You may want to change Dskpatch so that it doesn't read a new sector when you change drives. We just set it up so that it's very difficult to write a sector to the wrong disk.

F6 changes the sector number. Just press F6 and type a sector number, in decimal. Dskpatch will read that sector.

F7   changes Dskpatch to file mode. Just enter the file name and Dskpatch will read a sector from that file. From then on, F3 (Previous Sector) and F4 (Next Sector) read sectors from within that file. F5 ends file mode and switches back to absolute-sector mode.

F8   asks for an offset within a file. This is just like F4 (Sector) except that it reads sectors within a file. If you enter an offset of 3, Dskpatch will read the fourth sector in your file.

F10   exits from Dskpatch. If you accidentally press this key, you'll find yourself back in DOS, and you'll lose any changes you've made to the last sector. You may want to change Dskpatch so that it asks if you really want to leave Dskpatch.

A number of other changes aren't as obvious as those we just mentioned. For example, Dskpatch now scrolls the screen one line at a time. So, if you move the cursor to the bottom line of the display and press the Cursor-Down key, Dskpatch will scroll the display by one line, putting a new line at the bottom.

In addition, some of the other keys on the keyboard also work now:

Home moves the phantom cursor to the top of the half-sector display and scrolls the display so you see the first half-sector.

End moves the phantom cursor to the bottom right of the half-sector display and scrolls the display so you see the second half-sector.

PgUp scrolls the half-sector display by four lines. This is a nice feature when you want to move part way through the sector display. If you press PgUp four times, you'll see the last half sector.

PgDn scrolls the half-sector display by four lines in the opposite direction from PgUp.

If you like, you can modify the advanced Dskpatch to better suit your own needs. That's why the disk has all the source files for the advanced Dskpatch: So you can modify Dskpatch any way you like and learn from a complete example. For instance, you might spruce up the error-checking capabilities. As it stands, if pressing F4 causes you to fall off the end of a disk or file, Dskpatch doesn't reset the sector to the last sector on the disk or file. If you feel ambitious, see if you can modify Dskpatch so it catches and corrects such errors.

Or, you may want to speed up screen updates. To do this you'd have to rewrite some of the procedures, such as WRITE_CHAR and WRITE_ATTRIBUTE_N_TIMES, to write directly to screen memory. Now, they use the very slow ROM BIOS routines. If you're really ambitious, try to write your own character-output routines that send characters to the screen very quickly.

Good luck.

Chapter Number	DSKPATCH	DISPATCH	DISP_SEC	KBD_IO	CURSOR	EDITOR	PHANTOM	VIDEO_IO	DISK_IO	TEST
9								VIDEO_9.ASM		
10								VIDEO_10.ASM		
13								VIDEO_13.ASM		TEST13.ASM
14			DISP_S14.ASM		CURSOR14.ASM			VIDEO_14.ASM		
15			DISP_S15.ASM						DISK_I15.ASM	
16			DISP_S16.ASM					VIDEO_16.ASM	DISK_I16.ASM	
17	DSKPAT17.ASM		DISP_S17.ASM		CURSOR17.ASM			VIDEO_17.ASM	DISK_I17.ASM	
18			DISP_18.ASM		CURSOR18.ASM			VIDEO_18.ASM		
19	DSKPAT19.ASM	DISPAT19.ASM	DISP_19.ASM	KBD_IO19.ASM					DISK_I19.ASM	
21			DISP_S21.ASM				PHANT021.ASM	VIDEO_21.ASM		
22		DISPAT22.ASM				EDITOR22.ASM	PHANT022.ASM			
23				KBD_IO23.ASM						TEST23.ASM
24				KBD_IO24.ASM						
25		DISPAT25.ASM								
26		DISPAT26.ASM							DISK_I26.ASM	
27							PHANT027.ASM			
30	DSKPAT30.ASM			KBD_IO30.ASM	CURSOR30.ASM			VIDEO_3.0ASM		

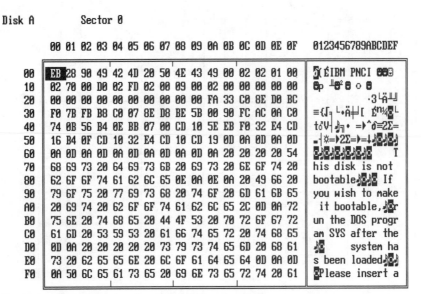

Disk A   Sector 0

```
   00 01 02 03 04 05 06 07 08 09 0A 0B 0C 0D 0E 0F   0123456789ABCDEF

00 EB 28 90 49 42 4D 20 50 4E 43 49 00 02 02 01 00   [)ÉIBM PNCI ◙◘◙
10 02 70 00 D0 02 FD 02 00 09 00 02 00 00 00 00 00   ◙p ⌐◙²◙ ○ ◙
20 00 00 00 00 00 00 00 00 00 00 FA 33 C0 8E D0 BC    ·3└Ä╨└
30 F0 7B FB B8 C0 07 8E D8 BE 5B 00 90 FC AC 0A C0   ≡{√╕└•Ä╪╛[ ⌠n¼└
40 74 0B 56 B4 0E BB 07 00 CD 10 5E EB F0 32 E4 CD   t∂V┤♫ ═►^δ≡2Σ═
50 16 B4 0F CD 10 32 E4 CD 10 CD 19 0D 0A 0D 0A 0D   ▬┤☼═►2Σ═►═↓♪♫♪♫♪
60 0A 0D 0A 0D 0A 0D 0A 0D 0A 0D 0A 20 20 20 20 54   ♫♪♫♪♫♪♫♪♫♪♫    T
70 68 69 73 20 64 69 73 6B 20 69 73 20 6E 6F 74 20   his disk is not
80 62 6F 6F 74 61 62 6C 65 0E 0A 0E 0A 20 49 66 20   bootable♫♪♫♪ If
90 79 6F 75 20 77 69 73 68 20 74 6F 20 6D 61 6B 65   you wish to make
A0 20 69 74 20 62 6F 6F 74 61 62 6C 65 2C 0D 0A 72    it bootable,♪♫r
B0 75 6E 20 74 68 65 20 44 4F 53 20 70 72 6F 67 72   un the DOS progr
C0 61 6D 20 53 59 53 20 61 66 74 65 72 20 74 68 65   am SYS after the
D0 0D 0A 20 20 20 20 20 73 79 73 74 65 6D 20 68 61   ♪♫     system ha
E0 73 20 62 65 65 6E 20 6C 6F 61 64 65 64 0D 0A 0D   s been loaded♪♫♪
F0 0A 50 6C 65 61 73 65 20 69 6E 73 65 72 74 20 61   ♫Please insert a
```

Press function key, or enter character or hex byte:

1   2↑Save 3Prev. 4Next 5Drive 6Sector 7File 8Offset 9   0Exit

Figure A-1. The Advanced Version of Dskpatch

APPENDIX B

LISTING OF DSKPATCH

Descriptions of Procedures

This appendix contains the final version of Dskpatch. If you're writing your own programs, you'll find many general-purpose procedures in this appendix that will help you on your way. We've included short descriptions of each procedure to help you find such procedures.

CURSOR.ASM

CLEAR_SCREEN   Like the BASIC CLS command; clears the text screen.

CLEAR_TO_END_OF_LINE   Clears all the characters from the cursor position to the end of the current line.

CURSOR_RIGHT   Moves the cursor one character position to the right, without writing a space over the old character.

GOTO_XY   Very much like the BASIC LOCATE command; moves the cursor on the screen.

SEND_CRLF   Sends a carriage-return/line-feed pair of characters to the screen. This procedure simply moves the cursor to the start of the next line.

UPDATE_REAL_CURSOR   Moves the real cursor to the location of the virtual cursor.

UPDATE_VIRTUAL_CURSOR   Moves the virtual cursor to the position of the real cursor.

DISK_IO.ASM

NEXT_SECTOR   Adds one to the current sector number, then reads that sector into memory and rewrites the Dskpatch screen.

PREVIOUS_SECTOR   Reads the previous sector. That is, the procedure subtracts one from the old sector number (CURRENT_SECTOR_NO) and reads the new sector into the memory variable SECTOR. It also rewrites the screen display.

READ_SECTOR Reads one sector (512 bytes) from the disk into the memory buffer, SECTOR.

WRITE_SECTOR Writes one sector (512 bytes) from the memory buffer, SECTOR, to the disk.

DISPATCH.ASM

DISPATCHER The central dispatcher, reads characters from the keyboard and then calls on other procedures to do all the work of Dskpatch. Add any new commands to DISPATCH_TABLE in this file.

DISP_SEC.ASM

DISP_HALF_SECTOR Does the work of displaying all the hex and ASCII characters that appear in the half-sector display by calling DISP_LINE 16 times.

DISP_LINE Displays just one line of the half-sector display. DISP_HALF_SECTOR calls this procedure 16 times to display all 16 lines of the half-sector display.

INIT_SEC_DISP Initializes the half-sector display you see in Dskpatch. This procedure redraws the half-sector display, along with the boundaries and top hex numbers, but does not write the header or the editor prompt.

WRITE_HEADER Writes the header at the top of the screen you see in Dskpatch. There, the procedure displays the disk-drive number and the number of the sector you see in the half-sector display.

WRITE_PROMPT_LINE Writes a string at the prompt line, then clears the rest of the line to remove any characters from the old prompt.

WRITE_TOP_HEX_NUMBERS Writes the line of hex numbers across the top of the half-sector display. The procedure is not useful for much else.

DSKPATCH.ASM

DISK_PATCH The (very short) main program of Dskpatch. DISK_PATCH simply calls a number of other procedures, which do all the work. It also includes many of the definitions for the variables that are used throughout Dskpatch.

EDITOR.ASM

EDIT_BYTE   *Edits* a byte in the half-sector display by changing one byte both in memory (SECTOR) and on the screen. Dskpatch uses this procedure to change bytes in a sector.

WRITE_TO_MEMORY   Called upon by EDIT_BYTE to change a single byte in SECTOR. This procedure changes the byte pointed to by the phantom cursor.

KBD_IO.ASM

BACK_SPACE   Used by the READ_STRING procedure to delete one character, both from the screen and from the keyboard buffer, whenever you press the Backspace key.

CONVERT_HEX_DIGIT   Converts a single ASCII character into its hexadecimal equivalent. For example, the procedure converts the letter A into the hex number 0AH. **Note**: CONVERT_HEX_DIGIT works only with upper-case letters.

HEX_TO_BYTE   Converts a two-character string of characters from a hexadecimal string, such as A5, into a single byte with that hex value. HEX_TO_BYTE expects the two characters to be digits or uppercase letters.

READ_BYTE   Uses READ_STRING to read a string of characters. This procedure returns the special function key, a single character, or a hex byte if you typed a two-digit hex number.

READ_DECIMAL   Reads an unsigned decimal number from the keyboard, using READ_STRING to read the characters. READ_DECIMAL can read numbers from 0 to 65535.

READ_KEY   Reads a single key from the keyboard and returns 0 through 255 for ordinary characters, and 100h plus the scan code for special keys.

READ_STRING   Reads a DOS-style string of characters from the keyboard. This procedure also reads special function keys, whereas the DOS READ_STRING function does not.

STRING_TO_UPPER   A general-purpose procedure, converts a DOS-style string to all uppercase letters.

PHANTOM.ASM

ERASE_PHANTOM   Removes the two phantom cursors from the screen by returning the character attribute to normal (7) for all characters under the phantom cursors.

MOV_TO_ASCII_POSITION   Moves the real cursor to the start of the phantom cursor in the ASCII window of the half-sector display.

MOV_TO_HEX_POSITION   Moves the real cursor to the start of the phantom cursor in the hex window of the half-sector display.

PHANTOM_DOWN   Moves the phantom cursor down and scrolls the screen if you try to move past the sixteenth line of the half-sector display.

PHANTOM_LEFT   Moves the phantom cursor left one entry but not past the left side of the half-sector display.

PHANTOM_RIGHT   Moves the phantom cursor right one entry but not past the right side of the half-sector display.

PHANTOM_UP   Moves the phantom cursor up one line in the half-sector display, or scrolls the display if you try to move the cursor off the top.

RESTORE_REAL_CURSOR   Moves the cursor back to the position recorded by SAVE_REAL_CURSOR.

SAVE_REAL_CURSOR   Saves the position of the real cursor in two variables. Call this procedure before you move the real cursor if you want to restore its position when you've finished making changes to the screen.

SCROLL_DOWN   Rather than scrolling the half-sector display, displays the first half of the sector. You'll find a more advanced version of SCROLL_DOWN on the disk available with this book. The advanced version scrolls the half-sector display by just one line.

SCROLL_UP   Called by PHANTOM_DOWN when you try to move the phantom cursor off the bottom of the half-sector display. The version in this book doesn't actually scroll the screen: It writes the second half of the sector. On the disk, more advanced versions of SCROLL_UP and SCROLL_DOWN scroll the display by one line, instead of 16.

WRITE_PHANTOM Draws the phantom cursors in the half-sector display: one in the hex window and one in the ASCII window. This procedure simply changes the character attributes to 70H to use black characters on a white background.

VIDEO_IO.ASM

Contains most of the general-purpose procedures you'll want to use in your own programs.

INIT_WRITE_CHAR Call this procedure before you call any of the other procedures in this file. It initializes the data used by the routines that write directly to screen memory.

WRITE_ATTRIBUTE_N_TIMES A handy procedure you can use to change the attributes for a group of N characters. WRITE_PHANTOM uses this procedure to draw the phantom cursors, and ERASE_PHANTOM uses it to remove the phantom cursors.

WRITE_CHAR Writes a character to the screen. Since it uses the ROM BIOS routines, this procedure doesn't attach special meaning to any characters. So, a carriage-return character will appear on the screen as a musical note (the character for 0DH). Call SEND_CRLF if you want to move the cursor to the start of the next line.

WRITE_CHAR_N_TIMES Writes N copies of one character to the screen. This procedure is useful for drawing lines of characters, such as the ones used in patterns.

WRITE_DECIMAL Writes a word to the screen as an unsigned decimal number in the range 0 to 65535.

WRITE_HEX Takes a one-byte number and writes it on the screen as a two-digit hex number.

WRITE_HEX_DIGIT Writes a single-digit hex number on the screen. This procedure converts a 4-bit nibble into the ASCII character and writes it to the screen.

WRITE_PATTERN Draws boxes around the half-sector display, as defined by a pattern. You can use WRITE_PATTERN to draw arbitrary patterns of characters on the screen.

WRITE_STRING A very useful, general-purpose procedure with which you can write a string of characters to the screen. The last character in your string must be a zero byte.

Program Listings for Dskpatch Procedures
DSKPATCH Make File

Here is the makefile that you can use with Microsoft's Make utility to build Dskpatch automatically.

```
DSKPATCH.OBJ:    DSKPATCH.ASM
        MASM DSKPATCH;

DISK_IO.OBJ:     DISK_IO.ASM
        MASM DISK_IO;

DISP_SEC.OBJ:    DISP_SEC.ASM
        MASM DISP_SEC;

VIDEO_IO.OBJ:    VIDEO_IO.ASM
        MASM VIDEO_IO;

CURSOR.OBJ:      CURSOR.ASM
        MASM CURSOR;

DISPATCH.OBJ:    DISPATCH.ASM
        MASM DISPATCH;

KBD_IO.OBJ:      KBD_IO.ASM
        MASM KBD_IO;

PHANTOM.OBJ:     PHANTOM.ASM
        MASM PHANTOM;

EDITOR.OBJ:      EDITOR.ASM
        MASM EDITOR;

DSKPATCH.EXE:    DSKPATCH.OBJ DISK_IO.OBJ DISP_SEC.OBJ VIDEO_IO.OBJ CURSOR.OBJ \
                 DISPATCH.OBJ KBD_IO.OBJ PHANTOM.OBJ EDITOR.OBJ
        LINK @LINKINFO
```

DSKPATCH Linkinfo File

And here is the linkinfo file:

```
DSKPATCH DISK_IO DISP_SEC VIDEO_IO CURSOR +
DISPATCH KBD_IO PHANTOM EDITOR
DSKPATCH
DSKPATCH /MAP;
```

CURSOR.ASM

```
CR        EQU      13                      ;Carriage return
LF        EQU      10                      ;Line feed

.MODEL    SMALL
.CODE

          PUBLIC   CLEAR_SCREEN
;-----------------------------------------------------------------------;
; This procedure clears the entire screen.                              ;
;-----------------------------------------------------------------------;
CLEAR_SCREEN    PROC
          PUSH     AX
          PUSH     BX
          PUSH     CX
          PUSH     DX
          XOR      AL,AL                   ;Blank entire window
          XOR      CX,CX                   ;Upper left corner is at (0,0)
          MOV      DH,24                   ;Bottom line of screen is line 24
          MOV      DL,79                   ;Right side is at column 79
          MOV      BH,7                    ;Use normal attribute for blanks
          MOV      AH,6                    ;Call for SCROLL-UP function
          INT      10h                     ;Clear the window
          POP      DX
          POP      CX
          POP      BX
          POP      AX
          RET
CLEAR_SCREEN    ENDP


          PUBLIC   GOTO_XY
.DATA
          EXTRN    SCREEN_PTR:WORD         ;Pointer to character under cursor
          EXTRN    SCREEN_X:BYTE, SCREEN_Y:BYTE
.CODE
;-----------------------------------------------------------------------;
; This procedure moves the cursor                                       ;
;                                                                       ;
; On entry:     DH       Row (Y)                                        ;
;               DL       Column (X)                                     ;
;-----------------------------------------------------------------------;
GOTO_XY         PROC
          PUSH     AX
          PUSH     BX
          MOV      BH,0                    ;Display page 0
          MOV      AH,2                    ;Call for SET CURSOR POSITION
          INT      10h

          MOV      AL,DH                   ;Get the row number
          MOV      BL,80                   ;Multiply by 80 chars per line
          MUL      BL                      ;AX = row * 80
          ADD      AL,DL                   ;Add column
          ADC      AH,0                    ;AX = row * 80 + column
          SHL      AX,1                    ;Convert to a byte offset
          MOV      SCREEN_PTR,AX           ;Save the cursor offset
          MOV      SCREEN_X,DL             ;Save the cursor position
          MOV      SCREEN_Y,DH

          POP      BX
          POP      AX
          RET
GOTO_XY        ENDP

          PUBLIC   CURSOR_RIGHT
.DATA
          EXTRN    SCREEN_PTR:WORD         ;Pointer to character under cursor
          EXTRN    SCREEN_X:BYTE, SCREEN_Y:BYTE
```

```
        .CODE
;------------------------------------------------------------------;
; This procedure moves the cursor one position to the right or to the  ;
; next line if the cursor was at the end of a line.                ;
;                                                                  ;
; Uses:          SEND_CRLF                                         ;
; Writes:        SCREEN_PTR, SCREEN_X, SCREEN_Y                    ;
;------------------------------------------------------------------;
CURSOR_RIGHT    PROC
        INC     SCREEN_PTR              ;Move to next character position (word)
        INC     SCREEN_PTR
        INC     SCREEN_X                ;Move to next column
        CMP     SCREEN_X,79             ;Make sure column <= 79
        JBE     OK
        CALL    SEND_CRLF               ;Go to next line
 OK:
        RET
CURSOR_RIGHT    ENDP

        PUBLIC  UPDATE_REAL_CURSOR
;------------------------------------------------------------------;
; This procedure moves the real cursor to the current virtual cursor  ;
; position.  You'll want to call it just before you wait for keyboard ;
; input.                                                           ;
;------------------------------------------------------------------;
UPDATE_REAL_CURSOR      PROC
        PUSH    DX
        MOV     DL,SCREEN_X             ;Get position of the virtual cursor
        MOV     DH,SCREEN_Y
        CALL    GOTO_XY                 ;Move real cursor to this position
        POP     DX
        RET
UPDATE_REAL_CURSOR          ENDP


        PUBLIC  UPDATE_VIRTUAL_CURSOR
;------------------------------------------------------------------;
; This procedure updates the position of our virtual cursor to agree  ;
; with the position of the real cursor.                            ;
;------------------------------------------------------------------;
UPDATE_VIRTUAL_CURSOR   PROC
        PUSH    AX
        PUSH    BX
        PUSH    CX
        PUSH    DX
        MOV     AH,3                    ;Ask for the cursor position
        XOR     BH,BH                   ;On page 0
        INT     10h                     ;Get cursor position into DH, DL
        CALL    GOTO_XY                 ;Move virtual cursor to this position
        POP     DX
        POP     CX
        POP     BX
        POP     AX
        RET
UPDATE_VIRTUAL_CURSOR   ENDP

        PUBLIC  CLEAR_TO_END_OF_LINE
;------------------------------------------------------------------;
; This procedure clears the line from the current cursor position to  ;
; the end of that line.                                            ;
;------------------------------------------------------------------;
CLEAR_TO_END_OF_LINE    PROC
        PUSH    AX
        PUSH    BX
        PUSH    CX
        PUSH    DX
        MOV     DL,SCREEN_X
        MOV     DH,SCREEN_Y
        MOV     AH,6                    ;Set up to clear to end of line
        XOR     AL,AL                   ;Clear window
        MOV     CH,DH                   ;All on same line
```

CURSOR.ASM *continued*

```
        MOV     CL,DL                   ;Start at the cursor position
        MOV     DL,79                   ;And stop at the end of the line
        MOV     BH,7                    ;Use normal attribute
        INT     10h
        POP     DX
        POP     CX
        POP     BX
        POP     AX
        RET
CLEAR_TO_END_OF_LINE     ENDP

        PUBLIC  SEND_CRLF
;-------------------------------------------------------------------------;
; This routine just sends a carriage return-line feed pair to the         ;
; display, using the DOS routines so that scrolling will be handled       ;
; correctly.                                                              ;
;                                                                         ;
; Uses:           UPDATE_VIRTUAL_CURSOR                                    ;
;-------------------------------------------------------------------------;
SEND_CRLF       PROC
        PUSH    AX
        PUSH    DX
        MOV     AH,2
        MOV     DL,CR
        INT     21h
        MOV     DL,LF
        INT     21h
        CALL    UPDATE_VIRTUAL_CURSOR   ;Update position of virtual cursor
        POP     DX
        POP     AX
        RET
SEND_CRLF       ENDP

        END
```

DISK_IO.ASM

```
        .MODEL   SMALL

        .DATA

        EXTRN    SECTOR:BYTE
        EXTRN    DISK_DRIVE_NO:BYTE
        EXTRN    CURRENT_SECTOR_NO:WORD

        .CODE

        PUBLIC   PREVIOUS_SECTOR
        EXTRN    INIT_SEC_DISP:PROC, WRITE_HEADER:PROC
        EXTRN    WRITE_PROMPT_LINE:PROC
        .DATA
        EXTRN    CURRENT_SECTOR_NO:WORD, EDITOR_PROMPT:BYTE
        .CODE
;------------------------------------------------------------------------;
; This procedure reads the previous sector, if possible.                 ;
;                                                                        ;
; Uses:          WRITE_HEADER, READ_SECTOR, INIT_SEC_DISP                 ;
;                WRITE_PROMPT_LINE                                        ;
; Reads:         CURRENT_SECTOR_NO, EDITOR_PROMPT                         ;
; Writes:        CURRENT_SECTOR_NO                                        ;
;------------------------------------------------------------------------;
PREVIOUS_SECTOR         PROC
        PUSH     AX
        PUSH     DX
        MOV      AX,CURRENT_SECTOR_NO   ;Get current sector number
        OR       AX,AX                  ;Don't decrement if already 0
        JZ       DONT_DECREMENT_SECTOR
        DEC      AX
        MOV      CURRENT_SECTOR_NO,AX   ;Save new sector number
        CALL     WRITE_HEADER
        CALL     READ_SECTOR
        CALL     INIT_SEC_DISP          ;Display new sector
        LEA      DX,EDITOR_PROMPT
        CALL     WRITE_PROMPT_LINE
DONT_DECREMENT_SECTOR:
        POP      DX
        POP      AX
        RET
PREVIOUS_SECTOR        ENDP


        PUBLIC   NEXT_SECTOR
        EXTRN    INIT_SEC_DISP:PROC, WRITE_HEADER:PROC
        EXTRN    WRITE_PROMPT_LINE:PROC
        .DATA
        EXTRN    CURRENT_SECTOR_NO:WORD, EDITOR_PROMPT:BYTE
        .CODE
;------------------------------------------------------------------------;
; Reads the next sector.                                                  ;
;                                                                        ;
; Uses:          WRITE_HEADER, READ_SECTOR, INIT_SEC_DISP                 ;
;                WRITE_PROMPT_LINE                                        ;
; Reads:         CURRENT_SECTOR_NO, EDITOR_PROMPT                         ;
; Writes:        CURRENT_SECTOR_NO                                        ;
;------------------------------------------------------------------------;
NEXT_SECTOR    PROC
        PUSH     AX
        PUSH     DX
        MOV      AX,CURRENT_SECTOR_NO
        INC      AX                     ;Move to next sector
        MOV      CURRENT_SECTOR_NO,AX
        CALL     WRITE_HEADER
        CALL     READ_SECTOR
        CALL     INIT_SEC_DISP          ;Display new sector
```

DISK_IO.ASM *continued*

```
        LEA     DX,EDITOR_PROMPT
        CALL    WRITE_PROMPT_LINE
        POP     DX
        POP     AX
        RET
NEXT_SECTOR     ENDP


        PUBLIC  READ_SECTOR
;-------------------------------------------------------------------;
; This procedure reads one sector (512 bytes) into SECTOR.          ;
;                                                                   ;
; Reads:        CURRENT_SECTOR_NO, DISK_DRIVE_NO                    ;
; Writes:       SECTOR                                              ;
;-------------------------------------------------------------------;
READ_SECTOR     PROC
        PUSH    AX
        PUSH    BX
        PUSH    CX
        PUSH    DX
        MOV     AL,DISK_DRIVE_NO        ;Drive number
        MOV     CX,1                    ;Read only 1 sector
        MOV     DX,CURRENT_SECTOR_NO    ;Logical sector number
        LEA     BX,SECTOR               ;Where to store this sector
        INT     25h                     ;Read the sector
        POPF                            ;Discard flags put on stack by DOS
        POP     DX
        POP     CX
        POP     BX
        POP     AX
        RET
READ_SECTOR     ENDP


        PUBLIC  WRITE_SECTOR
;-------------------------------------------------------------------;
; This procedure writes the sector back to the disk.               ;
;                                                                   ;
; Reads:        DISK_DRIVE_NO, CURRENT_SECTOR_NO, SECTOR           ;
;-------------------------------------------------------------------;
WRITE_SECTOR    PROC
        PUSH    AX
        PUSH    BX
        PUSH    CX
        PUSH    DX
        MOV     AL,DISK_DRIVE_NO        ;Drive number
        MOV     CX,1                    ;Write 1 sector
        MOV     DX,CURRENT_SECTOR_NO    ;Logical sector
        LEA     BX,SECTOR
        INT     26h                     ;Write the sector to disk
        POPF                            ;Discard the flag information
        POP     DX
        POP     CX
        POP     BX
        POP     AX
        RET
WRITE_SECTOR    ENDP

        END
```

DISPATCH.ASM

```
        .MODEL  SMALL

        .CODE
        EXTRN   NEXT_SECTOR:PROC                        ;In DISK_IO.ASM
        EXTRN   PREVIOUS_SECTOR:PROC                    ;In DISK_IO.ASM
        EXTRN   PHANTOM_UP:PROC, PHANTOM_DOWN:PROC      ;In PHANTOM.ASM
        EXTRN   PHANTOM_LEFT:PROC, PHANTOM_RIGHT:PROC
        EXTRN   WRITE_SECTOR:PROC                       ;In DISK_IO.ASM
        .DATA
;---------------------------------------------------------------------;
; This table contains the legal extended ASCII keys and the addresses ;
; of the procedures that should be called when each key is pressed.   ;
;                                                                     ;
; The format of the table is                                         ;
;               DB      72              ;Extended code for cursor up   ;
;               DW      OFFSET PHANTOM_UP                             ;
;---------------------------------------------------------------------;
DISPATCH_TABLE  LABEL   BYTE
        DB      61                              ;F3
        DW      OFFSET _TEXT:PREVIOUS_SECTOR
        DB      62                              ;F4
        DW      OFFSET _TEXT:NEXT_SECTOR
        DB      72                              ;Cursor up
        DW      OFFSET _TEXT:PHANTOM_UP
        DB      80                              ;Cursor down
        DW      OFFSET _TEXT:PHANTOM_DOWN
        DB      75                              ;Cursor left
        DW      OFFSET _TEXT:PHANTOM_LEFT
        DB      77                              ;Cursor right
        DW      OFFSET _TEXT:PHANTOM_RIGHT
        DB      85                              ;Shift F2
        DW      OFFSET _TEXT:WRITE_SECTOR
        DB      0                               ;End of the table

        .CODE

        PUBLIC  DISPATCHER
        EXTRN   READ_BYTE:PROC, EDIT_BYTE:PROC
        EXTRN   WRITE_PROMPT_LINE:PROC
        .DATA
        EXTRN   EDITOR_PROMPT:BYTE
        .CODE
;---------------------------------------------------------------------;
; This is the central dispatcher. During normal editing and viewing,  ;
; this procedure reads characters from the keyboard and, if the char  ;
; is a command key (such as a cursor key), DISPATCHER calls the       ;
; procedures that do the actual work.  This dispatching is done for   ;
; special keys listed in the table DISPATCH_TABLE, where the procedure ;
; addresses are stored just after the key names.                      ;
;                                                                     ;
; If the character is not a special key, then it should be placed     ;
; directly into the sector buffer--this is the editing mode.          ;
;                                                                     ;
; Uses:         READ_BYTE, EDIT_BYTE, WRITE_PROMPT_LINE               ;
; Reads:        EDITOR_PROMPT                                         ;
;---------------------------------------------------------------------;
DISPATCHER      PROC
        PUSH    AX
        PUSH    BX
        PUSH    DX
DISPATCH_LOOP:
        CALL    READ_BYTE               ;Read character into AX
        OR      AH,AH                   ;AX = -1 if no character read, 1
                                        ; for an extended code.
        JS      NO_CHARS_READ           ;No character read, try again
        JNZ     SPECIAL_KEY             ;Read extended code
        MOV     DL,AL
```

DISPATCH.ASM *continued*

```
            CALL    EDIT_BYTE               ;Was normal character, edit byte
            JMP     DISPATCH_LOOP           ;Read another character

SPECIAL_KEY:
            CMP     AL,68                   ;F10--exit?
            JE      END_DISPATCH            ;Yes, leave
                                            ;Use BX to look through table
            LEA     BX,DISPATCH_TABLE
SPECIAL_LOOP:
            CMP     BYTE PTR [BX],0         ;End of table?
            JE      NOT_IN_TABLE            ;Yes, key was not in the table
            CMP     AL,[BX]                 ;Is it this table entry?
            JE      DISPATCH                ;Yes, then dispatch
            ADD     BX,3                    ;No, try next entry
            JMP     SPECIAL_LOOP            ;Check next table entry

DISPATCH:
            INC     BX                      ;Point to address of procedure
            CALL    WORD PTR [BX]           ;Call procedure
            JMP     DISPATCH_LOOP           ;Wait for another key

NOT_IN_TABLE:                               ;Do nothing, just read next character
            JMP     DISPATCH_LOOP

NO_CHARS_READ:
            LEA     DX,EDITOR_PROMPT
            CALL    WRITE_PROMPT_LINE       ;Erase any invalid characters typed
            JMP     DISPATCH_LOOP           ;Try again

END_DISPATCH:
            POP     DX
            POP     BX
            POP     AX
            RET
DISPATCHER  ENDP


            END
```

DISP_SEC.ASM

```
        .MODEL   SMALL


;-----------------------------------------------------------------------;
; Graphics characters for border of sector.                            ;
;-----------------------------------------------------------------------;
VERTICAL_BAR      EQU      0BAh
HORIZONTAL_BAR    EQU      0CDh
UPPER_LEFT        EQU      0C9h
UPPER_RIGHT       EQU      0BBh
LOWER_LEFT        EQU      0C8h
LOWER_RIGHT       EQU      0BCh
TOP_T_BAR         EQU      0CBh
BOTTOM_T_BAR      EQU      0CAh
TOP_TICK          EQU      0D1h
BOTTOM_TICK       EQU      0CFh


        .DATA

TOP_LINE_PATTERN        LABEL    BYTE
        DB       ' ',7
        DB       UPPER_LEFT, 1
        DB       HORIZONTAL_BAR,12
        DB       TOP_TICK,1
        DB       HORIZONTAL_BAR,11
        DB       TOP_TICK,1
        DB       HORIZONTAL_BAR,11
        DB       TOP_TICK,1
        DB       HORIZONTAL_BAR,12
        DB       TOP_T_BAR,1
        DB       HORIZONTAL_BAR,18
        DB       UPPER_RIGHT,1
        DB       0
BOTTOM_LINE_PATTERN     LABEL    BYTE
        DB       ' ',7
        DB       LOWER_LEFT, 1
        DB       HORIZONTAL_BAR,12
        DB       BOTTOM_TICK,1
        DB       HORIZONTAL_BAR,11
        DB       BOTTOM_TICK,1
        DB       HORIZONTAL_BAR,11
        DB       BOTTOM_TICK,1
        DB       HORIZONTAL_BAR,12
        DB       BOTTOM_T_BAR,1
        DB       HORIZONTAL_BAR,18
        DB       LOWER_RIGHT,1
        DB       0

.DATA?

        EXTRN    SECTOR:BYTE

.CODE

        PUBLIC   INIT_SEC_DISP
        EXTRN    WRITE_PATTERN:PROC, SEND_CRLF:PROC
        EXTRN    GOTO_XY:PROC, WRITE_PHANTOM:PROC
.DATA
        EXTRN    LINES_BEFORE_SECTOR:BYTE
        EXTRN    SECTOR_OFFSET:WORD
.CODE
;-----------------------------------------------------------------------;
; This procedure initializes the half-sector display.                  ;
;                                                                       ;
; Uses:          WRITE_PATTERN, SEND_CRLF, DISP_HALF_SECTOR            ;
;                WRITE_TOP_HEX_NUMBERS, GOTO_XY, WRITE_PHANTOM         ;
```

DISP_SEC.ASM *continued*

```
; Reads:          TOP_LINE_PATTERN, BOTTOM_LINE_PATTERN            ;
;                 LINES_BEFORE_SECTOR                              ;
; Writes:         SECTOR_OFFSET                                    ;
;-----------------------------------------------------------------;
INIT_SEC_DISP   PROC
        PUSH    DX
        XOR     DL,DL                   ;Move cursor into position
        MOV     DH,LINES_BEFORE_SECTOR
        CALL    GOTO_XY
        CALL    WRITE_TOP_HEX_NUMBERS
        LEA     DX,TOP_LINE_PATTERN
        CALL    WRITE_PATTERN
        CALL    SEND_CRLF
        XOR     DX,DX                   ;Start at the beginning of the sector
        MOV     SECTOR_OFFSET,DX        ;Set sector offset to 0
        CALL    DISP_HALF_SECTOR
        LEA     DX,BOTTOM_LINE_PATTERN
        CALL    WRITE_PATTERN
        CALL    WRITE_PHANTOM           ;Display the phantom cursor
        POP     DX
        RET
INIT_SEC_DISP   ENDP


        PUBLIC  WRITE_HEADER
.DATA
        EXTRN   HEADER_LINE_NO:BYTE
        EXTRN   HEADER_PART_1:BYTE
        EXTRN   HEADER_PART_2:BYTE
        EXTRN   DISK_DRIVE_NO:BYTE
        EXTRN   CURRENT_SECTOR_NO:WORD
.CODE
        EXTRN   WRITE_STRING:PROC, WRITE_DECIMAL:PROC
        EXTRN   GOTO_XY:PROC, CLEAR_TO_END_OF_LINE:PROC
;-----------------------------------------------------------------;
; This procedure writes the header with disk-drive and sector number.  ;
;                                                                 ;
; Uses:           GOTO_XY, WRITE_STRING, WRITE_CHAR, WRITE_DECIMAL    ;
;                 CLEAR_TO_END_OF_LINE                            ;
; Reads:          HEADER_LINE_NO, HEADER_PART_1, HEADER_PART_2    ;
;                 DISK_DRIVE_NO, CURRENT_SECTOR_NO                ;
;-----------------------------------------------------------------;
WRITE_HEADER    PROC
        PUSH    DX
        XOR     DL,DL                   ;Move cursor to header line number
        MOV     DH,HEADER_LINE_NO
        CALL    GOTO_XY
        LEA     DX,HEADER_PART_1
        CALL    WRITE_STRING
        MOV     DL,DISK_DRIVE_NO
        ADD     DL,'A'                  ;Print drives A, B,...
        CALL    WRITE_CHAR
        LEA     DX,HEADER_PART_2
        CALL    WRITE_STRING
        MOV     DX,CURRENT_SECTOR_NO
        CALL    WRITE_DECIMAL
        CALL    CLEAR_TO_END_OF_LINE    ;Clear rest of sector number
        POP     DX
        RET
WRITE_HEADER    ENDP

        EXTRN   WRITE_CHAR_N_TIMES:PROC, WRITE_HEX:PROC, WRITE_CHAR:PROC
        EXTRN   WRITE_HEX_DIGIT:PROC, SEND_CRLF:PROC
;-----------------------------------------------------------------;
; This procedure writes the index numbers (0 through F) at the top of  ;
; the half-sector display.                                        ;
;                                                                 ;
; Uses:           WRITE_CHAR_N_TIMES, WRITE_HEX, WRITE_CHAR       ;
```

```
;                       WRITE_HEX_DIGIT, SEND_CRLF                        ;
;-------------------------------------------------------------------------;
WRITE_TOP_HEX_NUMBERS    PROC
        PUSH    CX
        PUSH    DX
        MOV     DL,' '                          ;Write 9 spaces for left side
        MOV     CX,9
        CALL    WRITE_CHAR_N_TIMES
        XOR     DH,DH                           ;Start with 0
HEX_NUMBER_LOOP:
        MOV     DL,DH
        CALL    WRITE_HEX
        MOV     DL,' '
        CALL    WRITE_CHAR
        INC     DH
        CMP     DH,10h                          ;Done yet?
        JB      HEX_NUMBER_LOOP

        MOV     DL,' '                          ;Write hex numbers over ASCII window
        MOV     CX,2
        CALL    WRITE_CHAR_N_TIMES
        XOR     DL,DL
HEX_DIGIT_LOOP:
        CALL    WRITE_HEX_DIGIT
        INC     DL
        CMP     DL,10h
        JB      HEX_DIGIT_LOOP
        CALL    SEND_CRLF
        POP     DX
        POP     CX
        RET
WRITE_TOP_HEX_NUMBERS    ENDP

        PUBLIC  DISP_HALF_SECTOR
        EXTRN   SEND_CRLF:PROC
;-------------------------------------------------------------------------;
; This procedure displays half a sector (256 bytes)                       ;
;                                                                         ;
; On entry:     DS:DX   Offset into sector, in bytes -- should be          ;
;                       multiple of 16.                                   ;
;                                                                         ;
; Uses:         DISP_LINE, SEND_CRLF                                      ;
;-------------------------------------------------------------------------;
DISP_HALF_SECTOR          PROC
        PUSH    CX
        PUSH    DX
        MOV     CX,16                           ;Display 16 lines
HALF_SECTOR:
        CALL    DISP_LINE
        CALL    SEND_CRLF
        ADD     DX,16
        LOOP    HALF_SECTOR
        POP     DX
        POP     CX
        RET
DISP_HALF_SECTOR          ENDP

        PUBLIC  DISP_LINE
        EXTRN   WRITE_HEX:PROC
        EXTRN   WRITE_CHAR:PROC
        EXTRN   WRITE_CHAR_N_TIMES:PROC
;-------------------------------------------------------------------------;
; This procedure displays one line of data, or 16 bytes, first in hex,    ;
; then in ASCII.                                                          ;
;                                                                         ;
; On entry:     DS:DX   Offset into sector, in bytes.                     ;
;                                                                         ;
; Uses:         WRITE_CHAR, WRITE_HEX, WRITE_CHAR_N_TIMES                 ;
; Reads:        SECTOR                                                    ;
;-------------------------------------------------------------------------;
```

DISP_SEC.ASM *continued*

```
DISP_LINE       PROC
        PUSH    BX
        PUSH    CX
        PUSH    DX
        MOV     BX,DX                   ;Offset is more useful in BX
        MOV     DL,' '
        MOV     CX,3                    ;Write 3 spaces before line
        CALL    WRITE_CHAR_N_TIMES
                                        ;Write offset in hex
        CMP     BX,100h                 ;Is the first digit a 1?
        JB      WRITE_ONE               ;No, write space already in DL
        MOV     DL,'1'                  ;Yes, then place '1' into DL for output
WRITE_ONE:
        CALL    WRITE_CHAR
        MOV     DL,BL                   ;Copy lower byte into DL for hex output
        CALL    WRITE_HEX
                                        ;Write separator
        MOV     DL,' '
        CALL    WRITE_CHAR
        MOV     DL,VERTICAL_BAR         ;Draw left side of box
        CALL    WRITE_CHAR
        MOV     DL,' '
        CALL    WRITE_CHAR
                                        ;Now write out 16 bytes
        MOV     CX,16                   ;Dump 16 bytes
        PUSH    BX                      ;Save the offset for ASCII_LOOP
HEX_LOOP:
        MOV     DL,SECTOR[BX]           ;Get 1 byte
        CALL    WRITE_HEX               ;Dump this byte in hex
        MOV     DL,' '                  ;Write a space between numbers
        CALL    WRITE_CHAR
        INC     BX
        LOOP    HEX_LOOP

        MOV     DL,VERTICAL_BAR         ;Write separator
        CALL    WRITE_CHAR
        MOV     DL,' '                  ;Add another space before characters
        CALL    WRITE_CHAR

        MOV     CX,16
        POP     BX                      ;Get back offset into SECTOR
ASCII_LOOP:
        MOV     DL,SECTOR[BX]
        CALL    WRITE_CHAR
        INC     BX
        LOOP    ASCII_LOOP

        MOV     DL,' '                  ;Draw right side of box
        CALL    WRITE_CHAR
        MOV     DL,VERTICAL_BAR
        CALL    WRITE_CHAR

        POP     DX
        POP     CX
        POP     BX
        RET
DISP_LINE       ENDP


        PUBLIC  WRITE_PROMPT_LINE
        EXTRN   CLEAR_TO_END_OF_LINE:PROC, WRITE_STRING:PROC
        EXTRN   GOTO_XY:PROC
.DATA
        EXTRN   PROMPT_LINE_NO:BYTE
.CODE
;----------------------------------------------------------------------;
; This procedure writes the prompt line to the screen and clears the   ;
; end of the line.                                                     ;
```

```
;                                                                       ;
; On entry:      DS:DX    Address of the prompt-line message            ;
;                                                                       ;
; Uses:          WRITE_STRING, CLEAR_TO_END_OF_LINE, GOTO_XY            ;
; Reads:         PROMPT_LINE_NO                                         ;
;-----------------------------------------------------------------------;
WRITE_PROMPT_LINE         PROC
        PUSH    DX
        XOR     DL,DL                      ;Write the prompt line and
        MOV     DH,PROMPT_LINE_NO          ; move the cursor there
        CALL    GOTO_XY
        POP     DX
        CALL    WRITE_STRING
        CALL    CLEAR_TO_END_OF_LINE
        RET
WRITE_PROMPT_LINE         ENDP


        END
```

DSKPATCH.ASM

```
DOSSEG
.MODEL  SMALL

.STACK

.DATA

        PUBLIC  SECTOR_OFFSET
;-----------------------------------------------;
; SECTOR_OFFSET is the offset of the half-      ;
; sector display into the full sector.  It must ;
; be a multiple of 16, and not greater than 256 ;
;-----------------------------------------------;
SECTOR_OFFSET   DW      0

        PUBLIC  CURRENT_SECTOR_NO, DISK_DRIVE_NO
CURRENT_SECTOR_NO       DW      0               ;Initially sector 0
DISK_DRIVE_NO           DB      0               ;Initially Drive A:

        PUBLIC  LINES_BEFORE_SECTOR, HEADER_LINE_NO
        PUBLIC  HEADER_PART_1, HEADER_PART_2
;-----------------------------------------------;
; LINES_BEFORE_SECTOR is the number of lines    ;
; at the top of the screen before the half-     ;
; sector display.                               ;
;-----------------------------------------------;
LINES_BEFORE_SECTOR     DB      2
HEADER_LINE_NO          DB      0
HEADER_PART_1           DB      'Disk ',0
HEADER_PART_2           DB      '        Sector ',0
        PUBLIC  PROMPT_LINE_NO, EDITOR_PROMPT
PROMPT_LINE_NO          DB      21
EDITOR_PROMPT           DB      'Press function key, or enter'
                        DB      ' character or hex byte: ',0

.DATA?

        PUBLIC  SECTOR
;-----------------------------------------------;
; The entire sector (up to 8192 bytes) is       ;
; stored in this part of memory.                ;
;-----------------------------------------------;
SECTOR  DB      8192 DUP (?)

.CODE

        EXTRN   CLEAR_SCREEN:PROC, READ_SECTOR:PROC
        EXTRN   INIT_SEC_DISP:PROC, WRITE_HEADER:PROC
        EXTRN   WRITE_PROMPT_LINE:PROC, DISPATCHER:PROC
        EXTRN   INIT_WRITE_CHAR:PROC
DISK_PATCH      PROC
        MOV     AX,DGROUP               ;Put data segment into AX
        MOV     DS,AX                   ;Set DS to point to data

        CALL    INIT_WRITE_CHAR
        CALL    CLEAR_SCREEN
        CALL    WRITE_HEADER
        CALL    READ_SECTOR
        CALL    INIT_SEC_DISP
        LEA     DX,EDITOR_PROMPT
        CALL    WRITE_PROMPT_LINE
        CALL    DISPATCHER
        MOV     AH,4Ch                  ;Return to DOS

        INT     21h
DISK_PATCH      ENDP

        END     DISK_PATCH
```

EDITOR.ASM

```
        .MODEL   SMALL

        .CODE

        .DATA
        EXTRN    SECTOR:BYTE
        EXTRN    SECTOR_OFFSET:WORD
        EXTRN    PHANTOM_CURSOR_X:BYTE
        EXTRN    PHANTOM_CURSOR_Y:BYTE
        .CODE
;-------------------------------------------------------------------------;
; This procedure writes one byte to SECTOR, at the memory location        ;
; pointed to by the phantom cursor.                                       ;
;                                                                         ;
; On entry:      DL      Byte to write to SECTOR                          ;
;                                                                         ;
; The offset is calculated by                                            ;
;   OFFSET = SECTOR_OFFSET + (16 * PHANTOM_CURSOR_Y) + PHANTOM_CURSOR_X   ;
;                                                                         ;
; Reads:         PHANTOM_CURSOR_X, PHANTOM_CURSOR_Y, SECTOR_OFFSET        ;
; Writes:        SECTOR                                                   ;
;-------------------------------------------------------------------------;
WRITE_TO_MEMORY PROC
        PUSH     AX
        PUSH     BX
        PUSH     CX
        MOV      BX,SECTOR_OFFSET
        MOV      AL,PHANTOM_CURSOR_Y
        XOR      AH,AH
        MOV      CL,4                    ;Multiply PHANTOM_CURSOR_Y by 16
        SHL      AX,CL
        ADD      BX,AX                   ;BX = SECTOR_OFFSET + (16 * Y)
        MOV      AL,PHANTOM_CURSOR_X
        XOR      AH,AH
        ADD      BX,AX                   ;That's the address!
        MOV      SECTOR[BX],DL           ;Now, store the byte
        POP      CX
        POP      BX
        POP      AX
        RET
WRITE_TO_MEMORY         ENDP

        PUBLIC   EDIT_BYTE
        EXTRN    SAVE_REAL_CURSOR:PROC, RESTORE_REAL_CURSOR:PROC
        EXTRN    MOV_TO_HEX_POSITION:PROC, MOV_TO_ASCII_POSITION:PROC
        EXTRN    WRITE_PHANTOM:PROC, WRITE_PROMPT_LINE:PROC
        EXTRN    CURSOR_RIGHT:PROC, WRITE_HEX:PROC, WRITE_CHAR:PROC
        .DATA
        EXTRN    EDITOR_PROMPT:BYTE
        .CODE
;-------------------------------------------------------------------------;
; This procedure changes a byte in memory and on the screen.              ;
;                                                                         ;
;         DL      Byte to write into SECTOR, and change on screen         ;
;                                                                         ;
; Uses:         SAVE_REAL_CURSOR, RESTORE_REAL_CURSOR                     ;
;               MOV_TO_HEX_POSITION, MOV_TO_ASCII_POSITION               ;
;               WRITE_PHANTOM, WRITE_PROMPT_LINE, CURSOR_RIGHT            ;
;               WRITE_HEX, WRITE_CHAR, WRITE_TO_MEMORY                    ;
; Reads:        EDITOR_PROMPT                                            ;
;-------------------------------------------------------------------------;
EDIT_BYTE       PROC
        PUSH     DX
        CALL     SAVE_REAL_CURSOR
        CALL     MOV_TO_HEX_POSITION     ;Move to the hex number in the
        CALL     CURSOR_RIGHT            ; hex window
        CALL     WRITE_HEX               ;Write the new number
```

EDITOR.ASM *continued*

```
        CALL    MOV_TO_ASCII_POSITION   ;Move to the char. in the ASCII window
        CALL    WRITE_CHAR              ;Write the new character
        CALL    RESTORE_REAL_CURSOR     ;Move cursor back where it belongs
        CALL    WRITE_PHANTOM           ;Rewrite the phantom cursor
        CALL    WRITE_TO_MEMORY         ;Save this new byte in SECTOR
        LEA     DX,EDITOR_PROMPT
        CALL    WRITE_PROMPT_LINE
        POP     DX
        RET
EDIT_BYTE       ENDP

        END
```

KBD_IO.ASM

```
.MODEL   SMALL


BS       EQU      8                      ;Backspace character
CR       EQU      13                     ;Carriage-return character
ESCAPE   EQU      27                     ;Escape character


.DATA

KEYBOARD_INPUT   LABEL BYTE
CHAR_NUM_LIMIT   DB       0              ;Length of input buffer
NUM_CHARS_READ   DB       0              ;Number of characters read
CHARS            DB       80 DUP (0)     ;A buffer for keyboard input

.CODE

         PUBLIC   STRING_TO_UPPER
;-----------------------------------------------------------------------;
; This procedure converts the string, using the DOS format for strings, ;
; to all uppercase letters.                                             ;
;                                                                       ;
;        DS:DX    Address of string buffer                              ;
;-----------------------------------------------------------------------;
STRING_TO_UPPER          PROC
         PUSH    AX
         PUSH    BX
         PUSH    CX
         MOV     BX,DX
         INC     BX                      ;Point to character count
         MOV     CL,[BX]                 ;Character count in 2nd byte of buffer
         XOR     CH,CH                   ;Clear upper byte of count
UPPER_LOOP:
         INC     BX                      ;Point to next character in buffer
         MOV     AL,[BX]
         CMP     AL,'a'                  ;See if it is a lowercase letter
         JB      NOT_LOWER               ;Nope
         CMP     AL,'z'
         JA      NOT_LOWER
         ADD     AL,'A'-'a'              ;Convert to uppercase letter
         MOV     [BX],AL
NOT_LOWER:
         LOOP    UPPER_LOOP
         POP     CX
         POP     BX
         POP     AX
         RET
STRING_TO_UPPER          ENDP


;-----------------------------------------------------------------------;
; This procedure converts a character from ASCII (hex) to a nibble (4   ;
; bits).                                                                ;
;                                                                       ;
;                AL       Character to convert                          ;
; Returns:       AL       Nibble                                        ;
;                DF       Set for error, cleared otherwise              ;
;-----------------------------------------------------------------------;
CONVERT_HEX_DIGIT        PROC
         CMP     AL,'0'                  ;Is it a legal digit?
         JB      BAD_DIGIT               ;Nope
         CMP     AL,'9'                  ;Not sure yet
         JA      TRY_HEX                 ;Might be hex digit
         SUB     AL,'0'                  ;Is decimal digit, convert to nibble
         CLC                             ;Clear the carry, no error
         RET
TRY_HEX:
         CMP     AL,'A'                  ;Not sure yet
```

KBD_IO.ASM *continued*

```
                JB        BAD_DIGIT               ;Not hex
                CMP       AL,'F'                  ;Not sure yet
                JA        BAD_DIGIT               ;Not hex
                SUB       AL,'A'-10               ;Is hex, convert to nibble
                CLC                               ;Clear the carry, no error
                RET
BAD_DIGIT:
                STC                               ;Set the carry, error
                RET
CONVERT_HEX_DIGIT         ENDP

        PUBLIC  HEX_TO_BYTE
;-----------------------------------------------------------------------;
; This procedure converts the two characters at DS:DX from hex to one   ;
; byte.                                                                 ;
;                                                                       ;
;       DS:DX     Address of two characters for hex number             ;
; Returns:                                                              ;
;       AL        Byte                                                  ;
;       CF        Set for error, clear if no error                     ;
;-----------------------------------------------------------------------;
HEX_TO_BYTE     PROC
                PUSH      BX
                PUSH      CX
                MOV       BX,DX                   ;Put address in BX for indirect addr
                MOV       AL,[BX]                 ;Get first digit
                CALL      CONVERT_HEX_DIGIT
                JC        BAD_HEX                 ;Bad hex digit if carry set
                MOV       CX,4                    ;Now multiply by 16
                SHL       AL,CL
                MOV       AH,AL                   ;Retain a copy
                INC       BX                      ;Get second digit
                MOV       AL,[BX]
                CALL      CONVERT_HEX_DIGIT
                JC        BAD_HEX                 ;Bad hex digit if carry set
                OR        AL,AH                   ;Combine two nibbles
                CLC                               ;Clear carry for no error
DONE_HEX:
                POP       CX
                POP       BX
                RET
BAD_HEX:
                STC                               ;Set carry for error
                JMP       DONE_HEX
HEX_TO_BYTE     ENDP

        PUBLIC  READ_STRING
        EXTRN   WRITE_CHAR:PROC
        EXTRN   UPDATE_REAL_CURSOR:PROC
;-----------------------------------------------------------------------;
; This procedure performs a function very similar to the DOS 0Ah        ;
; function.  But this function will return a special character if a     ;
; function or keyboard key is pressed--no return for these keys.  And   ;
; ESC will erase the input and start over again.                        ;
;                                                                       ;
;       DS:DX     Address for keyboard buffer.  The first byte must     ;
;                 contain the maximum number of characters to read (plus;
;                 one for the return).  And the second byte will be used;
;                 by this procedure to return the number of characters  ;
;                 actually read.                                        ;
;                         0       No characters read                    ;
;                        -1       One special character read            ;
;                         otherwise number actually read (not including ;
;                                 Enter key)                            ;
;                                                                       ;
; Uses:        BACK_SPACE, WRITE_CHAR, READ_KEY, UPDATE_REAL_CURSOR     ;
;-----------------------------------------------------------------------;
READ_STRING     PROC
```

```
                PUSH    AX
                PUSH    BX
                PUSH    SI
                MOV     SI,DX                   ;Use SI for index register and
START_OVER:
                CALL    UPDATE_REAL_CURSOR      ;Move to position of virtual cursor
                MOV     BX,2                    ;BX for offset to beginning of buffer
                CALL    READ_KEY                ;Read one key from the keyboard
                OR      AH,AH                   ;Is character extended ASCII?
                JNZ     EXTENDED                ;Yes, then process it.
STRING_NOT_EXTENDED:                            ;Extnd char is error unless buf empty
                CMP     AL,CR                   ;Is this a carriage return?
                JE      END_INPUT               ;Yes, we are done with input
                CMP     AL,BS                   ;Is it a backspace character?
                JNE     NOT_BS                  ;Nope
                CALL    BACK_SPACE              ;Yes, delete character
                CMP     BL,2                    ;Is buffer empty?
                JE      START_OVER              ;Yes, can now read extended ASCII again
                JMP     SHORT READ_NEXT_CHAR    ;No, continue reading normal characters
NOT_BS: CMP     AL,ESCAPE                       ;Is it an ESC--purge buffer?
                JE      PURGE_BUFFER            ;Yes, then purge the buffer
                CMP     BL,[SI]                 ;Check to see if buffer is full
                JA      BUFFER_FULL             ;Buffer is full
                MOV     [SI+BX],AL              ;Else save char in buffer
                INC     BX                      ;Point to next free character in buffer
                PUSH    DX
                MOV     DL,AL                   ;Echo character to screen
                CALL    WRITE_CHAR
                POP     DX
READ_NEXT_CHAR:
                CALL    UPDATE_REAL_CURSOR      ;Move real cursor to virtual cursor
                CALL    READ_KEY
                OR      AH,AH                   ;An extended ASCII char is not valid
                                                ; when the buffer is not empty
                JZ      STRING_NOT_EXTENDED     ;Char is valid

;-------------------------------------------------;
; Signal an error condition by sending a beep     ;
; character to the display: chr$(7).              ;
;-------------------------------------------------;
SIGNAL_ERROR:
                PUSH    DX
                MOV     DL,7                    ;Sound the bell by writing chr$(7)
                MOV     AH,2
                INT     21h
                POP     DX
                JMP     SHORT READ_NEXT_CHAR    ;Now read next character

;-------------------------------------------------;
; Empty the string buffer and erase all the       ;
; characters displayed on the screen.             ;
;-------------------------------------------------;
PURGE_BUFFER:
                PUSH    CX
                MOV     CL,[SI]                 ;Backspace over maximum number of
                XOR     CH,CH
PURGE_LOOP:                                     ; characters in buffer.  BACK_SPACE
                CALL    BACK_SPACE              ; will keep the cursor from moving too
                LOOP    PURGE_LOOP              ; far back
                POP     CX
                JMP     START_OVER              ;Can now read extended ASCII characters
                                                ; since the buffer is empty

;-------------------------------------------------;
; The buffer was full, so can't read another      ;
; character.  Send a beep to alert user of        ;
; buffer-full condition.                          ;
;-------------------------------------------------;
BUFFER_FULL:
                JMP     SHORT SIGNAL_ERROR      ;If buffer full, just beep
```

KBD_IO.ASM *continued*

```
;------------------------------------------------;
; Read the extended ASCII code and place this    ;
; in the buffer as the only character, then      ;
; return -1 as the number of characters read.    ;
;------------------------------------------------;
EXTENDED:                               ;Read an extended ASCII code
        MOV     [SI+2],AL               ;Place just this char in buffer
        MOV     BL,0FFh                 ;Num chars read = -1 for special
        JMP     SHORT END_STRING

;------------------------------------------------;
; Save the count of the number of characters     ;
; read and return.                               ;
;------------------------------------------------;
END_INPUT:                              ;Done with input
        SUB     BL,2                    ;Count of characters read
END_STRING:
        MOV     [SI+1],BL               ;Return number of chars read
        POP     SI
        POP     BX
        POP     AX
        RET
READ_STRING     ENDP


        PUBLIC  BACK_SPACE
        EXTRN   WRITE_CHAR:PROC
;--------------------------------------------------------------------;
; This procedure deletes characters, one at a time, from the buffer and ;
; the screen when the buffer is not empty.  BACK_SPACE simply returns ;
; when the buffer is empty.                                          ;
;                                                                    ;
;       DS:SI+BX        Most recent character still in buffer        ;
;                                                                    ;
; Uses:         WRITE_CHAR                                           ;
;--------------------------------------------------------------------;
BACK_SPACE      PROC                    ;Delete one character
        PUSH    AX
        PUSH    DX
        CMP     BX,2                    ;Is buffer empty?
        JE      END_BS                  ;Yes, read the next character
        DEC     BX                      ;Remove one character from buffer
        MOV     AH,2                    ;Remove character from screen
        MOV     DL,BS
        INT     21h
        MOV     DL,20h                  ;Write space there
        CALL    WRITE_CHAR
        MOV     DL,BS                   ;Back up again
        INT     21h
END_BS: POP     DX
        POP     AX
        RET
BACK_SPACE      ENDP

        PUBLIC  READ_BYTE
;--------------------------------------------------------------------;
; This procedure reads either a single ASCII character or a two-digit ;
; hex number.  This is just a test version of READ_BYTE.            ;
;                                                                    ;
; Returns byte in      AL      Character code (unless AH = 0)        ;
;                      AH      0 if read ASCII char                  ;
;                              1 if read a special key               ;
;                              -1 if no characters read              ;
;                                                                    ;
; Uses:         HEX_TO_BYTE, STRING_TO_UPPER, READ_STRING            ;
; Reads:        KEYBOARD_INPUT, etc.                                 ;
; Writes:       KEYBOARD_INPUT, etc.                                 ;
;--------------------------------------------------------------------;
```

```
READ_BYTE       PROC
        PUSH    DX
        MOV     CHAR_NUM_LIMIT,3            ;Allow only two characters (plus Enter)
        LEA     DX,KEYBOARD_INPUT
        CALL    READ_STRING
        CMP     NUM_CHARS_READ,1           ;See how many characters
        JE      ASCII_INPUT               ;Just one, treat as ASCII character
        JB      NO_CHARACTERS             ;Only Enter key hit
        CMP     BYTE PTR NUM_CHARS_READ,0FFh    ;Special function key?
        JE      SPECIAL_KEY               ;Yes
        CALL    STRING_TO_UPPER           ;No, convert string to uppercase
        LEA     DX,CHARS                  ;Address of string to convert
        CALL    HEX_TO_BYTE               ;Convert string from hex to byte
        JC      NO_CHARACTERS             ;Error, so return 'no characters read'
        XOR     AH,AH                     ;Signal read one byte
DONE_READ:
        POP     DX
        RET
NO_CHARACTERS:
        XOR     AH,AH                     ;Set to 'no characters read'
        NOT     AH                        ;Return -1 in AH
        JMP     DONE_READ
ASCII_INPUT:
        MOV     AL,CHARS                  ;Load character read
        XOR     AH,AH                     ;Signal read one byte
        JMP     DONE_READ
SPECIAL_KEY:
        MOV     AL,CHARS[0]               ;Return the scan code
        MOV     AH,1                      ;Signal special key with 1
        JMP     DONE_READ
READ_BYTE       ENDP


        PUBLIC  READ_KEY
;-----------------------------------------------------------------------;
; This procedure reads one key from the keyboard.                       ;
;                                                                       ;
; Returns:      AL      Character code (unless AH = 1)                  ;
;               AH      0 if read ASCII char                           ;
;                       1 if read a special key                        ;
;-----------------------------------------------------------------------;
READ_KEY        PROC
        XOR     AH,AH                     ;Ask for keyboard read function
        INT     16h                       ;Read character/scan code from keyboard
        OR      AL,AL                     ;Is it an extended code?
        JZ      EXTENDED_CODE             ;Yes
NOT_EXTENDED:
        XOR     AH,AH                     ;Return just the ASCII code
DONE_READING:
        RET

EXTENDED_CODE:
        MOV     AL,AH                     ;Put scan code into AL
        MOV     AH,1                      ;Signal extended code
        JMP     DONE_READING
READ_KEY        ENDP


        PUBLIC  READ_DECIMAL
;-----------------------------------------------------------------------;
; This procedure takes the output buffer of READ_STRING and converts    ;
; the string of decimal digits to a word.                               ;
;                                                                       ;
;       AX      Word converted from decimal                            ;
;       CF      Set if error, clear if no error                        ;
;                                                                       ;
; Uses:         READ_STRING                                            ;
; Reads:        KEYBOARD_INPUT, etc.                                   ;
; Writes:       KEYBOARD_INPUT, etc.                                   ;
;-----------------------------------------------------------------------;
READ_DECIMAL    PROC
```

KBD_IO.ASM *continued*

```
                PUSH    BX
                PUSH    CX
                PUSH    DX
                MOV     CHAR_NUM_LIMIT,6        ;Max number is 5 digits (65535)
                LEA     DX,KEYBOARD_INPUT
                CALL    READ_STRING
                MOV     CL,NUM_CHARS_READ       ;Get number of characters read
                XOR     CH,CH                   ;Set upper byte of count to 0
                CMP     CL,0                    ;Return error if no characters read
                JLE     BAD_DECIMAL_DIGIT       ;No chars read, signal error
                XOR     AX,AX                   ;Start with number set to 0
                XOR     BX,BX                   ;Start at beginning of string
CONVERT_DIGIT:
                MOV     DX,10                   ;Multiply number by 10
                MUL     DX                      ;Multiply AX by 10
                JC      BAD_DECIMAL_DIGIT       ;CF set if MUL overflowed one word
                MOV     DL,CHARS[BX]            ;Get the next digit
                SUB     DL,'0'                  ;And convert to a nibble (4 bits)
                JS      BAD_DECIMAL_DIGIT       ;Bad digit if < 0
                CMP     DL,9                    ;Is this a bad digit?
                JA      BAD_DECIMAL_DIGIT       ;Yes
                ADD     AX,DX                   ;No, so add it to number
                INC     BX                      ;Point to next character
                LOOP    CONVERT_DIGIT           ;Get the next digit
DONE_DECIMAL:
                POP     DX
                POP     CX
                POP     BX
                RET
BAD_DECIMAL_DIGIT:
                STC                             ;Set carry to signal error
                JMP     DONE_DECIMAL
READ_DECIMAL    ENDP


                END
```

PHANTOM.ASM

```
        .MODEL   SMALL

        .DATA

REAL_CURSOR_X          DB      0
REAL_CURSOR_Y          DB      0
        PUBLIC   PHANTOM_CURSOR_X, PHANTOM_CURSOR_Y
PHANTOM_CURSOR_X       DB      0
PHANTOM_CURSOR_Y       DB      0

        .CODE

;---------------------------------------------------------------------;
; These four procedures move the phantom cursors.                     ;
;                                                                     ;
; Uses:          ERASE_PHANTOM, WRITE_PHANTOM                         ;
;                SCROLL_DOWN, SCROLL_UP                               ;
; Reads:         PHANTOM_CURSOR_X, PHANTOM_CURSOR_Y                   ;
; Writes:        PHANTOM_CURSOR_X, PHANTOM_CURSOR_Y                   ;
;---------------------------------------------------------------------;
        PUBLIC   PHANTOM_UP
PHANTOM_UP      PROC
        CALL     ERASE_PHANTOM          ;Erase at current position
        DEC      PHANTOM_CURSOR_Y       ;Move cursor up one line
        JNS      WASNT_AT_TOP           ;Was not at the top, write cursor
        CALL     SCROLL_DOWN            ;Was at the top, scroll
WASNT_AT_TOP:
        CALL     WRITE_PHANTOM          ;Write the phantom at new position
        RET
PHANTOM_UP      ENDP

        PUBLIC   PHANTOM_DOWN
PHANTOM_DOWN    PROC
        CALL     ERASE_PHANTOM          ;Erase at current position
        INC      PHANTOM_CURSOR_Y       ;Move cursor down one line
        CMP      PHANTOM_CURSOR_Y,16    ;Was it at the bottom?
        JB       WASNT_AT_BOTTOM        ;No, so write phantom
        CALL     SCROLL_UP              ;Was at bottom, so put back there
WASNT_AT_BOTTOM:
        CALL     WRITE_PHANTOM          ;Write the phantom cursor
        RET
PHANTOM_DOWN    ENDP

        PUBLIC   PHANTOM_LEFT
PHANTOM_LEFT    PROC
        CALL     ERASE_PHANTOM          ;Erase at current position
        DEC      PHANTOM_CURSOR_X       ;Move cursor left one column
        JNS      WASNT_AT_LEFT          ;Was not at the left side, write cursor
        MOV      PHANTOM_CURSOR_X,0     ;Was at left, so put back there
WASNT_AT_LEFT:
        CALL     WRITE_PHANTOM          ;Write the phantom cursor
        RET
PHANTOM_LEFT    ENDP

        PUBLIC   PHANTOM_RIGHT
PHANTOM_RIGHT   PROC
        CALL     ERASE_PHANTOM          ;Erase at current position
        INC      PHANTOM_CURSOR_X       ;Move cursor right one column
        CMP      PHANTOM_CURSOR_X,16    ;Was it already at the right side?
        JB       WASNT_AT_RIGHT
        MOV      PHANTOM_CURSOR_X,15    ;Was at right, so put back there
WASNT_AT_RIGHT:
        CALL     WRITE_PHANTOM          ;Write the phantom cursor
        RET
PHANTOM_RIGHT   ENDP
```

PHANTOM.ASM *continued*

```
        PUBLIC   MOV_TO_HEX_POSITION
        EXTRN    GOTO_XY:PROC
.DATA
        EXTRN    LINES_BEFORE_SECTOR:BYTE
.CODE
;-----------------------------------------------------------------------;
; This procedure moves the real cursor to the position of the phantom   ;
; cursor in the hex window.                                             ;
;                                                                       ;
; Uses:          GOTO_XY                                                ;
; Reads:         LINES_BEFORE_SECTOR, PHANTOM_CURSOR_X, PHANTOM_CURSOR_Y ;
;-----------------------------------------------------------------------;
MOV_TO_HEX_POSITION     PROC
        PUSH     AX
        PUSH     CX
        PUSH     DX
        MOV      DH,LINES_BEFORE_SECTOR    ;Find row of phantom (0,0)
        ADD      DH,2                      ;Plus row of hex and horizontal bar
        ADD      DH,PHANTOM_CURSOR_Y       ;DH = row of phantom cursor
        MOV      DL,8                      ;Indent on left side
        MOV      CL,3                      ;Each column uses 3 characters, so
        MOV      AL,PHANTOM_CURSOR_X       ; we must multiply CURSOR_X by 3
        MUL      CL
        ADD      DL,AL                     ;And add to the indent, to get column
        CALL     GOTO_XY                   ; for phantom cursor
        POP      DX
        POP      CX
        POP      AX
        RET
MOV_TO_HEX_POSITION     ENDP


        PUBLIC   MOV_TO_ASCII_POSITION
        EXTRN    GOTO_XY:PROC
.DATA
        EXTRN    LINES_BEFORE_SECTOR:BYTE
.CODE
;-----------------------------------------------------------------------;
; This procedure moves the real cursor to the beginning of the phantom  ;
; cursor in the ASCII window.                                           ;
;                                                                       ;
; Uses:          GOTO_XY                                                ;
; Reads:         LINES_BEFORE_SECTOR, PHANTOM_CURSOR_X, PHANTOM_CURSOR_Y ;
;-----------------------------------------------------------------------;
MOV_TO_ASCII_POSITION     PROC
        PUSH     AX
        PUSH     DX
        MOV      DH,LINES_BEFORE_SECTOR    ;Find row of phantom (0,0)
        ADD      DH,2                      ;Plus row of hex and horizontal bar
        ADD      DH,PHANTOM_CURSOR_Y       ;DH = row of phantom cursor
        MOV      DL,59                     ;Indent on left side
        ADD      DL,PHANTOM_CURSOR_X       ;Add CURSOR_X to get X position
        CALL     GOTO_XY                   ; for phantom cursor
        POP      DX
        POP      AX
        RET
MOV_TO_ASCII_POSITION     ENDP


        PUBLIC   SAVE_REAL_CURSOR
;-----------------------------------------------------------------------;
; This procedure saves the position of the real cursor in the two       ;
; variables REAL_CURSOR_X and REAL_CURSOR_Y.                            ;
;                                                                       ;
; Writes:        REAL_CURSOR_X, REAL_CURSOR_Y                           ;
;-----------------------------------------------------------------------;
SAVE_REAL_CURSOR     PROC
        PUSH     AX
        PUSH     BX
        PUSH     CX
```

```
        PUSH    DX
        MOV     AH,3                         ;Read cursor position
        XOR     BH,BH                        ; on page 0
        INT     10h                          ;And return in DL,DH
        MOV     REAL_CURSOR_Y,DL             ;Save position
        MOV     REAL_CURSOR_X,DH
        POP     DX
        POP     CX
        POP     BX
        POP     AX
        RET
SAVE_REAL_CURSOR          ENDP

        PUBLIC  RESTORE_REAL_CURSOR
        EXTRN   GOTO_XY:PROC
;-----------------------------------------------------------------------;
; This procedure restores the real cursor to its old position, saved in ;
; REAL_CURSOR_X and REAL_CURSOR_Y.                                       ;
;                                                                        ;
; Uses:         GOTO_XY                                                  ;
; Reads:        REAL_CURSOR_X, REAL_CURSOR_Y                             ;
;-----------------------------------------------------------------------;
RESTORE_REAL_CURSOR       PROC
        PUSH    DX
        MOV     DL,REAL_CURSOR_Y
        MOV     DH,REAL_CURSOR_X
        CALL    GOTO_XY
        POP     DX
        RET
RESTORE_REAL_CURSOR       ENDP

        PUBLIC  WRITE_PHANTOM
        EXTRN   WRITE_ATTRIBUTE_N_TIMES:PROC
;-----------------------------------------------------------------------;
; This procedure uses CURSOR_X and CURSOR_Y, through MOV_TO..., as the   ;
; coordinates for the phantom cursor.  WRITE_PHANTOM writes this         ;
;                                                                        ;
; Uses:         WRITE_ATTRIBUTE_N_TIMES, SAVE_REAL_CURSOR                ;
;               RESTORE_REAL_CURSOR, MOV_TO_HEX_POSITION                 ;
;               MOV_TO_ASCII_POSITION                                    ;
;-----------------------------------------------------------------------;
WRITE_PHANTOM    PROC
        PUSH    CX
        PUSH    DX
        CALL    SAVE_REAL_CURSOR
        CALL    MOV_TO_HEX_POSITION          ;Coord. of cursor in hex window
        MOV     CX,4                         ;Make phantom cursor four chars wide
        MOV     DL,70h
        CALL    WRITE_ATTRIBUTE_N_TIMES
        CALL    MOV_TO_ASCII_POSITION        ;Coord. of cursor in ASCII window
        MOV     CX,1                         ;Cursor is one character wide here
        CALL    WRITE_ATTRIBUTE_N_TIMES
        CALL    RESTORE_REAL_CURSOR
        POP     DX
        POP     CX
        RET
WRITE_PHANTOM    ENDP

        PUBLIC  ERASE_PHANTOM
        EXTRN   WRITE_ATTRIBUTE_N_TIMES:PROC
;-----------------------------------------------------------------------;
; This procedure erases the phantom cursor, just the opposite of         ;
; WRITE_PHANTOM.                                                         ;
;                                                                        ;
; Uses:         WRITE_ATTRIBUTE_N_TIMES, SAVE_REAL_CURSOR                ;
;               RESTORE_REAL_CURSOR, MOV_TO_HEX_POSITION                 ;
;               MOV_TO_ASCII_POSITION                                    ;
;-----------------------------------------------------------------------;
ERASE_PHANTOM    PROC
        PUSH    CX
        PUSH    DX
```

PHANTOM.ASM *continued*

```
                CALL    SAVE_REAL_CURSOR
                CALL    MOV_TO_HEX_POSITION        ;Coord. of cursor in hex window
                MOV     CX,4                       ;Change back to white on black
                MOV     DL,7
                CALL    WRITE_ATTRIBUTE_N_TIMES
                CALL    MOV_TO_ASCII_POSITION
                MOV     CX,1
                CALL    WRITE_ATTRIBUTE_N_TIMES
                CALL    RESTORE_REAL_CURSOR
                POP     DX
                POP     CX
                RET
ERASE_PHANTOM   ENDP


                EXTRN   DISP_HALF_SECTOR:PROC, GOTO_XY:PROC
        .DATA
                EXTRN   SECTOR_OFFSET:WORD
                EXTRN   LINES_BEFORE_SECTOR:BYTE
        .CODE
;-------------------------------------------------------------------;
; These two procedures move between the two half-sector displays.   ;
;                                                                   ;
; Uses:         WRITE_PHANTOM, DISP_HALF_SECTOR, ERASE_PHANTOM, GOTO_XY ;
;               SAVE_REAL_CURSOR, RESTORE_REAL_CURSOR               ;
; Reads:        LINES_BEFORE_SECTOR                                 ;
; Writes:       SECTOR_OFFSET, PHANTOM_CURSOR_Y                     ;
;-------------------------------------------------------------------;
SCROLL_UP       PROC
                PUSH    DX
                CALL    ERASE_PHANTOM              ;Remove the phantom cursor
                CALL    SAVE_REAL_CURSOR           ;Save the real cursor position
                XOR     DL,DL                      ;Set cursor for half-sector display
                MOV     DH,LINES_BEFORE_SECTOR
                ADD     DH,2
                CALL    GOTO_XY
                MOV     DX,256                     ;Display the second half sector
                MOV     SECTOR_OFFSET,DX
                CALL    DISP_HALF_SECTOR
                CALL    RESTORE_REAL_CURSOR        ;Restore the real cursor position
                MOV     PHANTOM_CURSOR_Y,0         ;Cursor at top of second half sector
                CALL    WRITE_PHANTOM              ;Restore the phantom cursor
                POP     DX
                RET
SCROLL_UP       ENDP

SCROLL_DOWN     PROC
                PUSH    DX
                CALL    ERASE_PHANTOM              ;Remove the phantom cursor
                CALL    SAVE_REAL_CURSOR           ;Save the real cursor position
                XOR     DL,DL                      ;Set cursor for half-sector display
                MOV     DH,LINES_BEFORE_SECTOR
                ADD     DH,2
                CALL    GOTO_XY
                XOR     DX,DX                      ;Display the first half sector
                MOV     SECTOR_OFFSET,DX
                CALL    DISP_HALF_SECTOR
                CALL    RESTORE_REAL_CURSOR        ;Restore the real cursor position
                MOV     PHANTOM_CURSOR_Y,15        ;Cursor at bottom of first half sector
                CALL    WRITE_PHANTOM              ;Restore the phantom cursor
                POP     DX
                RET
SCROLL_DOWN     ENDP


                END
```

VIDEO_IO.ASM

```
.MODEL  SMALL

.DATA
        PUBLIC  SCREEN_PTR
        PUBLIC  SCREEN_X, SCREEN_Y
SCREEN_SEG      DW      0B800h          ;Segment of the screen buffer
SCREEN_PTR      DW      0               ;Offset into screen memory of cursor
SCREEN_X        DB      0               ;Position of the screen cursor
SCREEN_Y        DB      0


.CODE
        PUBLIC  WRITE_STRING
;-----------------------------------------------------------------------;
; This procedure writes a string of characters to the screen. The       ;
; string must end with          DB      0                               ;
;                                                                       ;
; On entry:      DS:DX   Address of the string                         ;
;                                                                       ;
; Uses:          WRITE_CHAR                                            ;
;-----------------------------------------------------------------------;
WRITE_STRING    PROC
        PUSH    AX
        PUSH    DX
        PUSH    SI
        PUSHF                           ;Save direction flag
        CLD                             ;Set direction for increment (forward)
        MOV     SI,DX                   ;Place address into SI for LODSB
STRING_LOOP:
        LODSB                           ;Get a character into the AL register
        OR      AL,AL                   ;Have we found the 0 yet?
        JZ      END_OF_STRING           ;Yes, we are done with the string
        MOV     DL,AL                   ;No, write character
        CALL    WRITE_CHAR
        JMP     STRING_LOOP
END_OF_STRING:
        POPF                            ;Restore direction flag
        POP     SI
        POP     DX
        POP     AX
        RET
WRITE_STRING    ENDP

        PUBLIC  WRITE_HEX
;-----------------------------------------------------------------------;
; This procedure converts the byte in the DL register to hex and writes ;
; the two hex digits at the current cursor position.                    ;
;                                                                       ;
; On entry:      DL      Byte to convert to hex.                        ;
;                                                                       ;
; Uses:          WRITE_HEX_DIGIT                                        ;
;-----------------------------------------------------------------------;
WRITE_HEX       PROC                    ;Entry point
        PUSH    CX                      ;Save registers used in this procedure
        PUSH    DX
        MOV     DH,DL                   ;Make a copy of byte
        MOV     CX,4                    ;Get the upper nibble in DL
        SHR     DL,CL
        CALL    WRITE_HEX_DIGIT         ;Display first hex digit
        MOV     DL,DH                   ;Get lower nibble into DL
        AND     DL,0Fh                  ;Remove the upper nibble
        CALL    WRITE_HEX_DIGIT         ;Display second hex digit
        POP     DX
        POP     CX
        RET
WRITE_HEX       ENDP
```

VIDEO_IO.ASM *continued*

```
        PUBLIC  WRITE_HEX_DIGIT
;---------------------------------------------------------------;
; This procedure converts the lower 4 bits of DL to a hex digit and ;
; writes it to the screen.                                       ;
;                                                                ;
; On entry:     DL      Lower 4 bits contain number to be printed ;
;                       in hex.                                  ;
;                                                                ;
; Uses:         WRITE_CHAR                                       ;
;---------------------------------------------------------------;
WRITE_HEX_DIGIT         PROC
        PUSH    DX                      ;Save registers used
        CMP     DL,10                   ;Is this nibble <10?
        JAE     HEX_LETTER              ;No, convert to a letter
        ADD     DL,"0"                  ;Yes, convert to a digit
        JMP     Short WRITE_DIGIT       ;Now write this character
HEX_LETTER:
        ADD     DL,"A"-10               ;Convert to hex letter
WRITE_DIGIT:
        CALL    WRITE_CHAR              ;Display the letter on the screen
        POP     DX                      ;Restore old value of DX
        RET
WRITE_HEX_DIGIT         ENDP


        PUBLIC  INIT_WRITE_CHAR
;---------------------------------------------------------------;
; You need to call this procedure before you call WRITE_CHAR since ;
; WRITE_CHAR uses information set by this procedure.             ;
;                                                                ;
; Writes:       SCREEN_SEG                                       ;
;---------------------------------------------------------------;
INIT_WRITE_CHAR         PROC
        PUSH    AX
        PUSH    BX
        MOV     BX,0B800h               ;Set for color graphics display
        INT     11h                     ;Get equipment information
        AND     AL,30h                  ;Keep just the video display type
        CMP     AL,30h                  ;Is this a monochrome display adapter?
        JNE     SET_BASE                ;No, it's color, so use B800
        MOV     BX,0B800h               ;Yes, it's monochrome, so use B000
SET_BASE:
        MOV     SCREEN_SEG,BX           ;Save the screen segment
        POP     BX
        POP     AX
        RET
INIT_WRITE_CHAR         ENDP

        PUBLIC  WRITE_CHAR
        EXTRN   CURSOR_RIGHT:PROC
;---------------------------------------------------------------;
; This procedure outputs a character to the screen by writing directly ;
; into screen memory, so that characters such as the backspace are ;
; treated as any other characters and are displayed.            ;
;                                                                ;
; This procedure must do a bit of work to update the cursor position. ;
;                                                                ;
; On entry:     DL      Byte to print on screen.                ;
;                                                                ;
; Uses:         CURSOR_RIGHT                                     ;
; Reads:        SCREEN_SEG, SCREEN_PTR                           ;
;---------------------------------------------------------------;
WRITE_CHAR      PROC
        PUSH    AX
        PUSH    BX
        PUSH    DX
        PUSH    ES

        MOV     AX,SCREEN_SEG           ;Get segment for screen memory
```

```
                MOV     ES,AX                   ;Point ES to screen memory
                MOV     BX,SCREEN_PTR           ;Pointer to character in screen memory

                MOV     DH,7                    ;Use the normal attribute
                MOV     ES:[BX],DX              ;Write character/attribute to screen
                CALL    CURSOR_RIGHT            ;Now move to next cursor position

                POP     ES
                POP     DX
                POP     BX
                POP     AX
                RET
WRITE_CHAR      ENDP

        PUBLIC  WRITE_DECIMAL
;-----------------------------------------------------------------------;
; This procedure writes a 16-bit, unsigned number in decimal notation.  ;
;                                                                       ;
; On entry:     DX      N : 16-bit, unsigned number.                    ;
;                                                                       ;
; Uses:         WRITE_HEX_DIGIT                                         ;
;-----------------------------------------------------------------------;
WRITE_DECIMAL   PROC
                PUSH    AX                      ;Save registers used here
                PUSH    CX
                PUSH    DX
                PUSH    SI
                MOV     AX,DX
                MOV     SI,10                   ;Will divide by 10 using SI
                XOR     CX,CX                   ;Count of digits placed on stack
NON_ZERO:
                XOR     DX,DX                   ;Set upper word of N to 0
                DIV     SI                      ;Calculate N/10 and (N mod 10)
                PUSH    DX                      ;Push one digit onto the stack
                INC     CX                      ;One more digit added
                OR      AX,AX                   ;N = 0 yet?
                JNE     NON_ZERO                ;Nope, continue
WRITE_DIGIT_LOOP:
                POP     DX                      ;Get the digits in reverse order
                CALL    WRITE_HEX_DIGIT
                LOOP    WRITE_DIGIT_LOOP
END_DECIMAL:
                POP     SI
                POP     DX
                POP     CX
                POP     AX
                RET
WRITE_DECIMAL   ENDP


        PUBLIC  WRITE_CHAR_N_TIMES
;-----------------------------------------------------------------------;
; This procedure writes more than one copy of a character               ;
;                                                                       ;
; On entry:     DL      Character code                                  ;
;               CX      Number of times to write the character          ;
;                                                                       ;
; Uses:         WRITE_CHAR                                              ;
;-----------------------------------------------------------------------;
WRITE_CHAR_N_TIMES      PROC
                PUSH    CX
N_TIMES:
                CALL    WRITE_CHAR
                LOOP    N_TIMES
                POP     CX
                RET
WRITE_CHAR_N_TIMES      ENDP


        PUBLIC  WRITE_ATTRIBUTE_N_TIMES
        EXTRN   CURSOR_RIGHT:PROC
```

VIDEO_IO.ASM *continued*

```
;--------------------------------------------------------------------;
; This procedure sets the attribute for N characters, starting at the ;
; current cursor position.                                            ;
;                                                                     ;
;       CX       Number of characters to set attribute for           ;
;       DL       New attribute for characters                        ;
;                                                                     ;
; Uses:          CURSOR_RIGHT                                         ;
; Reads:         SCREEN_SEG, SCREEN_PTR                               ;
;--------------------------------------------------------------------;
WRITE_ATTRIBUTE_N_TIMES         PROC
        PUSH    AX
        PUSH    CX
        PUSH    DI
        PUSH    ES

        MOV     AX,SCREEN_SEG           ;Set ES to point to screen segment
        MOV     ES,AX
        MOV     DI,SCREEN_PTR           ;Character under cursor
        INC     DI                      ;Point to the attribute under cursor
        MOV     AL,DL                   ;Put attribute into AL
ATTR_LOOP:
        STOSB                           ;Save one attribute
        INC     DI                      ;Move to next attribute
        INC     SCREEN_X                ;Move to next column
        LOOP    ATTR_LOOP               ;Write N attributes

        DEC     DI                      ;Point to start of next character
        MOV     SCREEN_PTR,DI           ;Remember where we are

        POP     ES
        POP     DI
        POP     CX
        POP     AX
        RET
WRITE_ATTRIBUTE_N_TIMES ENDP


        PUBLIC  WRITE_PATTERN
;--------------------------------------------------------------------;
; This procedure writes a line to the screen, based on data in the   ;
; form                                                               ;
;                                                                    ;
;       DB      (character, number of times to write character), 0   ;
; Where {x} means that x can be repeated any number of times          ;
;                                                                    ;
; On entry:      DS:DX   Address of the pattern to draw              ;
;                                                                    ;
; Uses:          WRITE_CHAR_N_TIMES                                  ;
;--------------------------------------------------------------------;
WRITE_PATTERN   PROC
        PUSH    AX
        PUSH    CX
        PUSH    DX
        PUSH    SI
        PUSHF                           ;Save the direction flag
        CLD                             ;Set direction flag for increment
        MOV     SI,DX                   ;Move offset into SI register for LODSB
PATTERN_LOOP:
        LODSB                           ;Get character data into AL
        OR      AL,AL                   ;Is it the end of data (0h)?
        JZ      END_PATTERN             ;Yes, return
        MOV     DL,AL                   ;No, set up to write character N times
        LODSB                           ;Get the repeat count into AL
        MOV     CL,AL                   ;And put in CX for WRITE_CHAR_N_TIMES
        XOR     CH,CH                   ;Zero upper byte of CX
        CALL    WRITE_CHAR_N_TIMES
        JMP     PATTERN_LOOP
```

```
END_PATTERN:
        POPF                        ;Restore direction flag
        POP     SI
        POP     DX
        POP     CX
        POP     AX
        RET
WRITE_PATTERN   ENDP

        END
```

APPENDIX C
COMMON ERROR MESSAGES

T his appendix lists many common error messages you may encounter as you use MASM, LINK, and EXE2BIN. If you don't find an error message listed here, check your macro assembler or your DOS manual.

The error messages are in three groups: one for MASM, one for LINK, and one for EXE2BIN. Within each section, error messages are listed alphabetically.

MASM

Block nesting error: You'll probably see this error message along with either an *Open procedures* or an *Open segments* message. See the following descriptions for these two error messages.

End of file, no END directive: This means you're either missing the END statement at the end of your file, or you need to add a blank line after the existing END statement. The Microsoft versions of the macro assembler expect to find a blank line at the very end of the file. If you don't have at least one blank line after END, MASM won't read the END statement.

Open procedures: This error message means that either you're missing a PROC or an ENDP statement, or that the names aren't the same on one PROC/ENDP pair. Make sure every PROC has a matching ENDP statement, and check the procedure name in both the PROC and the ENDP statements to make sure they match.

Open segments: This error message should only appear when you're using the full segment definitions. It means either that you're missing a SEGMENT or an ENDS statement, or that the names aren't the same on one SEG-MENT/ENDS pair. Make sure every SEGMENT has a matching ENDS statement, and check the segment name in both the SEGMENT and ENDS statements to make sure they match.

Symbol not defined: There are three things you should look for if you see this error message:
1. You may have misspelled a name. Check the line you see in the error display to make certain you've typed the name correctly.
2. You may have misspelled the name when you first declared a PROC or a variable. Check the spelling of the names you see in the faulty line against the names in the PROC or variable declarations.
3. You may be missing an EXTRN declaration, or the name in the EXTRN may be misspelled.

LINK

Fixup offset exceeds field width: This is a tricky one, and it's often the hardest bug to swat. This message usually means you've declared some procedure as a FAR procedure, but later declared that same procedure as a NEAR procedure in an EXTRN declaration.

It can also mean that your program has grown larger than the 64K limit for small programs. You can check for such errors by looking at the size field in the map file.

You should only see this message if you're using full segment definitions. This message can also appear when a segment has become fragmented. In such cases, the two fragments may be more than 64K apart, which means that CALLs must be FAR CALLs to work.

If that doesn't seem to be the problem, you'll have to search deeper. You may find a hint in the map file. For example, check the order of the segments. You may find they are out of order.

Symbol defined more than once: This message means you've probably defined the same procedure or variable in two source files. Make sure you've defined each name in only one source file, then use EXTRNs in other places where you need to use the same procedure or variable.

Unresolved externals: When you see this message, either a PUBLIC is missing from the file in which you declared the procedure or variable, or you misspelled the name in an EXTRN declaration and the CALLs in some other source file.

This error can also be caused by forgetting to link in a file. You may need to add the new file to your Make file or to the batch file you're using.

Warning: no stack segment: This isn't really an error message, it's simply a warning. You'll always see this message when creating .COM files. Ignore it in such cases.

EXE2BIN

You probably won't use EXE2BIN very often since you'll need it only when you're creating .COM programs. But when you do use it, there is probably only one error message you'll see:

File cannot be converted: This is not a very helpful message. Most of the time it can mean one of three things:

1. Your segments are in the wrong order, so you have a segment in memory before CODESEG. Check the load map to see if this is your problem.
2. Your main program is not the first file you listed in your LINK list. It must be, so try relinking to make sure this isn't the problem. Again, you can often spot this type of problem by looking at the load map.
3. Your main program does not have an ORG 100h as the first statement after the *CODESEG SEGMENT PUBLIC* declaration. Also, make sure the END statement in your main source file includes the label of the instruction at which you want to start—for example, *END DSKPATCH*.

APPENDIX D

MISCELLANEOUS TABLES

Table D-1. ASCII Character Codes

Dec	Hex	Char	Dec	Hex	Char	Dec	Hex	Char	Dec	Hex	Char
0	0		43	2B	+	86	56	V	129	81	ü
1	1	☺	44	2C	,	87	57	W	130	82	é
2	2	☻	45	2D	–	88	58	X	131	83	â
3	3	♥	46	2E	.	89	59	Y	132	84	ä
4	4	♦	47	2F	/	90	5A	Z	133	85	à
5	5	♣	48	30	0	91	5B	[	134	86	å
6	6	♠	49	31	1	92	5C	\	135	87	ç
7	7	•	50	32	2	93	5D	]	136	88	ê
8	8	◘	51	33	3	94	5E	^	137	89	ë
9	9	○	52	34	4	95	5F	_	138	8A	è
10	A	◙	53	35	5	96	60	`	139	8B	ï
11	B	♂	54	36	6	97	61	a	140	8C	î
12	C	♀	55	37	7	98	62	b	141	8D	ì
13	D	♪	56	38	8	99	63	c	142	8E	Ä
14	E	♫	57	39	9	100	64	d	143	8F	Å
15	F	☼	58	3A	:	101	65	e	144	90	É
16	0	►	59	3B	;	102	66	f	145	91	æ
17	11	◄	60	3C	<	103	67	g	146	92	Æ
18	12	↕	61	3D	=	104	68	h	147	93	ô
19	13	‼	62	3E	>	105	69	i	148	94	ö
20	14	¶	63	3F	?	106	6A	j	149	95	ò
21	15	§	64	40	@	107	6B	k	150	96	û
22	16	▬	65	41	A	108	6C	l	151	97	ù
23	17	‡	66	42	B	109	6D	m	152	98	ÿ
24	18	↑	67	43	C	110	6E	n	153	99	Ö
25	19	↓	68	44	D	111	6F	o	154	9A	Ü
26	1A	→	69	45	E	112	70	p	155	9B	¢
27	1B	←	70	46	F	113	71	q	156	9C	£
28	1C	∟	71	47	G	114	72	r	157	9D	¥
29	1D	↔	72	48	H	115	73	s	158	9E	₧
30	1E	▲	73	49	I	116	74	t	159	9F	ƒ
31	1F	▼	74	4A	J	117	75	u	160	A0	á
32	20		75	4B	K	118	76	v	161	A1	í
33	21	!	76	4C	L	119	77	w	162	A2	ó
34	22	"	77	4D	M	120	78	x	163	A3	ú
35	23	#	78	4E	N	121	79	y	164	A4	ñ
36	24	$	79	4F	O	122	7A	z	165	A5	Ñ
37	25	%	80	50	P	123	7B	{	166	A6	ª
38	26	&	81	51	Q	124	7C			167	A7	º
39	27	'	82	52	R	125	7D	}	168	A8	¿
40	28	(	83	53	S	126	7E	~	169	A9	⌐
41	29	)	84	54	T	127	7F	⌂	170	AA	¬
42	2A	*	85	55	U	128	80	Ç	171	AB	½

Table D-1. ASCII Character Codes *continued*

Dec	Hex	Char	Dec	Hex	Char	Dec	Hex	Char	Dec	Hex	Char
172	AC	¼	193	C1	⊥	214	D6		235	EB	δ
173	AD	¡	194	C2		215	D7		236	EC	•
174	AE	«	195	C3		216	D8		237	ED	
175	AF	»	196	C4	—	217	D9		238	EE	∈
176	B0		197	C5	┼	218	DA		239	EF	∩
177	B1		198	C6		219	DB		240	F0	≡
178	B2		199	C7		220	DC		241	F1	±
179	B3		200	C8		221	DD		242	F2	≥
180	B4		201	C9		222	DE		243	F3	≤
181	B5		202	CA		223	DF		244	F4	⌠
182	B6		203	CB		224	E0	α	245	F5	⌡
183	B7		204	CC		225	E1	β	246	F6	÷
184	B8		205	CD	=	226	E2	Γ	247	F7	≈
185	B9		206	CE		227	E3	π	248	F8	°
186	BA		207	CF		228	E4	Σ	249	F9	·
187	BB		208	D0		229	E5	σ	250	FA	·
188	BC		209	D1		230	E6	μ	251	FB	√
189	BD		210	D2		231	E7	τ	252	FC	ⁿ
190	BE		211	D3		232	E8	Φ	253	FD	²
191	BF		212	D4		233	E9	Θ	254	FE	■
192	C0	L	213	D5		234	EA	Ω	255	FF	

Table D-2. Color Codes

0	Black
1	Blue
2	Green
3	Cyan
4	Red
5	Violet
6	Brown
7	White

Attribute = background color * 16 + foreground color

Add 8 to the forground color for the bright versions, or add 8 to the to the background color to turn on blinking.

Many of the keys on the keyboard (such as the function keys) return a two-character code when you read the keys through DOS: A decimal 0 followed by a scan code. The following table shows the scan codes for all the keys that have no equivalent ASCII code.

Table D-3. Extended Keyboard Codes

15	Shift Tab
16-25	Alt keys for Q, W, E, R, T, Y, U, I, O, P
30-38	Alt keys for A, S, D, F, G, H, J, K, L
44-50	Alt keys for Z, X, C, V, B, N, M
59-68	F1 through F10
71	Home
72	Cursor Up
73	PgUp
75	Cursor Left
77	Cursor Right
79	End
80	Cursor Down
81	PgDn
82	Ins
83	Del
84-93	Shift F1 through F10
94-103	Control F1 through F10
104-113	Alt F1 through F10
114	Control PrtSc
115	Control Left Cursor
116	Control Right Cursor
117	Control End
118	Control PgDn
119	Control Home
120-131	Control Alt for 1, 2, 3, 4, 5, 6, 7, 8, 9, 0, -, =
132	Control PgUp

Table D-4. Table of Addressing Modes

Addressing Mode	Format of Address	Segment Register Used
Register	register (such as AX)	None
Immediate	data (such as 12345)	None
Memory Addressing Modes		
Register Indirect	[BX]	DS
	[BP]	SS
	[DI]	DS
	[SI]	DS
Base Relative*	label[BX]	DS
	label[BP]	SS
Direct Indexed*	label[DI]	DS
	label[SI]	DS
Base Indexed*	label[BX + SI]	DS
	label[BX + DI]	DS
	label [BP + SI]	SS
	label[BP + DI]	SS
String Commands: (MOVSW, LODSB, *and so on*)		Read from DS:SI Write to ES:DI

* Label[...] can be replaced by [disp + ...], where *disp* is a displacement. Thus, we could write [10 + BX] and the address would be 10 + BX.

Table D-5. INT 10h Functions

(AH) = 0   **Set the display mode.** The AL registers contains the mode number.

TEXT MODES

(AL) = 0   40 by 25, black and white mode
(AL) = 1   40 by 25, color
(AL) = 2   80 by 25, black and white
(AL) = 3   80 by 25, color
(AL) = 7   80 by 25, monochrome display adapter

GRAPHICS MODE

(AL) = 4   320 by 200, color
(AL) = 5   320 by 200, black and white
(AL) = 6   640 by 200, black and white

(AH) = 1   **Set the cursor size.**

(CH)   Starting scan line of the cursor. The top line is 0 on both the monochrome and color graphics displays, while the bottom line is 7 for the color graphics adapter and 13 for the monochrome adapter. Valid range: 0 to 31.

(CL)   Last scan line of the cursor.

The power-on setting for the color graphics adapter is CH = 6 and CL = 7. For the monochrome display: CH = 11 and CL = 12.

(AH) = 2   **Set the cursor position.**

(DH,DL)   Row, column of new cursor position; the upper, left corner is (0,0).

(BH)   Page number. This is the number of the display page. The color-graphics adapter has room for several display pages, but most programs use page 0.

Table D-5. INT 10h Functions *continued*

(AH) = 3   **Read the cursor position.**

(BH)	Page number	
On exit	(DH,DL)	Row, column of cursor
	(CH,CL)	Cursor size

(AH) = 4   **Read light pen position** (see Tech. Ref. Man.).

(AH) = 5   **Select active display page.**

         (AL)   New page number (from 0 to 7 for modes 0 and 1; from 0 to 3 for modes 2 and 3)

(AH) = 6   **Scroll up.**

         (AL)   Number of lines to blank at the bottom of the window. Normal scrolling blanks one line. Set to zero to blank entire window.

         (CH,CL)   Row, column of upper, left corner of window

         (DH,DL)   Row, column of lower, right corner of window

         (BH)   Display attribute to use for blank lines

(AH) = 7   **Scroll down.**

Same as scroll up (function 6), but lines are left blank at the top of the window instead of the bottom

(AH) = 8   **Read attribute and character under the cursor.**

         (BH)   Display page (text modes only)

         (AL)   Character read

         (AH)   Attribute of character read (text modes only)

(AH) = 9   **Write attribute and character under the cursor.**

         (BH)   Display page (text modes only)

         (CX)   Number of times to write character and attribute on screen

         (AL)   Character to write

         (BL)   Attribute to write

(AH) = 10   **Write character under cursor** (with normal attribute).

      (BH)   Display page
      (CX)   Number of times to write character
      (AL)   Character to write

(AH) = 11 to 13   **Various graphics functions.** (See Tech. Ref. Man. for the details)

(AH) = 14   **Write teletype.** Write one character to the screen and move the cursor to the next position.

      (AL)   Character to write
      (BL)   Color of character (graphics mode only)
      (BH)   Display page (text mode)

(AH) = 15   **Return current video state.**

      (AL)   Display mode currently set
      (AH)   Number of characters per line
      (BH)   Active display pages

This table contains the INT 16h functions used in this book to read characters from the keyboard.

Table D-6. INT 16h Functions

(AH) = 0   **Keyboard read.** This function waits for you to type a character on the keyboard. It returns the ASCII code in AL and the scan code in AH. For extended keys, AL will be set to 0. See Table D-2 for a list of scan codes for such keys.

                     (AL)   ASCII code of the key you press (0 for special keys).

                     (AH)   Scan code for the key you pressed.

(AH) = 1   **Keyboard status.** This function checks to see if there are any keys waiting to be read.

                     ZF   0, if a character is waiting
                                 1, if there are no characters waiting.

                     (AL)   ASCII code of character waiting to be read.

                     (AH)   Scan code of character waiting to be read.

(AH) = 2   **Shift status.** This function returns a byte with the state of the various shift keys:

                     (AL)   Status of the shift keys:

```
7 6 5 4 3 2 1
1 . . . . . . Insert on
. 1 . . . . . Caps Lock on
. . 1 . . . . Num Lock on
. . . 1 . . . Scroll Lock on
. . . . 1 . . Alt key down
. . . . . 1 . Left shift down
. . . . . . 1 Right shift down
```

This table contains the INT 21h functions used in this book. For a more complete list, you should buy the IBM *DOS Technical Reference* manual.

Table D-7. INT 21h Functions

(AH) = 1   **Keyboard input.** This function waits for you to type a character on the keyboard. It echos the character to the screen, and returns the ASCII code in the AL register. For extended keyboard codes, this function returns two characters: an ASCII 0 followed by the scan code (see Table D-2).

(AL)   Character read from the keyboard.

(AH) = 2   **Display output.** Displays one character on the screen. Several characters have special meaning to this function:

7   Beep: Send a one-second tone to the speaker.
8   Backspace: move the cursor left one character position.
9   Tab: Move to the next tab stop. Tab stops are set to every 8 characters.
0Ah   Line feed: Move to the next line.
0Dh   Carriage return: Move to the start of the current line.
(DL)   Character to display on the screen.

(AH) = 8   **Keyboard input without echo.** Reads a character from the keyboard, but doesn't display the character on the screen.

(AL)   Character read from keyboard.

(AH) = 9   **Display string.** Displays the string pointed to by the DS:DX pair of registers. You must mark the end of the string with the $ character.

DS:DX   Points to the string to display.

(AH) = 0Ah   **Read string.** Reads a strings from the keyboard. See Chapter 23 for more details.

Table D-7. INT 21h Functions *continued*

(AH) = 25h   **Set interrupt vector.** Sets an interrupt vector to point to a new routine.

(AL)	Interrupt number.
DS:DX	Address of the new interrupt handler.

(AH) = 35h   **Get interrupt vector.** Gets the address of the interrupt service routine for the interrupt number given in AL.

(AL)	Interrupt number.
ES:BX	Address of the interrupt handler.

(AH) = 4Ch   **Exit to DOS.** Returns to DOS, like INT 20h, but it works for *both* .COM and .EXE programs. The INT 20h function only works for .COM programs.

(AL)	Return code. Normally set to 0, but you can set it to any other number and use the DOS batch commands IF and ERRORLEVEL to detect errors.

The following two interrupts are DOS calls for reading and writing disk sectors.

Table D-8. Sector Read/Write Functions

INT 25h—Read Disk Sector

On entry:

(AL)	Drive number (0 = A, 1 = B, and so on)
(CX)	Number of sectors to read at one time
(DX)	Number of the first sector to read (the first sector is 0)
DS:BX	Transfer address: where to write the sectors read

INT 26h—Write Disk Sector

On entry:

(AL)	Drive number (0 = A, 1 = B, and so on)
(CX)	Number of sectors to write at one time
(DX)	Number of the first sector to write (the first sector is 0)
DS:BX	Transfer address: start of the data we want to write to the disk.

Information Returned by INT 25h, INT 26h

Both INT 25h and INT 26h return the following information in the AX register. They also leave the flags on the stack, so you'll want to use a POP or POPF to remove this word from the stack (see Chapter 15 for an example).

Returns:

Carry Flag	Set if there was an error, in which case the error information will be in AX.
(AL)	DOS error code
(AH)	Contains one of the following:
80h	The drive did not respond
40h	The Seek operation failed
08h	Bad CRC when we read the disk
04h	Could not find the sector we asked for
03h	Tried to write to a write-protected disk
02h	Some other error

Destroys

AX, BX, CX, DX, SI, DI, BP

INDEX

About the Authors

Peter Norton is well-known in the personal computing arena for both his writing and programming. Starting in the earliest days of the IBM Personal Computer, he began writing about the IBM/PC, helping other people understand how these wonderful machines work. He has written a half a dozen books on the PC family, including the best-selling *Inside the IBM/PC* and *The Peter Norton Programmer's Guide*. His set of programs called The Norton Utilities has helped many PC users rescue lost data and explore the inner workings of their computers. Peter grew up in Seattle, Washington, attended Reed College in Portland, Oregon; he now lives in Santa Monica, California with his wife and two children. He always wears his sleeves rolled up.

John Socha is better known for his public-domain utilities than by his name. In the early days of the IBM PC, he wrote a column for the now defunct magazine *Softalk*, where he published such programs as ScreenSave (the first screen blanker), KbdBuffer (extends the keyboard buffer), and Whereis (finds files on a hard disk). After the demise of *Softalk*, John concentrated on finishing his PhD in Physics and writing a commercial program called The Norton Commander. John grew up in Wisconsin, earned a BS degree in Electrical Engineering from the University of Wisconsin, an MS and a PhD in Applied Physics from Cornell University, and now lives in southern California. He always wears his WalkMan.

CUSTOMER SUPPORT PLAN

It is important that you register your purchase of any Simon & Schuster software package. By completing and returning your Owner Registration Card, you become eligible for:

- Software support directly from S & S.
- Diskette replacement when applicable.
- Purchase of future product upgrades at special prices.
- Subscriptions to Hint Books and newsletters where applicable.

Software Support Options

S & S will provide support to registered owners under the following programs:

30-day Startup Service - For the first 30 days after you purchase an S & S Software package, we will answer questions by telephone through our Technical Support Department. There is no additional charge for this service, but you must have registered your copy of the S & S Software package by sending the Owner Registration Card, or by calling S & S to register your purchase. During the 30-day Startup period, we will respond to your first call without having already received your Owner Registration Card.

Extended Support Service - Registered owners may purchase S & S Extended Support Service. This service provides up to three hours of telephone support from the S & S Technical Support Department for a period of one year. Extended Support costs $60, is renewable, and may be paid for when calling for support by Visa, Mastercard, American Express, or in advance by check.

Single-call Support Service - After the 30-day startup period, registered owners may obtain telephone support from the S & S Technical Support Department for $60 per hour, $10 minimum per call. These calls must be charged to an approved credit card. The customer must have card information available at the beginning of the call.

Mail-in Support Service - Registered owners may write to us with questions. We will respond in writing. There is no additional charge for this service.

We realize that our software packages are put to a wide variety of uses, however, we can only answer questions about the software package itself. You are required to have minimal experience using the hardware and operating system required to run our software packages. While we will do our best to answer your questions about the product, we must charge an extra $60 per hour fee for extensive consulting on problems not directly related to our products.

Before Calling Customer Support

Before calling our Technical Support Department, please make sure you have followed the steps in the "Pre-call Checklist" below.

Pre-call Checklist

1. If you are having difficulty understanding the program, have you read and performed the suggestions listed in the manual?

2. If you are not sure how to operate the program, have you used the help system (where available) to find the answer?

3. If there seems to be a problem in the software, can you reproduce the problem by following your steps again?

4. If the program displayed an error message, please write down the exact message.

5. You should be familiar with the hardware configuration you are using. We may need to know the brand/model of your computer, printer, the total amount of memory available, what video adaptor(s) you have in the system, the operating system version, etc.

6. When you call our Technical Support Department, please be at your computer or be prepared to repeat the sequence of steps leading up to the problem.

7. If applicable, please have your Visa, MasterCard, or American Express number and expiration date ready.

8. Our technical support number is (212) 373-7770. It is staffed on working days during normal business hours, 9:00 am to 5:00 pm, Eastern time.

Services and Prices

The above services and prices are subject to change without prior notice.

/////Brady Line

**Insights into
tomorrow's technology from
the authors and editors of
Brady Books**

You rely on Brady's bestselling computer books for up-to-date information about high technology. Now turn to *BradyLine* for the details behind the titles.

Find out what new trends in technology spark Brady's authors and editors. Read about what they're working on, and predicting, for the future. Get to know the authors through interviews and profiles, and get to know each other through your questions and comments.

BradyLine keeps you ahead of the trends with the stories behind the latest computer developments. Informative previews of forthcoming books and excerpts from new titles keep you apprised of what's going on in the fields that interest you most.

- Peter Norton on operating systems
- Winn Rosch on hardware
- Jerry Daniels, Mary Jane Mara, Robert Eckhardt, and
  Cynthia Harriman on Macintosh development, productivity,
  and connectivity

Get the Spark. Get *BradyLine*.

Published quarterly, beginning with the Summer 1990 issue. Free exclusively to our customers.
Just check the box on the Warranty/Registration card and mail it to begin your subscription now.

The Winn Rosch Hardware Bible

"Enhancing a computer is a matter of fitting connectors together and, at most, operating a screwdriver—almost anyone can do it, and that includes you."

—From the Introduction

PC journalist Winn Rosch walks you safely through the hardware jungle ... from processors to ports, from displays to storage. More than a guided tour, *The Hardware Bible* is hands-on all the way. Whether you want to just get along with your current system, or you're ready to enhance, upgrade, or even build a new machine.

- Covers the IBM PC, PC compatibles and IBM PS/2 hardware.
- Explains PC design and technology—you'll save time and money by making the right decisions up front.
- Spells out the standards for settings, adjustments, and compatibilities
- Offers you step-by-step install procedures with worry-free instructions.

ISBN 0-13-160979-3
$29.95